Praise for

THE TWENTY-FIRST-CENTURY CRISIS OF INTIMATE PARTNER VIOLENCE AMONG AFRICAN AMERICAN MALE VICTIMS

"This text offers the most thorough, well-researched, and well-documented examination to date on the subject of IPV. Dr. Gibson and a cadre of co-contributors from varied academic and specialized backgrounds and expertise provide the reader(s) with a comprehensive understanding of IPV and its impact on victims and the larger society—including the impact on both military veterans and active-duty servicemen/women.

"It is thought-provoking, shocking, and painful, especially the personal testimonies and experiences of family members and friends who grieve the losses of those who died as a result of IPV homicides. It is a must-read and a reliable source on the subject of IPV. Social workers, psychologists, criminologists, nurses, counselors, academicians, clergy, the general public, and survivors of IPV in particular will benefit from the information contained in this excellent resource."

—Deacon Milton Bailey, MSW
Retired DVA Readjustment Counseling Social Worker
Vietnam Veteran

"Superbly written and easy to comprehend the magnitude of a problem that is so often out of sight, and consequently out of mind. The personal stories add real value and vivid truth to the importance of the fact that much more attention should be given to the problem of IPV, particularly in the African American male community. Furthermore, these personal stories, along with the large volume of research data and analysis, make this work a valuable and powerful tool and resource, not only for the classroom, but for all professionals whose work is involved in social services."

—Dr. Theodus Drake Jr.
Pastor, Second Mt. Zion Baptist Church
Author of *The Fish Have Moved*

"No one can escape abuse. This is what Dr. Gibson and her son so eloquently detail in her book, *The Twenty-First-Century Crisis of Intimate Partner Violence among African American Male Victims.* In this personal, emotional, but extremely well-researched work, readers are invited into a world that is not often talked about. Unlike other books and journals out there, Dr. Gibson attempts to bring all sides into the conversation about IPV. This book is a must-read, and thank-you, Dr. Gibson, for educating me on this important subject!"

—Dr. Eddie Morris, PhD, MSW
Education Consultant

"This book is a guide for not only mothers raising their sons, but fathers too. The insight of the 'momma's boy' myth clears up the misperception that women cannot raise young boys. It is important for individuals to know how to respond to these situations, and it is imperative because the wrong decision can damage their fate with a criminal record! I am moved to do a domestic violence/IPV campaign to bring awareness to our community."

—Mr. Willie L. Batts Jr., EdS
Assistant Principal

THE TWENTY-FIRST-CENTURY CRISIS OF

INTIMATE PARTNER VIOLENCE

AMONG

AFRICAN AMERICAN MALE VICTIMS

THE TWENTY-FIRST-CENTURY CRISIS OF

INTIMATE PARTNER VIOLENCE

AMONG

AFRICAN AMERICAN MALE VICTIMS

UP CLOSE AND PERSONAL
WITH AN UNNOTICED POPULATION:
A SOCIAL WORK RESPONSE

To Casey, my new "childhood" friend. Thank you for supporting this awesome endeavor. Know that with God ALL things are possible!

Dr. Irma J. Gibson-Hall
Phillipians 4:13

DR. IRMA J. GIBSON

MOUNTAIN ARBOR
PRESS
Alpharetta, GA

The resources contained within this book are provided for informational purposes only and should not be used to replace formal therapy and specialized counseling in an individual or group therapeutic setting. Although most of the contributors are licensed practitioners in their various professions, the author of this work cannot be held responsible for the misuse of the information provided. Always consult a licensed mental health professional before making any decision regarding treatment of yourself or others.

Due to the sensitivity of the topic, some names have been changed to protect the identity of the subjects.

ISBN: 978-1-63183-519-3 - Paperback
eISBN: 978-1-63183-520-9 - ePub
eISBN: 978-1-63183-521-6 - mobi

Library of Congress Control Number: 2019914812

Printed in the United States of America 100819

⊗This paper meets the requirements of ANSI/NISO Z39.48-1992 (Permanence of Paper)

"Cause I ain't got no pencil," poem by Joshua Dickerson.

"Life Is a Theater," poem by Bill Prickett.

DEDICATION

To my parents: My mother, Ms. Doris Esther Shinholster-Davis, for your guidance and unwavering support throughout the years. As a momma's girl, the R & B group The Intruders expresses my feelings accurately with their lyrics in "I'll Always Love My Momma, She's My Favorite Girl": You are my "shero."

In memory of my late father, Mr. Sammie Lee "Junebug Gift of Gab" Davis, who at the age of eighty-six succumbed to his injuries on December 14, 2017, from a horrific car accident: Not only did he expose me to his love for the arts and saturate my childhood with a variety of music and entertainment, he also was the epitome of hard work and instilled in me a relentless "can do" spirit of excellence. It's because of his determined and confident nature that I don't give up, won't give up, or can't give up on my dreams and aspirations. It's not an option!

Lastly, to Terrell JaMar Gibson, my reason and my motivation for envisioning this prolific dissertation. Thank you for having the courage to tell your story despite being misjudged and regardless of what others might think. You are the wind beneath my wings, and I am so very proud of you. As the Lord orders your steps, continue to let the words of your mouth and the meditation of your heart be acceptable in His sight and continue to stand and let Him see you through.

EPIGRAPH

Life is a theater, so invite your audience carefully. . . . The more you seek respect, growth, peace of mind, love, and truth, the easier it will become for you to decide who sits in the front row and who should be moved to the balcony. In the finale, you cannot "change" most of the people around you, so you have to change the people you are around the most! Life is a theater, and YOU are the star.

—Bill Prickett

CONTENTS

FOREWORD

DR. JEROME H. SCHIELE

AUTHOR, ADMINISTRATOR, PROFESSOR OF SOCIAL WORK

Dr. Irma J. Gibson's book *The Twenty-First-Century Crisis of Intimate Partner Violence among African American Male Victims* is an important breakthrough in our understanding of domestic or intimate partner violence. This breakthrough is significant because most of the attention given to this devastating social problem has focused on women as the exclusive victims. Indeed, women are the primary victims of this horrible abuse and crime, and we should never deemphasize the harm and humiliation women experience, and the threat to their personhood. However, recent data demonstrate that men are increasingly becoming victims of domestic violence, yet very little attention has been given to this problem.

There are several reasons for the lack of attention given to the victimization of men in domestic violence. First, we live in a patriarchal society in which men are "supposed" to dominate all areas of social, economic, and political life. This androcentric paradigm portrays men as being prone to aggression and domination, and this is often the case. However, because of the advancement of various forms of feminism and womanism, patriarchy has come under enormous attack, and rightfully so. However, as women have gained more power to be autonomous and assert preferences that advance their individual and collective self-interest, they have become emboldened to challenge the assertions of men and their control over their lives. The resignation to male domination has increasingly been replaced by a kind of "insurrection" among women that may place some of them at risk of initiating violence against men. Thus, the challenge to patriarchy, which has been seen in many aspects of our society, may also be increasingly expressed in the domain of interpersonal relations.

Second, this lack of attention to male victims of domestic violence also may be a function of the orthodoxy of the academic and professional community. The study of domestic violence is viewed almost exclusively as a male-initiated problem that restricts and punishes any autonomy shown by women. Granted, this perspective is grounded in abundant evidence that speaks to the adverse consequences of androcentricity for the safety and freedom of women. However, this paradigm confines our understanding of interpersonal violence as a one-way-street phenomenon. It either excludes or marginalizes the potential and reality of women abusing men. It essentially creates and promotes a rigid narrative of intergender relations that affirms the nurturance and niceties of women and the selfishness and nefariousness of men. "Sugar and spice and everything nice" versus "snips and snails and puppy dog tails," without viewing the possibility that these polarities can coexist and interact.

A final reason for the lack of attention to male victims of domestic violence may be the underreporting of these episodes. We know from research there is significant underreporting of domestic violence among women, for a host of reasons. A major value that may guide this underreporting is that of privacy. The right and privilege of privacy is entrenched in our society and is even found in the first ten amendments of the US Constitution. Americans prioritize privacy and view it as a sacred practice and institution. Intimate, interpersonal relationships are immensely private, and due to the nature of these relationships, this privacy is often justifiable. This focus on privacy is enhanced when the actions that occur within its domain are shameful, embarrassing, and horrific. The action of violence within relationships that are ostensibly supposed to be loving is difficult to explain, let alone share. Because of the cultural and political overlay of patriarchy, this dilemma can be especially challenging for men who are abused by their female loved ones. Essentially, they may perceive that their "manhood" has been diminished and, thus, to report this abuse would only bring on severe ostracism and condemnation from both men and women. Indeed, this perception reflects the holistic dehumanization of patriarchy: its internalization for men not only places their wives and girlfriends at risk of abuse, but also themselves when they are the victims of violence and refuse to report.

Dr. Gibson's book boldly explores these issues, which are often uncomfortable for both professionals and the larger society. I deeply commend her for her courage to unearth and examine this topic, which for many is a taboo. Clearly, much more needs to be explored and known about this special form of abuse. Dr. Gibson's book significantly helps us to progress in that direction, and it gives us some ideas and recommendations about how we might prevent and alleviate this form of violence.

MR. LEON JONES
CHIEF CORONER, MACON (BIBB COUNTY), GEORGIA

I need your undivided attention! As you are reading this foreword, a domestic (intimate partner) violence incident is occurring. One happens every nine seconds. As a retired EMT with thirty-two years of overseeing ambulance services and twenty-eight years as coroner, I have seen my share of domestic "intimate partner" violence. Most incidents have been against women, but they are not limited by gender. The worst case that is indelibly in my memory is a young lady who was set on fire by her boyfriend. It was a horrific scene.

There are several reasons why people stay in an abusive relationship, and they all have a story. While it is up to your discretion to bring the serious nature of intimate partner violence to the forefront, there are implications for failing to do so. Additional exposure of the far-reaching effects of this debilitating social ill is long overdue. This book details why it's critical to start teaching and modeling social and emotional skills early in a child's life. These factors are precursors to IPV. This book also provides a comprehensive view of the many facets that must be explored as the origins of the problem are identified, risk and protective factors are calculated, and resolutions are strategized. Take heed . . . but tread lightly.

PREFACE

The foreword of this book is written by Dr. Jerome H. Schiele and Mr. Leon Jones, two distinguished and accomplished gentlemen who boast a significant level of expertise in their respective professions. Dr. Schiele is an author, researcher, and expert in his own right on the plight of people of color and the environmental and social justice issues that are addressed in social work education. In reference to his research agenda, he is particularly passionate about how human service professionals can help to eliminate cultural oppression and presents a new way of understanding human behavior in the social environment, attacking social problems and exploring social issues as is evident in his research repertoire. To his credit as an author, prior manuscript contributions are delivered in the form of a guide that shows how understanding the simultaneous forces of oppression and spiritual alienation in American society serves as a foundation for understanding the societal problems in various environments. His invaluable knowledge as an academician and statistician who has gathered evidence and disseminated factual information about a multitude of controversial topics (inside and outside the classroom) is laudable; thus he is immensely appropriate for introducing this teaching, real-world, "thinking outside the box" textbook.

Mr. Jones is a public figure who has the daunting and emotionally charged responsibility of addressing not only those victims who become the fatalities of failed IPV (intimate partner violence) prevention and interventions, but also those who succumb to other types of senseless violence that are being witnessed in our communities today. He was strategically selected due to his position as well as his personal philosophy and living legacy. He has a heart for publicly serving others as he embraces the values of the social work profession: respect for the dignity and worth of the person, respect for human relationships, social justice, integrity, and commitment, and service to those who are in need. Additionally, upon witnessing the live autopsy of a twenty-nine-year-old female Afrotrini victim of intimate partner violence in Trinidad and Tobago during the summer of 2018, one of the workers boldly stated to me and the two social work students: "This is what happens when you don't do your jobs!" That was a profound statement that resonated with me as I contemplated who would be most appropriate to introduce this manuscript. Due to the serious nature of the subject matter, I desired someone who was not just the status quo or the norm, but who could provide an up-close and personal wake-up call for the readers of this long overdue topic. Mr. Jones has saturated the Central Georgia news circuit with his show of concern for addressing the problems of drunk driving and community violence, and my initial impression of him was that he is passionate about what he does and goes above and beyond his normal duties to serve the people. As a coroner, he embraces the mission of the social work profession and practices the values of social work. Additionally, he truly represents the lives of those who could fall victim to the risk factors and the statistics of intimate partner violence if it were not for the "protective factors" that placed him on the trajectory to beat the odds and reach his destiny in life. Unequivocally and ideally, he represents what we aspire for all youth who are facing at-risk circumstances: to become socially conscious, lifelong productive citizens. Mr. Jones' testimony speaks volumes, and no one is more fitting to introduce this book than he and Dr. Schiele.

Because of the serious consequences of IPV, both the Centers for Disease Control and the World Health Organization identify IPV as a significant public health issue. Intimate partner violence is a critical issue that crosses a plethora of cultural boundaries, including age, race, religion, ethnicity, and economics, to name a few. Yet there is a population, the African American male, who is often overlooked as representing victims of this seriously debilitating problem. In addition to providing the readers with some early memories from my son's childhood and the foundation upon which he was raised, the introductory chapter will provide historical origins of IPV terminology and my reasons for writing a book to address this important public health issue. Included among the topics of discussion will be my personal experience as a mother of a black male victim of intimate partner violence and the conflicting thoughts, feelings, and emotions I encountered as a parent and as a clinical social worker who possessed specific knowledge and training about the problem and the process toward a resolution. Thus, the decisions I contemplated as a "professional" when I was subjected to the societal responses I witnessed from other "professionals" will also be addressed, in regard to the sensitivity and training, or lack thereof, of some of the first responders. What propelled my determination to expose this problem and to impact change via this prolific avenue, as well as my parenting style as a divorced single mother and the significance of the "family" foundation as a protective factor, will be the highlight of **chapter 1, "Torn AND Driven."**

Chapter 2, "Run with Your Hands Up: My Story," will present my son's personal encounters with this life-changing experience as a victim of IPV, and how he became the inspiration that propelled my vision. He will talk about his upbringing and some of his most memorable teaching moments about relationships and life from his parents, particularly his mother. He will also discuss the origin, the history, and the continuum of the relationship wherein he was a victim of intimate partner violence as specific events unfolded; the personal and professional interactions and encounters with friends, family, peers, school administrators, law enforcement, and the court system; and the details of some of his most personal low points, the disappointments he experienced as well as the invaluable lessons he gained as a result of the tragedy he avoided.

Chapter 3, "An Endangered Species: Gone Too Soon, but Never Forgotten," is the heartbreaking story of a family impacted by IPV who remain close friends of mine. They are prior neighbors in the subdivision where my son was reared between the ages of nine and seventeen. Our families are kindred spirits and share many childhood memories amongst our children as they grew into young adulthood. Unfortunately and tragically, one of the young men in the neighborhood circle met his fate at the hands of IPV and also propelled me to no longer delay the initiation of my book. This chapter will articulate Bobby's story and provide an up-close, real, and "no holds barred" depiction about intimate partner violence and what can happen if it is not addressed effectively. From the heart and the soul of Mrs. Tonica Gleaton, Bobby's mother, his story will be shared with the world. She will share what she wants the readers to know about him, his twenty-five years of living, and the horrific experience of losing her firstborn to a senseless tragedy. She was given the freedom to tell her story in her own way, and despite her pain, it was done with respect, compassion, agape love, and a phenomenal show of courage and strength. Additional information will focus upon statistical information about the dismal numbers depicting the state of the African American male population as an "endangered species." In this regard, IPV is just another social problem that is pertinent to the cradle-to-prison pipeline. Both contribute to the black male's demise as the signs and symptoms of IPV are also identified. Although this chapter is brief, its contents are profound and powerful.

Although the overall focus of this book is the male victim of IPV, IPV can't be comprehensively discussed without addressing the female victim, who has suffered for years and continues to suffer at the hands of male perpetrators. Everyone knows the story of the man with two distinct personalities: in an instant, he can go from being the morally conscious Dr. Jekyll to the morally bankrupt Mr. Hyde. Clearly men who abuse women fit this description. As a survivor of domestic violence, the author of this chapter is cognizant of how quickly the transformation from Jekyll to Hyde takes place. **Chapter 4, "Home: The New Prison,"** is the true story of how this female victim survived this horrible experience.

Chapter 5, "Why 'Big Boys' Don't Cry or Tell: African American Male College Students' Perception, Attitude, and Behavior toward Male Victims of Female-Perpetrated Intimate Partner Violence," will provide an overview of statistical data about IPV with a discussion pertaining to a university campus qualitative study that focuses on male victims. The responses of the participants and the results of the study may surprise you and will hopefully open your eyes to the attitudes and mentalities of the twenty-first-century male who appears to be negatively impacted and influenced by the stereotypical views of society.

Although the "mean girls" concept is somewhat related to bullying, the essence of **Chapter 6, "Mean Girls, Reality TV Media Influences, and Low Self-Esteem: A Twenty-First-Century Challenge,"** will focus more upon the "mean girl" theory as it relates to twenty-first-century influences such as reality television, social media, and the significance of the correlate of low self-esteem to these factors. It has even become a topic of study for the classroom, as is evident by a course description in the literature department of a Colorado college. The description states that the class is designed to explore the "motives behind why women seek authority and the actions they are willing to take in order to hold onto it." Females have long come under less scrutiny than males, leaving them free to perpetrate crimes of passion and bullying in relative anonymity. Only of late have females been receiving consequences equal to their male counterparts for similar acts. Therefore, it is no surprise that acceptance of female perpetrators of violent behaviors has developed gradually. It is this gradual acceptance that has allowed females to freely participate in bullying and IPV. Two wrongs don't make a right! The stigma of weakness and being dominated by a female translates into male victims being less likely than females to disclose that they are the victims of IPV. It is impacting society in unimaginable ways, and the time has come to address the implications for the present and future generations.

Because a significant component of aggressive behavior is bullying, it is imperative that this social issue is included in the discussion of IPV. This is the essence of **Chapter 7, "What Does Bullying Have to Do with It?: The K–12 Educational Environment."** Everything! Again, bullying is a social phenomenon generally associated with males. The behavior is repeated, or has the potential to be repeated, over time. Both youth who are bullied and who bully others may have serious, lasting problems. In order to be considered bullying, the behavior must be aggressive and include an imbalance of power: Youth who bully use their power—such as physical strength, access to embarrassing information, or popularity—to control or harm others. Power imbalances can change over time and in different situations, even if they involve the same people. Hence, the study of the social and legal aspects of bullying *within the school setting* is a necessary undertaking. It is certain that male victims of IPV cannot be ignored, and the speed with which the issue is addressed must exceed the snail's pace of debunking centuries of obsolete misconceptions.

Researchers claim the reason for officers' "reluctance or frustration" in responding to IPV is their lack of understanding of the complexities of these incidents and their insensitivity for victims. However, some believe these researchers themselves do not clearly understand the complex nature of IPV, nor the multifaceted "perceptions" of victimization it presents to law enforcement. As one report suggests, some IPV victimization can be more subjective than objective. The report also claims that individual officers' perceptions may actually be similar to those of many researchers and other professionals concerning IPV. It states that some officers are supportive of victims, while others are less supportive. **Chapter 8, "Exploring Intimate Partner Violence: A Law Enforcement Perspective,"** will explore these issues and provide an inside perspective geared toward providing clarity and understanding about IPV, its origin and how the climate of today's urban youth and family status have changed the rules of the game, and the dynamics involved from law enforcement's point of view.

Chapter 9, "Intimate Partner Violence and Its Impact on Military Personnel and Veterans," will discuss intimate partner violence as a serious public health problem that has received increased attention in the military. While various wartime eras are analyzed, the author discusses the factors that human service providers need to be aware in an effort to effectively address IPV issues pertaining to the US military armed forces. Over the past fifteen years, the US has been actively involved in Operation Iraqi Freedom (OIF) and Operation Enduring Freedom (OEF). During this period, there has been a significant increase in the number of IPV cases and occurrences across the spectrum of the armed forces. For both military veterans and active-duty servicemen, IPV results in significant victim injury and negative child outcomes, problematic substance use, depression, and antisocial characteristics which represent psychiatric correlates of IPV perpetration. A detailed and thorough analysis of these issues, the problem as it relates to culture, the military language and terminology, the guidelines, and the most effective interventions are presented in layman's but profound terms. It is a basic lesson in Military and War 101 infused with the impact of IPV.

Chapter 10, "The Boomerang Effect," will introduce theory, the crucial component of the social work perspective to this public health issue formally known as domestic violence. This brief chapter, with some statistical data, will provide thoughts and viewpoints strictly from a therapist's perspective that seek to explain the behaviors of this population, including those of the victims and the perpetrators. Basic feedback and reflections resulting from her experience utilizing the Boomerang Effect will clarify possible guidelines for constructing effective therapeutic interventions and techniques. In social psychology, the Boomerang Effect refers to the unintended consequences of an attempt to persuade, resulting in the adoption of an opposing position instead (Brehm and Brehm, 1981).

Intimate partner violence (IPV) can be defined in many ways and encompasses many different types of physical and emotional abuse. IPV affects the health, safety, and quality of life for women, men, and children worldwide, regardless of race, sexual orientation, or socioeconomic status. The mental health consequences of IPV can be severe and include post-traumatic stress disorder (PTSD), depression, anxiety, and eating disorders. IPV is also a major cause of mortality due to suicide and homicide. Thus, the health effects include acute trauma and a wide range of physical and emotional effects. Although evidence regarding the prevalence and characteristics of IPV worldwide has grown enormously during the past decade, there are still many gaps that have not been addressed. Research has confirmed that IPV is substantially "costly" to all of our well-being as a society: The lifetime per-victim cost is $103,767 for women and $23,414 for men. The lifetime economic cost to the US population is $3.6 trillion. This economic cost estimate includes almost 32 million women and 12 million men who have been victims of IPV. The $3.6 trillion economic cost estimate included:

- $2.1 trillion (59%) in medical costs
- $1.3 trillion (37%) in lost productivity among victims and perpetrators
- $73 billion (2%) in criminal justice costs
- $62 billion (2%) in other costs, such as victim property loss or damage

Chapter 11, "Intimate Partner Violence: A Miscalculated Weapon of Mass Destruction (The Behavioral Health Implications and Caveats)," will mainly present statistical data and contribute to the disclosure of the behavioral health dynamics and a synopsis of the physical health implications associated with intimate partner violence.

Chapter 12, "Intimate Partner Violence, Social Work, and the Law: The Dilemma of Victimhood," provides an analysis of social work and legal issues as related to intimate partner violence (IPV). Historical and contemporaneous data are used to highlight the magnitude of IPV on various population groups, with a particular emphasis being placed on male victims. In doing so, incidence and trends related to the types of IPV are examined to show how the "face" of IPV has evolved. Finally, the legal landscape—including state and federal statutes along with case law—is examined as potential means to address IPV. Implications for social work education, research, and practice are provided.

Chapter 13, "A Comprehensive, Psychoeducational, Therapeutic Social Work Response," will provide in-depth theoretical and therapeutic responses, resolutions, and interventions as well as primary, secondary, and tertiary prevention strategies to the issues and problems identified by the contributing authors from an ecological and social learning perspective. Additional micro, mezzo, and macro practice responses and resolutions will be provided in regard to other literature that pertains to intimate partner violence. Since the first social work class was offered in 1898 at Columbia University, social workers have led the way in addressing the needs of society from a perspective that includes examination of the environment from which the problem originates. This unique approach is referred to as the person in environment (PIE) perspective and will be applied to the examination of this public health issue.

Chapter 14, "Closing Reflections: A Call to Action," is the conclusion and will provide reflections on the overall findings via the various chapters. The most commonly asked question, "Why did the victim stay?", will also be addressed with "real-world" responses. Additionally, practical and pragmatic preventive responses and remarks will be shared and summarized in this chapter.

The vision to write this book was officially initiated approximately four years ago when I reached out to a group of constituents and colleagues whose areas of expertise were applicable to the various IPV topics that needed to be addressed from my professional perspective. These trailblazers answered the call and contributed their time and energy to the realization of this masterpiece. Despite overcoming many setbacks and delays, I kept my eye on the prize and never forgot that His delay is not a denial, and now this awesome project has become a reality.

Although the main focus is on black male victims of IPV, we can't write about this aspect without addressing the entire crisis of IPV, comprehensively, truthfully, and holistically. Thus, within the chapters, there will be overlap and redundancy pertaining to some of the statistical data and other information; however, this is a strategic move and is necessary for the reader to achieve full comprehension due to the complexity of the topic and the numerous factors involved. I am blessed, because we all are professional social workers as well as professionals in other disciplines, and we have either indirectly or personally experienced and survived this public health problem and/or know someone who has been impacted either directly or indirectly. The point is that the stories had to be told, subjectively and objectively, and I wanted to utilize this type of platform to do so, while educating, informing, and inspiring victims, advocates, educators, professionals, and the world alike.

The contributors' areas of expertise have been showcased and their deposits into your enlightenment have been told from a personal, research-based, practice-focused, and/or policy-based perspective. This book is purposefully unique and different from all others. It is nonfiction, inspiring, educational, and motivational, with a social work flavor. It is a classroom textbook *and* a "must read" on a personal level. The reviewers have also played an instrumental part in sharing their words of wisdom: Mr. Milton Bailey presents a wealth of experience as a retired social worker who has been exposed to violence and trauma as a Vietnam War veteran and a therapist involved in assisting others in picking up the pieces; Pastor Willie Batts Jr., as an educator and school administrator who has witnessed and intervened to address issues within the K–12 environment, speaks from a place of familiarity as our youth struggle to rise above the issues of the twenty-first century; Attorney Karen Baynes-Dunning, whose tireless work with children and families within and outside of the court system, personally and professionally shares her expertise in this plight to create solutions; and Dr. Theodus Drake, pastor of Second Mt. Zion Baptist Church, lends years of personal and professional experience and knowledge from counseling and guiding others through the storms of life with pragmatic feedback to persons young and old. This book consists of a powerful lineup of contributors, and I am thankful and blessed that as a result, you will be exposed to and educated about the reality of this public health problem as it has never been told before. Every chapter tells a story, and every story represents someone's real-world experience.

ACKNOWLEDGMENTS

First and foremost, the glory belongs to my Lord and Savior from whom all of my blessings flow. Your unconditional love has transformed my life, my will, and my ways. To all of those who are not here to tell their story, I honor their memory, and for all of those survivors who daily conjure up the courage to take a stand against intimate partner violence, I stand on your shoulders in my quest to reach multitudes via any means necessary. To all of my content contributors for taking this ride with me, I appreciate you. Your input, thoughts, opinions, feedback, reviews, expertise, and constructive criticism were invaluable. Even for the "setbacks," which I now realize were just a setup to propel me closer to my destiny and to the realization of this vision ordained by God, it wasn't in vain. I now know that the article submissions and proposals rejected by others over the years, because certain criteria were not met in their subjective perspectives, were a part of the divine plan to push me into something greater. I acknowledge and thank all of you too.

I recognize Dr. Eddie Morris, whose childhood exposed him to the woes of living within the cycle of abuse, addiction, crime, and violence, and who as an expert in prevailing against the hard knock lessons of life and in the profession and the field of social work has dedicated his life to addressing the issues of at-risk youth. Thank you for my wake-up call and for introducing me to the concept of Voices from a Broken Village and Burying the Pain, works that are still in progress. I acknowledge Attorney Jermario Davis, "the quiet storm" of his profession at Davis Legal, LLC, for his legal guidance and input throughout this project. To Dr. Sharon Bent-Harley, my extraordinary physician of twenty-four years, thank you for listening to and supporting my vision and for providing insight, expertise, and wisdom in the areas that were lacking. You are the best.

In every platform for which I am blessed to reach others, I attempt to educate, edify, encourage, and inspire. The contents of this book are strategic and purposeful in accomplishing these goals personally, professionally, and in the classroom. Thus, I acknowledge all of my past and present students who, in their own way, have taught and continue to teach me more than any book can ever deliver. Last but not least, I acknowledge my Mountain Arbor Press publishing team for their patience, guidance, and support throughout this tedious and sometimes cumbersome journey. You made it all worthwhile.

INTRODUCTION

According to the Centers for Disease Control and Prevention, intimate partner violence (IPV) is a community crime problem that costs the United States more than $5.8 billion every year. Intimate partner violence, often called domestic violence, is generally described as abuse within the context of an intimate relationship, where one partner asserts power and control over the other. While legal definitions vary by state, IPV can include physical, sexual, and psychological abuse, as well as economic coercion. It affects millions of individuals in our country regardless of marital status, sexual orientation, race, age, religion, education, or economic status. Because of the seriousness of the crime, the effects on victims and their families, and the difficulties in the criminal justice system response, victims of IPV may require sustained resources, including access to emergency shelter, housing assistance, protection orders and safety planning, support groups, and financial assistance. IPV is a major drain on law enforcement resources, involving a high volume of calls and repeated calls to the same location, consuming large amounts of time and often resulting in injuries or death. Intimate partner homicides make up 40–50 percent of all murders of women in the United States. Women who have experienced a history of IPV report more health problems than other women; they have a greater risk for substance abuse, unemployment, alcoholism, and suicide attempts (CDC). So how could a national problem, so costly and harmful to families and children, continue to persist and worsen year after year?

The latter part of the aforementioned excerpt is the opening statement of an article that pertains to IPV and is representative of the contents of what readers will view the majority of the time this subject is addressed. The focus is strictly upon women, although it does make mention of children and families (as it should); however, it lends credence to the reason and the justification of why this book is long overdue. Case in point, "When we discuss domestic violence, it is often assumed that the victims are women. And the statistics are truly astounding. The less-told story is that a striking number of men are victims, too, suffering physical, mental and sexual abuse in both heterosexual and same-sex relationships" (Weinstein, 2015). According to the CDC (as stated in Weinstein, 2015), one in four adult men in the US will become a victim of domestic violence during his lifetime. That's upward of three million male domestic violence victims every year, or one man in America abused by an intimate or domestic partner every 37.8 seconds. Welcome to the twenty-first century!

Attorney Weinstein has raised a valid point and eloquently conveys the essence of what this book specifically embodies in the following statements: "Highlighting these statistics is not meant to downplay in any way domestic violence among women. It is, however, intended to add to the growing conversation that anyone can be the victim of domestic abuse and everyone who needs protection deserves access to it." There is an unnoticed population that in the past might have received some research interest and even some limited attention in IPV presentations, but the extent appears to have been minimal. That unnoticed population is the male victim of IPV—more specifically, the African American male.

It is ironic that the title of the article from which a part of the opening statement was quoted is labeled "A Different Response to Intimate Partner Violence." That is the rationale that supports my vision to address this taboo and sensitive subject, and it began approximately seven years ago when God placed it in my spirit to create a platform for those victims who are lost in the depths of society's systemic double standards of gender role expectations and stereotypes, misconceptions and lack of interest in the minority on many levels, and from many genres of discrimination. The platform of the future must take a different approach than previous ones and must be addressed and embraced honestly, empathetically, and compassionately, yet totally without the fear of retribution due to the lack of political correctness. We must address the "elephant in the room." I introduce you to *The Twenty-First-Century Crisis of Intimate Partner Violence among African American Male Victims: Up Close and Personal with an Unnoticed Population (A Social Work Response).*

CHAPTER 1

TORN AND DRIVEN

DR. IRMA J. GIBSON

Historically called "domestic violence," intimate partner violence (IPV) describes physical, sexual, or psychological harm by a current or former intimate partner or spouse. This type of violence can occur among heterosexual or same-sex couples (Breiding, Chen & Black, 2014).

Today, the terms "domestic violence" and "intimate partner violence" are used synonymously to describe some form of abusive behavior by one individual upon another person in a [current or former] relationship. While these two terms are used interchangeably to describe the same criminal offense, they have different origins (Wallace, 2015; Smith et al., 2017).

HISTORICAL INFORMATION ABOUT DOMESTIC VIOLENCE

The origin of the term "domestic violence" stems from the traditional view of violence in a relationship that focused on two individuals in an opposite-sex (heterosexual) marriage. Typically, the abuser was the husband and the wife was the victim. The abusive behavior was viewed as a form of violence that existed within a domestic relationship (Smith et al., 2017).

According to Wallace (2015), women's rights groups began an organized campaign highlighting the need to address the issue of abuse perpetrated by husbands upon their wives in the early 1970s. In response, government and nonprofit agencies started providing emergency shelters and other advocacy services for women who were survivors of domestic violence. Thus, societal views expanded to better understand the types of violence that exist within relationships as well as the reality that the roles of abuser and victim are not gender specific. As a result, the term "intimate partner violence" was introduced to encompass a broader understanding of violence in relationships. While it is challenging to specifically identify when it came into existence, it appears to have gained momentum sometime around 2000.

Wallace (2015) further states that the use of the term "intimate partner violence" [challenges us to critically rethink] the old view that abusive violence only occurs in marital relationships (the husband was the abuser and the wife was the victim). Regardless of sexual orientation, marital status, or gender, the concept of intimate partner violence acknowledges that abuse can exist in any type of personal intimate relationship. Like "domestic violence," this new term does not assign the roles of the abuser and victim to one gender or the other. Intimate partner violence is a critical issue that crosses a variety of cultural boundaries, including age, race, religion, ethnicity, and economics, to name a few. Yet there is a population, males, particularly the African American male, that is often overlooked as representing victims of this seriously debilitating problem.

Though the terminology is changing, it remains challenging to identify victims who do not fit into the stereotypical model of females in opposite-sex relationships. Some areas of our society still view the typical male as being strong, which makes male victims in either opposite-sex or same-sex abusive relationships more hesitant to come forward and request assistance out of fear of rejection by their family, friends, and peers (Wallace, 2015). The author of the above history lesson conveys a powerful introduction to this chapter. He makes it plain for all readers to comprehend as he discusses in layman's terms how and why the terminology changed while summarizing and identifying the complexity of the issue as it relates to the societal and other implications.

Make no mistake, IPV can happen to anyone, no matter how much education or money he/she has. In the United States, about one in four women (or 27 percent) and one in ten men (or 11 percent) report having been harmed by sexual or physical violence, or by stalking by an intimate partner at some point in their lives (National Center for PTSD, 2015). My son, Terrell JaMar Gibson, can be counted as a number in this statistical data. Thus, I want to introduce you to my personal experience as a mother of a black male victim of intimate partner violence and the conflicting feelings and emotions I encountered as a parent *and* as a clinical social worker. I possessed specific knowledge and training about the problem, yet my up-close and personal experience rocked me to the core and challenged not only my educational training, but even more so my practice wisdom.

Educating others in the classroom setting and within the practice arena on these types of issues is a sharp contrast to actually experiencing problems of this caliber up close and personal. Self-awareness and self-regulation are major components that are infused throughout the social work curriculum. These crucial entities are the first steps toward becoming an effective and emotionally sound social worker in preparation for the unique, diverse, and culturally robust encounters the profession presents. Although this was not my first rodeo in regard to personally experiencing topics and subject matter addressed in the classroom, with my social work students and within my educator's role, there was something different about this experience. While I attempted to "think social work" during the ordeal, I was also propelled to think beyond the basic instincts of safely resolving the dilemmas and felt as though I was in a fight-or-flight impasse and that survival was the main goal for my son and for me.

After this ordeal, I now know the true meaning of "by any means necessary" and going above and beyond to make things happen. Short of breaking the law and losing my moral integrity, I found myself taking drastic actions to "save" my one and only son. I'm not sure whether I made certain "rational" decisions because of my social work training, or because of my parental upbringing and what I was taught via "family," one of the main agents of socialization. I could have easily "lost it" and allowed my emotions to overtake me. I do believe that as a result of my choices in handling the situation, a "bullet" and a catastrophe were avoided. I shudder to think what could have happened. Never judge another person if you haven't walked in his/her shoes.

In my introduction, intimate partner violence is defined in general, with more thorough and comprehensive definitions to follow in the subsequent chapters. To reiterate, IPV "includes physical violence, sexual violence, stalking and psychological aggression (including coercive tactics) by a current or former intimate partner (i.e. spouse, boyfriend/girlfriend, dating partner, or ongoing sexual partner)" (Breiding et al., 2015). As a social worker with over thirty-four years of clinical and administrative experience and practice wisdom, I thought I was equipped to handle anything thrown in my pathway. I thought I had seen and experienced it all. But no textbook, dialogue, lecture, or job could have sufficiently prepared me for the emotionally draining experience I faced as a result of my son's ordeal as a victim of IPV. It was surreal . . .

THE MIRACLE OF LIFE

On December 13, 1989, 11:11 a.m., in the labor and delivery section of the Bamberg, Germany, *Klinikum* (hospital), a six-pound, six-ounce baby boy was born to two proud parents. Four weeks premature, I considered him to be my miracle baby, as I had consistently prayed for his future while I carried him in my womb. Upon laying my eyes on this little creature I had a part in creating, I was in awe! I counted ten fingers and ten toes; there were no breathing tubes or anything that might indicate he wasn't healthy. And even if this were the case, it didn't change my feelings. He was perfect in my eyes, and that was all that mattered. I instantly knew my life had changed and would never be the same again. Little did I know the significance of that statement, as it reflects the ordeal my son and I experienced some twenty-one years later.

All but three of the coauthors of this book have either known and/or interacted with Terrell from birth and/or during various stages of his life. Some have watched him grow and mature into the young man he is today, and some have had the pleasure of interacting with him in other informal settings, or as a mentor or a spiritual advisor. I believe it's accurate to say that if they were asked about his personality, character, and/or their first impressions of him, you might hear such adjectives as intelligent, mannerly, polite, respectful, friendly, mild-mannered, and hardworking. In describing my role as a mother, I often tell others that if I had chosen to give him a sibling, I would have wanted a child identical to him. He was just a joy to raise, and he continues to be a joy to parent. Despite the "hard knock" lessons I have witnessed thus far in his life, I count it all joy and often think about the blessing he has been as a son. As he matures through young adulthood, he continues to be a work in progress. And while the challenges could have been worse, I can honestly state he has been an ideal son who has been willing to strive to be a model citizen and an example for others, learning from his mistakes and being receptive to the guidance and positive influence provided throughout his life. It hasn't always been easy raising this black male, but I have no regrets. Appendices 9, 10, and 11 provide some evidence about his temperament and his transformation from childhood to the present. On his twenty-fifth birthday, *he* gave *me* a card of thanks. Who does that?

THE EARLY YEARS

For I know the plans that I have for you . . . plans to prosper and not to harm you, plans to give you hope and a future. (Jeremiah 29:11)

Some of my most vivid memories occurred during Terrell's infancy through age seven, which are, in my professional opinion, the most impressionable years. Experts agree that the first five years of a child's life are fundamentally important. They are the foundation that shapes children's future health, happiness, growth, development, and learning achievement at school, in the family and community, and in life. Recent research confirms that the first five years are particularly important for the development of the child's brain, and the first three years are the most critical in shaping the child's brain architecture. Early experiences provide the base for the brain's organizational development and functioning throughout life. They have a direct impact on how children develop learning skills as well as social and emotional abilities. Children learn more quickly during their early years than at any other time in life. They need love and nurturing to develop a sense of trust and security that turns into confidence as they grow. Babies and young children grow, learn, and develop rapidly when they receive love and affection, attention, encouragement, and mental stimulation. In fact, children learn from the moment of birth. They grow and learn best when they receive attention, affection, and stimulation, in addition to good nutrition and proper healthcare. Understanding the stages of child development helps parents know what to expect and how to best support the child as she or he grows and develops. In many settings, early-childhood programs support parents and their children from infancy through age eight, which includes the important transition from home to school (Facts for Life, 2010).

Terrell taught me a lot and often made me laugh as he was transitioning through the various stages of early life. I remember one incident that occurred when he was about four and a half. His dad was standing while holding his newborn niece and Terrell looked up and asked, "Daddy, can we get one of these?" And he proceeded to specify the gender: "But I want a boy one." That was hilarious! Another fond memory occurred one night when he was about four or five years old. He was kneeling and repeating the prayer I was reciting and teaching him prior to his bedtime. As I recited, "Now I lay me down to sleep, I pray to the Lord my soul to keep; if I should die before I wake, I pray to the Lord my soul to take." Before I could recite another word, Terrell stopped midsentence and asked, "Why do I have to say 'if I should die before I wake'?" This is when I realized the time had come to switch to the Lord's Prayer, and that he was truly his mother's son. He was growing up, his cognitive development was on track, and the perception of words mattered.

As a kindergartener, he was blessed with the tutelage of Mrs. Lisa Curry Tolbert at Faith Academy. She was awesome and was the first educator to utilize rap culture to teach him important lessons in his young life. I and other family members were proud of the fact that he could "rap" the sixty-six books of the Bible just like that, and we often displayed his talent to anyone who cared to listen. He attempted one of his first negotiating and testing moments in primary school: a pitch to have an item from his list of "wants" fulfilled. His heartfelt response to my refusal to honor his request is stated in the letter listed in Appendix 10. And one of the most vivid and heartfelt memories and child/parental teaching moments of all occurred when he was celebrating one of his teen birthdays. As I was planning what I thought would be an awesome, special birthday celebration at Dave and Buster's, he shared that the best birthday he had ever had was when I had prepared cupcakes for him and brought them to school to share with his classmates. He stated I had not done that in a long time (elementary school, to be exact). This was a teaching moment that confirmed what research has consistently shown about effective parenting: spending quality time with children is much more effective in the demonstration of parental love and emotional support than material possessions. "Emotional intimacy in the parent-child relationship has been found to be important in the development of self-esteem, with the benefits lasting into adulthood. Maternal support [is] associated with emotional well-being" (Hutchison, 2015).

There is an idiom that states, from a parental perspective, "Children are heavy on your heart when they are young and heavy on your mind when they become older." I often ponder the truth behind this statement and reminisce about those early years and my experiences as a single co-parent from the time Terrell was the age of four. In addition to the memories I just shared, I remember everything about the primary, elementary, middle, junior, and high school years. I was concerned for his well-being and whether his kindness would be taken for weakness. And yes, bullying was a major concern also, because he was a victim at various stages of his school years. I often wondered if he would be able to defend himself, as I consistently stressed and instilled the nonviolent response for addressing the bullies he faced. I knew I could not be with him twenty-four hours a day, but I strategically involved myself in every aspect of his educational and other endeavors: PTA/PTO, field trips, school events, career day, honors programs, Boy Scouts, basketball, band, and all of the extracurricular activities in which he was interested and involved. Yes, I was an involved and active parent whose main goal was to raise a well-rounded, confident, model citizen who stood in his truth, displayed self-love, respected himself and others, believed in himself, and desired to make a positive impact in the world.

I purposely engaged him in conversations before and after school, even if he periodically had very little to say. He knew I was always there for support and to provide a listening ear. According to Facts for Life, 2010, encouraging girls and boys equally to observe and express themselves and to play and explore helps them learn and develop socially, physically, emotionally, and intellectually. Along with the planned family vacations, we embraced those precious moments and treasured quality and bonding time. And because I was cognizant of the fact that he was born into a category (an endangered species) in which he had no choice, I found myself having to occasionally defend my parenting style.

The discussion of my and other parenting styles is pertinent for a variety of reasons. This crucial factor is a common denominator in the research-based results that are explored throughout the chapters of this book, and it is aligned with various theories (to be thoroughly discussed in chapters 10 and 13) that provide explanations and a childhood blueprint for the behaviors and characteristics of both the victims and the perpetrators of IPV. As a single black woman raising a black male, the term "momma's boy" was the label and stereotype I found myself correcting, discussing, and defending to society and even some of my own friends and family members. My parenting strategy is something I don't apologize for, because the label of "momma's boy" was far less detrimental than being born in the "endangered species" category, which had a major impact on my parenting style and my determination to ensure Terrell would avoid becoming a disturbing statistic. It continues to be my priority.

TRAIN UP A CHILD THE WAY HE SHOULD GO: THE MOMMA'S BOY MYTH

To those who wrongly stereotype and label *all* sons raised by women as "momma's boys," I stand to correct you and to educate you from a personal and a professional perspective. Make no mistake, I wholeheartedly believe it was the "momma's boy" influence that kept Terrell sane and able to refrain from resorting to physical means and retaliation throughout this ordeal. The struggle was real! I have always wanted the best for my son, just as all concerned parents should want the best for their daughters or sons. All children have the right to protection. They have the right to survive, to be safe, to belong, to be heard, to receive adequate care, and to grow up in a protective environment. A family is the first line of protection for children. Parents or other caregivers are responsible for building a protective and loving home environment. Schools and communities are responsible for building a safe and child-friendly environment outside the child's home. In the family, school, and community, children should be fully protected so they can survive, grow, learn, and develop to their fullest potential (Facts of Life, 2010).

Since the beginning of time, double standards have existed in regard to how we teach and raise our young females and how we teach and raise our young males. And while I am 110 percent convinced there are some things only another female can teach a female and there are some things only another male can teach a male, good manners, accountability, values, and respect for self and others are the exception and are applicable and teachable by any gender, to all children and youth as they develop across their lifespan. Etiquette such as "keep your hands to yourself," respecting others, and treating others the way you want to be treated should not be gender specific—nor should the double standard which exhibits pride and boastfulness in proclaiming "She is a daddy's girl," but ridicule and criticism if a male is close to his mom. This double standard has to be challenged and discussed.

Why can't single mothers who are raising sons expect the same respect that is desired for our daughters? Unless you have experienced raising a male as a single mother, it is unfair to assume he is a "momma's boy." It's stereotypical to lump everyone in the same category without individually assessing each case and/or situation. And the media and arts often perpetuate this stereotype without considering the fact that stereotypes can be harmful and misleading. Author Kate Stone Lombardi contends in her new book, *The Mama's Boy Myth*, that having a close mother-son relationship makes boys stronger and ultimately helps them be better partners and husbands. Society fears the "blindly adoring mother, the emasculating mother, and the martyred mother. The myth is that any boy close to his mom will be a sissy, a wimp, forever dependent and never a man who can have a healthy relationship. And it's everywhere we look, in the movies, on TV." (James, 2012).

I don't apologize for teaching my son to expect to be treated like a king, no more than I do when I encourage young ladies to demand to be treated as queens. My son was initially taught the value of self-love, and then he was taught the importance of treating his future female companion as a queen. I have also instilled in him spiritual guidance ("He who findeth a wife, findeth a good thing," Proverbs 18:22, KJV) and the biblical principle which indicates that upon marriage, his wife has to be his first priority as he "leaves his mother and protects and honors his wife" (Mark 10:7, KJV).

According to James (2012), in one 2010 research project, Carlos Santos, a professor at Arizona State University, followed 426 middle school boys to determine to what extent they bought into traditional masculine roles. Those who had warm and supportive relationships with their mothers had better tools for communication and lower rates of depression and delinquency than their "tougher" peers. "These boys had a broader definition of masculinity and didn't buy into the idea that men had to be stoic and not fight back at every moment," says Lombardi. "Being close to mom was good for their mental health." She said research shows that these boys are less susceptible to peer pressure to do drugs and alcohol, and they tend to delay their first sexual experience and have less unprotected sex.

THE BIOLOGICAL TRUTH AND JUSTIFIED CONNECTION

I refused to let society regulate and dictate the manner in which I demonstrated my concern for my son's emotional growth and development toward becoming a strong, independent, and self-sufficient black man. It's unfair to judge, because I chose and still choose to base my parenting decisions and guidance on discoveries and factors that have been revealed as a result of the quality time I have expended toward getting to know my son as a unique individual instead of upon the basis of others' expectations. Why do I refuse to conform to everything society dictates for how we live our lives and how we raise our children, adolescents, and youth? One of the main reasons pertains to the fact that research has shown the human brain does not reach full maturity until at least the mid to late twenties (Giedd, 2004). The specific changes that follow young adulthood are not yet well studied, but it is known that they involve increased myelination and continued adding and pruning of neurons. As a number of researchers have put it, "The rental car companies have it right." The brain isn't fully mature at sixteen, when we are allowed to drive, or at eighteen, when we are allowed to vote, or at twenty-one, when we are allowed to drink, but closer to twenty-five, when we are allowed to rent a car without a lot of red tape. Achieving the legal age to participate in a given activity (e.g. driving, voting, marrying) often comes to be taken as synonymous with the developmental maturity required for it, and while I am by no means encouraging you to ignore these milestones, I caution you to avoid letting the standards of society always determine what is best for your children as you raise them.

In the last decade, a growing body of longitudinal neuroimaging research has demonstrated that adolescence is a period of continued brain growth and change, challenging longstanding assumptions that the brain was largely finished maturing by puberty (Giedd, 2004; Johnson, S. B., Blum, R., Giedd, J. N., 2009). The frontal lobes that are home to key components of the neural circuitry's underlying "executive functions," such as planning, working memory, and impulse control, are among the last areas of the brain to mature; *they may not be fully developed until halfway through the third decade of life* (Lahey, 2014). This finding has prompted interest in linking the stage of neuro-maturation to the maturity of judgment. Indeed, the promise of a biological explanation for often puzzling adolescent health-risk behavior has captured the attention of the media, parents, policymakers, and clinicians alike (Johnson et al., 2010). So if you are wondering what they are thinking when their decisions appear irrational, risky, or ill prepared, wonder no more. They probably were not. They truly are not always in a position to make adult decisions, although their behavior is prone to commit adult acts.

[Overall], recent research shows that the human brain continues to develop throughout adolescence, with the prefrontal cortex not fully developing until the midtwenties. Because adolescents' brains are not fully matured, their decision-making and thought processes differ from those of adults. For example, it is developmentally normative for adolescents to take greater risks and show greater susceptibility to peer influences than adults (Physicians for Human Rights, n.d.). These otherwise normal differences can contribute to behaviors that lead to involvement with the juvenile justice system. Beyond developmental influences, additional risk factors associated with youth ending up in the juvenile justice system are cognitive deficits, low school involvement, living in poverty, or being a runaway or homeless (Aratani, Y., 2009; Christle et al., 2007).

I want to reiterate via another crucial example that the frontal lobes of the teen brain are key players in the "executive functions" of planning, working memory, and impulse control. As a result, researchers have discovered pertinent differences between problem solving during adolescence. "Cold cognition" is problem solving when the adolescent is alone and calm, and the processing of information is independent of emotional involvement. "Hot cognition" is associated with cognitive and physiological arousal, in which a person is more responsive to environmental factors. It is automatic, rapid, and emotion-driven, and may consequently cause biased and low-quality decision-making (Hutchison, 2015). Although neuroscience has been called upon to determine adulthood, there is little research-based evidence to support age eighteen, the current legal age of majority, as an accurate marker of adult capacities. But as parents, many of us are guilty of making decisions based upon this societal viewpoint, which can be a disaster depending upon the circumstances and the environmental and social factors at play. Lombardi states it plainly: "Dads are important, too. Parenting is not a zero-sum game. You don't have to be close to one parent and not the other. They both bring something. [Unfortunately] many women fearing that a mother's love can be a 'dangerous influence' close the door on their sons too early. Some studies suggest boys are more fragile than girls, at least earlier in life. Sometimes that 'hearty shove' is premature and can be devastating" (James, 2012).

I have never been quick to allow society's values to dictate how I live my life. I will wear black in the summer, white after Labor Day, and open-toe shoes in the middle of winter without a second thought and with no worry about what others think. Thus my parental decisions were not influenced by the judgments of others, but upon more pragmatic factors. It was because of the aforementioned knowledge and my son's individuality that I strategically raised him with unconditional but tough love. My parenting style was not perfect, but it was executed in a manner that provided an environment wherein he was able to make mistakes, grow, and learn from them without fear of being judged, prematurely cast into situations he was not equipped to handle, or propelled into seeking emotional support from the wrong crowd. Spend quality time with your children and know that each one has his or her own unique personality and genetic makeup. What works for one may not work for the other, and it is up to you as a parent to effectively use your discretion to decide what is best for him or her, based upon a number of factors that have already been addressed. I realize parenting is difficult and that there is no such thing as a perfect parent. However, some parenting styles are more effective than others.

PARENTING STYLE AND THE DIFFERENCE IT CAN MAKE

In the social work curriculum, students are taught about the various types of parenting styles. According to McGoldrick et al. (2011), as cited in Zastrow and Kirst-Ashman (2015), the family environment is of crucial importance to children's socialization and is characterized by three main parenting styles. Permissive parents are nondirective and avoid trying to control their children. They may be either overly indulgent, easygoing, and unconventional, or show little if any affection, leaving their kids to fend for themselves. Authoritarian parents do not hesitate to make rules and tell their children what to do. They emphasize control and authority. The third style is authoritative, which is somewhere in the middle of the other two styles. Authoritative parents have definite standards for their children, who clearly understand what is expected of them; parents want their children to behave in a way that is age appropriate, and a warm, loving relationship exists between the parents and the children (Baumrind, 1996, as cited in Zastrow and Kirst-Ashman, 2015).

Parenting styles are prescribed in part by the community and the culture and can take on different connotations depending upon the community. Research has also indicated differences in parenting styles based upon the socioeconomic environment in which parenting occurs. Although it's not a certainty, middle-class parents consistently use subtle forms of control, while at the same time trying to instill autonomy in their children, who spend a large portion of their time under adult supervision in one activity or another. I am/was an authoritative parent whose ultimate goal is/was to display a high degree of warmth and nurturing, demonstrate positive reinforcement, and grant an increased level of autonomy, keeping in mind the genetic component of human behavior and the aspect of the brain affected by experience. Parents are a major part of that experience throughout life, and in early childhood, other people also come to be a part of the context of ongoing brain development, thus introducing the important role of social environment for regulating the genes (Hutchison, 2015). A good family environment provides nurturance, support, guidance, and a safe, secure place to which children can turn. In layman's terms, know your child and base your effective parenting decisions on this and the fact that positive parent-child relationships are crucial and a positive relationship with at least one parent helps children to feel secure and nurtured. Because Terrell is my and his father's only child together, with no older or younger siblings, this approach was more crucial than ever as he was being raised.

Dr. Laurence Steinberg, author of the book *Age of Opportunity: Lessons from the New Science of Adolescence,* indicates that children raised by warm, firm, and supportive parents, referred to as "authoritative" parenting, emerge from adolescence with more well-honed skills of self-regulation, and are much less likely to fall victim to delinquency, addiction, obesity, and premarital pregnancy (Lahey, 2014). Reflecting on the encounters and various incidents of the IPV experience, my parenting style, which may have been negatively misconstrued as a "momma's boy" approach, was a critical factor in the ultimate outcome of my son's IPV ordeal.

Last but certainly not least, my spiritual faith, my use of biblical principles, and my knowledge of Maslow's hierarchy of needs greatly influenced my parenting philosophy and provided me with an increased assurance that Terrell had the potential to grow and develop into a healthy, viable, and productive member of society with self-efficacy and self-esteem. Abraham Maslow (1954, 1968, 1971, as cited in Zastrow and Kirst-Ashman, 2015) viewed human beings as basically good and saw the thriving for self-actualization as a positive process because it leads people to identify their abilities, strive to develop them, feel good as they become themselves, and benefit society. In this positive process to grow, flourish, and reach their potential, he identified a hierarchy of needs that must be met and fulfilled within the environment: physiological needs, safety needs, needs for belonging and love, esteem needs (acceptance), needs for self-actualization (potentialities and capabilities), and the need for cognitive understanding. The significance of this theory will be discussed in detail in chapter 13.

In part, the daily morning and/or afternoon check-ins to discuss Terrell's day and his concerns, the active parent/teacher organization (PTO) participation and membership, chaperoning for school field trips, supporting him during honor's and other school activities, family vacations, and other avenues to spend quality time during every phase of his life were a part of my efforts to ensure his well-being was holistically addressed. I was on a mission to keep him out of the negative statistics about the black male child, and I was prepared to sacrifice and be more than the "average" parent. No, it was not based on society's values (driving at sixteen, doing this at eighteen, keeping up with the Joneses, etc.). He received his first cell phone at the age of sixteen and was appreciative and ecstatic. My son was only a number to society, and society didn't know his strengths or weaknesses or needs. I did. In fact, only after becoming a statistic as an "endangered species" does the spotlight truly shine on our young black males, and it is usually in a negative connotation and is sometimes too late. I couldn't allow this to happen under my watch.

I refused to buy into such a thwarted and warped philosophy of life as I instilled and spoke life into my one and only son. Negative labeling by society, low expectations, and negative media stereotypes were unacceptable to me as a parent raising a young black male. My line of work exposed me to the fact that millions of children are not protected from the wiles and woes of society. Many of them deal with violence, abuse, neglect, exploitation, exclusion, and/or discrimination every day from those authority figures whom they trust. "In 2010, state welfare authorities received a total of 3.3 million reports of suspected child maltreatment and 1,560 children died from child abuse or neglect. Eighty-one percent of the perpetrators of child maltreatment are parents of the child, with other relatives accounting for 6 percent" (Videka et al. in Gitterman, 2014). Such violations limit their chances of surviving, growing, developing, and pursuing their dreams.

As I raised Terrell, these kinds of facts were always at the forefront of my mind as I contemplated my parenting decisions. It was not my focus to be his friend, but his parent. So, please don't judge or assume what you don't know. As a respectable woman in society who has modeled for him what being treated as a queen entails, it is these kinds of examples I have attempted to set for him throughout his life. Along with his positive male influences and mentors, this invaluable strategy has given him the blueprint to make some young lady very happy in the future when he decides to settle down. It's no problem being a momma's boy if he is being effectively raised by the "right momma," under the "right" guidance, and in a thriving, effective, and productive environment, "exhibiting protection, initiation of the vetting process, deciphering the difference between a five year old and a 29 year old and knowing my boundaries" (James, 2012). Welcome to my "momma's boy" style of parenting. Nature (innate and genetic criteria) and nurture (environmental and social criteria) are powerful forces that must be considered, weighed, delicately balanced, and pragmatically applied. That was and still is my strategy. Please don't get it twisted.

FAST-FORWARD TO THE COLLEGE YEARS

During Terrell's senior year in high school, 2006, I made a career move that resulted in a relocation to southeast Georgia. Not surprisingly, Terrell was excited and supportive, and he actually looked forward to the transition into a new environment and, eventually, the college experience. After his graduation from high school in 2007, we relocated again to Pooler, a move that placed me closer to my job as a college professor. Terrell had been accepted into Savannah State University and was eagerly making preparations to embark upon the next chapter in his life. This was a life-changing decision in more ways than one. As an only child, his father and I decided that residing in campus housing was a necessity. We both agreed it was the best investment we could have made toward preparing him for his future and adulthood. This was the perfect venue to expound upon and enhance his socialization skills. This diverse environment is where lifelong friends are made, true characters are tested, roles are established to either become a leader or a follower, crucial decisions are made that can have a lasting impression upon one's life, and factors that often determine whether academic success and the ultimate goal of graduation are reached. These are some of the elements that predict if one's potential will be fully realized.

Terrell and I had a tradition of meeting for lunch each Saturday after my classes. School and life were our main topics of discussion, and this was his time to vent and address any concerns on his mind. Of course, I was always accessible if there was a crisis outside of our normal meeting times. While I had informed Terrell about the joys and pains of college life, what and whom to avoid, and how to succeed academically, I could never have prepared him for the ultimate lesson that he would eventually learn during his tenure toward furthering his education. Honestly, one of my biggest fears as a parent has been the unpredictable actions of others with whom Terrell directly and even indirectly interacts. I know him, but I don't know them. (And unfortunately, sometimes he is too trusting.) I frequently teach my social work students about the nature (innate qualities) versus nurture (environmental and learned qualities) theory and how human behavior is determined, in part, by those two main factors. Our beliefs and values are derived from the main agents of socialization: family, school, peers, media, social media, employers, and religion. Socialization is the process through which people are taught to be proficient members of society. It describes the ways people come to understand societal norms and expectations, accept society's beliefs, and be aware of societal values. It also describes the way people come to be aware of themselves and to reflect on the suitability of their behavior in their interactions with others. Socialization occurs as people engage and disengage in a series of roles throughout life (Little, 2016).

While I am confident a solid foundation has been laid for Terrell and that prosocial norms and values have been instilled for the various roles he will encounter throughout his life, I am not naïve to the fact that sometimes offspring are different in the absence of their parental figures. The agents of socialization outside of family can be equally influential. Terrell is not an exception. And while that's not necessarily a negative revelation, it is just reality. I am a firm believer that the true test of character is what you do when you believe no one else is looking. I wholeheartedly believe in Terrell, and I have made a conscious effort to allow him to make mistakes without being too critical and judgmental as long as there is a positive lesson to learn and a determination to do better today than yesterday, and even better tomorrow than today. I am also a firm believer that when we know and learn better, then we should do better. Yet, I am still leery of the unpredictable actions of others, and I constantly stressed this concern to Terrell and his "trusting" nature as he faced college life within the confines of his home away from home. I had no clue what he (we) were about to face.

A PARENT'S WORST NIGHTMARE

Overall, Savannah State University was a life changer for Terrell, filled with positives and negatives as is expected in any typical college experience. However, the nightmare that propelled me to write this book was my son's up-close and personal encounter with intimate partner violence. Although I don't quite remember the specific date I eventually discovered his livelihood was being impacted by this socially, emotionally, and physically debilitating social ill, I remember vividly how I felt: anger, disbelief, fear and disappointment, and a range of emotions that was overwhelming. As a parent, how did this happen? How did this skip my radar? I'm a perfectionist, and I felt as though I had failed him as a parent. As a social work practitioner, how did I not know? Months before the revelation, Terrell had become involved with a young lady with whom I can honestly say he had fallen in love. They were inseparable, and 20/20 hindsight indicates this should have been my first sign of an unhealthy relationship for such a young couple. But she appeared to be a fine young lady, "physically" attractive and friendly. Terrell appeared to be content and I became fond of her, accepting and welcoming her into my circle of friends, and more importantly, my family, Terrell's family. I missed all of the signs that were both subtle and at times profound: clinginess, neediness, insecurity, anger-management issues, dishonesty, deception, an oversensitive and overprotective attitude, and personality highs and lows. But Terrell appeared happy, and I was happy for him. Sadly, I couldn't see the forest for the trees.

However, the first sign of serious trouble occurred when I received a phone call from her father, who was concerned because he had received a "pocket call" from his daughter's phone that appeared to reveal a physical altercation between her and Terrell. He was concerned, as any parent would be. So was I. I remember that conversation and the both of us discussing the characters and personalities of our children. Of course, this was not like Terrell. He adored this young lady in a way I had never witnessed with prior relationships. Additionally, he didn't have a mean streak in his body. This was a young man whose compassion is so profound he will risk wrecking a car before he will hit a squirrel or other animal crossing the road. It didn't make sense. We later discovered she had actually intentionally dialed her father's number as she was having one of her tirades so he could listen to the commotion, which she managed to connive and twist. In actuality, Terrell was attempting to prevent her from destroying his computer, as she often resorted to physical means that included destroying physical property and electronic gadgets in her efforts to invade his privacy, a right to which she believed she was entitled. It was a part of her attempts to control.

After attempting to "change her" through love, patience, second chances, and support on every level, he confessed to me that he was emotionally bankrupt, depressed, and wanted to end the relationship because he was being physically and mentally abused. Researchers suggest that leaving an abusive partner is not a single event but a process that extends over time, involving temporary breakups and preparatory stages or strategy (Enander and Holmberg, 2008). I was flabbergasted and immediately knew I had to assist and save my son's life. This could end in tragedy, but I was not about to allow it to happen under my watch. The instincts of a mother's love and my social work practice wisdom kicked in. My mind and my emotions were all over the place, but I knew I had to consult others if I had any chance of effectively and successfully responding to Terrell's cry for help. The calls to her parents, with whom I had become "friends," fell on deaf ears. They denied that their daughter could be capable of this type of behavior and insisted the solution was to teach Terrell to "tolerate" her physical and emotional abuse if he indeed loved her. I couldn't believe what I was hearing. There were many instances prior to and even after the disclosure of IPV where I had supported her basic needs and even included her in our family and social gatherings (against my better judgment). Prior to the revelation, I extended Southern hospitality on many occasions and allowed her parents to stay overnight in my apartment after she became sick from food poisoning and was hospitalized. In an attempt to keep peace at the beginning of the ordeal, I extended the olive branch in vain. Needless to say, our relationship deteriorated, and the next few weeks and months were filled with harrowing interactions and verbal conversations that were sometimes hostile, irrational, lacking insight, accusatory, and full of denial.

DISBELIEF AND DISAPPOINTMENT

It should be noted that after Terrell revealed he was being abused, he followed my advice and dissolved the relationship. In his mind, it was a last resort and was done so ambivalently. Remember, he truly loved this young lady. Many people who have experienced IPV have a hard time talking about it. Experiencing IPV can bring up feelings of shame and low self-esteem. These feelings can make it hard to seek help or reach out to others for support. Also, since violent partners often try to control and keep their partners away from their loved ones, experiencing IPV can make you feel alone (National Center for PTSD, 2015). However, despite his actions to distance himself from the chaos, including changing his cell phone numbers and pairing with friends as a measure of added protection when he moved about campus, he continued to face daily stalking and other attempts to make contact with him.

Stalking is a pattern of repeated, unwanted attention and contact that causes fear or concern for one's own safety or the safety of someone else (e.g. family member or friend). Some examples include repeated unwanted phone calls, emails, or texts; leaving cards, letters, flowers, or other items when the victim does not want them; watching or following from a distance; spying; approaching or showing up in places when the victim does not want to see them; sneaking into the victim's home or car; damaging the victim's personal property; harming or threatening the victim's pet; and making threats to physically harm the victim (Tjaden and Thoennes, 2000). She wouldn't give up, and she was relentless in her efforts to salvage the relationship. And I didn't make it any better. In my attempts to "save" my son, I did not handle the breakup as I should have. I didn't break clean from the interactions with her. A part of me was attempting to control the situation by blindly and naïvely treating her with kindness in hopes that she would take the advice and move on. It became worse. Her promises to move on were never kept; her trust was never gained or provided.

In the midst of the ordeal, I arranged flight reservations, airport transportation, and even purchased an airline ticket during the holidays because it meant my son could have some peace during the winter break. Sometimes, I also kept her at my apartment (away from campus) in an effort to provide Terrell with some solace and some peace. It didn't occur to me that my life could have been in danger, and it speaks to the lack of emotional stability that can overtake someone in these types of situations and how decisions based upon emotions lack intellectual and rational reasoning. The stories of the measures I took to protect Terrell are surreal. One of her family members even resorted to terroristic threats, and a couple of them simply telephoned Terrell to initiate a warning, then exited from the verbal fray upon learning the truth.

Although there were several awful encounters, one incident in particular left an indelible impression in my psyche. After one campus ordeal that turned physical (there were many), the young lady called her parents, who traveled twelve hours to campus with the intent to confront Terrell. I was in Oregon on university business and received a call in the middle of the morning about the looming, unknown threat awaiting Terrell, who just happened to be away from his dormitory and was alerted by his roommate that the family was waiting for his return. Upon receiving the call about the situation, I contacted his dad in Atlanta and requested that he remain on standby. I subsequently placed a call to the young lady's father. I knew I couldn't threaten him, so I chose my words carefully and warned him of the consequences if he hurt my son in any way. He denied any intent other than to have a conversation with my son; however, I informed him that Terrell was off limits and his best plan was to leave campus and return home with his daughter. By the grace of God, Terrell managed to avoid the family without further incident. This ordeal was just one of many that occurred during the course of that rocky journey. The truth of the matter is that the experiences were traumatic, and when I read about the tragic experiences and outcomes of other victims, I realize how very blessed and fortunate we are to be a living testimony. I would not wish this harrowing experience on anyone. It was emotionally and physically draining.

The reports to and the responses from the Office of Student Affairs were documented and consistent; however, they appeared to be of little or no help. Additionally, responses from some of the campus police appeared to present insensitivity and resulted in a one-on-one meeting with the chief of police. Not all of his staff responded in this manner, though some of the males found it hard to believe that a twenty-year-old male could be the victim of abuse. "You're a man," "She's a female," and "Just let it go, man" were some of the comments made by a few of the first responders. Remember that she was an extremely "attractive" young lady. Was this a factor in the response that was sometimes provided by the male police officers? Because many of the incidents occurred in campus housing, we met with and involved the housing director as well as Student Affairs. Restraining orders were filed and paper trails were created in hopes of eventually resolving the issue. This meant nothing to her. Terrell constantly had to watch his back throughout campus, in and out of class. (She even managed to enroll in one of his courses, even though it was not in her major discipline.)

THE JAIL EXPERIENCE AND EVENTUAL RELIEF

According to Woods (2017), while it is often assumed that domestic violence involves physical abuse, this is not always the case. Domestic violence can involve psychological, verbal, sexual, or economic abuse. Contributing to the isolation frequently experienced by victims, these forms of domestic violence can be difficult to spot. Abusers often exhibit certain attributes, however, that can serve as warning signs, including jealousy, controlling behavior, isolation of their partner from friends and family members, hypersensitivity or being quick to anger, and cruelty toward animals or children.

"As with many personal or family-related problems, there is a tremendous stigma that prevents victims from coming forward to share their experiences and to seek help. This stigma, along with overwhelming feelings of shame or embarrassment, can be particularly damaging for male domestic violence survivors. Men often don't want to be seen as weak and thus remain silent about their experiences" (Woods, 2017). It is so important to periodically stop and remind readers of the significance of this book as they continue to embellish their insight throughout the remainder of the chapters. Opportunities to initiate conversations about this subject are crucial. Through them, we can begin to normalize such discussions and create an acceptable and safe environment for victims to come forward.

Student Affairs officially took action when the last incident resulted in a violation of student conduct and the expulsion from campus housing (standard policy procedure, and a part of the plan). They intervened administratively by forcing him to move off campus. This action created an official university forum for Terrell to finally disclose and document the history of his problems with the perpetrator (enclosed in Appendix 5). This time, the responding campus police staff was a female officer who listened to Terrell's story and set a plan in motion. She assured him that if his story was legitimate, her plan would prevail, and she finally set him free via the judicial system and the court of law. She proceeded to arrest both of them, and I found myself reporting to the same jail I had visited with my students during classroom field trips. How ironic! But this paradox resulted in the first sign of relief for the beginning of the end to this nightmare. Just as the female officer predicted, the truth prevailed and Terrell was vindicated. The case was eventually forwarded to family court, where the young lady was found guilty of being the perpetrator. The stipulations that the judge implemented placed serious restrictions on the young lady and her ability to contact Terrell. The judge covered every avenue possible, including social media, and offered Terrell relief to which he had not been privileged for a long time. The system was finally working on his behalf, and he could once again begin to focus on completing his education and the ultimate reason he had decided to attend college. For many months, he received letters from the district attorney's office of victim assistance (Appendix 4), alerting him to scheduled court dates she was facing in regard to the incidents.

I reflect on the experience and how it impacted me as a parent, who feared losing her one and only son to something that could have been prevented. And as a professional, while my social work practice wisdom resulted from years of experience, this ordeal was surreal as it unfolded, and at times it appeared my pleas were falling on deaf ears. But I knew that despite the disappointment and even the periodic embarrassment I experienced, this story had to be told. I was torn, yet I was driven. I am one who follows protocol, rules, and procedures at all costs. But this was my son, and sometimes it felt as though we were losing the battle and the good guys were finishing last. My belief in the criminal justice system was truly being tested. But the consequences could be dire if I (we) resorted to an eye-for-an-eye mentality, although some of the persons in our family and friend circle suggested just that. We were all frustrated that she was allowed to "get away" with her manipulating tactics and conniving behavior. At least, it appeared that way. Why was she not being held accountable for her actions? Terrell was not the only person to whom she was exhibiting aggression. Why wasn't she held accountable for the encounters she had with other females on campus? And what if Terrell had truly defended himself? He was emotionally bankrupt and drained, and so was I. Surely he would be judged, condemned, and even locked up if he responded in any other way than walking away.

Although I wasn't willing to take that chance, it was difficult! I remember his dad engaging in a heated conversation with her father (there were many with both parents), and his exact words to him were: "Even a dog will come out fighting if you back it into a corner long enough!" It had truly become critical. And while I still couldn't allow this to happen, I knew I had to stay the course and encourage Terrell to do the same. I hoped and prayed that sooner or later, this dangerous charade would end before someone was hurt. And it finally did, but not before taking an emotional and social toll on everyone involved, especially Terrell.

How many others are in the same predicament, but are suffering in silence? How many other black male victims are too proud to disclose their vulnerability to others for fear of being judged as "weak"? Male victims of intimate partner violence, just like female victims, often deal with intense self-doubt and anxiety before reaching out for help. Victims may fear their abusers will seek retribution if they go to the police, or they feel great uncertainty about leaving their home for temporary shelter. Men and women can both experience these kinds of worries. But one barrier that tends to only apply to male victims is the belief that domestic violence laws and resources don't apply to them (Weinberger, 2016). These questions and more propelled me to write this book, and I invite you to keep an open mind and lend yourself to gaining insight into this twenty-first-century crisis as you indulge in the remaining chapters depicting challenges, heartache, grief, disappointments, triumph, and hope.

CHAPTER 2

RUN WITH YOUR HANDS UP: MY STORY

TERRELL J. GIBSON

"You're an endangered species." All my life, my mother has reminded me that I already have two strikes against me: the first being African American, and the second being male. As harsh as that sounds, it is reality. Besides, she is a no-nonsense type of parent who has always kept it one hundred with me. And she was preparing me for the hard-knock lessons of life and the real world. I used to always think about that statement as I found myself in the different situations I had to face while growing up. However, the second point is what stood out to me in the dating world. I would see other males growing up and being taught the basic alpha male things like "boys don't cry," no matter what position they were put in. I'm thankful my mother didn't conform to society's way of thinking with this belief, and I believe it is why I am not an angry or aggressive person today. She encouraged me to always show my emotions and to release any negative vibes I was harboring in spite of what others thought about me. I remember that her rationale for expressing my feelings without shame, even if it meant shedding a tear or two, is that "Jesus wept." I didn't quite understand it then, but as I have matured, I recognize what that statement and the entire lesson meant. But what most don't understand or positively learn from their environment is that the African American male is human just like everyone else. We have feelings, and we should be able to express them just like any other being. It may be a part of the reason why so many of our black males have problems resolving conflict effectively. They have not been taught (or allowed) to (effectively) deal with emotions such as anger, which really is considered a normal feeling to have. But many of us are oblivious to this fact because of how boys and girls are expected to behave from the time we are born. Chapter 6 is so on point with describing how society is biased and flawed about how males and females are expected to behave in emotional situations.

But in all honesty, for some reason, I still sometimes feel like the stereotypical man in regard to relationships—that is, feeling and thinking that I/we am/are supposed to show no emotion no matter what, especially in the presence of women or in public. Society's double standards, unfortunately, can still impact us despite the best of teachings. In my particular situation, which resulted in the writing of this chapter, I feel as though all of those stereotypical sayings and beliefs weren't and still aren't fair. And please don't judge, because you never know what situation you will be put in until it happens.

Being my mother's only child, my college years were when I explored who I am—discovering my inner self, finding myself, figuring out who I am, and things of that nature. They say your college years are supposed to be some of the best years of your life for numerous reasons. I can truly say they were, but at the same time, they were probably my worst. I met a very attractive female, and as a male I know the majority of us go by looks when we find "love" in a spouse or partner. But what a lot of us fail to realize is that these females who catch our eyes are also human and have a story. They might have been through things in the past, and they probably have also been raised a certain way. They possibly can come with issues that haven't been resolved that can affect how they treat us and how they react to what we do, and it can make or break a relationship.

When we started dating, everything was smooth. I was so head over heels that I ignored a lot of the red flags I should've paid attention to from the beginning. Right around December of 2009 was when we met, at a college party to be exact. We lived in different states, so phone "convos" were an everyday thing. When we got back to school for the second semester (spring 2010), the bond became stronger. We were talking, hanging out, chilling with each other on a daily basis, but we weren't giving each other time to be by ourselves. Since that chapter in my life, I've come to find it's not good to not have time apart from your significant other. As I was getting to know her, things weren't adding up on who she claimed to be or who she was. As far as her parents' occupations and where she resided, it didn't add up. But even as much as I questioned those half-truths, in my head none of that seemed to matter, and definitely not in my heart. I was blinded by the light—and yes, love is blinding. It led me to overlook and excuse a lot of inconsistencies within the relationship.

To me, she was beautiful and could have no flaw. I thought she was the one. It's crazy how physical appearance can make you forget about any other thing that matters in life. My mom warned me early in life and today that men are visual, and that I need to get to know the heart because "eye candy" can be deceiving. Her favorite saying is, "Don't be fooled by dressed-up trash cans." That's just another way of saying that some of us like to dress up the outside while harboring unresolved emotional baggage and unaddressed hurts and pain from prior experiences. Everything that glitters isn't gold. It doesn't make you a bad person, it just means there are some unresolved issues that need to be brought to the surface. If it's not acknowledged, then what's on the inside is eventually going to surface, and it may not be a pretty picture. Mom also likes to state: "To thine own self be true." And while I am a good person, I'm not perfect, but I am aware of my flaws.

In my situation, one red flag is that the relationship was rushed. Every day, she would always ask and push for the boyfriend and girlfriend title, only after a month of talking. After about a month and a half, I gave in and honored her wishes, even though I didn't know her that well and wasn't comfortable. Yes, I was still getting to know her, but I still accepted the idea and made it official. I should not have given in to the pressure, but I did. That was a major mistake. The control factor was already in motion . . .

Another major red flag was her temper when we had disagreements. She would throw things around the room, yell, shout, and eventually become physical and try to express her anger in ways that were out of control. But me being the person I am, I believe in second chances and giving others the benefit of the doubt, thinking they will change. Anyone can change, and I thought that about her. But I finally realized that if she was raised in that environment, it would take a lot more than just trying to be there for her to bring about a positive change.

Additionally, another red flag is that she was always questioning where I was going and wanted me to be under her watch 24/7. This behavior showed that she was very insecure. Her trust had been messed up because of other guys in her past, and she carried it into the relationship with me, which caused more stress and problems. The relationship carried on for a few months, and in addition to the serious stuff, it had its ups and downs as any other "normal" relationship. The first time I knew I could be in possible danger was when she tried to jerk the steering wheel during a disagreement while I was driving.

Anyone who's willing to put his/her own life in danger to express his/her emotions and feelings definitely isn't healthy or ready to be in a relationship. Things got shakier after that. Not long after that incident, there was another where we were in two separate rooms, due to another disagreement where her temper had flared and the double standards took effect. I was listening to music through my stereo system and playing a video game. I later discovered she had called her dad and had him on the phone while she came into the room. Her motive was to act like I was the aggressor so while he couldn't see what was going on, he could only go by what he heard. So she started trying to pull cords out and unhook everything. I tried to stop her, but at the slightest grab of her hand she screamed, "Stop! Don't touch me!" Initially, I didn't realize her dad was on the phone until I heard him comment, "Don't touch her! What's going on? Is he hitting you?" Then she picked up the phone and walked out the room, responding, "I'm fine." I was in complete disbelief. He assumed I was being abusive or trying to physically attack her without asking or getting a truthful answer to what was really going on, or inquiring about how I was raised. It was a setup that resulted in a totally different story. I'm sure her dad never viewed me the same way.

The common domestic/intimate partner abuse we observe in the news is the male being the abuser or the physical one. Why is that? Besides the awful true statistics, I think it is because with men being physically stronger, society cannot fathom women doing those things. But in my case, she was the aggressive one. And it wasn't the first time it had happened, as far as false accusations of me hitting her. Earlier that same year, we were on a Spring Break trip in Panama City Beach, Florida. Money was tight because a bunch of us college kids were trying to live beyond our means and have a good, fun Spring Break. However, the complete opposite happened. We had gotten our spring refund checks right before the trip. She had to send her money home to her family (all of it), so due to that, the things she had budgeted for were no longer an option. Honestly, we should've cancelled the trip at that point, but we went anyway. I was the driver and had maintenance done to my mom's car with some of my refund check before the trip, since her friends didn't have cars and I was the only one with access to one. My mother was in the Dominican Republic with her students for alternative Spring Break and academic service learning, and she had granted me permission to use her car. So that's where the majority of my refund check was spent, and of course for room and board. We arrived at our destination and from the jump, money became the main conflict. It shouldn't have been a surprise.

She eventually let us know she had only twenty dollars for a five-day trip. I only had $120 after most of the expenses, but I knew to follow everything I had budgeted for and planned to do. However, I couldn't do it for two people, especially in a tourist spot like Panama City. Although my mom and dad chastised me and gave me the "come to Jesus" lecture, they eventually arranged to have additional money transferred to my account, but it wasn't before I encountered her friends' wrath. They had a lot of negative comments to say since I was the male in the relationship and couldn't pay for her wants on that particular trip. In their heads, the male was supposed to "provide no matter what." So at that point, I didn't want to be around any of them, and I decided to just go to the downstairs patio area of the resort for some fresh air and alone time. My girlfriend thought I was going out to ignore her, and she followed me and started yelling out of control, which brought attention from strangers and other people in public. As I was getting off the elevator on the first floor, the security guard happened to be there, so my girlfriend proceeded to storm off and scream in the opposite direction. His first question to her was, "Ma'am, did he hit you?" That is one of the stereotypes a black male in a relationship is subjected to from society. Both incidents were an eye opener for me in that she could always act and play off lies in public. Those lies and dramatic tirades could have cost me my freedom, countless other losses, and the unthinkable—MY LIFE! With me being me, I stayed in the relationship and continued to try to change her. Both of these incidents happened all in the same year, between March and July.

But the question that came to my mind every time her temper flared up was, "What did I do to make her do that?" It's crazy how people think the male has to provoke the female for her to act a certain way, which I now know firsthand isn't true at all. In relationship talks with my mom, she has constantly drilled in my psyche that we all have control over how we allow others to impact us and that we should never give up that power. There is no excuse for placing blame on another person for our own behavior and the actions we choose to display. I can truly say no relationship is perfect and no one is perfect in a relationship, but what we can communicate on, compromise on, and tolerate plays a very big role.

The main reason for our disagreements and issues was because even though I was (and still am) easygoing with a lot of situations, I was attempting to make sure I wouldn't be controlled. I've come to realize on a personal level that a lot of people who are insecure and have had their trust broken in the past are afraid it will keep happening to them in the future. When those prior relationship issues are not resolved and that baggage is allowed into the next relationship, the aspect of "controlling" gets to a point where the significant other wants to know where you are at all times or wants to be around you 24/7. That was also the type of relationship her mom appeared to have with her dad, so it was evident that this was the type of relationship she was used to seeing and being around. Unfortunately for me, what she was looking for with me and our relationship was all she knew. The need to control appeared to be what she had learned.

During July of 2010, I had taken a trip with her, her mother, and her sister to Florida to visit some other family members. This was my opportunity to witness where more of the controlling part came from with her mom. I had driven 80 percent of the route, on an estimated ten-hour drive. I was taught that the driver is supposed to be comfortable, but this brought more light to what I was saying earlier when everyone isn't raised the same. I was forced to stop when and where they wanted to stop. The mother had stipulations on everything. She only used hotel restrooms and not those located in restaurants, gas stations, or rest areas. I had to listen to their choice of music, even though they were asleep most of the time. It didn't matter. The control was mind boggling.

Upon arriving at our destination and settling in, I had more eye-opening experiences. We were all staying under the same roof at their relative's home. It got so bad that her mother would call or text me (as we all were in the same house) to bring her an item or something specific from upstairs or even from within the same room. I honestly felt more like a butler or slave than a boyfriend to her daughter at that point. I had to ask myself, *Is all of this worth my happiness and sanity?* As I was nearing my last two years of college, I knew this relationship would cause more stress, as her tirades escalated every time there was an argument or disagreement. I knew my safety, my life, and my future could possibly be in danger. It was time for a change. I had had discussions with her about her temper and ways we could've solved those issues without the situation getting out of hand. Time and time again she would say things like "I'll control it" or "I'll get better" and "It won't happen again," but in all reality it continued happening and it was getting worse.

The breaking point was the first week of school (fall 2010), and my mother witnessed her temper firsthand. I was walking to my mom's classroom for us to go on our Saturday-morning errands. We would often exercise together, and she would help me with grocery shopping, treat me to lunch, and things of that nature. My girlfriend would sometimes come with us on these outings, but this time I wanted to talk to my mom about my decision to call it quits and put an end to the unhealthy relationship. I wanted her advice, so I needed this time alone with her to bring light to the situation and what had been going on. Once I told my girlfriend what I was doing and that she was not invited to come, she completely lost it. The walk from my on-campus apartment to the building was about four minutes. That morning, it seemed like forever. She hit, pushed, and shoved all the way over. I was silent, emotionally and physically taking everything she was doing as I walked. Other college students looked on, and some were amused while others were in awe. But even as all of this was going on, no one said a thing. Some of the people who witnessed it thought it was funny. In my head, it appeared society was more acceptable of a female abuser, but we all know intimate partner violence is never okay.

As I neared the building, I can honestly say God was in the plan. The architecture of the building was constructed with a huge glass entrance and the doors were mirrorlike. From the outside walking in, you saw your reflection, but you couldn't see what was inside. However, everyone inside the building could observe the happenings outside. In other words, you could see from the inside out, but you couldn't see from the outside in. My mother just happened to be waiting for me in the lobby and having a conversation with her students and colleagues. She saw what was going on. As my girlfriend attacked me with one last hard shove, I had my hands in the air, and that's when my mother opened the door in panic and yelled, "Hey!" to bring it to an abrupt end. My mother had always instructed me to "run with my hands up" if I ever found myself in a situation where a female was attacking me or becoming physical. She had taught me to place myself in the presence of another person, if possible, and to run for my life. When my mom surprised her, my girlfriend turned her anger into sudden sadness. Turning her tears on and off was something she was very good at. She began to cry and sob as if she were the victim. Luckily, people had been watching from inside the building and knew that wasn't the case at all. My mother had a forty-five-minute-to-an-hour conversation with us, not only as a concerned parent and mother seeing her son in a tough situation, but as a college professor. She let us know across the board that no type of violence is tolerated on campus or in the world. She stated to us both that we could not raise each other and that it is never acceptable to put your hands on another person, period! And if this is the case, then the relationship isn't healthy and needs to end. I already knew that, but my girlfriend obviously didn't. Of course, that was the last straw. It had to come to an end, and the relationship needed to be called off for our best interest. I ended it, but once this was done, the real nightmare began. The next few months were a living hell I wouldn't wish on anybody.

She wouldn't accept my decision at all. She said us breaking up was not an option. Every day, things got worse. She managed to go into complete stalking mode, many times throwing rocks at my window throughout the night. She changed her class schedule to a replica of mine, she found out what apartment I lived in, and due to careless roommates I had randomly been placed with that year, she would often have access to come in uninvited. Whether she was telling them I had invited her into the apartment or telling people we were still together when in all actuality we weren't, the dishonesty magnified. Sometimes she entered the apartment forcefully, sometimes she would just walk in because so many people went in and out of the apartment that they would often leave the door unlocked. There were nights I would get back to my room and she would be sitting in the dark in the living room. No one actually knew she was there because the bedrooms were upstairs in the townhouse-style apartments. Constant phone calls were made from her number, then from other people's numbers around campus. The alternate phones she used displayed blocked numbers. She bombarded me with constant messages on social media, wanting me to answer her, to keep the relationship active and requesting to talk, saying she had changed. She informed me that regardless of what I said, it didn't matter because I wasn't single and we were together. She even went to the extreme of faking a pregnancy and telling others she was pregnant, but she didn't want to take a pregnancy test. I knew that with the cautious measures I had taken in that regard within our relationship, it just didn't add up. It was a part of her desperate scheme to hold on to what could never be.

"Why not tell anyone?" "Why don't you call campus law enforcement?" were questions posed to me by the people in power and who handled the dangerous scenarios and issues on campus. The crazy thing about those questions was that I had done just that. I reported to them numerous times, and each time they had responses like "We aren't here to fix relationships" and "We aren't here to mediate." The most common response was, "That's a female; you shouldn't even be here complaining about that." They told me not to bother them, and if I kept on in the future, they would take both of us to jail. There were times she would pop up at my friends' and associates' apartments on campus. When we were dating, she had been introduced to them, so she knew my whereabouts and common hangout spots. Oftentimes she called the campus police when I was at my friends' place and they would show up asking for me. She reported to them that I was bothering her, and it seemed when she reported a made-up story, due to being a female, they took the matter more seriously than when I reported her, even with evidence. When I say I presented evidence to them, I mean witnesses, scratches, physical marks, even items that were broken. I knew hitting a female wasn't the right thing to do, so I restrained her in these situations until someone showed up to help or assist. It would be a serious note and matter until they arrived on scene and saw it was a female. She would put on an act every single time to get out of those situations. It was unbelievable but at the same time a wake-up call because my mom had provided me with reality checks and real-world current events all during my childhood. A part of her parenting style was to keep it honest and be transparent about what I had to face as a black man in the world.

I changed my phone number plenty of times and blocked her from social media. But with the small student body mixed with her ability to manipulate people, she somehow got the new number each time. Even reaching out to her parents wasn't a help. With them being who they were, nothing I said mattered. She would tell them it wasn't true and that everything was fine. Then the situation escalated more when her mother found out that in reality we weren't even together and we were no longer a couple. Her mom dialed my phone to call me names including punk, momma's boy, and coward. She also stated I was not a child of God. She told me I wasn't good enough for her daughter, nor anyone for that matter. This behavior didn't match with someone who claimed to be an evangelist, and I was in complete shock that someone, especially an adult, would stoop that low to try and belittle another person, particularly because her daughter was the culprit. I felt like I needed to fight fire with fire, so I informed my mother about the phone calls and what was going on. Some people looked down on me for doing this. Their judgment of my decision to inform my parents was harsh. To me, it was crazy that in their eyes I couldn't go to my parents for an answer and a solution. These are the people who raised me and always gave me advice throughout the years. But it was okay for her to involve her parents, because I was a male and she was a female. It was unbelievable!

Her mom wasn't the only family member who called. I got calls from a cousin who tried to persuade me to give her another chance and encourage me to stick with her. When I told him what was really going on, he didn't even argue. The reply was, "I didn't know all of that. Yeah, we know how she is." At one point, I felt like I had nowhere to turn and no one to talk to. During this time, I was in a slight depression. Besides going to class, I shielded myself from the world, disengaging from everything I had normally been doing and loved to do. I cut out playing basketball at the gym. Going to the cafeteria—I would grab a quick lunch at one of the eating venues and return to my room. I discontinued going out to social parties, for fear of getting into a bad situation with her. There were times when she said she would leave me alone, and then she would go on public rants, calling me a "momma's boy" or telling me, "Yeah, that's right, go on and tell your mom" when I would walk out and not acknowledge her. She would say these hateful things and within the same day approach my mom to request items she wanted or needed. My mom, being who she is, would oblige. I know it sounds unreal and may appear irrational, but it happened, and it speaks to the crazy decisions that can originate from a bruised and drained emotional state. Besides, my mother had become fond of her despite the ugly behavior that had been exhibited and worsened since the breakup. My mother has a good heart.

However, the cutoff point for my mother was taking her to Disney World for her birthday in October 2010. Yes, after all of those awful encounters, the planned trip was not cancelled. The motive wasn't to get us back together, it was because my mom is a woman of her word and had promised her during our active relationship that she would take her there as a birthday gift. But she made it clear to her it was only to honor her word and nothing more. We took my grandma as added security, and for the extra pair of eyes and ears. Not surprisingly, her mother called and made disrespectful comments while she was on the trip with us, but we made it through without incident.

While my mom continued to show acts of kindness until the end of the ordeal, it was more of a strategy to stay two steps ahead of the "game plan" and to protect me than to risk losing me to the nonsense. However, due to the breakup, my girlfriend's name was removed from the end of the fall semester cruise we had planned and she was replaced with my roommate at the time. Yet, my mom still paid for her airfare to spend the winter holidays with her family and even arranged for my cousin to drop her off at the Jacksonville airport as she was en route to Fort Lauderdale to join everyone for the cruise. Even after all of that, she called everyone near me on the trip. This irrational behavior was negatively impacting her livelihood as well.

Because she was so obsessed with me, she neglected her schoolwork and was placed on academic suspension. As a result, she wasn't enrolled in school the following semester, spring 2011. That was a breather for me and gave me less to worry about. But when my senior year rolled around, fall 2011, it all started back up again. I went on a Fall Break trip, and once again, she called all the people who she knew were on the trip with me, from cousins to friends and associates. On the first day back from Fall Break, she followed me to class questioning me about why I had been ignoring her and began to strike me in broad daylight, again. I had no choice but to restrain her by just pinning her to the ground until her friends came out to aid her and to relieve me. Out of confusion and panic, I just went to my room to call my mother, and then she (the perpetrator) went to the campus law enforcement. They knocked on my door and proceeded to take me to the station, where she was sitting.

Her story was that I had attacked her, but luckily I had a witness with me who had gone on the trip the week before and knew everything that was going on. The only question they were concerned about, though, was if I had hit her or not during the whole altercation, despite all of the times I had complained and called them in the past. My mom had indicated that a paper trail of the incidents had to be established, regardless of what they thought. When the incident presented in a court of law, that would be crucial evidence. On a sidenote, my mom and I had already involved the Office of Student Affairs, director of housing, the campus police, and anyone we thought could help. However, it seemed like she (the perpetrator) was all they were concerned about. I felt like giving up. I couldn't win for losing. Do the good guys really finish last? Once again, I was trying to allow them to handle the situation and bring it to their attention lawfully. I can recognize why so many lose hope in situations such as this. Thank God for my supportive family and friends, and thank God for my supportive parents.

They were going to take me to jail if I became physical with her, no matter what she did, even with the hard evidence I had presented: my headphones being broken, a few bodily scratches, and a witness saying she had attacked me. Statements were written and hours went by. The strategic move of a black female officer changed the course of this saga—I say strategic because she assured me that if my story was true, then the system would work for me. It actually had to get worse before it got better. Because of her discretion, they decided to take both of us in for "fighting on a college campus," which led to both of us being kicked off for a week (Appendix 5).

As we were being transported to the county lockup facility, from the manner in which the African American female officer placed my phone in my pocket (strategic), I was able to send a text to my mom letting her know we were going to jail. I was in there all day because my mom had to attend a conference in another town. However, she bailed me out as soon as she returned to the area. Although she has always indicated I was entitled to one "get-out-of-jail-free card," she assured me this incident did not count. It was still one letdown after another, and it was emotionally draining, to say the least.

As I was returning to campus to retrieve my belongings, I had gotten calls from private numbers—her family members were calling to threaten me. My mother became fed up with the whole situation and had some choice words for them before they abruptly hung up. I had to write a letter for an early reinstatement so my education and academic endeavors could remain on track (Appendix 6). (This letter also confirms, in detail, my recall of the specific events, conversations, etc.) My mom also wrote a letter (Appendix 7).

Shortly after being reinstated to academics and campus life, I was out eating breakfast a few weeks later and got a call from my roommate saying her dad was at the door looking for me. I could hear shouting and wailing in the background from her younger teenage sister and conversation from her mother. They had driven from the Northeast all night to arrive on campus that morning. I immediately informed my mom, who was attending a conference in Oregon, and she informed my dad, and they both gave her dad a call to confront him and intervene in the situation. Her dad's solution was to run away from her whenever she attacked me. My mom informed him that it was his responsibility to teach his daughter to respect others, manage her anger, and refrain from hitting anyone. My dad wasn't so understanding and told him that even a dog will fight to defend itself if it is backed in a corner and forced to choose between life or death. This was just one of several intensive conversations between my parents and hers.

As a result of the October 2011 arrest, we went to court for the incident. Due to us being on a college campus, no restraining order could be granted, so they just ordered a no-contact rule along with thirty hours of community service. This didn't necessarily work, but it was the beginning of some much-needed support from the courts. During my last semester of school, a similar situation happened when she attacked me as I was washing clothes. It was as if the arrest and court orders had never happened. She had been drinking and watching me from the laundry room. Luckily this time a resident assistant (RA) had observed the incident from his window. Someone called the police, and it felt like déjà vu. The officers asked the same question—did I hit her—but this time the RA stepped in and told them no. He had witnessed the entire incident. Once again, people in public were disgusted with me, like I had done something wrong, because she was going to jail. And this time it was her alone. This was the beginning of the peace and the relief I had been seeking all those months.

By the grace of God, midway through the semester when the graduation list was emailed and distributed, she abruptly withdrew from all her classes and went home. Call it divine intervention. It was like a huge weight had been lifted. I knew then I was free from that stress, at least temporarily. Since my ordeal, I have strategically taken steps to protect myself from any effort she may expend to contact me and/or my associates on social media. I am always aware of the fact that anything can happen, and therefore I must keep a vigilant watch over what I disclose about me and my endeavors. It's hard to explain, but I believe and feel that remaining cautious is still necessary. The ordeal changed my life!

While I did not tell you about every single incident and setback during this nightmare, I tried my best to put the timeline of events in order and to be as detailed as possible so you can at least visualize how complicated the problem is as well as the extremes perpetrators will employ to get their way. As time goes on, it's harder to remember the exact sequence in which these occurrences happened. This might be a conscious or unconscious defense mechanism. I'm not sure. Nevertheless, I will not forget how I felt during the overall ordeal. I would never wish what I went through on anyone, and I share my story to try and prevent it from happening to others.

This saga was a definite eye-opener for me about the double standard for men and women in society and how the persons of the world, personally and professionally, can change and affect other people's lives in more ways than you can imagine. This entire experience made me feel that as a black man, we have the hardest trials and tribulations in regard to gender and race. I embraced this whole encounter as a life lesson and keep it in mind when approaching all relationships. It made me wiser, and it forced me to pay attention to contradictions and red flags when I date and get to know women who interest me and whom I allow in my circle. It taught me that you cannot be misled into thinking someone is all good because of your physical attraction to them, to focus more on the inside and get to know her for who she really is. I know this might be easier said than done, because physical attraction is what catches the eye nine times out of ten—and let's be honest, everyone wants someone who is physically attractive as a significant other. But the inside and the character are far more important. Still, flesh can get the best of us. I'm warning you!

Depending on the family upbringing and other important factors, there may be some hidden problems and issues that have not been resolved, and because of "untamed" emotions, you might be walking into a situational nightmare that will change the course of your entire life. Intimate partner violence is real, and it does not discriminate. I'm a living witness, which is why it's important for me to acknowledge the memory of my friend Bobby Jr. and those who lost the battle and paid the ultimate price. I tell my story in your honor so your untimely deaths won't be in vain. Millions didn't make it, and I don't take it for granted that I'm one of the ones who did.

CHAPTER 3

AN ENDANGERED SPECIES: GONE TOO SOON, BUT NEVER FORGOTTEN

MRS. TONICA GLEATON AND DR. IRMA J. GIBSON

Blessed be the ties that bind.

—English Hymn

At the age of twenty-five, Bobby Lee Gleaton Jr. suddenly lost his life in April 2015, after being hit by his girlfriend's car in Metropolitan Atlanta following an argument. From this love/hate relationship originated a history of verbal and physical altercations, make up to break up, and other unhealthy decisions. Amongst the investigation that eventually became labeled as a criminal/homicide case, friends, family, a mother, a father, and a brother struggled to make sense of the ordeal while attempting to begin the grieving process, which was delayed, in part, by the mystery of the tragedy. How and why did this happen? What were the factors that led to such a tragedy? What were the signs that were overlooked, ignored, and missed? There were so many unanswered questions and so many entangled emotions: anger, bitterness, sadness, and disbelief. Bobby's story provides an up-close, real, and "no holds barred" depiction about intimate partner violence and what can happen if it is not addressed effectively. What do you do after the horrific experience of losing your firstborn to a senseless, preventable tragedy?

I remember the first time I saw the Gleaton brothers, Bobby Jr. and Brandon. Terrell and I were driving through the Decatur neighborhood to our new home on which I had just closed and purchased a few days prior; and as I turned on the street in front of their home, there they were in the driveway, frolicking around in their football uniforms, appearing to be free from any of the worries of the world. They looked adorable and appeared to be around the same age as Terrell, so yes, they could very well be playmates for him. After all, we were new to the neighborhood and had not had a chance to meet any of our neighbors. Little did I know that they, their parents, Terrell and I, and our families would become extremely close and form an extended kinship. We had a lot in common, mainly the belief in and fear of God, our federal government careers, the military cultural connection, and the Germany experience.

Bobby Jr. was also born in Germany in October 1989, approximately two months prior to Terrell's birth there. How coincidental is that? Actually, it was not by happenstance. Our paths were destined to cross. The bond and the memories we created and shared during the years to come (the late '90s and beyond) are nothing short of God's strategic plan. Celebrations, milestones, emotional support, guidance, family gatherings, and worshipping together were all factors that intertwined our hearts and Christian love, and we were truly a fellowship of kindred minds. They are good people with good hearts, and it didn't take a rocket scientist to recognize that we were going to remain in each other's circle and create a bond to last a lifetime. As a parent, I trusted Terrell with the Gleaton family, and as parents, they trusted Bobby and Brandon with the Davis-Gibson family. Their dog Ginger was the mother of Terrell's first puppy, Tara. And yes, we kept each other's pets as well. We were truly kindred spirits. And despite the transition in 2006 to the Hinesville location, four hours away, the friendship remained intact, along with the great memories. However, there is one unfortunate recollection that stays with me more, and it is that dreadful day in April 2015.

In the late morning of Saturday, April 4, 2015, I received a disturbing phone call from my son that rocked me to my core. He frantically stated that Bobby was dead but did not know the circumstances nor the details surrounding his untimely death. It was surreal, and I would later find out that intimate partner violence had once again hit close to home, and this time, it was fatal, tragic, and even more costly than what Terrell had experienced. The price that was paid was the loss of a precious human life.

Intimate partner violence (IPV) is violence or aggression that occurs in a close relationship. The term "intimate partner" includes current and former spouses and dating partners. IPV can vary in frequency and severity and occurs on a continuum, ranging from one episode that might or might not have a lasting impact, to chronic and severe episodes over a period of years. IPV is a serious, preventable public health problem that affects millions of Americans (NDICCDVP, 2017).

According to the Bureau of Justice Statistics, based on FBI (2011) data, in 2010 an estimated 241 men (110 husbands and 131 boyfriends) and 1,095 women (603 wives and 492 girlfriends) were victims of IPV homicides. Any life that is lost is one too many. In order to understand the nature of an individual's use of violence in an intimate relationship, you have to understand his/her role in the general control dynamics of that relationship. Unlike the feminist perspective, which posits IPV as a problem strictly against women where men use control and violence that escalates and won't stop on its own, the family violence perspective has described intimate partner violence as behavior initiated by either men or women that is not necessarily frequent or escalating in severity, and not always motivated by the desire to control an intimate partner. The debate entails two different perspectives, and as a result, the following viewpoints have emerged. Intimate terrorism involves the perpetrator's use of violence in the service of general control over his or her partner and situational couple violence in which the perpetrator is violent (and his or her partner may be as well); however, neither of them uses violence to attempt to exert general control (Johnson, 2008 as cited in Gitterman, 2014).

The possible detrimental consequences that can result from intimate partner abuse are numerous, with the most serious outcomes being homicide and suicide. Unfortunately, the Gleaton family's tragedy places them in a statistical category in which no one wants to be identified. The following heart-piercing account that led to Bobby Jr.'s demise is told by his mother, and the inclusion of the term "endangered species" in the title is done so appropriately and intentionally. According to Dublin (2017), "endangered species" is defined by Britannica as any species that is at risk of extinction because of a sudden rapid decrease in its population or a loss of its critical habitat. Additionally, certain criteria have to be met in order to be considered an endangered species, including certain factors or hazards within the environment that are causing eventual extermination. Although some of these hazards occur naturally (innate hopelessness and emotional bankruptcy), most are caused by human beings (systemic and structural racism, discrimination, and unfair criminal justice system/sentencing laws and practices) and their economic (poverty and high unemployment rates) and cultural activities (addiction, mental health challenges, and other social ills). Thus, the endangered species definition is profoundly on point in describing the African American male population, especially when we consider the state of black males in the twenty-first century and the historical battles and woes they have faced throughout time and continue to endure.

"Compared to all males in America Black males are on average younger at 31 years old compared to the age of 'all males' (36 years old). However, when looking at a breakdown of age, Black male children under 18 years old are at the same percentage as 'all male children' (51%). The percent of the population who are males, declines much quicker for Black males as they get older due to a higher mortality rate than males on average. This considering that men of all races and ethnicities have a shorter lifespan than women" (Black demographics, n.d.).

Additionally, Black Demographics (n.d.) reports that about 6 percent of working-age (eighteen to sixty-four years old) black men are currently in state or federal prison, or in a municipal jail. This is three times higher than the 2 percent of "all men" in the same age group. What's even more concerning is that approximately 34 percent of all working-age black men who are not incarcerated are ex-offenders, compared to 12 percent of "all men," which means they have at one point in their lives been convicted of a felony. This data coincides with the increased absence of Black men in the labor force, because ex-offenders are prevented from obtaining a large percentage of occupations by law and are often legally discriminated against by private employers.

These statistics place black males at a disadvantage and on a trajectory that leads to less-than-stellar destinies and failed potentials. They are up against insurmountable odds that have to be delicately and strategically addressed to avoid premature extinction. And so the term "endangered species" has always been at the forefront of my mind, especially since fate charged me with the responsibility of raising a black male child. I often reminded Terrell of this fact and exposed him to every lesson of survival that could be derived from each teaching moment. One of those teaching moments occurred in the Gleatons' front yard during a late-evening gathering with most of the neighborhood male youth. Most of the time, they gathered at this house or mine. I don't recall the exact reason I felt compelled to have one of my informal encouragement sessions with the young males, but it had something to do with a verbal encounter and language I had overheard and considered to be disrespectful by a male visitor from another part of the neighborhood. As I addressed the importance of respect, the other lesson to them was to remember that as black males, they should support each other and make choices that will propel them to become successful because they are considered an endangered species. One statement that I so vividly remember is the focus I placed on the age of twenty-five, stressing to them that I would like to see all of them live and make it past this number. I was attempting to "speak life" into every single one of them, not realizing their fate was not based upon my will nor my thoughts nor my ways. That gathering is forever etched in my memory because I never would have fathomed that less than eleven years later, one amongst them would lose his life to such a senseless and preventable social ill.

During that particular gathering, my reference to the analogy of "endangered species" pertained to the cradle-to-prison pipeline I often introduce to my students, the younger generations, and those advocates who take an interest in at-risk youth. "Nationally, one in three Black boys and one in six Latino boys born in 2001 are at risk of going to prison during their lifetimes. Although boys are more than five times as likely to be incarcerated as girls, the number of girls in the juvenile justice system is significant and growing. This shamefully high incarceration rate of Black youth is endangering our children at younger and younger ages and poses a huge threat to our nation's future. America's cradle to prison pipeline is putting thousands of young people on a trajectory that leads to marginalized lives, imprisonment, and often premature death. Third grade reading levels are one of the criteria that are used to determine the probability" (Children's Defense Fund, 2008). Almost two million of the seventy-two million minor children in the United States have a parent who is currently incarcerated. Ninety-three percent of the incarcerated parents are fathers. Black children are nine times and Latino children are three times more likely to have an incarcerated parent than are white children (US Department of Justice, 2000, as cited in Cook, 2005).

Another fact that aligns with the "endangered species" hypothesis and fuels the prison pipeline is "that millions of American children [particularly children of color] get to fourth grade without learning to read proficiently, and that puts them on the high school dropout track. The ability to read is critical to a child's success in school, life-long earning potential and their ability to contribute to the nation's economy and its security. Children can succeed at reading proficiency if policymakers focus on school readiness, school attendance, summer learning, family support and high-quality teaching" (Annie E. Casey Foundation, 2010).

The age of twenty-five is significant in this case and to the longevity of black male survival for another reason. Research has consistently found that individuals become susceptible to intimate partner abuse at a young age, with a majority of female and male survivors experiencing their first incident of relationship abuse before twenty-five years of age. Intimate partner homicide is the most serious form of intimate partner violence, and is generally the result of an escalating pattern of abuse (Black et al., 2011, as cited in Gitterman, 2014). IPV was not on my radar during my dialogue that night. In fact, it didn't occur to me that this was a serious problem, even when a good friend and business associate of mine was shot in the head by a girlfriend around the same time period and lived to tell his story with a full recovery, physically. Bobby Jr.'s death was my cue to move forward with my vision to expose this social problem. From the pen, the heart, the mind, and the soul of Mrs. Tonica Gleaton, I present to you . . .

BOBBY'S STORY

Bobby Jr., Adidas Bob, Little Bobby, Lah Man, and Bob were a few of Bobby's names. Bobby was the oldest of two. He and his brother, Brandon, were the best of friends, two peas in a pod. They were inseparable, the two of them against the world! No one could mess with Brandon but Bobby. Bobby Jr. was very overprotective of his six-foot-five "little" brother. Bobby was loved and respected by many. He was relentless and unstoppable. He enjoyed the limelight, and it enjoyed him. Although he was raised in church under the reverence and fear of God, Bobby enjoyed going to parties, and the party didn't start until he arrived!

Bobby and Sasha were in a relationship for two to three years, give or take. Sadly, this relationship was a toxic one. They fought a lot. Bobby Jr. spoke to his dad about how best to deal with the issues they were experiencing, and many times he encouraged Bobby to break it off. But Bobby loved her, a lot, and wasn't able to pull the plug. Sasha often reached out to me for relationship guidance, and I too asked her to break it off. Like many relationships, this one was much like a roller coaster. It had highs, but *lots* of lows, which concerned Bobby Sr. and me enough to encourage them to part ways. Sadly, it seemed the more we'd say, "Break up," the more determined they were to be together.

On Friday, April 3, 2015, Easter weekend, I was in the kitchen preparing dinner. Sasha dropped by with two of her friends. Her birthday was coming up, and she and a group of friends were making plans to go to the club to celebrate. I cleaned up the kitchen, said goodnight to Bobby Jr., and went upstairs to get ready for bed. I had no knowledge that Bobby was planning to tag along.

Around 3:45 to 4:00 a.m., Bobby Sr.'s cell phone rang, startling him from a deep sleep. The caller ID read Dale Williams, but it was Sasha who was frantically asking him to come to where they were. "Bobby hit my car," she said. Bobby lay back down but wasn't able to get back to sleep. I asked him who it was and where were they, and he told me. We got up, got dressed, and drove to the Sonic restaurant to see what was going on. It was dark, and it was raining hard. We arrived to find Sasha, one of her girlfriends, two guy friends, and Dale. It was obvious Sasha had been drinking. Her speech was slurred and her demeanor was different than usual. She was adamant about us knowing her car wasn't drivable and she had to be to work later that day, and that her grandfather and mom were going to be mad at her. We asked her what happened and she said Bobby hit her car with his fist. We looked at her car and there was no way damage of that magnitude could have been caused by a fist. It looked as if a body had been dropped on her car, but there was no way of knowing what had hit it. We took her word.

It was strange that among the small group of kids at the restaurant, no one spoke up, yet they all shared the same possessed look, like they knew something but didn't want to say anything. I asked her where Bobby Jr. was and she stated that she didn't know, he had gone walking. Bobby was a walker, so it was nothing that he'd walk to clear his head. Bobby Sr. and I left the restaurant and returned home with the hopes he'd be there so we could talk to him and tell him to break off the relationship. We arrived home and went to his room, but he wasn't there. We called his cell phone, left messages, and texted him, but to no avail.

We got back in bed to get a few hours of sleep because Bobby Sr. had overtime and was to report to work at 7:00 a.m. At 6:00 a.m., the alarm went off. Bobby Sr. said something wasn't right. I agreed, I got dressed, and announced that I was going to patrol the area and see what I could find out. Bobby Sr. called 911 to see if anyone had been arrested, or taken to the hospital or the morgue. The operator gave him a hard time and wasn't much help at all. While driving around, I saw a DeKalb County patrol car parked in an office plaza. I later learned he was a detective. I asked him a few questions to see if anyone had been transported or arrested the night before, because my son was missing and although it hadn't been twenty-four hours, this behavior wasn't like him. The investigator asked me some questions, which I answered best I could, but I didn't like where they were headed. I called Bobby Sr. to tell him where I was, and he joined me. While he was en route, the investigator warned me that he had some pictures, but the person hadn't made it. He asked if I was able to view the pictures, and I shook my head no. Bobby Sr. pulled up, asked what was going on, and the investigator took over the conversation. He shared the pictures with him, and that's how Bobby Jr.'s body was identified. Brandon shortly joined us and we shared the news with him. The investigator gave us his condolences and left us to process the news.

We all drove home, where we made a few calls to family members to share the news. The news of his death was all over various social media sites. Within an hour, I received a text message from Sasha saying how sorry she was, that she would never do anything like that, and that she loved Bobby. At this time it still wasn't confirmed that Sasha had hit Bobby Jr., but the puzzle was quickly being put together. Her mother called me in distress and asked what could she do, but I wasn't in a frame of mind to have an intelligent conversation, as I was still processing that I was now minus one child. I told her I didn't know and I needed to make funeral arrangements, and ended the call.

The influx of people visiting and extending their condolences helped a lot. The love we felt during that time was amazing, but the pain is unshakable because it doesn't go away. We got through the funeral. We asked that it be short, and our request was honored.

There is one extremely painful image in my head that I will never be able to erase, and that is my younger son sitting by his brother's grave listening to his music. He sits there peacefully, reminiscing about their relationship and maybe blaming himself—if he had gone to the club with Bobby Jr. that night, he may still be with him. Brandon aches, Bobby Sr. aches, and I do too. He is sorely missed. I've asked God to heal us, and even though He is, the loss is so great. It still hurts.

Since 2015, I have learned a lot about the legal process in regard to my son's case, and it's nothing like what is on television. It's a very, very, very long and drawn-out process, and there are many layers to each step. I've grown closer to God through prayer, and He has given me patience and peace. I will honestly admit it hasn't been pleasant or painless, but the outcome outweighed all the angst leading up to and going through the trial.

I am now a proud grandmommy of a busy two-year-old boy, by way of my youngest son, Brandon. His name is Braylen Lebron Gleaton, also known as "Mr. Gleaton." Since his birth, this little guy has stolen and captivated my heart, and is one of the main reasons my heart still beats. He was a timely blessing from God and has filled a large part of the void in our lives.

April 4, 2018, marked another year of my son's death, but I've been able to find a little more peace knowing his killer is finally behind bars. Sasha was convicted to serve all fifteen years of her sentence. I empathize with her parents because there are no winners in this situation, but as a victimized parent, she will never be able to serve enough time for taking my son away from us.

I share my story with family, friends, and others so they will see that God is able to heal and keep your heart, mind, and soul in perfect peace in spite of great pain and adversity.

STAY WOKE: RISK FACTORS FOR INTIMATE PARTNER VIOLENCE

The following information comes from a CDC fact sheet and provides valuable data about the criteria that can breed intimate partner violence (IPV). Persons with certain risk factors are more likely to become perpetrators or victims of IPV. Those risk factors contribute to IPV but might not be direct causes, and not everyone who is identified as "at risk" becomes involved in violence.

Some risk factors for IPV victimization and perpetration are the same, while others are associated with one another. A combination of individual, relational, community, and societal factors contribute to the risk of becoming an IPV perpetrator or victim. Only the individual and relational factors will be identified in this chapter, while the latter two will be addressed in chapter 13. Understanding these multilevel factors can help identify various opportunities for prevention.

Individual Risk Factors

- Low self-esteem
- Low income
- Low academic achievement
- Young age
- Aggressive or delinquent behavior as a youth
- Heavy alcohol and drug use
- Depression
- Anger and hostility
- Antisocial personality traits
- Borderline personality traits
- Prior history of being physically abusive
- Having few friends and being isolated from other people
- Unemployment
- Emotional dependence and insecurity
- Belief in strict gender roles (e.g. male dominance and aggression in relationships)
- Desire for power and control in relationships
- Perpetrating psychological aggression
- Being a victim of physical or psychological abuse (consistently one of the strongest predictors of perpetration)
- History of experiencing poor parenting as a child
- History of experiencing physical discipline as a child

Relationship Factors

- Marital conflict—fights, tension, and other struggles
- Marital instability—divorces or separations

- Dominance and control of the relationship by one partner over the other
- Economic stress
- Unhealthy family relationships and interactions (National Center for Injury Prevention and Control, Division of Violence Prevention, 2017)

This profound and heartfelt story is evidence that the will to follow one's mind and heart, despite the best support and love from family, is powerful and that this tragedy can happen to anyone. It speaks volumes about the twenty-first century and the main agents of socialization outside of family: specifically, peers, school, media, and social media.

CHAPTER 4

HOME: THE NEW PRISON

SABRINA MANNING-PRINCE

Intimate partner violence (IPV), also known as domestic violence (DV), has been defined by the US Department of Justice as a pattern of abusive behavior by one partner in a relationship over the other partner. This abuse can be physical, sexual, emotional, economic, or psychological in nature. IPV is neither gender nor relationship specific; males, as well as individuals in same-sex relationships, can also be IPV victims. The first step to ending IPV is recognizing the signs that abuse may be occurring in a relationship. Victims of IPV often suffer in silence due to the control the abuser establishes over them. Victims typically will not self-report IPV until the violence has reached a point that it can no longer be tolerated (Wallace, 2015). IPV can't be comprehensively discussed without addressing the female victim, who has suffered for years and continues to suffer at the hands of male perpetrators. The following saga is representative of the evidence-based data that has been published and written about the survivors of the IPV traumatic experience. The struggle is real.

Everyone knows the story of the man with two distinct personalities. In an instant, he could go from being the morally conscious Dr. Jekyll to the morally bankrupt Mr. Hyde. Clearly men who abuse women fit this description. As a survivor of domestic violence, I am cognizant of how quickly the transformation from Jekyll to Hyde takes place. If I turned to the left, it was wrong and Hyde appeared. If I went right, that too was wrong, and Hyde would appear. In the eyes of my abuser, I could do nothing right, and he could not allow Jekyll with his normalcy to accept the fact that I was not perfect. On the other hand, he allowed Hyde to punish me for not being perfect. My Hyde's desire to have everything perfect meant he had to control me in order to maintain his elusive environment of perfection. Little did he know his attempt to control me belied his claim to perfection. Perfection is not controlled, but it is allowed to blossom and grow.

My growth was stunted over nearly six years of abuse. I soon become someone only Hyde could recognize. That is exactly the way he wanted it. He wanted to keep me within the confines of our home, where he could control my every action, my every thought, and my every desire. Literally, my home became my prison. It is not often a prisoner contemplates and carries out a prison break, yet I knew I was going to have to attempt it or one of us was not going make it out of this volatile marriage alive. I did get out, but I often wondered just how I allowed it to get to that point. Why would I stay with a man who abused me? Why did I allow this Mr. Hyde to have so much power that he caused Dr. Jekyll to vanish? To answer those questions and others that some might have, I am going to share portions of my book, *Home: The New Prison*, as an insight into my world of living with Mr. Hyde.

MY DR. JEKYLL

In the fall of 1990, when I was twenty-two, I met my Dr. Jekyll. He was everything a girl could want in a potential husband, and he treated me like a queen. He was chivalrous, and took an old-school approach in courting. We did not "go Dutch"; he paid for my meals. Never did he allow me to open a door. He did all the traveling to see me, driving two hours one way every weekend to spend time with me. While he still lived at home with his parents, he had his own car and worked two jobs while he saved for a place of his own.

MY MR. HYDE

Six months after meeting, dating, and being courted by my Dr. Jekyll, he and I officially became Mr. and Mrs. on that fateful day, my wedding, May 18, 1991. My own private justice system indicted me and sentenced me to a life imprisonment of marriage. Within the first two weeks, my "Mr. Right" became "Mr. Wrong"—Dr. Jekyll to Mr. Hyde. Mr. Hyde made his first appearance the day I came home from job hunting. As I mentioned previously, he worked two jobs: in the a.m. as a package handler for a global courier company and in the p.m. for a medicinal dispensary. I was to seek, at a minimum, part-time employment. So, I began my search for a job. I started with a temp service. They required that I take tests to determine my skill set. I scored extremely high on their tests and was told I had done the best of anyone ever tested. They said they would be calling me within days to place me at a job site.

When my husband got home from work, I excitedly told him about how well I had done at the employment agency. Boy, was I not ready for what came out of his mouth. He said, "You are not that smart. My sister did not go to school, and she has a job as a secretary. You have not done anything special." That was the beginning of the end. Here you have a man who was attracted to me because of my intellect, but now he was condemning me for being intelligent. Oftentimes throughout our marriage, he would tell me I was not that smart or that I thought I was so smart. The verbal abuse began. Considering that he was a very intelligent and professional young man, one would think he would appreciate his wife being likewise. I was. However, I soon discovered that he viewed me as competition.

Not only was he attracted to my brains, but he also was attracted to my looks. Again, the very thing about me to which he was attracted became something he detested. He is light-complexioned and I am bronze/brown-skinned, so I was constantly referred to as "your black self." Did he not realize we are both black? Hmmm! The third thing to which he was attracted was my spirituality. Yet that, too, become a source of contention for him. You see, in his warped sense of right he would use the scriptures to browbeat me, saying I was usurping his headship anytime I did anything he thought was wrong, according to his standards, not God's. What should have been a solid foundation for a marriage was actually a rocky foundation of dislike for me in the area of intellect, physical attractiveness, and spirituality. He was my judge and jury. I was in shock and disbelief that someone who had doted on me so much during our courtship could make a complete 180-degree change to become a man who would sentence me to a life of misery and who seemed to despise the ground upon which I walked. No longer would I tread the path of freedom and independence, but I was now enslaved to him and his desires. Oh, I felt as if I needed to leave, but I was married now. As a Christian woman, it is not acceptable to up and leave without just cause. He had not hit me, but he had slaughtered me with his words. I soon found out the saying "Sticks and stones may break my bones, but words will never hurt me" was far from the truth. The invisible wounds inflicted by his tongue were painful and cut to the core of my existence.

He began controlling my every move and every aspect of my life. That, too, I did not readily recognize because I thought his actions were those of care and concern. He further felt the need to control me because he did not want anyone to find out about the abuse. If he knew where I was at all times, whom I was with, and what I was doing, he could keep tight reins on my mouth. As the saying goes, he was afraid my loose lips would sink our already sinking "ship" of a marriage. His initial degree of control was a gateway to emotional, verbal, and physical abuse and neglect. While he never sexually assaulted me, I soon found out that his desire to control me was greater than his intimate desire to have me as his wife.

Allow me to rewind to the early years of the marriage through a series of flashbacks. They are not in chronological order, which is often the case with victims of most types of abuse. Yet I cannot continue without asking you to allow me to point out something to all readers. No two cases of domestic violence are identical, but there will always be two common denominators: an abuser and the abused. Each victim has her own "mountain." It may seem like a molehill to some, but until one lives through abuse, no one can say what is minor for anyone else. Abuse is abuse, whether perceived as minor, major, acute, or severe.

I have broken down my imprisonment into three categories: Home, Work, and Play. Yes! Most readers can easily grasp the Home category, but the other two may not be so readily grasped. Well, know that prisoners do have work detail, and with good behavior some are granted some time for leisure.

HOME

Negligence is a form of abuse, and the first time negligence was evident was shortly after we were married. I came down with honeymoon cystitis, a urinary tract infection accompanied by a burning sensation that causes one to have the frequent urge to urinate even though the bladder is empty. In severe cases, there may even be the visible presence of blood.

Well, my case became severe. Since I was new to the area and had not yet found a family practitioner, I relied upon my husband for guidance. After nearly two weeks of suffering, he did not take me to the doctor until I told him there was blood. Prior to my seeing blood, he ignored my cries as if the symptoms were going to just up and disappear. When he finally decided to take me to the doctor, we found out just how severe my situation was. Did he apologize for being inconsiderate and negligent? No way! His treatment of me in this situation was indicative of how he would treat me anytime I was sick or not feeling well. However, when he was sick, it was my wifely duty to make sure he had the best of care.

Next came the verbal and physical abuse. Within the first six months of marriage, I saw the real-life Dr. Jekyll/Mr. Hyde play out right before my eyes. They were both my warden in this prison called home. How so? After each dangerously explosive episode with Mr. Hyde in the leading role, Dr. Jekyll would, with his cunning ways, give me a false sense of security as if he truly loved me and wanted to please me. Imprisonment, as we all well know, is the removal of freedom to roam and make one's own decisions. One is told when to lie down and when to get up, when to speak and when to keep quiet, when one can have visitors and when one is to be alone, etc. Another aspect of imprisonment is punishment. Usually one will be punished more readily for noncompliance or the perception thereof. Again, step back with me in time to my days of being incarcerated right in my own home.

***

I do not know about other women, but I think a man's whereabouts after midnight should be only one place—at home with his wife. An occasional outing with the boys is to be understood, but it should not be the norm. It did not start out this way, but later in the marriage, he would leave home around midnight. He would tell me he was going to his best friend's house. I never felt comfortable with this, but what could I do? When he wanted to go out and do whatever it was he was doing, he orchestrated a way to have total warden control. I can see that sleek, red-and-charcoal corded telephone as clear as day. SMH! Anyway, he would take the cord that connects the handset to the base so I could not make any outgoing calls. I was to talk to no one while he was away. He would call back periodically to make sure I had not left. When the phone rang, I was to simply lift the handset so he knew I was still there.

One night when the phone was usable, I decided I would call his best friend. I was wondering why my husband had to leave our house to go somewhere else at midnight. So, I asked his friend, "What is my husband getting at your house that he cannot get at home?" Not knowing what to say, the best friend stumbled over his own words. Well, my husband was there, and boy did he let me have it over the phone for calling his friend to spy on him. He told me he was on his way home, and I could tell in his voice that meant trouble. I went downstairs to make sure the door was locked and the security chain was in place. For added protection, I locked our bedroom door. I was a sitting duck, hoping he would calm down by the time he got home. Hoping, too, that when he realized the door was chained he would get back in his car, go back to his friend's house, and spend the night there. Oh, no! Although our front door was metal, he broke the chain by kicking the door. The sound I dreaded, his barging up the stairway, was one of the most chilling moments of my imprisonment. When he discovered the bedroom door was locked, he kicked it in—knocking a hole from the outside of the door through to the other side. He came over to where I was, took off his belt, and beat me with his belt buckle. I feared he would kill me, but he knew how to aim his blows and use his "weapons" to minimize visible signs. He did, however, break the skin, but I knew the drill: wear long sleeves to hide the injury. After this episode, that same night/morning, he told me we were going to have to replace the door. I thought to myself, *Now, I did not break the door, but replacing it is an "us issue."* My thinking, too, was how in the world were we going to bring a door in without the neighbors seeing what we are bringing into the apartment? Well, we went to one of the franchised building supply stores to purchase the door. We also bought some black outdoor trash bags. We then drove to an area out of public view, and we covered the door to make it look as if we were protecting a piece of artwork. When we got home, we casually and inconspicuously walked the door inside our townhouse. We took it upstairs and hung the door. Of course, we had to cover the damaged door in the same manner as we had the new door so we could take it outside to dispose of it. I do not recall where, but we discarded that door off the property. Of course, the blame was placed where he thought it should have been—it was my fault that we had to go through all of that. Go figure.

***

This is one of many hair experiences I had with him. Again, during one of his tirades, he used what was nearby to humiliate me. Just hours before this particular episode, I had come home from the beauty salon with a fresh new do. He became so outraged over something trivial that he opened a gallon jug of water and emptied it over my head. I was devastated.

***

He was not opposed to taking a strong drink, and I have never felt that drinking is wrong; it is the extent of one's drinking that poses a problem. Oftentimes, he would get behind the wheel of the car with me in it after he had been drinking. When he did not have anything in thc house on Sunday and he wanted a little buzz, we would drive to the neighboring state line to pick up a "package." I recall on one occasion when he got mad at me about something trivial. He tortured me by driving at excessive speeds on the interstate. I feared for my life. If I cried and screamed, he hit me to try to silence me. This lasted for about fifteen miles.

WORK

Immediately after we were married, we would meet at home every day for his lunch break at 2:00 p.m. While it started out with my not wanting to be late, I soon found out I had better not be. Going to lunch with coworkers was not entirely forbidden, but it was monitored. Just where did I work? The temporary agency that had been so pleased with my skills placed me at the corporate office of a national home health agency. This turned out to be a dream job for me. I am a people person, and my coworkers and I had a mutual fondness for each other, which made for an amiable work environment. My supervisors valued me as an employee and took the opportunity to reward my drive, my dedication, and my loyalty by recommending me for promotions as positions became available or necessary within my department. I went from being a temporary employee to a full-time quality assurance assistant. Then, I was promoted to department secretary. After my supervisor received her distinction as vice president, I was promoted to take on the role of her executive secretary. I took that position beyond its written tasks and made it into something new—no longer was I just a secretary. Finally for me, the recognition of all recognitions came when my supervisor decided to reward me for growing that position. She created a position for me to serve in a supervisory role and as the department's liaison to other corporate departments. The coolest part was that I was charged with the task of coming up with a name for the position. I love words, and lots of them, so I came up with quality management operations coordinator (QMOC).

Well, when I went home and told my husband about it, I was told I could not accept the position. If memory serves me, the position was going to pay between eighteen and twenty dollars per hour. To avoid chaos and confusion, I complied with his demands and turned down the offer. In the meantime, someone else filled the position that had been created for me. Well, when this position was later vacated, again it was offered to me. However, now the hourly pay was less—$13.04 per hour. Because the previous incumbent had a higher degree and I had only a technical college diploma, the company could not justify paying me the same. That is a standard business practice in some places, and I understood. This time, my husband agreed to my promotion. It was a bittersweet moment because I knew what I had given up the first time I turned down the position.

***

Another controlling situation came about when our department relocated to a building right up the highway. Before my first day at the new site, we took a drive from home to the job site so he could time me to see how long it would take me to get back home. I was told what time I should be home. If I was not at home on time, there were consequences—episodes of interrogation and physical abuse.

***

Once when we were separated, I went outside to leave from work to go to lunch and my car was not there. He had taken it because he did not think I should have it since I was not living at home, where he thought I should be. Shamed and hurt, I played it off like my husband had picked the car up from my job to have something repaired on it. I had good credit, so I called up the credit union and had them take an application for an auto loan over the phone.

Fortunately for me, I qualified for a new car with no money down. Buying my own car and having my own means of transportation to work may have seemed to be a victory. Partially, it was. You see, when he would go on abusive rages, he feared I would leave. What would he do? He would take my keys and lock them away in his briefcase. This bondage was so unsettling. My thinking: You do not want me to leave, yet you give me every reason to want to.

PLAY

Our "play," for the most part, rarely involved others. It was as if our lives had to be this well-kept secret. The secret part was that he did not want anyone to get close enough to recognize the abuse that was taking place behind closed doors. On the rare occasions that I was allowed to hang out with the girls, I was interrogated upon my return home. First of all, he never had to ask my whereabouts because he knew prior to my departure. It was a prerequisite for my going. What he would ask was what did we talk about, who did I talk with, and what did I tell them? Even when it came to attending religious services, I would arrive right after the opening prayer, and with my hand clutching my pocketbook handle, I would be sitting at the rear after the closing prayer to make my exit before anyone could get in a hello. I knew if I was not home shortly after the services ended, I would have to face his wrath. Rather than dealing with the interrogations, I had become a recluse in my own home. I did not have the strength to squabble over words about where I had been and what I was doing. He knew I was faithful, and I did not feel like having to prove that every time I left home.

FALSE SENSE OF HOPE

During my imprisonment—halfway through the marriage—my warden, Mr. Hyde, had agreed to seek professional help for his abusive behavior. When the counselor sat down with us, she heard from us briefly as a couple, and then she met with us separately. It was her assessment of our situation that broke my spirit and ultimately led to my decision to cease and desist with her services. She told me I may have been the one with the problem because I did not want him to hang out with his friends. Really? I cried all the way back to work. Prior to walking into work, I was trying to regain my composure. I thought I had it all together. I did not! When I walked back into work to discover that a major employee violation had taken place and someone was being relieved of her duties, my tears began to flow once again. Folks thought I was crying about the fallen employee, but I was crying about the counselor's perception of my fall from grace. I was not beating on him and abusing him. He was not the abused, he was the abuser. The counselor had shifted the blame to me! Go figure. What I thought would be relief turned into prolonged grief. Even more so then, I had to hear from him that I was the problem.

MY PRISON BREAK

I was reared in a household where education was important, but was I not educated enough to know when it was time to leave an abuser? Academic education has no bearing on whether I was knowledgeable in dealing with domestic violence. I was not! I did successfully make my prison break, but not without incident. You would have to read the full book to find out the details, but just know I am still gracing the earth with my presence and am forever thankful I got out. Yes, there was a complete and utter sense of relief and incomparable sense of independence as I left and escaped to freedom. However, I felt as if a part of me had died. It was not the fact that when I walked out the door of my private prison that I would potentially end my marriage. It was, though, the guilt I felt for not loving myself. Loving myself? Yes! I realized why I left. It was not because I loved myself. I left because I loved my mother so much that I did not want her to have to visit me in prison or bury me beside my father. I had lost myself. My love for self was buried among the pain I had experienced at the hands of the man who said he would love and protect me, my Dr. Jekyll. Was there something lacking within me that would cause me to manifest such a warped sense of love for others and not love myself first? Would not love for myself have led to an earlier escape from my abuser? The answer to both of those questions is YES!

Some folks think a woman who stays in an abusive relationship must be crazy. Crazy I was not. Interestingly, for me and many other women who become victims of domestic violence, there is an underlying common thread from our past. Not having done years of theoretical research and conducting a formal study, I can only speak from experience and from the knowledge I gained from talking with other victims. Subconsciously, we were on a quest to be loved, and the desire for love became stronger than the love we had for ourselves. There is nothing crazy about wanting to give and receive love; that is a natural human desire. Sadly, though, that warped sense of love might have stemmed from several things that happened to us in our childhood, a past failed relationship, etc.

SIGNS TO LOOK FOR IN A MR. HYDE

In addition to wondering if there was something wrong with me as to why I stayed in an abusive marriage, oftentimes, folks will ask if there were warning signs that my husband would become an infamous Mr. Hyde. That is a good question. There were some missed warning signs. "But he loves me! That is why he comes every weekend on Friday and stays through Sunday." I wish that truly had been the case. No! He came so regularly so he could control my weekends and know with whom I was spending time and what I was doing. Because I had not personally experienced abuse, I did not know the signs, and I had never even thought about making myself aware of the signs. I thought I had married a man who wanted to do God's work, and that nothing like this could ever happen to me. Did I notice any signs that would have indicated he was a potential abuser? No. However, they were there! If I had been made aware of just general stuff about domestic violence, I would have recognized the signs. Here are some of the signs I missed:

- Wanting to be around all the time when the both of you are not working, allowing no time to "breathe"—obsessive and controlling.
- Tying up my free time with phone calls. That leaves no time to get involved with anyone else and no time for old friends or developing new friendships.
- Having a temper. You can find out a lot from someone's family members if only you listen to the things not said. Case in point, when I asked his mother if there was anything about him I should know, she stated that he had a little temper. Hmmm! That was the main thing I missed. That temper was far from being little.
- Standing up for me against others. In this one instance, I recall my youngest brother getting a little flipped with me, and before he knew what hit him, my then boyfriend had pushed my brother to the floor. At that time, I thought how chivalrous to stand up for me. Hindsight is 20/20; he was being controlling. As I would find out later, he was the only one who had the "right" to hit me.
- Keeping everything about one's relationship a secret. Some things can be transparent.
- Exercising male dominance in extreme excess. He demonstrated this at a wedding shower some of my family and friends had for us. One of my fifth-grade teachers has remained a constant in my life, and she was invited to the shower. Well, in passing she asked my future husband if he knew how smart his future wife is and that she could have been a doctor or lawyer. In a most disrespectful voice and matter-of-fact tone, he told her his wife would not be going to college and rudely walked off.

These are the most obvious warning signs I missed during my courtship. Of course, this list is not inclusive of all the signs a potential abuser may exhibit.

LIFE AFTER MY MR. HYDE

I had been given a death sentence, yet I was resurrected. However, the road was still rocky, and I thought I would never stop grieving the loss of my marriage. For me, marriage was not something I went into thinking, "If it does not work, we can just get a divorce." I could never imagine using the word "divorce" and my name in the same sentence. One of the first things I attempted to do to aid in my recovery and make my "parole" a lot easier was to pray to get my ex-husband out of my system. I cried buckets of tears, to the point that I felt my tear ducts had dried up. I recall the last night of a teary flood. I could not seem to stop crying. I cried, I prayed, I cried, I prayed, and so on. The next morning, my mind was in a hazy fog. I began thinking to myself, "Now who is that guy I was married to?" My closure had arrived. He was a mere fleeting thought.

That was truly refreshing for me; however, I wanted a more tangible, definitive closure. I had previously filed for and was granted a legal separation, but I wanted more. So, I had my attorney draw up the divorce papers. He was contacted on numerous occasions to make arrangements to sign them, and he refused. He eventually signed the papers, and we were divorced. One day before my thirtieth birthday, my divorce was final. I was paroled for life. No more Mr. Hyde. The divorce came nearly one and a half years after I left him for the final time. Freedom had never felt so sweet. I could now begin to regain the "me" I had lost. I had become so consumed with loving him I forgot to love myself. I forgot what it felt like to just rest, relax, and meditate on the more important things in life. I had become so broken I could not even remember where I was born. Could it have been that I wanted to forget I was born? Did I want to die? Was I contemplating suicide? Honestly, I cannot say. However, I found it quite disturbing that I actually had to call my mother to find out my place of birth. I cried during my conversation with her. Knowing my mother, I know she was crying inside. Well, I was now free, so she did not have to worry anymore.

The time had finally arrived for me to get back to being me. However, that "me" was no longer there. Previously, I had been someone who dared not take risks. I was someone who needed someone to hold my hand for every first in life. I was afraid to go things alone, and I was afraid of being alone. LOL! I just thought about how scared I used to be in my adolescent and teenage years. My little sister, who is six years younger, used to walk with me as I passed the back door of our mobile home going to the bathroom. I always feared someone would open the door and snatch me away from my family.

Well, I was no longer afraid to do things alone when what needed to be done was of importance to me. I eventually moved into my own apartment. I learned how to maneuver my car in big-city traffic, and I took long-distance trips by myself. I could go to a restaurant or movie all by myself. I went to the mall by myself and shopped until I dropped. While I never lost confidence in my work abilities, I had, however, been stuck in the mindset that I could only do certain kinds of work. The new "me" became adventurous in work. I tried several different lines of work that opened up doors for my career. That foundation of growth is the basis for my success now as an entrepreneur.

The shackles that limited my movement to establish new friendships were removed. I blossomed into a friendlier woman who knew the value of a smile to enhance the brightness of someone else's day and the priceless worth of a hug that sends a message to others that you embrace their friendship. It felt good to be able to demonstrate kindness and generosity on behalf of others. Previously, I felt so selfish in that prison of a marriage because we did very little giving of ourselves or resources to others. I truly learned one of life's most important lessons: "There is more happiness in giving than there is in receiving." The greatest joy in giving that I experienced after my "parole" was being able to serve God without restrictions. I could go to worship and not have to rush out to avoid the wrath of my abusive husband. I got to experience warm Christian love before and after worship and could talk freely without worrying about being interrogated once I arrived home. I could dine out with my friends after service.

My second greatest joy was reconnecting with my mother, brothers, and sister. He had become so consumed with controlling me that he did not allow me to go home to visit my folks often. Neither did he want them at "his" house. He had made them feel so uncomfortable that they rarely came to visit us in our home. No longer was he an obstacle to showing love to my most loyal support system—my family. I was determined to never again allow anyone to put a wedge between my family and me. Our familial bonds become tighter than ever. While the two greatest loves a human can have are for one's Creator and his/her biological family, intertwined with that love would be one's romantic desires to feel love for another. One may think my desire for romantic love was held captive with me in my private prison and that it may have died. No, it did not!

The abuse did nearly snuff the life out of my desire to be with someone. However, I never stopped loving the man I had married, I stopped loving the man he had become. Oftentimes a woman's nurturing nature calls for her to become a therapist/counselor of sorts for her husband. Like some other victims, I could not walk away without having tried everything I could do to help my husband to want to change. Notice I did not say I thought I could change him. My reality was that I knew I could not. If that were the case, my love for him would have been enough for him to want to change. As can be noted, that was not enough. That is the answer to the million-dollar question: Why did she stay? After all those years of abuse and being mistreated by a man who should have given me the royal treatment, would I be able to love again? Yes, I would and I did.

Prior to getting married to my Dr. Jekyll/Mr. Hyde, I had dated only one other guy, to whom I had been engaged, so I did not completely fear returning to the dating scene since I had done it once before. Dating was not easy, for now I had the baggage of a failed, abusive marriage. I had to sift through many layers to allow the real me to love again. I was so scared of attracting another abuser, since that seems to be the norm for some women whose first relationships or first marriages are riddled with domestic violence. The new "me" arose from the rubble of abuse as a more confident, self-motivated woman. While I was already a deep thinker, I became even more logical and analytical. I balanced the serious confident persona with a more fun-loving self. I learned how to laugh at myself and not take myself so seriously.

With a heightened sense of self and reclaiming my balance, there was still something with which I struggled. I had cried so much and felt such deep pain of heart that I had become numb. I could not feel pain of heart on the normal level. When a loved one was sick or someone I loved dearly died, I was not touched as deeply as my former tenderhearted self would have been. I could not shed empathetic or sympathetic tears naturally. I had to fake condolences. I had become a shell of a woman in the area of emotions. Knowing I was nearly devoid of feelings, I had to be careful not to make any decisions that required being emotionally aware. Even now, I take my time in making decisions because I want to make sure I am not doing so callously.

Through it all, I am still standing. I feel so alive. If ever a girl has exhaled, I certainly did once I realized I had gotten "me" back—a new and improved me.

Of course, I did not just get back on my feet on my own, for I was suffering from battered woman syndrome. At one point after my separation from my Mr. Hyde, a group of clinicians recommended I be hospitalized in a mental health facility. During my abusive marriage, I had gotten on a course of self-destruction. When I shared some of the potentially deadly things I had done to myself during the evaluation, the staff felt I was a threat to myself, but not to the point where they would have "forced" the issue of hospitalization. I guess what I shared with them would have made anyone wonder if I was losing ground. I told them about throwing myself down a flight of stairs. Then, there was the time my ex-husband and I were driving through a parking lot, and I opened the door and tried to jump out of the car. Finally, I recounted the time when after one of his violent episodes, I ended up with a pair of scissors in my hand. I recall wanting to use them on him, but instead I took those scissors and cut my own hair at an angle.

After some careful research, I found a mental health counselor forty-five minutes away from my home in a nearby city. During my first couple of sessions, I found myself trying to protect the identity of my abusive husband. Here I was, allowing him to still control me. Eventually, though, I began to really open up to the counselor and share with her everything that had transpired. My healing slowly began to take place. After a year of counseling, I was a brand-new woman with a renewed sense of self. Now, it is my turn to help someone else get out of an abusive relationship. A year after completing my therapy, which was three years after my divorce, my quest to raise awareness began. I wanted to hold an annual event during National Domestic Violence Awareness Month to draw attention to this social ill. Fourteen years later, I held my first event in November 2015 and published my book the following month. If I was sitting on the couch opposite a renowned talk show host on national television, I would take advantage of that opportunity to raise awareness among the viewing audience. I would not seek my fifteen minutes of fame. I would seek to help some victim realize how she can reclaim her life, dignity, and name. The first thing I will tell any person living in an unhealthy state of fear of an abuser is to make your plans to get out. You are at the center of a potentially volatile situation. Being that you are the center, when the center moves the situation can be dissolved before something fatal happens. It is time to come up with an escape plan. You must not wait around for a prison release, for you must get out now! This takes careful planning and forethought.

THE PRISON BREAK: PLANNING TO LEAVE

All too often victims are threatened with violence or death if they have any plans of leaving. Unless your abuser is around you 24/7, you will have a window of time for your prison break. As much as you may not want to, you should contact your local authorities to make them aware of your situation. This does not mean you are seeking his arrest. It simply means you are putting them on notice in the event something happens to you. If you have photos or any other valid proof of prior incidents of abuse, it is to your advantage to keep a copy for yourself and to give a copy to the authorities. Do not be afraid to take out a restraining order if you feel your life is in danger. That is your right to protect yourself and your children. Laws have changed, and you should exercise your right. Also, if you find it necessary to leave your abuser, it is wise to put distance between you and him. Do not move two streets over or to another apartment in the same complex. Distance tends to be a deterrent.

Order the following steps carefully and in the order you deem most logical for you:

1. Buy a prepaid cell phone that cannot be traced by your abuser so you can make all the calls necessary for your escape. If your abuser is the account holder for your personal cell phone or home phone, he can easily gain access to details of your calls.
2. Contact the battered women's shelter that serves your county to determine if there is a place for you (and your children) at the shelter. If there is not a place for you at the shelter, someone there should be able to make a recommendation or referral for a safe haven. In the event you stay with family or friends, your whereabouts need to be made known to the authorities and the members of the household where you are staying all need to keep your whereabouts hush-hush.
3. Take just what is necessary for your continued existence and survival. You would want to take clothes for the next couple of days, important papers and documents, prescription medications, a list of important contacts (if not stored in your phone), etc. While the abuser may destroy your other belongings, those things are material and can be replaced. You must move swiftly to preserve your greatest possession—your life and the life of your children.
4. Do not use any form of traceable payments when buying anything. It is best to use cash, and do not shop at your usual places. Abusers are the most skilled stalkers, and they generally know your every move and the places you frequent.
5. While you want to notify your closest family members and friends, tread carefully. Because you have probably kept the abuse a secret, some friends and family may not believe you are telling the truth, and they may tell him things that would put you in harm's way.
6. If it is at all possible, hide your vehicle in an inconspicuous place and use another means of transportation.
7. If you have children, it may be necessary for them to get permission to be absent from school. The school should be instructed not to give out any information to ensure the safety of the children.
8. If you must use any form of technology for communication, refrain from using any to which your abuser may have access. Always clear the browsing history. Again, abusers are good trackers/tracers.

Again, how each victim orders these steps is an individual decision. No two abusive environments will be the same. Unfortunately, abusers are really not as predictable as we may think. How many times have we heard folks say, after a domestic violence fatality, that they are shocked because "he was such a nice guy and we never saw any signs of him being violent"? Abusers do not generally go public with their abuse, and victims keep the abuse private—confined to the walls of their prison cell called home. Be in the know about ways to protect yourself if ever you are in an abusive situation or if you know someone who is being abused. **Everyone needs to know the number to the battered women's shelter that provides services for residents of your town/city.**

Store all emergency contact numbers in your cell phone or on a secret piece of paper that you can easily find. Some of the numbers to include are as follows:

- **The National Domestic Violence Hotline:** 1-800-799-7233
- Police and sheriff department
- Fire department
- Emergency medical services
- Health department, medical centers, and physicians. Abusers may attempt to stop providing medical care and coverage that victims and their children must have for chronic illnesses.
- Mental health services. Many victims are traumatized and suffer from battered woman syndrome and post-traumatic stress disorder. Counseling and support are a must for recovery.
- Department of Family and Children Services
- Goodwill. There are times when victims have to flee and leave all clothing and personal belongings behind.
- Housing authority. Many victims and their children will need housing that can only be provided for a limited time at shelters.

Love yourself despite the fact that your abuser does not know how to love you! He may never learn, and he may not want to know how. Some folks bask in doing what feels good to them, and being abusive may feel good to him. He may expect you to conform to his ways and accept the abuse despite how well he cares for you financially and sexually. You, however, have to continue to live with you. Get back to loving you. You just might have the opportunity to love again. You cannot love someone else unless you first love yourself.

Say goodbye to your prison cell of a home, and say hello to a new you. You may not be the same you, but you still have your life, health, and strength. That is more than some victims of abuse can say. Relish the moments you have awaiting in the future, and be wise when allowing love to choose you the next time.

"Domestic violence" is by far one of the greatest oxymorons ever coined. He who is domesticated should only have to fight against things outside of one's home or domestic place of dwelling. He should never fight the very one he is supposed to protect and thus provide for her well-being and ultimate survival. Yet, abusers who are guilty of domestic violence know very little about survival. They themselves cannot even protect themselves from themselves.

I shared my story of becoming victorious over domestic violence because I hope to not only reach women who are plagued by these circumstances, but also to reach the men who set the environment for the circumstances. Not all men are bad, and not all abusers grasp the concept of *not* abusing. Abuse is oftentimes a learned behavior, or it is the direct result of misogynistic thinking that is oftentimes perpetuated by society or within the households in which young boys become men.

CHAPTER 5

WHY "BIG BOYS" DON'T CRY OR TELL: AFRICAN AMERICAN MALE COLLEGE STUDENTS' PERCEPTION, ATTITUDE, AND BEHAVIOR TOWARD MALE VICTIMS OF FEMALE-PERPETRATED INTIMATE PARTNER VIOLENCE

DR. ROENIA DELOACH

ABSTRACT

Existing research shows that while intimate partner violence (IPV) is a major concern in the United States, most research has focused on female victimization. To fill this gap in the literature, the present research examines male victims of IPV by conducting focus groups and interviews with eight African American male college students. The aim is to explore their perception, attitude, and behavior toward male victims of female-perpetrated intimate partner violence. Ultimately, a seven-item, semi-structured interview guide was developed to elicit information from participants. All interviews were audio-recorded, transcribed, and coded for analysis. The analysis revealed emergent themes from the focus groups and interviews concerning the role that society and family played in shaping the participants' perception of male victims of female-perpetrated violence. Subsequently, the participants' perceptions impacted their attitude and behavior, which led to them stigmatizing and blaming the male victims for their circumstances. Findings suggest "big boys" do not cry or tell because of the lack of empathy, sensitivity, male-oriented victimization resources, and support from family, friends, and society as a whole.

PREVALENCE OF MALE VICTIMS OF INTIMATE PARTNER VIOLENCE

Intimate partner violence (IPV) is a serious public health problem that can be detrimental to the physical and psychological health of the victim. IPV includes acts of sexual, physical, and psychological violence and stalking against a current or former partner. In the US, one in four women and one in nine men have been victims of some form of sexual and/or physical violence, and/or stalking by an intimate partner in their lifetime (Smith, Chen, Basile, Gilbert, Merrick, Patal, Walling, and Jain, 2017). IPV is often hidden and only a small percentage of victims seek help. Women are more likely than men to report frequent and brutal levels of IPV (Archer 2000; Jaden and Thoennes, 2000), which influences societal perception that men rarely experience IPV from female perpetrators. Conversely, men who experience IPV from female perpetrators are viewed and treated differently (Coney and Mackey, 1999). It is not surprising that male IPV victims may view themselves as failures at masculinity, especially given societal stigmatization of men as inappropriate victims. Although most victims are pressured to remain silent about their experiences, in a patriarchal society like the US, men are further pressured to repress weaknesses or feelings resulting from being a victim of IPV (Kimmel, 2006).

Male victims of intimate partner violence is a phenomenon that has received little interest. Despite this paucity of attention, research on IPV has shown that men are frequently the target of IPV by their female partners (Tsui, Cheung, and Leung 2012a, b). Additionally, Straus (2006) reports "that there are more than 150 studies showing equal or higher rates of assault by women" (p. 1086). As cited in Hines and Douglas (2009, p. 1), the 2000 National Violence Against Women Survey reported that during a one-year period, "female perpetrated violence accounted for 40% of all injuries due to IPV, 27% of all injuries requiring medical attention and 31% of all victims fearing bodily harm." Reportedly, in the last twenty to thirty years, there has been a decrease in incidence of family violence to include male-perpetrated IPV against female. However, nonfatal female-perpetrated IPV against men has not changed quite so precipitously (Hines and Douglas, 2009). Crime statistics and hospitals report higher incidents of women victims of IPV. However, community-based studies suggest there are high occurrences of women perpetrating IPV. Contrariwise, it is challenging to establish reliable estimates of male victims of domestic violence because few men are willing to report being a victim of IPV and consequently do not seek professional resources (Leonard, 2003).

The expected social role of men as head of household and family protector makes it difficult to access victims and perpetrators. Men who have the courage to report their abuse often face stigma from friends, family, and their community, as well as authority figures. In fact, their stories are often disbelieved and/or ridiculed. Even when they have suffered severe violence, the public indifference to them deters them from reporting the abuse. Worst of all, very little is being done to help male victims report the abuse they suffer at the hands of women (Tsiko, 2016). Adding to this troubling phenomenon is the dismissing of earlier research that revealed that women are equally likely to be perpetrators of IPV (Straus and Gelles, 1990).

Intimate partner violence acts committed by females are often dismissed or viewed as humorous or trivial, or seen as acts of vindication (Cook, 2009). Interestingly, men generally do not consider physical violence to be threatening when it is perpetrated by women (Nybergh, Enander, and Krantz, 2016; Rhatigan, Stewart, and Moore, 2011). Because male physical injury is not seen the same as female and occurs to some extent less than female (Archer, 2000), bystanders may be less likely to intervene or contact the authorities when they witness a female assault a male partner (Sorenson and Taylor, 2005). In a study on college students' views on IPV, Sylaska and Walters (2014) found that males were held at a higher level of accountability for the victimization of women. However, both male and female students viewed IPV as less serious when the male was the victim. This suggests that females and males, including male victims, are more tolerant of female use of violence in relationships. For males, this may be potentially due to gentlemanly expectations (Robertson and Murachver, 2009) and a part of the role of social-emotional development.

SOCIAL-EMOTIONAL DEVELOPMENT OF MEN

Social-emotional development is the extent to which children can socially adjust and interact with family and other members of society and the ability to regulate their emotions to effectively achieve their goals (Squires, Bricker, and Twombly, 2005). There is a correlation between social-emotional development and gender-role attitudes as it relates to female-perpetrated violence against men. Family provides social-emotional development to strengthen children's capacity to learn and develop. Moreover, relationships with parents, family members, caregivers, and members of society provide the key context for men's social-emotional development. In their youth, children depend on the family for safety assurance, social approval, encouragement, and help with emotional regulation (Kim and Kim, 2011). Family interaction affects children's understanding of the meaning of emotions, the developing knowledge of which circumstances lead to which emotional outcomes, and their learning about which emotions are suitable to exhibit in which circumstances. Boys are socialized to withhold their emotions in certain circumstances, whereas girls are encouraged to show their emotions. Boys are told not to hit girls and to just walk away. When they are hit by a girl, they might hear comments such as "You know that did not hurt" or "Do not hit your sister." This type of upbringing has a profound effect on their social-emotional development in adulthood.

In keeping with their childhood experiences and societal expectations, men have been socialized to downplay acts of violence perpetrated by women. For example, when slapped or pushed, a man may say, "Come on now, girl, stop playing," or use humor, which both minimize the abusive situation. Oftentimes, the man may fear being labeled as a "wimp," weak, or a pushover. At the same time, a bystander might also downplay the situation by assuming the female was defending herself, responding to being provoked (Scarduzio, Carlyle, Harris, and Savage, 2016), or retaliating because the man was unfaithful or abusive (Carlyle, Scarduzio, and Slater, 2014). Reportedly, only a small minority of females who use violence against a male partner act in self-defense (Kernsmith, 2005). Researchers found that females, as well as males, arrested for violence against intimate partners minimize their abusive actions when describing the violent acts (Archer, 1999; Henning, Jones, and Holdford, 2005).

In a patriarchal society, men are expected to be dominant, have control, avoid weakness, and restrict or hide emotions. Daily, men must prove their masculinity, and if they falter, they feel and are treated as if they are less than a man. Social rules have played a major role in the social-emotional development of men and have contributed to a widespread perspective that minimizes male victimization and female perpetration of IPV. As noted in White (2009), Pasick compiled a list of typical social rules (Figure 1) for men to adhere to. The rules compel men to remain in control and to avoid situations that will make them appear weak. These rules certainly impact the social-emotional development of a man, especially if he is the victim of intimate partner violence. Being a victim means he would be considered weak, not in control of himself, and has allowed intimacy to weaken his self-reliance. Furthermore, because he is a victim, he lacks the capacity to take the necessary actions to fix a problem he has encountered.

Figure 1. Pasick List of Social Rules for Men

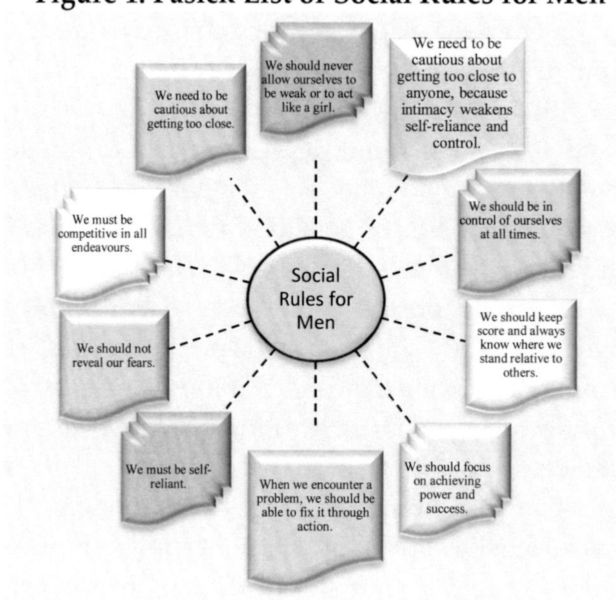

Society places great emphasis on the maintenance of appropriate standards of behavior. Oftentimes, this pressure impinges on the normal tendencies and preferences of the individual, thus precipitating an unfathomable sense of humiliation if the behavior is in opposition to the standards. In other words, if a male victim of IPV experiences become known, his subsequent identity performances often fail to meet society's expectations for appropriate roles and he is not perceived as a healthy, functioning adult (Hertzog and Rowley, 2014). As cited in Eckstein (2016, p. 216), Goffman posits that this failed performance can result in the "victims' attempts to reconcile expectation or to face stigmatization."

Stigmatization

Researchers have concluded that stigmatization plays a major role in the help-seeking attitude of men. Stigmatization refers to having negative perceptions of an individual based on perceived difference from the population at large. It includes humiliating, segregating, and discrediting those who experience IPV. Stigmatization has a major impact on persons' decisions to conceal their victimization (Murray, Crowe, and Overstreet, 2015; Murray, Crowe, and Brinkley, 2015; Overstreet and Quinn, 2013; Trotter and Allen, 2009; Tsui, Cheung, and Leung, 2010). It is not uncommon for a male victim to stigmatize another male victim of IPV (Arnocky and Vaillancourt, 2014). This is partly due to the association of the undesirable trait of being a victim (Rudman, Feinberg, and Fairchild, 2002). Again, this attitude is related to the expectation that society places on male masculinity and his ability to oversee the relationship and not be a victim.

Despite the possibility of being stigmatized, researchers have found that some victims do disclose to family members. The supportive reaction of family members and friends can be a mediating factor to the negative effects IPV has on the victim (Sylaska and Edwards, 2014). However, an unsupportive social system can lead to greater psychological distress and may also impact the victim's decision to disclose IPV to others or seek professional help.

Legal and Administrative Aggression

Stigmatization is not the only reason a male victim does not reveal IPV. Some do not tell in fear of legal aggression. Legal and administrative (LA) aggression occurs when one partner uses the legal or administrative system as a source of retribution (Hines, Douglas, and Berger, 2015). It might encompass trivial lawsuits, false allegations of child abuse, and "other system-related legal manipulations" (Berger, Douglas, and Hines, 2014). Although LA aggression can be pursued by male or female perpetrators of violence, there are several reasons why it is more frequently used by females. Women are given the benefit of the doubt when they seek legal repercussion even if they are the perpetrator. In this case, men are revictimized by the failure of the system to intervene (Tilbrook, Allan, and Dear, 2010). Society, the legal system, and domestic violence service organizations' prejudice against men being victims of IPV are to blame for the failure to protect men against LA aggression. (This fact is discussed further in chapter 12.)

Researchers have found that the threat of LA aggression also prevents male victims from seeking help or revealing IPV. Similarly, in another study of heterosexual males who seek help for IPV, when asked what prevents men from leaving an abusive female partner, one of the most commonly cited reasons was a fear they would never see their children again (Hines and Douglas, 2010). Findings from a qualitative study conducted by Tilbrook et al. (2010) suggest that restraining orders and false allegations against male victims of IPV have resulted in the unfortunate allocation of time, money, and resources to prove they are in fact the victim. Law enforcement and domestic abuse services are inclined to believe the woman to be the victim. Also, when female victims seek restraining orders, judges are more inclined to award the order to a female victim more so than in the case of a male victim seeking protection (Basile, 2005).

In a study on IPV, Cook (2009) provided evidence to support the use of LA aggression when male victims reported losing their home and other possessions by females who manipulated the system. The manipulation also included threats of ruining male victims' reputation in the community and at work. To further complicate the matter, some men in the study feared they might be accused of physically or sexually abusing their children.

Much has been discussed about the impact society, family, legal and administrative systems, and domestic violence service organizations have on male victims revealing and seeking help for female-perpetrated IPV. However, one of the shortcomings of the existing research on IPV is that very little has focused on the impact other men play on the decision for a male victim to tell or seek help for victimization. The current study addresses this gap by exploring African American male college students' perception, attitude, and behavior toward male victims of female-perpetrated IPV.

METHOD

Sample and Study Procedure

The author and a graduate research assistant developed a flyer and recruited twelve African American males between the ages of twenty-two to twenty-five from various buildings on a university campus to participate in the study on IPV. Participants were offered a Visa gift card for their participation in the study. The researcher scheduled two focus groups with a total of four participants each. However, only two participants showed for each of the focus groups. The four participants who did not attend the focus group contacted the researcher and were granted individual interviews. A total of eight males participated in the study.

Given the explorative aim of the study, two semi-structured focus groups and four semi-structured interviews were conducted by the author and graduate assistant. One focus group was held in a classroom and the other focus group and interviews were held in a conference room at the university. The participants were fully informed about the study, including the goals of the research. None of the participants reported being a victim of IPV but had strong views about IPV. Prior to signing the consent form, participants were assured of confidentiality and given an opportunity to ask questions. They all agreed to participate in the focus group/interview and for the session to be tape-recorded and quotes to be used. The interviews began with the participant being invited to talk about intimate partner violence. The length of the interviews and focus group ranged from forty-five minutes to one hour. Half of the interviews were transcribed verbatim by the author and the other half by the graduate assistant. Names, places, and similar information that might compromise the participants' anonymity were omitted during the transcription process. Ethical approval for this study was granted by the university's Human Subject Review Board.

Data Analysis

The researcher employed qualitative methodology based on heuristic principles of grounded theory to explore the subjective world of African American males' perception and attitude on male victims of female-perpetrated IPV. Qualitative research seeks to understand the meaning of experience by understanding real-life phenomena in real-world settings. The grounded theory method, as developed by Glaser and Strauss (1967), was considered suitable for the aim of the study. In grounded theory it is the attitude and perception, not the individuals, which are categorized. The grounded theory method is used to build a theoretical model of what is perceived and what is the attitude about male victims of female-perpetrated IPV. In the present study, the perceptions and attitudes are those described by African American male college students.

The analysis of data included a line-by-line review of all text. Notes and sidebars were written to highlight important elements. Operational notes were used to record practical issues. Using colored marker, the research highlighted words and phrases based on emerging themes. A table was designed based on the words and phrases, and categories were subsequently developed. The next phase was to develop subheadings in each category. This was done by returning to the literature and rereading the transcribed data. The researcher began by analyzing key words and phrases. This process continued until all mutually exclusive categories had been exhausted and all key words and phrases had been categorized. Categories and subcategories were processed through a matrix of thematic headings in order to develop a paradigm that would aid in describing African American males' perception, attitude, and behavior toward male victims of female-perpetrated IPV. The analysis focused on three key concepts, i.e. perception, attitude, and behavior. Notice in Figure 2 how the subcategories have taken form. For example, in the first subcategory, society's and family's influence on the social and emotional development of men played a major role in the participants' perception of male victims of female-perpetrated IPV. And as far as the participants' attitudes and behaviors, stigmatization and blaming the victim for his circumstances were noted in a second subcategory.

Figure 2. Thematic Headings

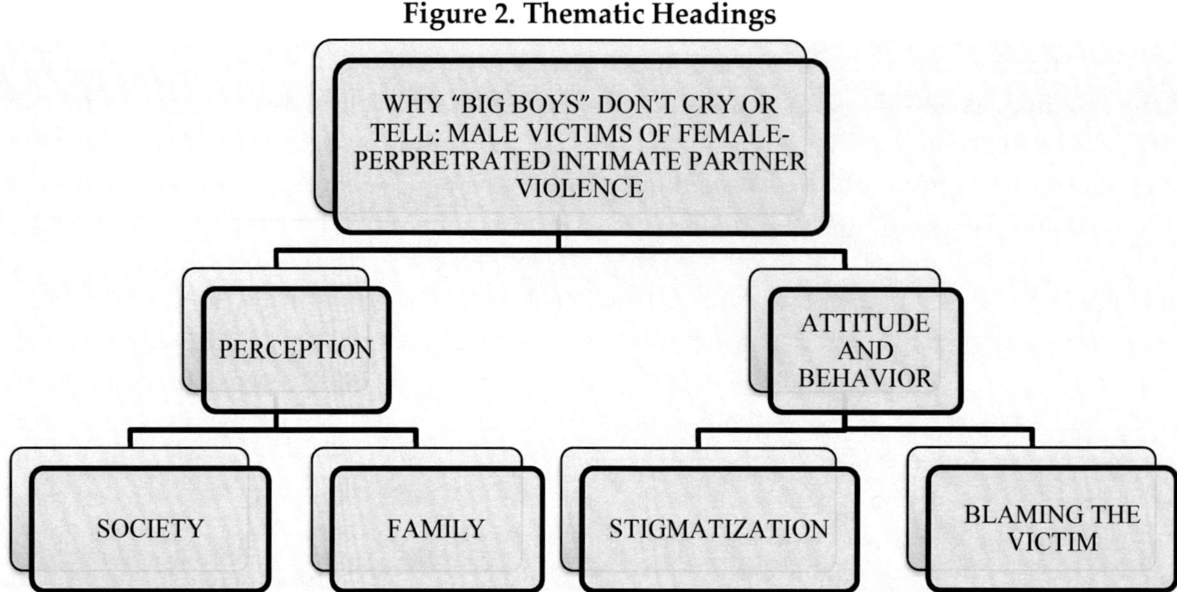

Analysis of texts. The analysis of text (Figures 3 and 4) focused on the induction and construction of meanings. Several categories and subcategories of themes emerged. Examples of data used to develop the subcategory "society" include "Black men are victims because you got this thing going on the outside of the world that affects us," "It does matter which gender is the aggressor," "Men should just walk away," and "Female is more natural to love and care for you." Examples of data used to develop the subcategory "family" include "Whatever happens, just take it in and keep moving," "We men are raised not to show emotions or feelings," "Maybe it was how she was raised," "Just like growing up, you try not to break a tear," and "What happened in his childhood that makes him a recessive person?"

Figure 3. Society's Role

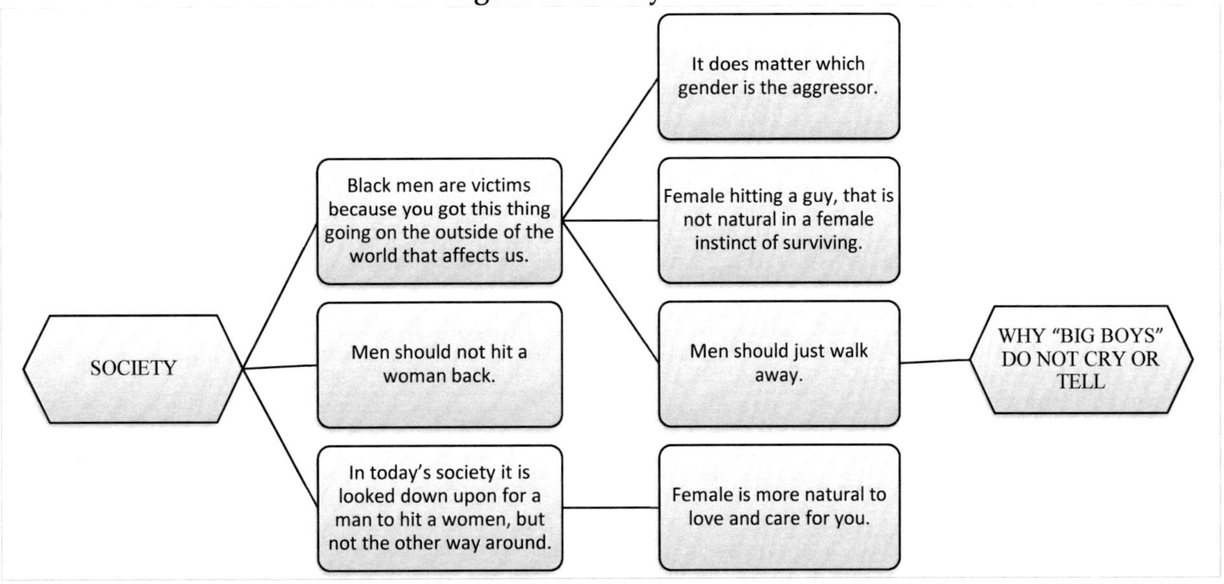

Figure 4: Family's Role

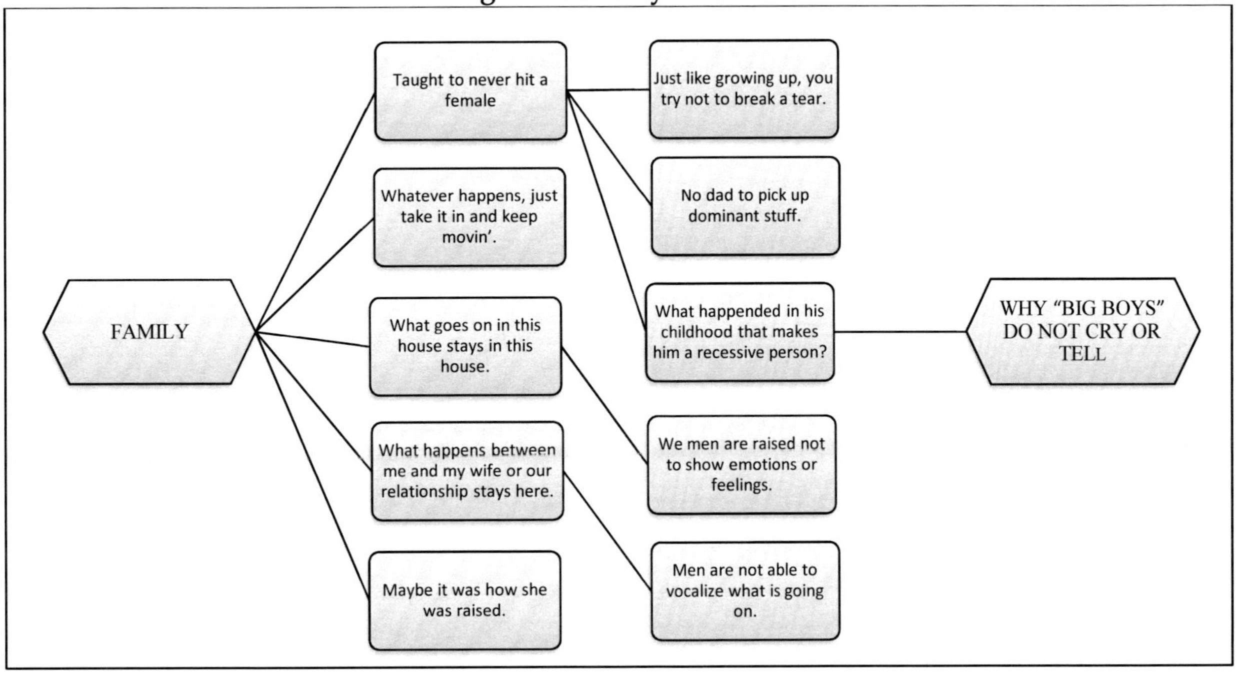

The analysis of text in Figure 5 focused on the induction and construction of meanings to describe the participants' attitude and behavior toward male victims of female-perpetrated IPV. For the concepts attitude and behavior, two subcategories, "stigmatization" and "blaming the victim,"

emerged from the data. Examples of data used to develop the subcategory "stigmatization" include "feminine qualities," "It is not a good thing to call him," "weak . . . wimp . . . ruined reputation . . . embarrassing . . . looked down upon," "bitch ass," and "pushover." When it came to the subcategory "blaming the victim," the participants expressed their attitude with statements such as "If I saw a female hit a man, I would look away. He does not know how to handle his business," "If people are mature they wouldn't just let someone hit him," "Some guys be doing stuff to piss a female off," "You are getting walked over because you cannot put your feet down," and "What is going on with you? A deeper meaning behind this."

Figure 5. Stigmatization and Blaming the Victim

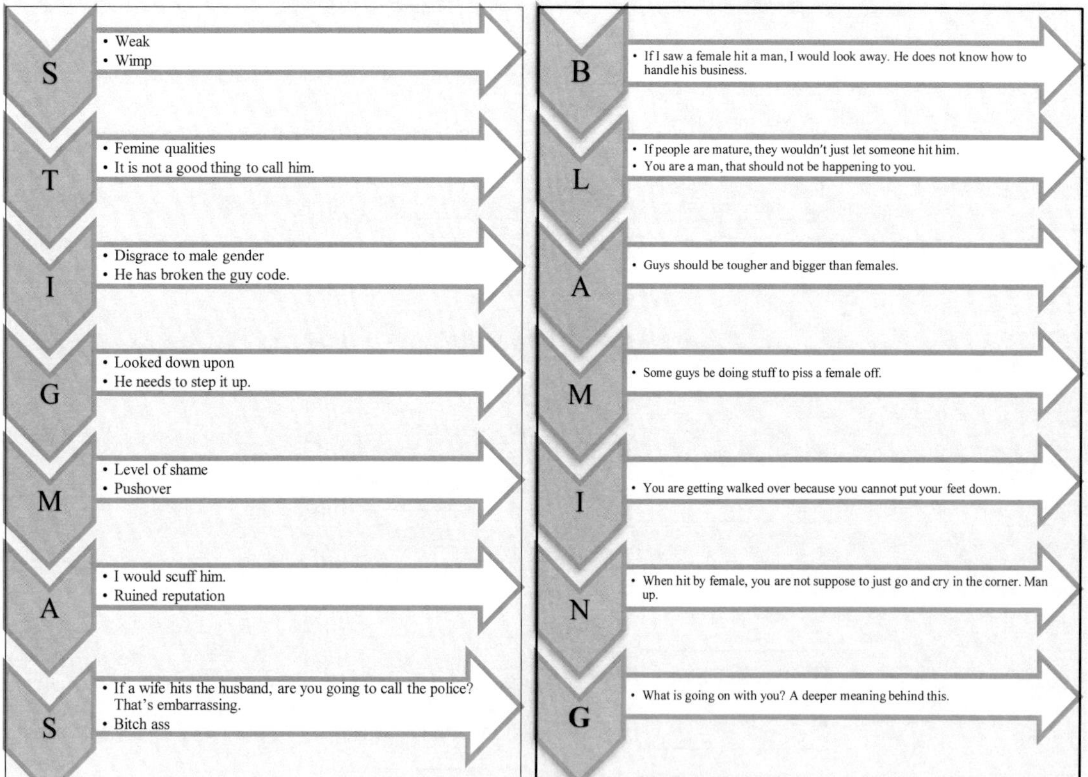

Findings

The interviews revealed four overarching themes related to the perceptions, attitudes, and behaviors that African American male college students have about male victims of female-perpetrated IPV. In the case of perception, two themes, society and family, emerged as sources that help to shape the participants' discernment of the male victims. Stigmatization and blaming the victim emerged as the themes associated with the participants' attitude and behaviors about the victims.

Initially, the participants were asked to talk about their personal experience with IPV. All participants stated they had never been in an IPV relationship. Two participants stated they had been playing around with their girlfriends, and when things looked like they were going to get "serious," they stopped.

One participant expressively stated, "I mean, it has been times where I've been in relationships and you know, and girls like to play a little too much and, you know, start like hitting and stuff, but I end that right then and there because I don't do that, so they start trying to be funny and little too handsy. I guess we just going to stop right there and we are not going to be putting our hands on each other, and you know, I will feel some type of way you touch me that way, you don't want me to hit you, so don't hit me. So, it never got to the next level, past the little playful stage. It never got taken there!"

When asked if they had witnessed a man hitting a female in public, would they intervene? All participants stated they would intervene. One stated, "I would have no problem intervening," and another added, "To me in public, you know, these days people film fights and everything. I feel if people are matured people, they wouldn't just let someone hit on a female in public; to me that will be wrong in my opinion. If I was outside I would try to stop it. Man to man is different, female to female is different, but a man hitting a female in public, to me something has to be done about it."

Participants were asked if they had witnessed a man being assaulted by a woman. Six of the participants stated they had witnessed some form of IPV (i.e. more words, profanity, arguing, pushing, or "just" slapping the face) where the female was the aggressor. All participants stated that a female abusing a male is a little different and they would hesitate to intervene. They did not view it as a major concern unless there was a "weapon or a lot of blood." These attitudes support the notion that men have been socialized to "downplay" acts of violence perpetrated by women (Scarduzio, Carlyle, Harris, and Savage, 2016).

The next set of questions focused on male victims of female-perpetrated IPV. It is at this point the themes began emerging. When asked the question "Why is female-perpetrated IPV against men different from male-perpetrated IPV against women?" participants' responses led to two central themes, i.e. society and family values on what is considered appropriate male characteristics and the ascribed male-female gender roles.

Theme I: Perception—Society

Participants identified the role society played in shaping their perception of male victims of IPV. Several of their statements about the expected roles for men are also noted in the aforementioned list of social rules for men drafted by Pasick (as cited in White, 2009). Gender roles were exquisitely described in the participants' statements.

If the male does not conform to society's image of a male, then "in society someone is looked down upon; you are the man, like, that shouldn't be happening and it is happening. What's going on. . . . A man should be able to do something about the situation." Similar responses about male-female roles included, "Like, it occurs in high school. You know for guys, they play contact sports, and violent things [Pasick refers to this as competitiveness in all endeavors] and ladies do simple things like take care of the home, play with dolls," and "So it's like when you get older you are thinking, like, only the guy has to be strong."

One participant shared, "All right, because it's kind of, in today's society it's kind of looked down on, just like if the wife hits the husband, are you going to call the police? Because that's embarrassing, I am not saying it's right to hit the woman back." Another stated, "It does matter which gender is the aggressor. It is not natural for a female to be violent; a female's role is to love and support her man. Most women in society are loving and supportive, it is just the natural thing to do." And, a third participant joined, "To me females are more natural to want to love you and care for you than to want to hurt you." "It is the responsibility of the man to be in control and have power over the situation at all times."

All participants agreed society has a hand in the way male victims of IPV are treated. One participant took the issue a little further: "Society has a big hand in what is happening to men, especially the black man. Because we got all these things in the outside world that affects us too. We have to try not to break a tear. We must be strong and show no fear." Another participant stated, "To add to his comment, we cannot show no sign of weakness." These participants alluded to the fact that for black males, IPV was a double whammy. "Black males are perceived by society to be strong and fearless. They are less receptive to being the victim of a woman."

A final comment was made by a participant who felt that men becoming victims is a more recent phenomenon. He also commented on how the man not being able to protect himself is at odds with the social norms. "Let a disagreement go down and she starts swinging on him and he don't know how to fight, and it's like she is really attacking him, like, the younger age group is breaking the social norm."

Theme I: Perception—Family

Family plays a major role in the social-emotional development of children (Kim and Kim, 2011). Parents teach and model how to regulate emotions based on the situation at hand. Like society, family also ascribes gender roles to emotions and activities. This can be observed in the comments made by the participants when responding to the question "How is female-perpetrated violence against men different?"

One participant described his upbringing. "You know we men were kind of raised as like, we men are not supposed to show our emotions or feeling, I mean I don't mind talking about it because, I can handle it. . . . Whatever happens, just take it in, you know, keep on moving, you can only take so much. We all have feelings at the end of the day, so, so much going on, and say you got school, work, you know, you got his personal life, you know how things, like, you know things get stressful, but everything going on, but you do not have an outlet; you could just be pushing on."

Another participant commented on how he was raised: "Usually guys are tougher and bigger than females, so you know, when a female's hitting you, you not supposed to just go cry in the corner about the issue, you just can walk away from it; to me that's what I was taught, to you know, never hit a female back, 'cause I have sisters and of course, I was raised by a good mother and father, and um, you know, I just walk away if anything . . ."

Statements by others included:

"Like growing up, one thing my parent used to always say is that what happens in the house stays in the house, and so that's the same thing that most men take, that what happens between me and my wife or in our relationship stays here . . . I may need help, but I am not going to ask for help."

"As a guy you don't have the proper support, like, a male presence, or like, you don't have a father. All he has is his mama to look to, and then he becomes, like, feminine, kind of pick up feminine qualities. And, then he becomes recessive, and it's like you been a girl who may not have had a dad to pick up the dominant stuff, and then you put them together; it is like a bad combination." This participant implied that it is important for a guy to have a male figure to teach and model the role and emotions of a man. If he does not have a male role model, then he might take on more of the feminine qualities of his mother.

Overall, the participants held strong views about the role family and society play in the socialization of men. It is evident by their voices that their perception of male victims of IPV has been shaped by their upbringing and the expectation of our society. The participants were also aware of how their perceptions shaped their attitude and behavior. The next section provides a view of the participants' attitude and behavior toward male victims.

Theme II—Attitude and Behavior: Stigmatization and Blaming the Victim

The identified themes related to participants' attitude and behavior toward male victims of female-perpetrated violence were stigmatization and blaming the victim. In some cases, the participants reflected the view that wider society does not fully endorse the idea that men can be victims of female-perpetrated IPV. Most of the participants did not perceive the male victims to be "real men." In this sense, they resorted to labeling the male victims and blaming them for their circumstances.

Theme II—Attitude and Behavior: Stigmatization. Throughout the interview, many stigmatizing words and phrases were used to describe male victims of female-perpetrated IPV. These observations reflect the participants' attitude and behavior toward male victims who do not espouse the characteristic Pasick (as noted in White, 2009) exclaims men should possess. There were many instances where the attitude of the participants alluded to the notion that the male victims deviated from the male masculine gender "code." Their expressions of disfavor toward these men is reflected in their behavior, i.e. name calling.

The participants were asked how they would characterize a male friend who is being abused by a woman. The participants quickly chimed in on this question. One stated, "If that was my friend, I would be like, I would try to help him at first, and then if it was still happening, I'd be like, your girl is beating on you, like, you are maybe a wimp. I would scoff him. You know, guys, it's like maybe like . . . well, I don't know, it's just that. It is not going to be a good thing, it is not going to be good." Another responded, "Weak, somebody that is getting walked over or doesn't put their foot down." One participant referred to a man calling the police because his wife hits him as an "embarrassment to men," and another replied, "Do not go to the cops, like a girl." Other phrases and words included feminine qualities, bitch ass, level of shame, ruined reputation, disgrace to the male gender, pushover, looked down upon, something is wrong with him, he broke the guy code, he is a recessive person, vulnerable, and he is not a mature man. The participants' stigmatization of male victims is similar to those found in previous studies.

Theme II—Attitude and Behavior: Blaming the Victim. Evidence suggests the participants' attitude and behavior about male victims of female-perpetrated IPV have been shaped by their past and present teachings and experiences. Notably, society and family have played a significant role in their attitude and behavior toward male victims. Most of the participants expressed some empathy toward the male victims, howbeit only if the man immediately got out of the situation or he "fixed" the problem. When the participants believed the abuse was a long-term issue, they resorted to demoralizing the victim by blaming him for the abuse he was experiencing. Several of the participants believed the guy had done something to deserve the abuse: "Out in public I have seen this, yes, but you never know what was behind it because a guy would have done something the night before, the day before, but yes, I have seen a woman be the aggressor. It was more words and then slapping in the face, things of that sort," and "Some guys be doing stuff that piss a female off to the extent that she has to put her hands on him."

One of the participants candidly responded to the question "What do you think about a guy who gets beat up by a woman?": "I would say he doesn't treat that woman with respect, whether they are in a relationship, a family, or whether a personal thing they have going on, or either that guy did something to deserve it, because to me for a female to hit a guy or be . . . with a guy outside of intimacy, that's not natural in a female's instinct of surviving. To me females are more natural to want to love you and care for you than to want to hurt you. So usually if a female goes out of her way to hurt, you know that you have pushed her out to a point where there is no return or either you have hurt her pretty bad by doing something personally." Another participant stated, "A female acts awkward because a man has done something to her." Yet another participant implied the man is to blame because he is not mature: "If people are mature they wouldn't just let someone hit them." Blaming the victim is further illustrated in the following quotes:

- "That guy did something to deserve it."
- "You have hurt her pretty bad."
- "Do something about it, if she is beating him for no reason. Leave."
- "Talk to the guy to see what is going on and if his wife is beating him for no reason."
- "If there's blood, or if he has to be rushed to the hospital or if she sends you to the hospital, at this point you will need to step up."
- "Move away, you know you can do something about it."

Not only are participants blaming the male victims for their circumstances, but they are also holding them responsible for solving the problems. In this sense, the victims are less likely to seek help if their informal support system is exacerbating the situation by blaming them. Attitudes that place the responsibility for violence on the victim show a lack of empathy or insensitivity toward victims, and this can further isolate the victims and minimize the opportunity for them to seek help.

With further probing about male victims' help-seeking attitudes, several comments were made by the participants as to why they believed men do not pursue legal help (including calling the police) or services from community domestic violence organizations. One participant stated, "Honestly, it is a pride thing . . . even if I know I needed help, I am not going to ask for help." Another reasoned, "Because, you know that you cannot go to the police officer . . . like me, I wouldn't want to ruin not just my reputation but also hers, even though she may need it. I wouldn't want to just send her to jail for that and ruin her life completely." Others expressed concerns about the lack of appropriate shelters and resources specifically designed to deal with male victims. They complained that most advertisements and resources are designed to address women and children and not men and children. They then alluded to the notion that male victims' needs are far different than female needs.

Discussion

In this study, the researcher explored African American male college students' perception, attitude, and behavior toward male victims of female-perpetrated intimate partner violence. Several themes observed in the literature have reemerged in this study. Like other studies, our findings revealed that family (Kim and Kim, 2011) and society (Hertzog and Rowley, 2014) played a major role in the shaping of the participants' perception of the male victims. Overall, the participants perceived male victims as lacking the socially acceptable masculine characteristics. The participants' attitudes and behaviors were subsequently influenced by their perceptions, and they resorted to stigmatizing and blaming the male victims for failing to control and/or escape the abusive situation.

IPV against men is not a highly recognized social problem, and it is also underreported. For these reasons, it is important that we put forth the effort to change the perceptions, attitudes, and behaviors of stigmatizing and blaming the male victims. Society, family, and friends' tolerance toward this form of violence can influence males' responses to their abuse by discouraging them from seeking services or reporting the violence. Arguably, those who blame victims for their own misfortunes are less willing to help them. This was expressed by one of the participants who explained that he could not understand how a man would allow for abuse to occur more than twice. This participant conveyed that his upbringing asserts a man should be strong and able to handle his household. Values such as this support previous findings that imply attitudes toward IPV are largely influenced by experiences in the family system (Copp, Giordano, Longmore, and Manning, 2016). Likewise, many parents raise their sons to cry privately, if at all. It is ingrained in many men that masculine identity means holding back tears and showing no signs of weakness.

The idea that "big boys don't cry" is imparted in boys during early social-emotional development. As reported by the participants, boys are taught that crying is a sign of weakness, powerlessness, and pain. This is demonstrated in the way parents console boys and girls. For example, if a girl cries, she may be cuddled with warmth, whereas when a boy cries he may be scorned and told, "You are a big boy; that did not hurt." Parents often do not cuddle boys, citing that it will make them soft. Boys who cry might also be taunted and or called names (i.e. crybaby, sissy, mama's boy) by friends as well as parents and other family members (Grant, 2004). Parents oftentimes model their own views about masculinity roles and impose those perceptions and attitude in children, which may be intentionally or unintentionally. Therefore, boys learn at an early age what are acceptable and unacceptable emotions and behaviors. We must ask, if a boy is taught not to cry or show certain emotions when he is hurt, then, as a man, how is he going to tell others he is being victimized by a woman in a society that has prescribed these gender roles and expectations? This and other factors condition men not to "cry or tell," even in the most hurtful situations.

Why "big boys" do not tell is partly due to the insensitivity, lack of empathy, and the anticipated backlash from family, friends, the legal system, and the community. Unfortunately, men who fail to exhibit societal-ascribed masculine characteristics or perform macho-projected roles are marginalized and stigmatized. It is not uncommon for a male victim to stigmatize another male victim of IPV (Arnocky and Vaillancourt, 2014). This is partly due to the association of the undesirable trait of being a victim (Rudman, Feinberg, and Fairchild, 2002). Research has also shown that gender bias exists against male victims who report female-perpetrated IPV to legal and law enforcement (Shernock and Russel, 2012). Brown (2004) found that men who protect themselves from the abuser are less likely to be believed by law enforcement, and according to Dewar (2008) are most often arrested or threatened to be arrested. Other researchers have found that men are less likely to receive protective orders (Basile, 2005; Muftic and Bouffard, 2007; Muller, Desmaraise, and Hamel, 2009).

Limitations

Though this study is a unique contribution to the literature, it was not without its limitations. One limitation was the small sample size. The researcher had anticipated conducting two focus groups with a total of six participants each; however, four of the participants were not able to participate. Perhaps the researcher should have invited more participants in the event some did not show up. A second limitation is that four of the participants were interviewed face to face rather than as participants of a focus group. Noticeably more dialogues (verbal and nonverbal) were made between the participants in the focus group. The data were based on eight African American male students and may not necessarily represent general male college student perceptions, attitude, and behavior toward female-perpetrated IPV.

Recommendations

The present study constitutes an analysis of men's perception, attitude, and behavior toward male victims of IPV. It provides valuable information for families, the legal community, mental health and social service practitioners, and policy makers. Early education on interpersonal relationships and intimate partner violence should be made available to youth so that they are knowledgeable about healthy relationships. Public education programs that focus on discrimination against men is equally important. The impact of gender-biased social-emotional development on children later in life should be addressed with families. Reading materials should be made available in physician offices and clinics that service children and families. Adjustment in cultural practices is also important. Men who report abuse by a female partner should not be refused help, discounted, or made to feel helpless because they are in an abusive situation. Similar to those supporting women victims, concerted efforts should be made in advertising and campaigning for male victims to report female-perpetrated IPV. Mental health and social service practitioners must consider a variation of intervention mechanisms that best fit the unique needs of male victims of IPV.

ACKNOWLEDGMENTS

The author is grateful to her graduate research assistant, Ms. Itunu Ilesamni, MSW, for assisting with the recruitment of participants and focus groups and transcribing some of the data.

CHAPTER 6

MEAN GIRLS, REALITY MEDIA INFLUENCES, AND LOW SELF-ESTEEM: A TWENTY-FIRST-CENTURY CHALLENGE

DR. IRMA J. GIBSON

What are little girls made of? Sugar and spice and everything nice. This statement was etched into my early childhood memories as the Mother Goose nursery rhyme alluded to the goodness and innocence of the female species while placing an opposite label on the male species: What are little boys made of? Snips and snails and puppy dog tails. What a stark difference! And it should not be a surprise. Gender roles and expressions have been in existence since the beginning of time. Gender roles are the "attitudes, behaviors, rights and responsibilities that society associates with" being male or female. "They are societal expectations of how individuals should act, think or feel based upon their assigned gender or biological sex (and based upon the predominant binary system: male/female)." Gender expression refers to how individuals express their socially constructed gender and may include how they dress, their general appearance, the way they articulate, or the way they carry themselves (Hutchison, 2015). From the onset of birth, it is what society has socially created and constructed, and it can also be influenced by culture.

Although I wasn't aware at the time, the Mother Goose nursery rhyme is the first example I can recall of the social construction of gender. That was the 1960s. It is a fact that so much has changed in every aspect of society and the world since that time. Fast-forward to the twenty-first century and the expectations continue to be in existence, but the dynamics are changing and the stakes have elevated to another level of complexity, especially for youth and young adults. The social-constructionist perspective posits that the perception of reality is shaped by people's experiences and is socially created and influenced by their beliefs and actions (gender roles, expressions, etc.). How people think about situations as they interact with others becomes their reality. Encounters don't just happen to us; meaning is attached to all of our experiences regardless of whether they are negative or positive, good or bad, bitter or sweet. And because the social-constructionist approach incorporates human diversity, people learn how they are supposed to behave through their interactions with others, thus their behavior will change depending upon the circumstances in which they find themselves (Zastrow and Kirst-Ashman, 2015). This conceptual social work framework lays the foundation for and lends credence to the mean girls hypothesis, the connection to intimate partner violence (IPV), and the essence of this chapter.

The mean girls label can be traced back to the 1955 movie *Queen Bee*. However, as a result of technology, social media, and reality TV influences, the twenty-first century presents a multitude of additional challenges that surpasses any factor that was prevalent in the '50s or '60s. It has become an overwhelming phenomenon that is addressed in many conferences that pertain to youth who are at risk. It's not unusual to hear the phrase "girls gone wild" to describe the physical altercations that are often caught on tape and seem to comically amuse those who take pleasure in videotaping and witnessing these horrible acts of wretched behavior. And what is alarming is research has shown that the problems of some youth and these acts of aggression start early and extend across their lifespan into young adulthood. It has become so critical that college courses are being offered to explain the phenomenon. One such course is designed to explore the "motives behind why women seek authority and the actions they are willing to take in order to hold onto it." Another is titled "Mad Men and Mad Women" and examines the changing tides of masculinity and femininity in twentieth-century America and focuses specifically on the connections between postwar mass communication and formation of gender roles, consumption, and cultural expectations. While the demands to be respected are applauded, to do so at the expense of hurting others, causing harm and creating a toxic environment, should not be the acceptable norm, regardless of gender. The societal stereotype "you fight like a girl" is no longer a valid comparative persona to describe an altercation between two males due to the changing dynamics of the female species' physical prowess.

Enter into the equation the factor of reality television, which depicts all types of aggression, controversy, inability to control anger, and verbal and physical altercations. Reality TV is one of today's most popular genres of media entertainment, and youth are exposed to these antics on a level that exceeds moderation. "Americans watch TV as their main leisure activity. In 2011, the average American spent 2.8 hours a day in front of the TV, which accounts for about 50 percent of total leisure time activities" ("American Time Use Survey," as cited in Lehmann, 2012). Pressing the power button on the television remote provides instant access to a wide variety of shows that target different audiences and vary in concept; they all share the genre of "reality TV." It was initially introduced in the 1970s, but did not become successful until MTV launched *The Real World* in 1992, which achieved widespread popularity (Singer, as cited in Lehmann, 2012).

Today, reality TV shows air during prime time and are fully immersed within US television culture (Andrejeciv, as cited in Lehmann, 2012). Whether the message is positive or negative is up to interpretation; however, *Mom at Sixteen, Dating Naked, Growing Up Hip Hop, Married at First Sight, Big Brother, Marriage Boot Camp,* and *Hoarders* are in the lineup of choices, and as the genre indicates, reality TV features everyday people in unscripted situations dealing with "real-world" problems. Perhaps this is one of the factors that makes it so appealing to viewers, despite the staged drama often witnessed. It is relatable and, possibly, the norm.

According to Lehmann (2012), besides the lack of authenticity and accusation of audience manipulation, critics concern themselves with the moral issue of reality TV. A 2011 investigative report published by the Parents Television Council reveals that "gender portrayals on MTV reality programming" reinforce the discussion about reality TV and its negative influences on US society. The report also states that "only 24% of what females said about themselves [was] positive." The influence reality TV has on US society is significant, especially its influence on youth since television is a widely accessible form of mass culture. Studies confirm an alarming negative trend in girls' social behavior verifying that "[teens] who [are] exposed to high levels of television sexual content [are] twice as likely to experience a pregnancy" (Chandra et al., p. 1047, as cited in Lehmann, 2012). Negative notions about reality TV therefore give a reasonable cause for concern in addition to the fact that nearly every channel is home to reality television.

Christenson coauthored a study in 2006 that analyzed reality television programs with medical and health themes. He found that while the shows did seem to inspire healthier behavior in some viewers, there was a lot of emphasis placed on superficiality—something which, over time, he said, may have an effect on viewers' body image and self-esteem (Fahner, 2012). This is critical for the young female viewer and will be discussed later in this chapter.

According to Fahner (2012), Jaime Riccio, a graduate student at the Samuel Irving (SI) Newhouse School of Public Communications at Syracuse University, researches reality television and the effect it's having on youth culture in the United States. In 2010, Riccio said she began conducting a series of focus groups, interviews, and surveys on the subject. What she found is that reality television is leading to more dramatic tendencies in everyday life among young adults. "Because there is so much of that now that is being broadcast and that people are consuming, it is having an overarching effect on our youth culture," Riccio said. "It's an interesting area to look at, because it's so new, and I think it's something we're going to have to look at even further in the future."

MASS MEDIA, BULLYING, AGGRESSION, AND THE IPV CONNECTION

The "future" is here, the "future" is now. Research consistently shows that viewers, young viewers especially, are influenced by the behavior they see modeled on TV. As reality TV continues to spread, we need to be mindful of the messages and values these shows are communicating to young viewers. What's a young viewer likely to learn from reality TV? There is justification for concern not just in the case of vulnerable females, but all youth and young adults. Television serves as a model for social behavior and interaction, especially for young viewers, many of whom pick up social cues from how they see their favorite TV personalities behave (Rankin, n.d.). The exposure and the influences are inevitable because the main agents of socialization impact all persons in the environment: family, school, peers, media, social media, religion, and employers, 365 days of the year. The degree of influence varies based upon a number of biological, psychological, and social factors, some of which are discussed in the behavioral and mental health chapter (chapter 11).

Rankin (n.d.) asks us to consider the lessons children and young adults are learning from reality programs and their content. "It appears those who brutalize others are brutalized in the process, even if it means they might be willing to personally humiliate somebody, because they have seen it being done and think it is good fun. It [might] be good fun, but it is also a form of mental cruelty. [Intimate partner violence] is not just physical, it includes mental violence, so what is the difference? Being cruel to somebody isn't just beating them up. Reality television appears to be here to stay, and parents need to be aware that these [short TV] series are promoted heavily and often tailor-made for young viewers [and young adults]." However, "they are almost never appropriate for impressionable young minds. The consequences and the implications for our families, future generations and our communities are far reaching and serious."

Additionally, the influence of media on society has expanded exponentially and into ever diversified forms. Reality TV allows Americans to fantasize about gaining status through automatic fame. Ordinary people can watch the shows, see people like themselves, and imagine that they too could become celebrities by being on television. It does not matter as much that the contestants often are shown in an unfavorable light; the fact that millions of Americans are paying attention means the contestants are important. Media, in all their various forms, are today shaping our world in more ways than ever (Reiss and Wiltz, 2001). Gone are the days when the television networks discontinued broadcasting at midnight and viewers were greeted with the Star-Spangled Banner as the stations sounded off until the next morning.

Presently, beyond what children may see at home, they are continuously surrounded by messages and images in community institutions, advertisements, TV shows, songs, and other spheres that reinforce gender stereotypes—such as expectations of the subservience of women, or men exhibiting force as a display of strength—that often correlate with abusive behavior (Seabrook, 2017). Therefore, addressing the "mean girl" hypothesis as it relates to the influence of twenty-first-century woes is critical in moving forward with IPV primary prevention efforts. And these efforts have to originate from research and the collection and assessment of a plethora of data from the micro, mezzo, and macro environmental influences.

ADDITIONAL AGENTS OF ENVIRONMENTAL AND SOCIALIZATION INFLUENCES

One agency that has answered the call is "the National Institute of Justice (NIJ) which has a long history of research on intimate partner violence and recognizes the importance of understanding the factors during adolescence that put individuals at risk for intimate partner violence as adults. The researchers found that young adults who had unskilled parents or parents who experienced intimate partner violence were at an increased risk of exhibiting antisocial behavior as a teenager. In turn, antisocial teens were at a heightened risk of experiencing intimate partner violence in their young adult relationships. This pattern was stronger for males than females. The researchers also found that aggressive children who engaged with delinquent peers in adolescence led to intimate partner violence victimization and perpetration in young adulthood. These findings on developmental and familial factors give us insight on the possible origins and maintenance of behaviors that lead to intimate partner violence in young adulthood" (NIJ, 2017).

Additionally, partner [and significant other] influences on the relationship were critical. Lower levels of relationship satisfaction were related to increased levels of physical and psychological victimization. If a partner used alcohol or marijuana, it increased the likelihood of IPV perpetration. For instance, women's substance use was associated with increases of perpetrating physical violence, and men's substance use was associated with increases in perpetrating sexual violence. These findings provide additional research on how the use or abuse of multiple substances may influence the likelihood of intimate partner violence (NIJ, 2017).

Of equal importance, "an NIJ-funded longitudinal study of 1,162 students in the Midwest examined factors that led teens to engage in bullying, sexual harassment and dating violence while in middle and high school. The researchers found that youths who bullied other students while in middle school were more likely to engage in more serious forms of interpersonal aggression connected with dating and romantic relationships as they grew older" (NIJ, 2017). This is confirmation of a pattern of antisocial behavior that appears to produce different results for the genders as the various stages of the life span are experienced. Case in point:

> Bullying behavior in middle school predicted bullying behavior in high school, which, in turn, was linked to perpetrating teen dating violence. In middle school, aggression toward a sibling was a predictor of bullying behavior for both girls and boys. For girls, family conflict and having delinquent friends were also predictors of bullying behavior. For boys, family conflict was not a predictor of bullying behavior, but both having delinquent friends and self-reported delinquency were predictors. Among high school students, researchers found direct links between those who bullied and those who perpetrated teen dating violence. Female teens who bullied others were likely to perpetrate sexual, verbal and physical dating violence. Male teens who bullied others were likely to perpetrate verbal and physical dating violence. (NIJ, 2015)

The issue of bullying is a significant factor in the IPV saga and will be discussed in depth in the following chapter. Besides bullying, aggressive behavior, and other forms of violence, what are the other risk factors that may be exacerbated as a result of too much exposure to reality TV, which has become a household word and a staple in the twenty-first century's mass communication and social media lineup?

SELF-ESTEEM AND THE MEDIA AS POWERFUL AGENTS OF SOCIALIZATION

Despite the questionable influence of this popular form of "entertainment," if truth be told, some of us possess a guilty pleasure for reality television—the home of love and hip-hop, "real" housewives, celebrities, catfights, and drama. One of the infamous moments on *Flavor of Love* involved a woman spitting on another woman after being eliminated from the show. This show and others were a great way of showcasing sex, physical violence, profanity, and constant controversy. Reality TV shows have a major involvement in the behaviors of our society. And it's evident the reality television universe is emerging, and not always in the best way. The debate will continue in regard to whether reality TV is detrimental. After all, the behaviors we view on television, like verbal and physical altercations, shameless partying, and profanity, are what occur in society as well. Welcome to the twenty-first century. When it comes to reality television, people may think it's entertaining, but others take it seriously, and here's another reason why. Reality television, according to Brad Gorham of Syracuse University, has an effect on the behaviors of people in society. He claims people are easily influenced by reality television because they eventually copy the behaviors portrayed on television and use them in real life. Our young females are not exempt.

> That unfriendly behavior is good for TV ratings, but it might be bad news for [young adults], the viewers. A new study led by Bryan Gibson, a psychologist at Central Michigan University, finds watching reality shows with lots of what's called relational aggression—bullying, exclusion and manipulation—can make people more aggressive in their real lives. "We knew from past research that people who see relational aggression in media tend to become more aggressive," he explains to Tess Vigeland, guest host of NPR's [National Public Radio] weekends on *All Things Considered*. "Gossiping and nastiness is prevalent on these shows, so we wanted to find out whether it affected how aggressive people were after they watched." The experiment that exposed the research subjects to aggressive TV episodes confirmed that there was an increased aggression among the participants' response at the conclusion of the experiment. Gibson is quick to point out that these findings are not a reason to censor what television content makes it on air. But, he says, it's probably worth taking note if you're a parent. "This is one form of media that may appear harmless, [but] the research provides a little bit of evidence that there can be some negative outcomes as well," he says. (NPR Staff, 2014)

Up to this point in the discussion, numerous studies have confirmed that reality television and media exposure influences our youth and young adults in one way or another. However, this is just one factor in the matter. Although many youth are exposed to reality TV, all don't conform to and act out the negativity and loss of control that are exhibited. A popular saying is that imitation is the highest form of flattery. In social work, that is taught and academically assessed under the social learning theoretical framework that will be thoroughly addressed in chapter 13. The experts in the field of child and family welfare have their professional opinions also. Jane Addams, a social worker extraordinaire, expresses the power of social learning in the following statement: "America's future will be determined by the home and the school. The child becomes largely what he is taught; hence we must watch what we teach and how we live" (NYARCP, 2011). And Marian Edleman of the Children's Defense Fund bluntly states her position on the matter as follows: "What's [really] wrong with our children who are at risk?" According to Edelman (2007), in part, the culprit includes:

> Parents letting children raise themselves or be raised by television or the internet, adults telling children one thing and doing another, adults making promises we don't keep and preaching what we don't practice, adults telling children not to be violent while marketing and glorifying violence and adults telling children to be honest while lying and cheating in our homes, offices and public life.

Although family influence plays a significant role in the lives of children and youth specifically between ages zero and eight, the theoretical frameworks clearly state that the "person in environment" model is a powerful determinant of learned behavior across the lifespan. (This theoretical framework will be discussed thoroughly in chapter 13.) The saying "Children do as we do and not as we say" could not be more truthful than the examples in the earlier stated data that have been the subjects of discussion. What is occurring in the female psyche that results in the mean girl mentality is the question at hand. So many factors have raised eyebrows, including loss of control, various forms of violence, excessive aggression, verbal and physical attacks, and the inability to manage and control anger. How particular stimuli in the environment (reality TV and social media) impact these factors has already been elaborated and proven that whatever the culprit, it starts early in life and has the potential to escalate across the lifespan. Therefore it is necessary to explore another piece of the puzzle in this mean girl persona: the psychological and emotional components, specifically low self-esteem.

> Domestic violence is the maltreatment of an intimate partner in order to gain or maintain control. The U.S. Surgeon General recently declared domestic violence as the number one health concern in the USA today. Domestic violence is not gender specific, however; research shows that aggressive behavior is more often associated with males than with females and therefore more women than men are victims of partner abuse. It is reasonable to think that persons with low self-esteem tend to have chaotic relationships. Persons with low self-esteem are insecure and their self-images are often clouded by inaccurate [and negative] information from their [environments]. (Bradshaw, 2013)

It is ironic that much of the literature written about self-esteem and IPV assigns the label of low self-esteem to the victim instead of the perpetrator. My approach is different, and I challenge the readers to carefully examine the characteristics of persons who suffer from low self-esteem. These persons can easily be categorized as "mean persons/girls" and placed in the bully (perpetrator) grouping also. Remember that one of the common denominators is the desire to be "in control." While some of the characteristics of low self-esteem are identified above (insecurity, negative self-image, etc.), this is not an all-inclusive list. The fact is that persons who suffer from low self-esteem tend to believe they don't deserve healthy relationships. This may be another form of mental and psychological sabotage on the behalf of the mean girls/bullies. "Their subconscious belief of unworthiness leads to the avoidance of those who truly care; instead gravitating to chaotic relationships that leave them deeply psychologically and developmentally scared—greatly hampering the building and maintenance of healthy relationships" (Bradshaw, 2013). If the thoughts and feelings are negative, evidence of this will be disclosed in words and conversation, which eventually will be displayed in behaviors and actions.

According to Bradshaw (2013), the adage "hurt people hurt people" rings true. As a result of pain and insecurities, abusers often feel depleted or out of control, lacking the ability to nurture and to love. I often state to my students: *"You can't give what you don't have, and you can't teach what you don't know."* The victim endures being hurt because of lack of self-awareness or worth. The fact remains that persons with high self-esteem are less vulnerable to abuse. They tend to choose partners who understand and who honor their worth, bringing value to the relationship. A positive link exists between high self-esteem and healthy relationships. The fact of the matter is that IPV is at a critical state, and mean girl bullies, cliques, and gangs are contributing to the demise, although due to a number of factors, the research is still limited and has yet to yield accurate statistical data in this regard.

In closing, I want to bring your attention to the following study, which confirms that gender does matter in regard to self-esteem and the perception of IPV. I also cite the following definition to highlight the overarching themes present in almost every discussion about bullying, IPV, and the connection to the mean girl disposition. Convoluting the behavior is a combination of social and psychological defense mechanisms, mainly domination, control, and intimidation. These are important points that are crucial in understanding the derivation of this highly complex topic that will no doubt stir up one debate after another in pinpointing the origin as well as the dialogue about a primary prevention.

> Intimate Partner Violence (IPV) is a public health issue defined as "a constellation of abusive and controlling behaviors including psychological abuse, isolation, threats, stalking, and physical violence that taken together create a climate of fear and intimidation that maintain one partner in a position of domination and control with the other partner in a position of subordination and compliance" (Hall, 2012). The current study was carried out at the University of Massachusetts at Boston (UMB), and explores

> the relationship between being a victim of IPV, self-esteem, and stigma across gender and other characteristics. Approximately 250 male and female undergraduate students responded to a survey examining attitudes about abuse in an intimate partnership after reading an IPV vignette where they are depicted as a victim of IPV. Respondents answered questions about self-esteem and stigma after imagining themselves as an IPV victim. The findings from the study suggest that male respondents report significantly higher levels of self-esteem and lower levels of perceived stigma than the female respondents. The results also suggest that income, race, and setting of upbringing influence respondents' previous knowledge of IPV. This study offers some insight to gender differences in self-esteem and stigma as they relate to all victims of IPV. (Hall, 2012)

With cases of bullying on the rise, it is becoming more apparent than ever that female bullying is just as common as bullying with males. It is a common misconception that boys and teen males are the most dominant types of bullies. In fact, girls can be just as ruthless, especially when it comes to bullying that is not as physical. Types of bullying like cyberbullying are often spearheaded by teen girls placing an attack on their peers verbally. However, harsh words, lies, and rumors can be just as devastating to a child or teen as being physically attacked (library.thinkquest.org, n.d.).

There are many different types of bullies, including female bullies. This type of behavior has been happening for decades, and likely even before that. However, now that bullying is becoming more and more recognized, cases of female bullies have increased. The classic type of bullying includes the mean boy on the playground, but now it is clear that female bullying is just as prominent and severe as bullying with males. Female bullies can be even worse, possibly as a result of low self-esteem. Self-esteem issues appear to be a major factor associated with female perpetration, which is why it is also a major factor in the discussion about resolutions. With this in mind, one of the best ways to prevent bullying of any kind is to help build your child's self-esteem. Children and teens with higher self-esteem and more friends are less likely to become the victims [and perpetrators] of bullying (library.thinkquest.org, n.d.). Consequently, self-esteem-building tools can be vital in the prevention of intimate partner violence. It can also be a part of the critical answer to the problem of social and other media influences in regard to the promotion of aggressive behavior.

As a professor of social work who frequently interacts with predominantly female students, ranging in ages from nineteen and up, I have taken the liberty to conduct an informal survey over the past few years. As a sibling of one older sister, five older brothers, and one younger, I was raised in an environment where I was taught to "keep my hands to myself." In several of my classes, I shared with them that in my household, my siblings and I were forbidden to "pass a lick" upon each other. The same rule that applied to my brothers applied to my sister and me. We didn't get a pass to touch our brothers out of aggression just because we were females. Our parents made it clear that behavior of this type was unacceptable under any circumstances. In an informal poll of each class I posed the following question to several of my female students: How many of you were taught in your household that females *should not initiate* hitting males and/or were taught to keep your hands to yourselves just as males are forbidden to lay hands on females and should keep their hands to themselves? In each poll, less than a fraction of the female students who were polled raised their hands. The results were disturbing and confirm that the differences in gender expectations and gender bias are still viable today, despite the statistics that indicate a new way of teaching and modeling relationship etiquette is crucial. Remember, this isn't about classic cases of self-defense, wherein females have every right to defend themselves. It's about drawing attention to the progression of unprovoked aggressive behavior conducted by female perpetrators.

> Twenty Five years ago, for every 10 boys arrested for assault, there was one girl. Now there are only four boys arrested for each girl arrested. Simply put, the official arrest data indicate that girls today assault people and get arrested more often than did the girls of generations past. According to the U.S. Department of Justice, while criminal violence among teenage boys today still far exceeds criminal violence among teenage girls, the gap is narrowing. (Gabarino, 2006)

This confirms the critical need to be concerned about the increased violence and aggressive behavior society is witnessing in the twenty-first century among the female gender. Not only have the dynamics changed in regard to the female persona, female perpetrators are now being arrested for the crime of intimate partner violence.

> According to Henning, Renauer, and Holdford, 2006 (as cited in Schuler, 2010), there has been a substantial increase in females being arrested for intimate partner violence. Women now account for a quarter of arrests for this crime (Henning, Renauer, and Holdford, 2006). As a result, the criminal justice system has had to refocus on both women and men perpetrators of this crime. Society's ongoing debate on female use of aggression and possible gender favoritism within the criminal justice system has begun to be noted within the criminological research. (Schuler, 2010)

> Once again, gender biasness is a problem in the 21st century. In a social experiment with Deborah Roberts as the interviewer featured on *Good Morning America* in November 2017, male teens spoke openly about the negative effects of the traditional ideas of masculinity when it comes to their relationships with those around them. Unbeknownst to them, their fathers listened in to their conversations from behind a glass mirror. A group of fathers were surprised to discover the struggles their sons face as a teenager today, especially when it comes to navigating traditional ideas of masculinity and making good decisions about drugs and alcohol. "There's a lot of pressure on being a teenage boy, guys go through a couple of things not many people talk about," Nathaniel

> Harrison, 15, told ABC News' Deborah Roberts during the experiment. "Girls can like sleepover at other girls houses and stuff, but when you say that you are going to sleep over at a guy's house, then everybody's like 'Oh really, well what are you going to do there?'" he added. "And it's like we're just hanging out, we're friends." Griffin Reiner, 15, agreed with his peer, saying "people just don't think it's acceptable," to become emotionally close or connected to other boys. "I've never seen anyone in my school, any guy in my school start crying or like freak out about anything," he added. Griffin called being a teenage boy today "confusing," and Nathaniel described it as "frustrating." Nathaniel added that some people may not realize how scary it can be to open up about your feelings. "It takes real courage and real bravery to walk up to somebody and tell them how you feel," Nathaniel said. Most of the boys said they felt like they could not talk to their fathers about some of the struggles they were facing. "I don't tell them much," Griffin added of his relationship with his parents. "But when I do tell them stuff, **it's more to my Mom than to my Dad."** (Yeo, 2017)

This is another real-world example of how gender bias continues to be an issue that not only negatively impacts our female youth but our male youth as well. Thus, it's time for a change as the twenty-first century presents an array of ecological and cultural issues that require a new way of responding to all of our youth.

Dr. Logan Levkoff, an expert in parent-child communications, told ABC News it is important for parents to enforce rules for their teens that are in their best interest, even if it may be different from what their teens say they want. Levkoff added that one of the most important skills parents can teach teens is "resilience." "While we want to protect our kids, it is important for them to feel hurt or disappointment," she said. "Our job as parents is to teach our kids resilience, and to teach our kids how to overcome those challenges." Levkoff said that when your teen is feeling distressed emotionally, "pretending that those feelings don't exist is unhealthy." "Putting a bandage over it doesn't acknowledge all the feelings that are very real," she added (Yeo, 2017).

The title of this article documenting the results of the social experiment, "Teen boys discuss the pressures of becoming a man: 'Confusing' and 'frustrating,'" is hardcore proof and clearly states and alerts us that all teens need to feel comfortable with expressing their emotions, despite their gender. These findings again resonate with the evidence-based research I present and the concerns I raise in chapter 1 about society's double standards. In fact, chapter 5 also presents research pertinent to this fact. These are truly valid issues that must be met with a different mindset, mentality, and approach than previously demonstrated. We owe them nothing less.

In conclusion, as the topic of "mean girls" is debated and discussed, it should be stressed that gender is a critical factor that must be considered in pinpointing the complex problems of increased aggression and IPV and with targeting a resolution. Research has confirmed there are gender differences in the types of bullying children experience, such that boys are more likely than girls to report being physically bullied by their peers (Harris, Petrie, and Willoughby, 2002) and girls are more likely than boys to report being targets of rumor-spreading and sexual comments (Nansel et al., 2001). Girls report being bullied by boys and girls, while boys report being bullied primarily by other boys (Melton et al., 1998).

Additionally, bullying has been found to be related to negative psychosocial functioning among children who are victimized, including lowered self-esteem, higher rates of depression, anxiety (Hodges and Perry, 1996), feelings of loneliness (Nansel et al., 2001), suicidal ideation, and higher rates of school absenteeism (Rigby, 1996). While research suggests there is no single cause of bullying, overall, individual, familial, peer, school, and community factors may place a child or youth at risk for bullying his or her peers (Limber, 2000). These findings mirror consistently what has been reflected in the prior chapters as well as the data that is forthcoming. We must take heed to these critical evidence-based revelations and the "person in the environment" theory. This charge and the mindset challenge definitely include changing the culture of how we address our youth as it relates to gender, among other recommendations. Twenty-first-century issues call for twenty-first-century interventions.

CHAPTER 7

WHAT DOES BULLYING HAVE TO DO WITH IT?: AN ANALYSIS OF THE K–12 EDUCATIONAL ENVIRONMENT

DR. TREVIS KILLEN, DR. IRMA J. GIBSON, AND RICARLO WILLIAMS

Bullying is widespread in the United States. In the public school system, bullying is at an all-time high. One can observe it as early as kindergarten. While the magnitude and types of bullying can vary across communities and demographic groups, bullying negatively impacts all youth involved—*victims, bullies, and bystanders*.

- Bullying is common. One in five high school students reported being bullied on school property in the last year (CDCP, 2017).
- Bullying is frequent. Bullying is among the most commonly reported discipline problems in public schools. Twelve percent of public schools report that bullying happens at least once a week. Rates are highest for middle schools (22 percent) compared to high schools (15 percent), combined schools (11 percent), and primary schools (8 percent) (CDCP, 2017).
- Bullying can happen online. For example, over 15 percent of high school students reported being cyberbullied in the last year (Dilliberti et al., 2017).
- In a 2011 nationwide survey, 20 percent of high school students reported being bullied on school property in the twelve months preceding the survey (CDC, 2013). A higher percentage of middle school students reported being bullied than high school students. (Robers et al., 2013).

The school environment has drastically changed from the days of old. And while all who are called to prepare the next generation of leaders play an important role in addressing these issues, school social workers and social work administrators are in unique positions and are governed by the NASW Code of Ethics (NASW, 2008) to enhance human well-being and to help meet the basic human needs of all people, with particular attention to the needs and empowerment of people who are vulnerable, oppressed, and living in poverty. To promote social justice and social change with and on behalf of clients/students, the climate of the school sets the stage and must be sustained under ideal and supportive circumstances, from the top down. One can tell the climate of a school simply by entering the building.

The school climate refers to the social and working relationships of staff and administrators. The climate of a school affects its culture, the belief system, and the manner in which tasks are accomplished. School climate is important when evaluating bullying. O'Malley Olsen et al. (2014) concluded based on the findings of their study that a school's climate has a direct link to the rate of victimization within a school. Thus, as the problem of bullying is addressed, there are many pieces to the school's climate that should be considered: the culture within the school, staff/student relationships, student/peer relationships, parental involvement, and student perceptions. When we look at a school's culture, each school is going to look and feel different for a variety of reasons.

Bullying is no exception and varies depending upon the setting, and unfortunately it is common for a variety of reasons—social status, degree of racial tensions, and sexual identification issues are some examples (Klein, 2012; O'Malley Olsen, Kann, Vivolo-Kantor, Kinchen, and McManus, 2014). Large-scale incidents of school bullying can impact schools and their students, especially when they include [factors] such as cyberbullying, suicides, and school shootings (Kalish and Kimmel, 2010; Rice et al., 2015). Let's examine the properties of bullying.

CHARACTERISTICS OF BULLYING

To better understand the specific characteristics of bullying, several pieces of literature have been analyzed. The common themes are gender differences, sexual orientation in bullying, and friends and acquaintances in bullying.

According to the CDC (2013), a number of factors can increase the risk of a youth engaging in or experiencing bullying. However, the presence of these factors does not always mean that a young person will become a bully or a victim. Some of the factors associated with a higher likelihood of engaging in bullying behavior include:

- Externalizing problems such as defiant and disruptive behavior
- Harsh parenting by caregivers
- Attitudes accepting of violence

Some of the factors associated with a higher likelihood of victimization include:

- Poor peer relationships
- Low self-esteem
- Perceived by peers as different or quiet

GENDER DIFFERENCES IN BULLYING

There are many differences in how a female student handles a situation from how a male student handles a situation. This has to do with hormones, puberty, and a variety of other things that may be going on in the body at any given time. This factor is addressed more in depth in the previous chapter.

THE BULLY-VICTIM

Bullying can result in physical injury, social and emotional distress, self-harm, and even death. It also increases the risk for depression, anxiety, sleep difficulties, lower academic achievement, [poor school adjustment], and dropping out of school. Youth who bully others are at increased risk for substance use, academic problems, and experiencing violence later in adolescence and adulthood (NCIPC, 2017). Compared to youth who only bully, or who are only victims, bully-victims suffer the most serious consequences and are at greater risk for both mental health and behavior problems (Haynie et al., 2011).

Bullying was ignored for years by school employees, and the public viewed bullying as a part of the childhood experience. However, research has found that bullying is not a harmless phenomenon; rather, it is a widespread and serious problem that must be addressed (Espelage, and Swearer, 2003b). Terrell was a victim of bullying and this unfortunate type of scenario and response during his middle school years. I can honestly say the research is spot on, and a supportive parent (a strong family foundation) is a protective factor and worked on his behalf. My and his dad's actions and intervention with the school faculty and administrators proved to be effective, but not before I wrote a letter of displeasure about their ineffective responses to his pleas for help. (That crucial letter is listed in appendix 3.) At the time, I had no clue this awful ordeal would be directly connected to Terrell's IPV experience or that it was an early sign of this public health epidemic. But my letter identifies the concern I had then and that I continue to have: confirmation that the issue of bullying can be frustrating and requires a collaborative and consistent effort by all parties.

Now, legislation statutes and landmark court cases require schools to investigate incidences of bullying, which has contributed to a heightened awareness that no report of bullying should be ignored. As a part of this heightened awareness to help victims of bullying, school administrators are tasked with the sometimes challenging responsibility of determining who is a victim of bullying and who is the perpetrator. For example, sometimes a student who reports being a victim of bullying may retaliate in self-defense and thus will victimize peers. Terrell didn't resort to bullying others, but he did defend himself, which prompted me and his dad to call a meeting with the administrators. It was worth it.

This blurry line creates dilemmas for victims and school districts. To reduce situations that create bully-victims (or someone who both perpetrates bullying and is victimized by it), schools should encourage bystanders to report when they witness bullying. The various terminology that defines the types of bullying participants continues to provide a defined view of the overall aspects of the bullying saga and what we should be cognizant of as we decipher the players who are involved either directly and/or indirectly and how we can intervene. All are crucial to resolving this social issue, as you will be enlightened to the fact that doing nothing contributes to the problem also.

BYSTANDER

Students who observe bullying can intervene by reporting bullying to an adult, but some may fail to do so out of fear the bully will retaliate against them. Sometimes when bystanders do not report bullying, they develop guilt and anxiety, and may avoid offering personal support to the victim. By allowing bystanders to discuss their thoughts, feelings, and emotions, along with role-play to develop assertiveness skills and exploration of options for responding to bullying, schools can empower bystanders to serve as advocates for victims (CDC, 2017).

CYBERBULLYING

Bullying is not limited to face-to-face acts of harassment or aggression. Cyberbullying is a type of intentional bullying in which the individual uses electronic technology to feel powerful toward another person; examples include spreading rumors or sharing embarrassing photographs. Victimization involves more than just computers, but other devices also. Electronic devices can include cell phones, tablets, and e-readers. These devices have the ability to message other devices and have a wide variety of applications that can be downloaded to them, such as Facebook, Snapchat, Instagram, and Twitter. These social media outlets have the ability to access websites as well. With the variety of ways to connect, children are now opting to use their devices to communicate instead of picking up a phone and calling their friends. This allows for interaction anytime, day or night. It can happen alone, or with a group of friends. A problem with this is that parents are buying their children these devices, with little or no supervision (Upton, Patton, Sung Hong, Ranney et al., 2014). Another issue is that cyberbullying is not just being done at home, but it's being done at schools as well.

On a local Albany, Georgia, gospel radio program, a local church was highlighting the end of summer and supporting the return of the students and staff to school. An educational administrator was delivering the keynote address, and within his message, he talked about the most common issues and problems under his administration. He identified cell phones as the number-one issue, the manner in which the female students dress as number two, and third in line was social media. These three culprits result in the most disruptions from the academic and social learning environment within his school setting. This revelation supports the research that has been presented and that currently exists about the school environment. Cell phones and social media are two of the top three distractions.

Additional clarity is that perpetrators sometime use technology to deliberately and repeatedly inflict harm to victims through text messages, emails, websites, chatrooms, etc. Thus, bullying may take many forms, including physical bullying; teasing or name calling; social exclusion; peer sexual harassment; bullying about race, ethnicity, religion, disability, sexual orientation, and gender identity; and cyberbullying (bullying through email, text messaging, or other digital means) (APA, 2004). Cyberbullying can have a far-reaching span, especially considering that a hurtful post on social media can go viral within seconds. As a solution to reduce cyberbullying, some school districts require students to participate in internet safety-awareness training, which may include discussion on reporting cyberbullying to school staff, parents, or police. This strategy empowers student bystanders to intervene when they witness cyberbullying. When cyberbullying occurs off campus, school administrators are tasked with assessing when limits of free speech create or threaten to create a substantial disruption to the school or to a student's health or safety. Therefore, staff must be knowledgeable of when to report threats to police, and a best practice is to address off-campus cyberbullying by the implementation of policies that prohibit bullying through communication with school-issued electronic devices or networks.

RESPONDING TO BULLIES

School administrators may be quick to punish (in-school suspension, out-of-school suspension, expulsion, etc.) the aggressor for a bullying offense, but the student is not provided the opportunity to participate in a facilitated social-emotional learning (SEL) activity with a professional school counselor, school social worker, or school psychologist. Without this opportunity to process thoughts, feelings, and actions with a student services professional, the pathology of aggressive behavior may escalate for some students. Exposure to SEL curriculum will help students learn how to (a) recognize and manage emotions, (b) develop empathy, (c) develop healthy relationships, (d) make responsible decisions, and (e) handle conflict appropriately. Schools should teach these basic skills to help at-risk students function as productive members of society (Massat, Kelley, and Constable, 2016).

EVALUATING THE DATA AND RESPONSES IN TWO SOUTHERN STATES

As part of a comprehensive strategy to creating a healthy school climate in which bullying is not tolerated, it is important to assess students' perceptions of the school environment by including questions on topics such as bullying, school safety, peer victimization, school connectedness, peer social support, and adult social support. One comprehensive school climate survey that includes a compendium of questions on school safety, bullying, and peer victimization is the Georgia Student Health Survey 2.0, which is administered to students in grades six through twelve. Based on findings from the Georgia Student Health Survey, schools can then make informed decisions about the types of programs, services, technology, and safety measures to best meet the needs of their students. School climate survey data may be helpful when applying for grants and as justification for hiring student support services professionals (i.e. school counselors, school social workers, school psychologists, and school nurses). Undoubtedly, with access to an array of interventions tailored to school safety, school climate, and bullying, schools should have a systematic way for deciding which interventions will be most effective.

ADMINISTRATIVE CHALLENGES

Compliance with legislative statutes for bullying is no longer an option, but is a requirement in most states. However, some school district staff members embrace the notion that bullying is a natural part of child development. "The purpose of anti-bullying laws is to demonstrate that the legislature recognizes bullying as something that must be addressed, but the laws do not and cannot serve as the mechanism by which to actually address the behavior." Instead, as Secretary Duncan wrote, "When responding to bullying incidents, schools and districts should remember that maintenance of a safe and equitable learning environment for all students, including both victims and perpetrators of bullying, often requires a more comprehensive approach" (Temkin, 2015).

Some states have sought to overcome this limitation by expanding the scopes of their anti-bullying laws to not only require schools to have a policy, but criminalize bullying for those who engage in the behavior. This mindset creates a toxic school climate in which victims of bullying do not feel supported by staff who are charged with protecting their well-being. Failure to follow policies and procedures for reporting and investigating reports of bullying should not be tolerated. To create a school climate in which staff understand their role in reporting and investigating bullying, administrators should require all staff to participate in an annual training on bullying. A comprehensive overview of school policy, procedures, and best practices should be included in the presentation. In schools with more comprehensive anti-bullying policies, the prevalence of relational bullying was higher than in schools with less-clear policies. It is important for schools to examine their school safety policies and reconsider what constitutes violence. Schools must recognize the damaging effects of all types of bullying and include all types of bullying in their anti-violence policies (Woods and Wolke (2003).

BULLYING AND INTIMATE PARTNER VIOLENCE

Understanding the phenomenon of bullying is important, as it provides the earliest opportunity to intervene in the lives of adolescents. If left unchecked, bullying victimization or perpetration can alter normal childhood development and establish patterns of maladaptive behavior into adulthood (Fredland, 2008). Adolescent bullying may become a prelude for intimate partner violence as patterns of abuse are established and continue with adult partners. According to the Centers for Disease Control (2017), teen victims of intimate dating violence do not report it because they are afraid to tell friends and family. In addition, the 2013 National Youth Risk Behavior Survey found that approximately 10 percent of high school students reported physical victimization and 10 percent reported sexual victimization from a dating partner. These findings may suggest that bullying and teen dating violence (TDV) are interrelated.

As victims of bullying develop sexual identity and attitudes, they may be at risk for being verbally, emotionally, physically, and sexually abused by a partner. Considering that adolescence is usually the period when students begin to date, school districts should require eighth and ninth graders to participate in teen dating violence–prevention programs. To address the relationship between bullying and teen dating violence (TDV), school interventions should focus on preventing bullying, aggression, and sexual harassment, which are precursors to intimate partner violence. Moreover, legislation may help to promote awareness of teen dating violence and abuse.

BEST PRACTICES AND EDUCATIONAL INTERVENTIONS/POLICIES

One example of this type of legislative intervention is found in Section 1006.148, Florida Statute (F.S.), which requires school districts to adopt and implement a policy prohibiting dating violence and abuse.

According to Section 1006.148 F.S.:

1) Each district school board shall adopt and implement a dating violence and abuse policy. The policy shall:
    (a) Prohibit dating violence and abuse by any student on school property, during a school-sponsored activity, or during school-sponsored transportation.
    (b) Provide procedures for responding to such incidents of dating violence or abuse, including accommodations for students experiencing dating violence or abuse.
    (c) Define dating violence and abuse and provide for a teen dating violence and abuse component in the health education curriculum, according to s. 1003.42(2)(n), with emphasis on prevention education.
    (d) Be implemented in a manner that is integrated with a school district's discipline policies.
2) Each district school board shall provide training for teachers, staff, and school administrators to implement this section.

A clarion call for state legislatures to adopt laws aimed at reducing bullying in schools is in response to advocacy from groups that include students, parents, educators, and community stakeholders. In response to this call, legislative efforts to reduce bullying in schools differ across states, including a general definition of "bullying." A cursory review of research on bullying reveals that some definitions for bullying focus on specific actions, others look at intent of the aggressor, and some definitions focus on degree of harm (Angold et al., 2013). Best practices for school district policy on bullying should include the following actions: notification to parents/guardians of the victim and aggressor, developmentally appropriate consequences and interventions, annual mandatory professional development for all school personnel, workshops for parents/guardians, classroom guidance lessons for students, and school district policy for bullying included in the student code of conduct and the employee handbook.

Some of these best practices are already reflected in the Official Code of Georgia Annotated (O.C.G.A.) 20-2-751.4 statute, which requires school districts to adopt policies that prohibit bullying. In the proceeding sections of this chapter, we will review the O.C.G.A. 20-2-751.4, and consider how the K–12 educational environment can more effectively support victims of bullying and their aggressors through macro, mezzo, and micro-level interventions.

A MACRO-LEVEL RESPONSE: BULLYING DEFINED IN GEORGIA

The O.C.G.A. 20-2-751.4 includes a broad definition for bullying. According to this code, bullying is defined as an act that is:

1) Any willful attempt to threaten to inflict injury on another person, when accompanied by an apparent present ability to do so;
2) Any intentional display of force such as would give the victim reason to fear or expect immediate bodily harm; or
3) Any intentional written, verbal, or physical act, which a reasonable person would perceive as intended to threaten, harass, or intimidate, that:
    a) Causes another person substantial physical harm within the meaning of Code Section 16-5-23.1 or visible bodily harm such as is defined in Code Section 16-5-23.1;
    b) Has the effect of substantially interfering with a student's education;
    c) Is so severe, persistent, or pervasive that it creates an intimidating or threatening educational environment; or
    d) Has the effect of substantially disrupting the orderly operation of the school.

The term bullying applies to acts which occur on school property, on/in school vehicles, at designated school bus stops, at school-related functions or activities, or by the use of data or software accessed through a computer, computer system, computer network, or other electronic technology of a local school system. This term also applies to acts of cyberbullying originated on or within school property or with school equipment, if the electronic communication (1) is directed specifically at students or school personnel, (2) is maliciously intended for the purpose of threatening the safety of those specified or substantially disrupting the orderly operation of the school, and (3) creates a reasonable fear of harm to the students' or school personnel's person or property or has the likelihood of succeeding in that purpose. For the purpose of this code section, electronic communication includes but is not limited to any transfer of signs, signals, writings, images, sounds, data, or intelligence of any nature transmitted in whole or in part by a wire, radio, electromagnetic, photo-electronic, or photo-optical system.

The specified date selected by the school district that is adopting the anti-bullying policy should be inserted here. Following this date is a continuation of O.C.G.A. 20-2-751.4:

1) Each local board of education shall adopt a policy that prohibits bullying of a student by another student and shall require such prohibition to be included in the student code of conduct for schools in that school system;
2) Each local board policy shall require that, upon a finding by the disciplinary hearing officer, panel, or tribunal of school officials provided for in this subpart that a student in grades 6 through 12 has committed the offense of bullying for the third time in a school year, such student shall be assigned to the alternative school;

3) Each local board of education shall establish and publish in its local board policy a method to notify the parent, guardian, or other person who has control or charge of a student upon a finding by a school administrator that the student has committed an offense of bullying or is a victim of bullying; and
4) Each local board of education shall ensure that students and parents of students are notified of the prohibition against bullying, and the penalties for violating the prohibition, by positing such information at each school and by including such information in student and parent handbooks.

School district policy for bullying is necessary to hold students accountable for willful and intentional attempts to harm another student and to ensure that all school personnel clearly understand their role with reporting bullying to school administrators and know how to intervene to help victims of bullying. Therefore, board of education policy for bullying helps to establish a climate and culture of nonnegotiable expectations for bullying acts. This underpinning is needed to create a learning environment in which students and staff feel safe so that teaching and learning can occur. In the absence of a school district bullying policy, school districts are left vulnerable to lawsuits, experience loss of support from parents of bullying victims, and fail at their primary role, which is to keep students safe. In layman's terms, a part of the confusion and the uncertainty that school personnel experience when addressing the issue of bullying originates from the root of the problem, which is role ambiguity that hinders the establishment of a solid and effective anti-bullying policy. This lone factor breeds more problems within the school environment and culture because who is responsible for reporting what, to whom, and when are questionable. The answers to these questions vary depending upon who is providing the response: parent, teacher, or administrator. These barriers result in a ripple effect within the culture and to eventually establishing a clear and supportive policy. Until these culprits are addressed sufficiently, the absence of a policy or the lack of a clear policy will negatively impact the school's effective response to bullying.

CREATING A CULTURE OF AWARENESS: MEZZO-LEVEL INTERVENTIONS

Among some adults, being a victim or aggressor of bullying is commonly considered to be a "normal rite of passage" as children transition to adulthood (Woods, 2015). To debunk this thought, schools should implement mezzo-level interventions that heighten awareness of bullying behaviors as well as teach and empower members of the entire school community to move from passive "bystanders" to "upstanders" who report bullying acts to school personnel. By focusing on mezzo-level interventions to address bullying, schools will acknowledge the relationship between the student and environment (including peer group, school, family, and community), as well as those influences which help to create a responsive school climate and community in which bullying is not accepted. To create this type of school climate and culture, members of the school community must have a general understanding of the district's definition of bullying. To achieve this goal, developmentally appropriate classroom guidance lessons on learning how to recognize and report bullying must be offered in grades pre-K through twelve. Additionally, schoolwide programs such as Positive Behavior Interventions and Supports (PBIS) should reinforce expectations for student behavior by incorporating motivational systems to reward positive behavior (Massat, Kelley, and Constable, 2016). PBIS is a systems-based approach that is designed to promote prosocial behavior by acknowledging and rewarding "upstanders" who report bullying to school personnel. PBIS and developmentally appropriate classroom guidance activities are vital to creating a safe and effective learning environment that debunks the misconception that bullying is a "normal rite of passage" from childhood to adulthood. Some bullying acts may be covert and not seen by school staff, thus schools should train and empower students to become upstanders who report bullying.

Teaching and Engaging Adults about Bullying

Collaboration with parents and staff is essential to reducing bullying in school. This partnership is necessary to help both aggressors and victims of bullying. Unfortunately, schools sometimes miss opportunities to proactively educate and engage parents in conversation about the warning signs of victimization and pathology of bullying behavior. In fact, some school and district-level administrators fear that hosting a parent workshop on bullying will result in mass reports of bullying, while the reality is that awareness of bullying behavior can decrease reports of bullying, increase student achievement and school attendance, and create a safe and healthy school environment. To create a healthy and responsive school climate in which bullying is not accepted, schools should host annual workshops for parents that focus on bullying prevention and intervention. These annual workshops should include an overview of the school district's policy for bullying, protocol for reporting bullying, warning signs of victimization, and local counseling resource list. Although notification of a bullying offense to the parents/guardians of the aggressor and victim is a legally sound practice, as a best practice school districts should strive to be proactive by offering bullying workshops annually for parents and mandating participation for staff (Olweus, 1993; Olweus, D., 2001).

Although bullying and other issues related to school climate are often viewed independently from academic performance, student achievement will not reach the levels that truly reflect the potential of Georgia's students unless more attention is given to the relationship between school climate and academic achievement. Students cannot be expected to reach their full academic potential in an environment of fear and intimidation. Therefore, it is critical for schools to provide a safe and positive school climate for their students. A positive school climate will yield an increase in academic achievement and high school graduation rates (Woods, 2015).

ADDITIONAL SOLUTIONS: MICRO-LEVEL INTERVENTIONS

Short-term and long-term effects of bullying are well documented in the literature. According to Angold et al. (2013), victims of bullying between the ages of six and seventeen were found to be at risk for somatic problems, psychosomatic problems, and internalizing problems such as anxiety disorder or depression disorder. As this population ages, they are at increased risk for suicidal ideations, suicidal attempts, and death by suicide (Angold et al., 2013). In addition to affecting students' health, bullying impacts student attendance and academic achievement. Results from focus groups reveal bullying was reported by students as a common theme and reason for truancy, according to the Gastic (2008) study. Therefore, micro-level interventions are necessary to help victims of bullying to develop intrapersonal and interpersonal skills. Micro-level intervention in the school setting should focus on students' needs, strengths, and the problem. These micro interventions also should focus on the person in environment, while recognizing the innate characteristics that are unique to the individual student's resiliency.

CONCLUDING THOUGHTS

The K–12 educational environment has a critical role in mitigating the interplay of bullying and intimate partner violence. In this chapter, macro, mezzo, and micro interventions that directly or indirectly prevent bullying and intimate partner violence are discussed. Such interventions are effective means to reducing correlates associated with bullying and intimate partner violence, including school climate, aggression, maladaptive behavior, and sexual harassment. Existing research indicates that bullying at school may be significantly reduced through comprehensive, schoolwide programs that are designed to change norms for behavior (Olweus, Limber, and Mihalic, 1999). Interventions included in this chapter can be implemented at the K–12 levels as a classroom guidance activity or with individual students, and can include workshops for parents and staff. Policy for a school or school district should provide the framework for all interventions. Additionally, schools can empower student bystanders to intervene and report bullying to school staff. This support combined with interventions included in this chapter will help to create a responsive K–12 environment in which bullying is not tolerated and social-emotional supports are provided to help victims of bullying and their aggressors. The examples discussed address the lead that two southern states have taken to combat the problem. These examples as well as the following practical recommendations are applicable to nationwide school settings.

Former First Lady Michelle Obama, during a White House–sponsored function about bullying and the modeling of character, stated that parents aren't the only ones who have a responsibility.

> We all need to play a role—as teachers, coaches, as faith leaders, elected officials, and anyone who's involved in our children's lives. And that doesn't just mean working to change our kids' behavior and recognize and reward kids who are already doing the right thing, it means thinking about our own behavior as adults as well. (Munsey, 2011)

To effectively reach and empower youth in the twenty-first century, parents, educators, social workers, counselors, administrators, leaders, and citizens of the community have to wholeheartedly answer their cries. All have to elevate, set, and demonstrate the standards of expectation for them. They are the future and require twenty-first-century strategies for the twenty-first-century issues they face: untrustworthy and uncommitted adults and leaders; lack of positive, dependable "role models"; technology and social media (a blessing and a curse); bullying and cyberbullying; peer pressure; issues with self-worth; alcohol and drugs; crime and poverty. What youth frequently witness in regard to the negative behavior and character of leaders and authority figures is not fair, nor is it healthy. Adults should provide the front-line positive examples for youth to witness on a daily basis, so it is critical that the actions and behaviors of those adults and role models mirror their expectations of the youth. Truly, "the test of the morality of a society is what it does for its children" (Dietrich Bonhoeffer, as cited in NYARCP, 2011).

Additionally and of equal importance, the American Psychological Association (APA) (2004) encourages appropriate public and private funding agencies to support ecologically valid and culturally sensitive research on bullying behavior and anti-bullying interventions. It recommends integration of its bullying-prevention work into initiatives with other associations, governmental entities, and other interested parties in the dissemination of information that will help school administrators and staff, parents, mental health professionals, children and youth, and others to prevent bullying within and outside of the school setting. The APA encourages vigorous evaluations of bullying-prevention programs used in schools, after-school programs, and other settings; and encourages the implementation and dissemination of bullying-prevention programs and interventions that have demonstrated effectiveness in schools and communities and that are culturally sensitive.

In sync with these collaborative research-based prevention interventions recommended by the APA, the Alberti Center for Bullying Abuse Prevention seeks to reduce bullying by developing effective tools to change the language, attitudes, and behaviors of educators, parents, students, and society (Serwacki and Nicholson, 2012). While a part of the solution is to assess and target the overall state of society, the true and most significant assessing starts with each individual citizen ("the man in the mirror") and from within. Irresponsible behavior, lack of scruples, and inability to manage anger are issues with which adults appear to be grappling in the twenty-first century, and these behaviors appear to be paraded in the presence of children and youth via the media and social media. Many of them, as youth, have been victims of the same social ills, resulting in a vicious cycle and generational curses. Thus, the impact on this generation of children and youth as they struggle with unique twenty-first-century issues is subject to be repeated if this learned behavior is not arrested in a strategic and calculated therapeutic manner, beginning with self-awareness, self-assessment, and self-regulation.

Bullying and aggressive behavior have placed the future of society's youth at a critical and morbid state. To begin to address the issue, all, including adults, whether from a victim and/or perpetrator perspective need to seriously self-assess. Knowing one's strengths and weaknesses (acknowledging one's flaws) is an ongoing process that requires introspection as well as seeking out others' self-observations. "Children have more need of models than of critics" (Joseph Joubert, NYARCP, 2011).

IPV starts early and continues throughout the lifespan when it's not effectively addressed. An estimated 8.5 million women (7 percent) in the US and over 4 million men (4 percent) reported experiencing physical violence, rape (or being made to penetrate someone else), or stalking from an intimate partner in their lifetime and indicated they first experienced these or other forms of violence by that partner before the age of eighteen (NCIPC, 2018). A nationally representative survey of US high school students also indicates high levels of teen dating violence, a risk factor for IPV in adulthood. Among students who reported dating, 12 percent of girls and 7 percent of boys had experienced physical dating violence, and 16 percent of girls and 5 percent of boys had experienced sexual dating violence in the past twelve months. Supporting the development of healthy, respectful, and nonviolent relationships has the potential to reduce the occurrence of IPV and prevent its harmful and long-lasting effects on individuals, families, and their communities. Recommendations include the following: create protective environments, improve school climate and safety, teach safe and healthy relationship skills, develop social-emotional learning programs for youth, and promote bystander empowerment and education (NCIPC, 2018).

Youth violence is a significant public health problem that affects thousands of young people each day, and in turn, their families, schools, and communities. Youth violence typically involves young people hurting other peers who are unrelated to them and whom they may or may not know well. Youth violence can take different forms. Examples include fights, bullying, threats with weapons, and gang-related violence. A young person can be involved with youth violence as a victim, offender, or witness. [However], youth violence is preventable. The ultimate goal is to stop youth violence before it starts (NCICP, 2017). The ripple effects are chilling and long lasting, and they transcend a number of boundaries.

A case in point is that children and youth with disabilities and children and youth who are lesbian, gay, or transgender, or who are perceived to be so, may be at particularly high risk of being bullied by their peers (Rigby, 2002). Children and youth who bully are more likely than their peers to hold beliefs supportive of violence (Bosworth, Espelage, and Simon, 1999) and are more likely to influence their peers to engage in bullying others over time (Espelage et al., 2003a).

Finally, we close this chapter with some true and profound words of advice from the UN's International Day for the Elimination of Violence against Women summit: "We must consider how we can break the cycle of abuse and stop young people who are subjected to and witness domestic violence during their upbringing, and where they can grow up thinking abusive relationships are the norm. Domestic violence is all too often rooted in early upbringing and the family environment. Those who are subject to or witness abuse at a young age are much more likely to become victims or perpetrators later on in life."

And while the main agent of socialization, family, is pivotal in the quest to address this crisis, so is another, the school system. Next to the family, the educational environment is where many of the social ills and problems are identified, addressed, and sometimes resolved. Statistics from the Children's Defense Fund (2008) indicate that youth come to school carrying their burdens and issues with them. And that it is safe to assume that many of the children and adolescents are, indeed, at risk of having decreased horizons of success. By default our schools have become the focus of efforts to address at-risk issues. However, schools alone are not equipped for this immense task, but this has not stopped many of them from making a concerted effort. Other advocates must collectively join them in this fight to save society's most precious resources.

For starters, educating young people about what is a healthy and nonabusive relationship is key to preventing [intimate partner] and sexual violence in the future. This means ensuring that sex and relationship education is provided to all young people, and it should be compulsory. "I've come to the frightening conclusion that I am the decisive element in the classroom. It's my daily mood that makes the weather. As a teacher, I possess a tremendous power to make a child's life miserable or joyous. I can be a tool of torture or an instrument of inspiration. I can humiliate or humor, hurt or heal. In all situations, it is my response that decides whether a crisis will be escalated or de-escalated and a child humanized or dehumanized" (NYAR, Haim Ginott, 2011). We have a charge to keep.

I woke myself up
Because we ain't got an alarm clock
Dug in the dirty clothes basket,
Cause ain't nobody washed my uniform
Brushed my hair and teeth in the dark,
Cause the lights ain't on
Even got my baby sister ready,
Cause my mama wasn't home.
Got us both to school on time,
To eat us a good breakfast.
Then when I got to class the teacher fussed
Cause I ain't got no pencil
—Joshua Dickerson

The poet's main message is that "you must continue to fight, regardless of circumstances."

Keep your thoughts positive, because your thoughts become your words. Keep your words positive, because your words become your behavior. Keep your behavior positive, because your behavior becomes your habits. Keep your habits positive, because your habits become your values. Keep your values positive, because your values become your destiny.
—Mahatma Gandhi

Life and death are in the power of the tongue!

CHAPTER 8

EXPLORING INTIMATE PARTNER VIOLENCE: A LAW ENFORCEMENT PERSPECTIVE

DR. IRMA J. GIBSON AND MAJOR TONNIE WILLIAMS

The cost of intimate partner violence (IPV) has been assessed to exceed $5.8 billion (Menard et al., 2009). These costs consist of such things as police cost to domestic violence disputes, court cost to prosecute, shelters (mainly for women victims), hotlines for both men and women, mandated treatment programs, hospital cost for reported injuries, and prison maintenance. Homicides caused through IPV and the associated financial costs have caused the criminal justice system to change its responses to this type of crime. This change is in conflict with the societal perspective of how victims of IPV are viewed in terms of assistance from police, the court system, and support services for victims and perpetrators (Schuler, 2010).

Intimate partner violence accounts for 15 percent of all crime (Truman and Morgan, 2014) and is one of the most chronically underreported crimes (USDJ, 2003). Unlike most other crimes, IPV has a history of being regarded reproachfully by police. Officers historically were reluctant to become involved in IPV cases typically because they viewed IPV as a private matter falling outside police purview (Ford, 1983). However, the women's movement of the 1970s helped to advance IPV as a matter of serious concern in the criminal justice system generally (Mills, 1998) and in police departments specifically. Thirty years later, both state laws and departmental policies define IPV as a serious crime, although it is unclear to what extent individual officers endorse this view (Dejong, Proctor, Ellis, 2008). It is important to note that IPV is a major drain on law enforcement resources, involving a high volume of calls and repeated calls to the same location, consuming large amounts of time and often resulting in injuries or death. Intimate partner homicides make up 40–50 percent of all murders of women in the United States (Sumner, 2014). In fact, from 2010 to 2014, 22 percent of law enforcement officer "line of duty" deaths occurred while responding to a call for service involving a domestic dispute (Bruel and Smith, 2015).

My experience as I witnessed my son's ordeal as a victim raised some serious concerns in regard to how some of the officers responded and is one of the reasons I felt the need to address this issue as a crucial part of the IPV educational agenda. It is also the reason I sought the expertise and the perspective of the cowriter for this chapter. It appeared that some of those who responded to my son's 911 campus calls usually showed a lack of sensitivity and respect. Officers' "reluctance or frustration" in responding to IPV [may be attributed] to law enforcement's lack of understanding of the complexities of IPV and their insensitivity for victims. After all, the nature of IPV is complex, the "perceptions" of victimization are multifaceted, and some IPV victimization can be more subjective than objective. Some officers are supportive of victims, while other officers are less supportive (Dejong, Proctor, and Ellis, 2008).

My son's and my experience mirrored these findings, and it was discouraging and disheartening, to say the least. He was consistently encouraged to "let it go." However, dependence on the responding officers to take action was his only option, literally. He was truly at their mercy, because if he responded in any other way, fighting back and even simply defending himself from the physical attacks could mean the difference between ostracism by society, a false arrest, incarceration, and/or losing his life, and the battle to rid himself of the consistent harassment that had resulted in his weariness. It shouldn't have mattered that he was a male victim or she was a female perpetrator. None of these were options, with the exception of the last: successful resolution of the issue! What was occurring was discriminatory and gender-biased in nature, as well as stereotypical. My son was becoming a statistic, he was being victimized all over again, and I was desperate because I trusted the "system" to protect him and to hold her accountable for her actions. "Intimate partner assault is not reported to police most often for the following reasons: 'police couldn't do anything,' 'police didn't believe me,' 'wanted to protect attacker, relationship or children' and 'didn't want police or court involvement'" (CDC, 2000).

It was surreal and led me to take additional measures with a visit to the chief of campus police, who was very professional in his response. He wasn't surprised about the first-responder encounters, and he proceeded to inform me of the culture of law enforcement and, equally important, the male psyche and ego. Our conversation provided some relief and some guidance for possible future action to arrest the matter. These were professionals who had been called to protect and to serve and abide by a code of ethics, and my extensive social work training as a first responder and a mandated reporter suddenly took on a new meaning. I was so desperate I was willing and offered to provide sensitivity classes to the campus police. I needed assurance that my son would not be unfairly judged and had protection, understanding, and support on campus, and I was willing to go the extra mile to do my part in this regard. It was emotionally and mentally draining, but it was just that serious to me. [Intimate partner] violence–related police calls have been found to constitute the single largest category of calls received by police, accounting for 15 to more than 50 percent of all calls (Friday, Lord, Exum, and Hartman, 2006).

Law enforcement and the courts play an important role in helping victims escape violence and in bringing abusers to justice, including investigating domestic violence cases, promoting deterrence, assisting victims, and interrupting the continuation of violence. The statistics below demonstrate the challenges faced by these public servants and domestic violence victims in bringing perpetrators to justice (Law Enforcement, Justice System, and Domestic Violence, 2015).

> One in three women and one in four men in the United States have been physically abused by an intimate partner, and intimate-partner homicides account for 40 to 50 percent of femicides. Violence against women ranks among the top calls for service to police departments nationwide, yet over half of these types of crimes—including four-fifths of rapes—go unreported to law enforcement.
>
> There is no mystery as to why this is the case. The trauma that victims experience from intimate-partner violence (IPV) can make them particularly reluctant to engage with the criminal justice system. They fear being re-traumatized by the system's response, or that there will be no response at all. Indeed, the majority of IPV victims cite a belief that the police will not or cannot do anything to protect them. (Law Enforcement, Justice System, and Domestic Violence, 2015)

Yet this belief and lack of trust in the criminal justice system further endangers victims—not only by discouraging them from accessing available public-safety resources, but also by leading them to withhold crucial information from law enforcement. That undermines the ability of the criminal-justice system to properly investigate, prosecute, and deter these crimes (Teicher, 2017). For male victims, these scenarios are even more familiar. Certain aspects of the law enforcement response to sexual assault and domestic violence appear particularly susceptible to explicit and implicit bias based on gender, increasing the potential for discrimination (DOJ, n.d.).

In responding to a report of sexual assault or domestic violence, law enforcement officers should not base their judgments as to the credibility of a victim's account on assumptions or stereotypes about the "types" of people who can be victims of sexual assault, or about how victims of sexual assault and domestic violence "should" respond or behave. The following examples, as well as the scenarios my son faced as he sought assistance, can be added to the long list of responses that illustrate the application of assumptions or stereotypes to victims to gauge a victim's credibility, which undermines an effective investigation:

> **Example:** A young woman enters a police station and reports that, two weeks earlier, she was raped at a house party by a colleague from work. The woman reports that she had been drinking that evening. The police officer on duty asks how often the woman drinks excessively at house parties and asks her what she was wearing that night. The officer then tells her she should really watch how much she consumes when she goes out at night, especially if she is getting dressed up.

Example: A tall man, in good physical condition and with no visible injuries, goes to the local police precinct and reports that his boyfriend, with whom he lives, has been sending him threatening text and voice messages over the past several weeks, and that, the night before, his boyfriend had assaulted him. The responding officer looks at the man skeptically and tells him he's not sure he can take a report based on this situation. The officer tells the man to think carefully about whether he has a crime to report and to come back another day if he still believes he needs assistance.

Example: A woman who has been known to engage in prostitution flags down a police officer who frequently patrols her neighborhood. She reports to the officer that she was just raped. The police officer on duty writes down her statement, but when he returns to the police station, he immediately classifies the complaint as "unfounded," and takes no further action because of the woman's sexual and criminal history (DOJ, n.d.).

[There is no doubt that] prevention of violence between intimate partners is an important public health goal. National estimates indicate that approximately 25 percent of women report being victims of a partner's physical or sexual violence at some point in their life, and approximately 1.5 million women and 835,000 men are physically assaulted or raped by intimate partners in the United States annually (Tjaden and Thoennes, 1998).

[It should be noted that] the women's movement brought initial attention to the problem of partner violence directed at women and to the need for funding to address that problem (Dobash and Dobash, 1979). Much of the initial research on IPV was conducted with severely abused women and supported the assumption that IPV is primarily perpetrated by men against women. Data is mounting, however, that suggests IPV is often perpetrated by both men and women against their partner (Archer, 2000; Brush, 1990; Straus and Gelles, 1995). It is also becoming recognized that perpetration of IPV by both partners within a relationship is fairly common. This phenomenon has been described with terms such as mutual violence, symmetrical violence, or reciprocal violence. [A crucial reminder is that] reciprocal partner violence does not appear to be only comprised of self-defensive acts. Several studies have found that men and women initiate violence against an intimate partner at approximately the same rate (Whitaker et al., 2007). Additionally, in the National Family Violence Survey, both men and women reported that violence was initiated by each partner at least 40 percent of the time (Straus, 2004). This is significant, as it is yet another factor that changes the dynamics related to the possible reasons why women are sometimes viewed sympathetically by law enforcement in IPV male-victim cases even when they are the perpetrators and the aggressors.

There is now an ever-growing number of studies that document females can often be as assertive and aggressive in IPV incidents as males, though the incidents may not result in equivalent injury or fatality. A 2004 NIJ Journal documents that females often initiate IPV. Thus, it is difficult to understand how or why the officers did not make a single arrest of a female offender when a recent study from the Centers for Disease Control and Prevention concluded that women are the perpetrators in more than 70 percent of nonreciprocal IPV incidents (Davis, 2009). Due to my factual knowledge about the nature versus nurture theory, I am of the professional opinion that the perceptions, beliefs, values, and even the personal and professional experiences of the first responders can make the difference in whether an arrest is made. Self-awareness and self-regulation pertaining to our biases are critical when our line of work addresses and involves other people's lives. Our decisions can literally and figuratively mean the difference between life or death. The nature versus nurture theory will be addressed in detail in chapter 13.

A paradox pertaining to the failure to arrest female perpetrators in the CDC study mentioned above is evidence that all law enforcement don't respond in the same manner, despite their "consistent" training, and all research data are not consistently correlated. Case in point: A US Department of Justice (USDOJ) funded study documents a high rate of IPV conviction for females arrested and a much lower conviction rate for males. [Besides the fact that other crucial factors may be influencing the responding officers' discretion], this study also raises the concern about subjective versus objective decision factors; the study may also demonstrate that officers continue to arrest females based on traditional and proper "probable cause," but they arrest males based on IPV "gender clues" and on the content of an IPV training curriculum. The guide creates a gender bias about who is guilty and who is innocent before officers arrive at an IPV call. These factors, coupled with the hypothesis by IPV trainers that all IPV incidents will become a serious problem for females, results in inconsistencies in the female/male arrest criteria ratio and rates (Davis, 2009). IPV and the entire process of addressing the dynamics involved while searching for solutions are truly complex in nature and will definitely require additional studies and interventions on the micro, mezzo, and macro environmental levels.

This up-close and personal ordeal propelled me to seek answers directly from the source, and the response from Major Tonnie Williams, who is a decorated member of law enforcement with years of experience, enlightened me to another factor that further complicates the public health issue; and it has a significant impact on the entire culture of the criminal justice system and the fact that the twenty-first century has resulted in and mandated drastic changes pertaining to how the entire judicial process is lawfully and procedurally addressed in this regard. It involves every aspect, from training to internal and external community/police matters. Major Williams has seen and experienced a lot! And because the literature has consistently supported the fact that the aggressive behavior associated with IPV can be traced back to the early-childhood phase, this/his analogy makes sense and is eye opening. The following is strictly his professional insight of the matter based upon his extensive years of expertise.

INTIMATE PARTNER VIOLENCE AND SOCIAL CHANGE AMONG URBAN AFRICAN AMERICAN YOUTH

Over the past thirty years, I have witnessed the urban African American youth undergo a substantial social transformation. As a professional in law enforcement, the shift has been clear as the youth have become fearless, unforgiving, and disrespectful to the societal values and norms. Defiance is a common trait in this group of individuals with whom I interact on a daily basis. The youth appear to be angry about the world and appear to lack the motivation to achieve just like other persons of their age. With overall incarceration rates more than 500 percent higher than they were forty years ago, black Millennials and post-Millennials are at greater risk of contact with the system than any previous generation (The Sentencing Project, 2015).

As I carry out my duties to protect and to serve, I have also witnessed a rise in the number of single mothers. And because African Americans are overrepresented in the criminal justice system, millions of black women suffer from the stress associated with having a family member incarcerated. This indirect contact with the criminal justice system increases the risk of family instability, unemployment, socioeconomic disadvantage, substance use disorders, and mental health problems (Wakefield and Wildeman, 2011). Such households may rely on fixed government subsidies to cater for the basic needs. Some of the single mothers have limited education, and the structural support is inadequate to enable them to provide for their families. The societal pressures result in the commission of crimes, which also lead to fathers being incarcerated. In fact, an analysis from CDC data finds that one in four black Millennials had an incarcerated loved one before they even turned eighteen. For those born in the early 1990s, the rate is almost one in three (CDC, 2012). The outcome is poor or there is lack of support for the children and youth, who in turn embrace defiance in response to the strains they face.

Having interacted with peers from other racial demographics, some of the African American youth get angry at the feeling of the world being against them. Some of the youth in other racial groups appear to enjoy structural social support and functional families that contribute to the realization of dreams. Racial disparities in indirect contact with the criminal justice system are valid and persist long after childhood. In fact, more than one in four African American Baby Boomers—26.4 percent—report having an immediate family member incarcerated at some point in their lifetime, compared with just 15.1 percent of white Baby Boomers (AP-Norc Center, 2017). Large disparities exist even after controlling for other important variables, such as income and education. As Millennials and post-Millennials have come—or are coming—of age during a period of mass incarceration, they will likely report even higher rates of contact with the system during their lifetimes. Consequently, the African American youth find solace in the street gangs that act like their families. The youth join the illegal groupings for emotional support and attainment of financial stability. The engagement in criminal activities affords the African American youth the money to afford expensive jewelry, watches, label shoes, the latest video games, smartphones, and good food. The move aims at living lifestyles similar to those of their peers who have family support.

The community witnessed a rise in the number of teenagers born in the 1990s to single mothers. The mothers appear to be school dropouts in some cases. The children follow the example. They drop out of school at an early age to engage in antisocial behaviors. Consequently, the juvenile delinquencies land the teenagers in state prisons and county jails. The youth become ardent criminals with no patience in life. They want the best things in life in an instant without the resources. This forces them to engage in criminal activities. The United States has the highest incarceration rate in the world, and the overwhelming burden of contact with the system has fallen on communities of color, especially African Americans (Kaeble and Cowhig, 2016). To this group of individuals, the parents' opinions do not matter. What is important is the perception of their peers. Social media networks are more important than education. They prefer to learn about video games as opposed to going through school learning materials. To meet their needs, the urban African American youth appear ready to steal, engage in burglary, and break into cars. Drug addiction and peddling is also a common practice as the youth seek to achieve a certain status.

Social media networks such as Facebook, Twitter, and Instagram contribute to the social challenges facing the urban African American youth. The nudity and pornographic content prevalent in these and other networks is a bad influence, resulting in prostitution tendencies. In addition, these networks expose juveniles to antisocial habits including drug addiction, rapes, mass shootings, peer pressure, and disrespect to others. (These issues were also raised in chapter 6.) Lack of self-control among this population results in misleading endorsements from social media peers. Unknown to the youth, the law enforcement's keen eye is on social networks, which results in arrests and incarceration because of the leads provided by the teenagers' online posts. Social media exposure also leads to online bullying, which contributes to stress and depression among teenagers who feel noncompliant. (This factor was discussed in the chapter 7.)

It is heartbreaking to see the high level of addiction of urban African American youth to the social media. The online networks blind the young adults through misleading posts that contribute negatively to individual development. Images and news of destructive youth across the globe appear to inspire the young individuals to engage in illegal activities, such as mob justice, looting, and the destruction of property. Despite the youth's defiance and antisocial behavior, society views them stereotypically. The urban African American youth hate the negative perception but do little to develop a positive image. For instance, the baggy pants, dreadlocks, hoodies, and gold grills portray them as dangerous people to avoid.

In conclusion and from my professional viewpoint, society continues to witness defiant and antisocial behaviors among the urban African American youth. Various reasons as elaborated in this discussion contribute to this problem. Failure to implement substantial changes results in detrimental consequences for the country and society. The economic prosperity of the affected areas is in trouble as investors move away to safer areas. For example, businesspeople and residents of troubled areas move into suburbs and the countryside. Consequently, there is a loss of revenue and tax for the economy to prosper. The results include a negative impact on education, job opportunities, the quality of life, and the ability to invest in new businesses. The cycle goes on as criminal gangs move to find new opportunities, thereby propagating the culture of defiance and antisocial behavior among the urban African American youth. My message: "People need to understand that in communities in which family units have broken apart and there are few, if any, economic opportunities, gangs become like surrogate families, identities" (Davis, 2011). A meeting of the minds to seriously and collectively address these crises is long overdue.

***

These firsthand experiences and encounters from a seasoned law enforcement professional speak volumes about the various factors that impact the state of IPV in the twenty-first century and add credence and enlightenment to the content that has been discussed throughout this book, as well as the additional challenges that law enforcement have to consider as they proceed with fulfilling their job responsibilities to protect and to serve. The approach to resolving and mitigating this public health nightmare is truly compounded by the extenuating factors and the dynamics of child and family welfare issues, just as the literature has confirmed. The extent of violence occurring at alarming rates breeds a type of aggression and a lack of fear that require innovative thinking and interventions.

A study of intimate partner homicides found that 20 percent of victims were not the intimate partners themselves, but family members, friends, neighbors, persons who intervened, law enforcement responders, or bystanders (Smith, Fowler, and Niolon, 2014). Not only is this a national trend, it's universal and alarming, and it has to be addressed on micro, mezzo, and macro levels via policy, legislation, people, and programs. And while this is just a part of the solution, it's a crucial start.

Violence and abuse at the hands of a loved one or acquaintance is frightening, degrading, and confusing. In 1994, Congress passed the Violence Against Women Act (VAWA). This act, and the additions made in 1996, recognize that domestic intimate partner violence is a national crime and that federal laws can help an overburdened state and local criminal justice system. In 1994 and 1996, Congress also passed changes to the Gun Control Act, making it a federal crime in certain situations for domestic violence abusers to possess guns. The majority of domestic violence cases will continue to be handled by your state and local authorities. In some cases, however, the federal laws, and the benefits gained from applying these laws, may be the most appropriate course of action (USDJ, 2017).

A victim in a VAWA case shall have the right to speak to the judge at a bail hearing to inform the judge of any danger posed by the release of the defendant. Any victim of a crime of violence shall also have the right to address the court in person at the time of sentencing. Appendix 4 contains the document that confirms this law worked in my son's case, despite the fact that he was a male victim. He was notified each time his perpetrator had a court date, as it was located in the vicinity where he resided.

VICTIMS' RIGHTS

A federal domestic violence victim has the following rights under 42 U.S.C. Section 10606(b):

1) The right to be treated with fairness and with respect for the victim's dignity and privacy;
2) The right to be reasonably protected from the accused offender;
3) The right to be notified of court proceedings;
4) The right to be present at all public court proceedings related to the offense, unless the court determines that testimony by the victim would be materially affected if the victim heard other testimony at the trial;
5) The right to confer with the attorney for the Government in the case;
6) The right to restitution;
7) The right to information about the conviction, sentencing, imprisonment, and release of the offender (USDJ, 2017).

I have worked with many social workers and victim advocates, whose specific education and extensive training is intended to prepare them for "family interventions." Regardless, some social workers express "frustration" when dealing with families in conflict and victims who appear to exhibit self-destructive behavior. This frustration is not unique to law enforcement, and I am not sure what level of training will quell that frustration (Davis, 2009)

Every partner in the criminal-justice system—from an officer responding to a domestic disturbance call to a prosecutor conducting interviews with a victim to a judge presiding over a criminal court case—is in a position to send a message to IPV victims that the system is trustworthy, fair, and a place to seek help. But while procedural justice training can dramatically improve effectiveness in this effort, there are many small steps that can be taken immediately to achieve a powerful impact. It can be as simple as a police officer listening empathetically to a victim, offering information about services available, connecting the victim with a counselor, consistently enforcing protective orders, or clearly communicating to a sexual-assault victim what happens after a rape kit is completed and who will follow up about the case (Tiecher, 2017).

The single most appreciated service officers can deliver to the greatest number of victims is the arrest of their abusers. Specialized domestic violence law enforcement units that focus on arrests can enhance the likelihood of successful prosecution and increase victim satisfaction and safety (Klein, 2009). Several studies suggest general domestic violence training for law enforcement officers does not necessarily change attitudes toward domestic violence or, more important, change police behavior in terms of arrests of abusers or responses to domestic violence incidents. Although knowing a department's policy regarding domestic violence arrest preference increases the likelihood that officers will arrest alleged domestic violence suspects, the amount of domestic violence training received does not (Feder, 1999; Finn et al., 2004; Smithey, Green, and Giacomazzi, 2000).

Research suggests domestic violence arrest decisions are influenced more by an officer's assessment of the legal variables involved than by his or her attitudes (Hirschel et al., 1997). At least one study suggests failure of police managers to hold police officers accountable for failure to arrest in contravention of statutory requirements is responsible for their poor performance, not their lack of training (Rigakos, 1997). Clear policy pronouncements from the top administration may be more likely to change officer responses to domestic violence than is general domestic violence training aimed at education and attitude change (Klein, 2009).

However, research strongly supports the connection, regardless of the case outcome, between enhanced procedural justice and improvements in a victim's experience and long-term recovery. When victims perceive fairness, respect, and sincerity, they are more likely to engage meaningfully with police, prosecutors, and the court system. By integrating procedural justice practices into law enforcement's response to IPV, criminal justice practitioners create the opportunity to reframe how these crimes are handled, enhance victim safety, improve case outcomes, and repair a vulnerable community's trust in the system (Tiecher, 2017). While the previous chapters have solidified much of the data and the professional views presented in this discussion, chapter 12 will provide additional information and a more detailed discussion about the judicial process and IPV.

CHAPTER 9

INTIMATE PARTNER VIOLENCE AND THE IMPACT ON MILITARY PERSONNEL AND VETERANS

LTC (RETIRED) SAMMIE L. DAVIS JR.

Intimate partner violence (IPV) is defined in many terms, many of which include concepts and terminologies like physical violence, sexual violence, stalking and psychological aggression, and coercive acts from a current or former partner. In many cases, these actions are perpetrated predominantly against females and recorded as domestic violence incidents and crimes. Whatever the situation or circumstances, the predictable ending is harm against or toward the recipient. This author would like to view this disease, phenomenon, or syndrome from the eyes of a military member with thirty-four years of service, multiple deployments, and extensive hours of interaction with my brothers and sisters in arms. This chapter will address the research on IPV and provide a personal testimony of the uniqueness IPV has with respect to the military services, families, and society as a whole. This is just one service member's perspective on IPV combined with evidence-based content and its relationship to military services.

Based upon the Center of Disease Control (CDC), intimate partner violence is a serious, preventable public health problem that affects millions of Americans. The following comparison highlights the association with the CDC definition and the corresponding military elements that impact or contribute to IPV.

An intimate partner is a person with whom one has a close personal relationship that can be characterized by the following:

CDC Description	Military Connection
Emotional connectedness	Military personnel are interrelated from basic training throughout career
Regular contact	Daily interaction via Army Physical Fitness Test (APFT), work, training, and now social media
Ongoing physical contact	Intimate relationship developed though shared and/or sexual behavior common experiences (daily interactions, training, mobilization, and deployment)
Identity as a couple	Identified in the military as a "battle buddy"
Familiarity and knowledge about each other's lives	Association and assimilation based upon common and daily interaction (unit, squad, section, and individual)

The military relationship need not involve all of these dimensions, but one can see the systemic conditioning it has with respect to IPV as it relates to the definition. The CDC also indicates there are four main types of IPV:

1. **Physical violence** is the intentional use of physical force with the potential for causing death, disability, injury, or harm. Physical violence includes, but is not limited to, scratching; pushing; shoving; throwing; grabbing; biting; choking; shaking; aggressive hair pulling; slapping; punching; hitting; burning; use of a weapon; and use of restraints or one's body, size, or strength against another person. Physical violence also includes coercing other people to commit any of the above acts. This category has been commonly known as domestic violence and can be traced back to the earliest recorded history of 1874. These offenses are covered under Articles 92, 108–109, 117, 120, 124, 128, and 134 (NCDSV.org, 2015).
2. **Sexual violence** is divided into five categories. Any of these acts constitutes sexual violence, whether attempted or completed. Additionally, all of these acts occur without the victim's freely given consent, including cases in which the victim is unable to consent due to being too intoxicated (e.g. incapacitation, lack of consciousness, or lack of awareness) through their voluntary or involuntary use of alcohol or drugs.
   1) *Rape or penetration of victim***.** This includes completed or attempted, forced, or alcohol/drug-facilitated unwanted vaginal, oral, or anal insertion. Forced

penetration occurs through the perpetrator's use of physical force against the victim or threats to physically harm the victim.

2) *Victim was made to penetrate someone else.* This includes completed or attempted, forced, or alcohol/drug-facilitated incidents when the victim was made to sexually penetrate a perpetrator or someone else without the victim's consent.
3) *Non-physically pressured unwanted penetration.* This includes incidents in which the victim was pressured verbally or through intimidation or misuse of authority to consent or acquiesce to being penetrated.
4) *Unwanted sexual contact.* This includes intentional touching of the victim or making the victim touch the perpetrator, either directly or through the clothing, on the genitalia, anus, groin, breast, inner thigh, or buttocks without the victim's consent.
5) *Non-contact unwanted sexual experiences.* This includes unwanted sexual events that are not of a physical nature that occur without the victim's consent. Examples include unwanted exposure to sexual situations (e.g. pornography); verbal or behavioral sexual harassment; threats of sexual violence to accomplish some other end; and/or unwanted filming, taking, or disseminating photographs of a sexual nature of another person.

3. **Stalking** is a pattern of repeated, unwanted attention and contact that causes fear or concern for one's own safety or the safety of someone else (e.g. family member or friend). Some examples include repeated, unwanted phone calls, emails, or texts; leaving cards, letters, flowers, or other items when the victim does not want them; watching or following from a distance; spying; approaching or showing up in places when the victim does not want to see them; sneaking into the victim's home or car; damaging the victim's personal property; harming or threatening the victim's pet; and making threats to physically harm the victim.
4. **Psychological aggression** is the use of verbal and nonverbal communication with the intent to harm another person mentally or emotionally and/or to exert control over another person. Psychological aggression can include expressive aggression (e.g. name calling, humiliating); coercive control (e.g. limiting access to transportation, money, friends, and family; excessive monitoring of whereabouts); threats of physical or sexual violence; control of reproductive or sexual health (e.g. refusal to use birth control, coerced pregnancy termination); exploitation of victim's vulnerability (e.g. immigration status, disability); exploitation of perpetrator's vulnerability; and presenting false information to the victim with the intent of making them doubt their own memory or perception (e.g. mind games).

There is no doubt these characteristics are the critical validation and confirmation of IPV and what is defined in the military as sexual harassment and assault. Even more disheartening is that many of the incidents go unreported by the victim due to a lack of understanding of the warrior ethos and the military philosophy of "never leaving a buddy on the battlefield." Ultimately, this stigma has both physical and psychological impacts that lead to the worst-case scenario of harm and/or death to the victim. The author is also including the victims of suicide, which is from this perspective, IPV perpetrated against yourself.

Evidence shows that violence against women is a pervasive problem within the military, just as it is among civilians. However, women in the military are particularly vulnerable to abuse due to geographical isolation from family and friends, and the potential for social isolation within the military culture. Recently, a series of high-profile reports, articles, and documentaries have raised public awareness about the true nature of violence against women in the military. The 2012 Academy Award–nominated documentary *The Invisible War* distilled a sea of information and highlighted some of the most egregious problems:

- The Department of Defense (DoD) estimates more than 19,000 military sexual assaults occurred in 2010, yet less than 14 percent were reported.
- Of the 19,000 estimated military sexual assaults, the 3,192 reports only led to 191 convictions at courts-martial.
- One in three convicted military sex offenders remain in the military (Service Women's Action Network, 2012).
- In 2011 alone, the Veterans Administration spent close to $900 million, or $10,880 per military sexual assault survivor, on health services related to sexual assault.

In addition:

- The victim of domestic violence in the military is predominantly the female, civilian spouse of active-duty personnel. Victims normally have children and more than half have been married two years or less (Hansen, 2001).
- Substantiated spousal abuse involving members of the military is predominantly perpetrated by male, active-duty personnel (Caliber Associates for DoD, 1996).
- Among the Services, the Army consistently has shown the highest rates of domestic violence, followed by the Marines, Navy, and Air Force (Caliber Associates for DoD, 1996).
- Abused women in military communities are often fearful of reporting incidents due to the lack of confidentiality and privacy as well as limited victim services (Hansen, 2001).
- In the sample of active-duty military women from the greater Washington, DC, metropolitan area, 29.9 percent reported adult lifetime intimate partner violence, defined as physical and/or sexual assault from a current or former intimate partner. African American women were significantly less likely to be abused during military service than were white women, but ethnic group membership was not a risk factor for lifetime abuse (Campbell and Wolf, 2002).

In regard to the male victim, one-third of domestic violence victims in active-duty military families are men, Defense Department data shows. Married male service members and civilian husbands of active-duty wives lodge more than 2,500 domestic violence complaints per year, averaging about seven per day. In fact, inside the military, some studies suggest women are more likely to be abusive.

> A 2010 study by the Naval Health Research Center focused on sailors in their second year of service who were either married or cohabiting. The study found that 15 percent of men and 32 percent of women reported committing some level of physical aggression toward their partner during the prior year. Pentagon officials say family advocacy programs across the military are designed to respond to all types of domestic abuse, including the minority of reported cases involving female aggressors. "Abusive behavior may look different in women than in men," said Lt. Cmdr. Nate Christensen, a Pentagon spokesman. "Furthermore, all women who abuse do not abuse in the same way or for the same reasons," he said. "These differences may make it more difficult for some to recognize abusive behavior in women. A lack of knowledge concerning female offenders can lead to bias and negatively impact services to both offenders and victims." (*Military Times*, 2014)

HISTORY OF MILITARY INTIMATE PARTNER VIOLENCE

Knowing the Culture and the Environment

The history and evolution of the military is as vast and old as recorded time itself. When we look at IPV and its relationship to the military, we must first look and understand the culture in which the military operates. C. J. Heck states it best: "We are all products of our environment; every person we meet, every new experience or adventure, every book we read, touches and changes us, making us the unique being we are." As we seek to understand why IPV is so prevalent here, we need to look back at our history and the way we as soldiers, sailors, Marines, and air personnel train, think, and function regardless of our gender, sexual orientation, cultural background, or geographical location. The mindset is established through our initial entry training, assignments, colleagues, and experiences in this culture and environment. The goal in this section is to understand the military culture and the potential correlation within IPV. This understanding will be key to identifying risk factors in screening for IPV with veterans and military families. This understanding will help ultimately assist in identifying appropriate treatment and intervention strategies for military personnel experiencing IPV.

As we look at the clientele who will be receiving this service, I am reminded of a quote by then President Abraham Lincoln. In it, he addresses the nation's obligation to its service members, and I quote, "We are to care for him who shall have borne the battle and for his widow and his orphan." If we could go back into time following each of these periods in the evolution of the US military, I believe we would see evidence of how the military and combat experiences contributed to this condition known as IPV. There are thirteen periods of military development from colonial periods to the present. It is my theory that IPV, post-traumatic stress disorder

(PTSD), traumatic brain injury (TBI), and other conditions related to combat engagements spike during these times and decrease as the force exposure declines following the event.

US military history is both immense and complex, but its pluralistic military institutions, dual force of professional and citizen soldiers, and commitment to civilian control of the military have been consistent themes. As of 2007, the term "military" encompasses the Army, Navy, Air Force, Coast Guard, and Marine Corps, which are all under the command of the Department of Defense. The US president is commander in chief of each of these branches and also has authority to assume control of individual state militia or National Guard units. Today, America still stands as the world's premier military superpower, but it has not always been this way. There have been periods of war that have impacted the US military culture and society since 1512 with the onset of the colonial wars, the beginning of a civilian military (1512–1774). The earliest English settlers arrived in a dangerous New World. In response to not only unfriendly Native American tribes but also raiding European rivals, English settlers began developing a civilian militia in each colony in which the militiamen were required to maintain and provide their own weapons (Millett and Maslowski, 1984). Within each colony, civilian authority controlled military matters, thus establishing America's revered tradition of civilian control of the military. During this time, militia primarily engaged Native Americans in the Pequot War 1637, King Philip's War 1675, and the Yamasee War 1715 (Bradford, 2003). Though the colonists fought together with the British during the French and Indian Wars (1754–1763), tension between Britain and its colonies soon grew untenable. The following are synopses of the subsequent periods of war in which the US military indulged.

Revolutionary War: Establishing the Common Defense, 1775–1783

Convinced Great Britain was illegally subverting their liberties, colonists created the Second Continental Congress, which then formed the Continental Army. On April 19, 1775, shooting began in Lexington and Concord (Bradford, 2003).

Post-Revolutionary Era: Moving toward a Nationalized Military, 1783–1815

The New Republic had to both survive on a dangerous international stage while at the same time trying to reconcile its ideological concerns for liberty with military effectiveness. This task was further complicated when the Continental Army began making demands that reawakened fears of a standing army. In addition, the lack of an institutionalized response to Shay's Rebellion (1786–87) led leaders to question the nature of their military force (Millett and Maslowski, 1984).

The military, which had previously been involved in Europe's affairs, consciously tried to avoid further entanglement and assumed a passive defense policy while playing a key role in America's own domestic development and expansion (Bradford, 2004).

US Civil War: The Beginning of Modern Total Warfare, 1861–1865

The Civil War began at 4:30 a.m. on April 12, 1861, in South Carolina when Confederates fired on Fort Sumter. No one knows exactly what caused the war, though thoughtful explanations include moral disagreements regarding slavery, slavery's expansion into the territories, and states' rights versus national authority (Millett and Maslowski, 1984). Most people at the time thought the war would be brief and romantic; instead, it was the beginning of modern total warfare (Weigley, 1975). Though twice as many soldiers died from disease than from battle, the fact of Civil War battles is that technology had outpaced tactics. The Civil War Napoleonic formations based on frontal assaults with bayonets were not suited for more rifled weapons that would blast scores of men into bloody masses. In many respects, the North won by sheer numbers (Millett and Maslowski, 1984). Such a large coordination of logistical and strategic matters could not be left to individual states. Massive mobilization required an unprecedented degree of centralized control over military policy, and the country saw the military's balance of power shift further from the states to the national government. After the war, the military, which now included African Americans and Native Americans as permanent soldiers, returned to its traditional missions in support of national policy of expansion.

American Indian Wars: Continental Expansion, 1866–1890

These wars—which ranged from the seventeenth century's King Philip's War to the Wounded Knee massacre in 1890—were a result of several complex influences on the US military, including America's emerging imperialistic impulses, technological military advances, officers' concerns about their own careers, and social Darwinism (Millett and Maslowski, 1984). What these wars did was open the frontier to further colonization and force Native American assimilation. While these wars did not significantly change military policy or doctrine, the military gained experience using guerrilla-style tactics that would aid them in the next century.

Spanish-American War: The Beginning of a Military Superpower, 1898

With the diminishing frontier, America began to abandon its "continental" policy in favor of more aggressive competition for world trade, and it turned its eye toward Spain. The war began after Spain rejected American demands that Spain resolve the Cuban fight of independence peacefully (Bradford, 2003). America eventually won Spain's remaining overseas territories and, in doing so, acquired a colonial empire. Acquiring vast amounts of land had several important implications for the US military. Aware that its new possessions placed them on an international stage rife with economic and imperialistic competition and that more land also meant more area to defend, the US military sought to increase its forces. The next two decades saw unprecedented accelerated military change and development. By World War I, the American Navy battle fleet was second only to the British and Germans, and the American Army transitioned from frontier constabulary to a force equipped with air and motor power.

World War I: America's Debut as a Superpower, 1917–1918

America entered World War I reluctantly in 1917, abandoning its official policy of neutrality. Despite pleas from President Woodrow Wilson, German submarines continued to attack US ships carrying aid to Britain, forcing the US to join the war with the objective to "make the world safe for democracy" (Bradford, 2003). President Woodrow Wilson successfully framed the first peacetime draft in such terms, reciting ideals such as democracy, freedom, and national self-determinism. In practical terms, however, the military struggled with a new concept of twentieth-century war: the economic implications of national mobilization. The Department of War's procurement efforts coupled with the government attempts toward centralizing economic regulations overcame initial mobilization challenges. Though the US military initially struggled with the economic realities of twentieth-century war, it had gone to Europe and successfully fought a massive industrialized war against a nation known for its military strength and expertise and emerged a formidable superpower (Millett and Maslowski, 1984).

World War II: Military Golden Age, 1939–1945

On December 7, 1941, Japan pushed America into World War II by bombing Pearl Harbor, Hawaii. Seven days later, Germany declared war on the US, and President Franklin D. Roosevelt quickly mobilized the military. In the Pacific, the Japanese were defeated in the carrier battles of the Coral Sea and Midway. The exceptionally bloody battles at Iwo Jima and Okinawa in 1945 prompted the US to use atomic bombs on Hiroshima and Nagasaki, which quickly ended the war in the Pacific. Between 1942 and 1945, the US deployed millions of men to fight in Europe. Nazi Germany surrendered in May 1945 after the Allied forces invaded North Africa in 1942, Italy in 1943, and France in 1944 (Bradford, 2003). Due to its use of atomic weapons and impressive ground forces, the US military emerged as one of only two new superpowers. The advent of nuclear weapons sharpened interservice competition among the military as the Air Force, Navy, and Marine Corps vied to adapt to the new technology. Most notably, the US changed its policy to emphasize deterrence, and it was decided that the creation of nuclear weapons seemed to be the best form.

Cold War: Nuclear Deterrence, 1946–1990

The Cold War was a political, ideological, strategic, and military conflict between the two post-WWII superpowers, the US and the Soviet Union (Bradford, 2003). US Cold War military policy was defined by two themes: communist containment and strategic nuclear deterrence. Such a policy highlighted the move from a crisis-oriented military policy to a policy devoted to creating programs that would last as long as the Soviet Union. In fact, until the end of the 1960s, the public polls favored maintaining long-term military superiority. Significantly, the US joined the North Atlantic Treaty Organization (NATO), which both allowed the military to create a "nuclear umbrella" by stationing missiles in NATO countries, but at the same time tied the military to the behavior of NATO allies. Though the US and the Soviet Union rarely fought each other, the Cold War nevertheless was a global struggle that prompted several wars, including the Korean and Vietnam Wars, and soon competing East/West ideologies were felt in developing nations across the globe. It wasn't until the break-up of the Soviet Union in the early 1990s that the Cold War effectively ended.

Korean War: Military Containment, 1950–1953

The Korean War, sometimes called the "Forgotten War," was essentially a proxy Cold War. When communist North Korea invaded South Korea on June 25, 1950, the US became involved under the auspices of the United Nations (Millett and Maslowski, 1984). This was the first war in the nuclear age and the first war in which communist "containment" became a military rather than a political endeavor. Though the war ended in a stalemate, it solidified the US as the world's policeman and strengthened its relationships with Western European allies. After the war, rather than demobilize as the US military traditionally did, it remained strong. The defense budget quadrupled, creating the world's most powerful military, one that could skillfully combine land, sea, and air forces. The war was also interesting in its extensive use of the helicopter for reconnaissance, evacuation, and rescue work (Bradford, 2003).

Vietnam War: Erosion of US Military Power, 1959–1975

The roots of the Vietnam War lie in the US Cold War policy of communism containment, for it was containment that prompted the US military to become involved during the First Indochina War (1946–1954) and to continue its involvement unabated until Saigon was conquered by the Communist People's Army of China in 1975. When actual US military combat units first entered the conflict between North and South Vietnam in 1965, they were accompanied by huge logistical support by land, sea, and air. Such a powerful arsenal guaranteed that the US never lost a major battle in Vietnam; however, the fact that the US never achieved its objective of stabilizing an independent, noncommunist state highlights the war's significant complexity.

Though the US military had superior military power, the communists waged an effective psychological "hide-and-seek" war in oppressive jungle conditions by using ambush, night attacks, suicide bombers, snipers, and booby traps. Hoping to nourish the growing anti-war movement in the US, the communists also bombed key US administration sites, such as the Saigon Embassy. In addition, US politicians' own political motives and their confusion about war goals made it difficult for them to create an effective strategy in Vietnam. Under pressure from strong anti-war protests, military policy shifted mid-war from battlefield victory to negotiated settlement and withdrawal. The soldiers perceived this shift as further lack of support for the war, and reports of troop misconduct and demoralization increased domestic war-weariness. In a continued attempt to defuse the anti-war movement, the US government also ended the draft, but military technology could not compensate for the decline in manpower. Consequently, the US military was forced to reduce its spending on operations and maintenance, and after signing the Paris Peace Accord, finally withdrew from Vietnam in 1975. The war left the US military demoralized and materially crippled. Defense spending dropped, and the power of the president to conduct war fell under attack. Because the US failed to win its political objectives in Vietnam, the military's ability to use military force anywhere else in the war became seriously compromised. In addition, containment, at least as a military policy, was not a success. While the Vietnam War did not end the Cold War, it did cast doubt on twenty-five years of US military superiority.

Persian Gulf War: The Computer War and a Military Redemption, 1990–1991

When Iraqi dictator Saddam Hussein invaded Kuwait, coalition forces led by the United States responded swiftly in the largest US wartime engagement since Vietnam (Bradford, 2003). Using lessons gleaned from the Vietnam War, the UN coalition that attacked Iraqi forces was able to synchronize powerful air strikes. The Gulf War was technologically the fastest and most dramatic war in history and is often referred to as the "computer" war because of its use of "smart" bombs and guided missiles (Bradford, 2003). After just one hundred hours of ground combat, the US had Kuwait and southern Iraq under control. Though highly controversial, President Bush Sr. decided to keep Saddam Hussein in power to act as a counterweight in the region.

September 11 and the War in Iraq: The Beginning of the War on Terror, 2011–Present

Prompted by the September 11, 2001, terrorist attacks and on the assumption that Saddam Hussein was hiding weapons of mass destruction, a coalition led by the United States and Great Britain invaded Iraq in 2003 (Bradford, 2003). After three weeks of fighting, the United States military captured Saddam Hussein in a hole, and the Iraqi government executed him on December 30, 2006. Though President Bush consistently stated that the Iraq War was the central front on the War on Terror, the war has been severely criticized. With heavy coverage by modern media in addition to operations in a country with little modern infrastructure or political stability, the war has been compared to Vietnam. However, several milestones have been reached, including the capture of Saddam Hussein and democratic elections. Currently, the US military budget is the highest of any country, and by 2008, US military funds were projected to surpass the combined defense funds of the rest of the world.

THE EFFECTS OF WAR ON MILITARY CULTURE AND SOCIETY

Throughout the course of our military history, our men and women of the Armed Forces have been exposed to extreme danger and circumstances. As technology improved, more lethal and effective weapons have been developed to allow for engagement at a distance. However, the resulting effects are still evident with the carnage inflicted by these weapons to limbs, life, and mental stability. To understand how damaging this type of exposure is to the subconscious, one most understand the psychology of the military personnel.

Factors Leading to IPV

We are indoctrinated and conditioned through our training to put the mission first. These philosophies have been echoed through our history in phrases like, "Don't give up the ship," "We have not yet begun to fight"; "No mission too difficult, no sacrifice too great" and "Duty first"(US Army); "Ready to lead, ready to follow, never quit" (US Navy); "Aim high," "Fly, fight, win," and "We do the impossible every day" (US Air Force); "Semper fi," "First to fight," and "The few. The proud" (US Marine Corps).

We are trained to never quit, to put duty, honor, and country first, and this is represented in every aspect of our being without regret. This is where the issue with IPV starts, in that we refuse to admit defeat or show weakness. This is true of all service members, regardless of gender, and this tends to prevent us from seeking treatment for psychological ailments such as post-traumatic stress disorder (PTSD) and traumatic brain injury (TBI). It is this author's belief that these ailments have a direct relationship to intimate partner violence due to this systemic programming that is necessary and required for the military to continue to be successful. These variables also eventually lead to incidents of IPV if not detected early and treated.

As a military member with six combat deployments over the past thirteen years, I can attest to the impact of PTSD; the attempts to avoid feelings and thoughts that either remind you of the traumatic event or that trigger similar feelings; irritability or angry outbursts; hypersensitivity, including at least two of the following reactions: trouble sleeping, being angry, having difficulty concentrating, startling easily, or having a physical reaction (rapid heart rate or breathing, increase in blood pressure); and feeling detached or unable to connect with loved ones. Thank God, I am fortunate that my condition didn't lead to an incident of IPV due to family awareness and support that eventually inspired me to put my pride aside and seek treatment for my condition. Unlike many of my comrades in arms, the treatment, counseling, and therapy session worked to my advantage and allowed me to open up about what I was feeling. This type of dialogue proved to be very beneficial to my recovery and return to a sense of normalcy.

Factors Leading to Intimate Partner Violence

Based upon research, there are many factors that lead and influence the occurrence of IPV. These include many social factors that are applicable to both the military and the civilian culture. The statistics on IPV incidents are currently compiled, tracked, and analyzed and trends identified to better understand the complexity of this phenomenon. Based upon chapter 1 of *Family Violence across the Lifespan*, published by Sage, IPV can be influenced by the following:

- **Structural factors**: Many structural factors make families particularly prone to violence. One of these is the amount of time family members spend together, which increases the opportunity for violence. In addition, power differentials often exist among family members, and those who are less powerful run a greater risk for victimization. Children are subordinate to parents, wives often must be subordinate to husbands, and sometimes elderly parents are subordinate to their adult children. Further complicating matters is that children and women usually cannot fight back, nor can they always choose with whom they will or will not interact. Children are dependent on their parents, and wives are very frequently dependent on their husbands. Whereas many interpersonal conflicts can be resolved simply through the dissolution of relationships, most family relationships are protected by law and are not so easily severed. Even when child maltreatment comes to the attention of authorities, states are reluctant to break up families. Instead, authorities give dysfunctional families multiple opportunities to change. Finally, the privacy and autonomy traditionally granted to families make violence relatively easy to hide (Brinkerhoff and Lupri, 1988).

- **Cultural factors**: Cultural factors can also be useful in explaining male-to-female intimate partner violence (MFIPV). Some cultures accept violence; others condemn it. In some cultures, such as Brazil and the Arab world, a husband's violence against an unfaithful wife presumably restores the husband's honor (Kulwicki, 2002; Vandello and Cohen, 2003). Many authorities place partial blame for the widespread acceptance of violence in US culture on the content of television programming as well as movies, sports, toys, and video games (Bushman and Anderson, 2001). Others cite approval of violence within the home as a contributing factor. For some, the most crucial element is cultural acceptance of male dominance.

- **Individual factors**: In addition to powerful social forces that may foster family violence, there are a number of more individual factors that do so as well. One factor, of course, is some type of mental illness or mental disorder, such as schizophrenia. Another factor is individual differences, such as vulnerability to jealousy or anger. One powerful precursor of family violence that may flow across the lifespan is level of attachment. Attachment refers to the affectional bond between a parent and a child or, later as an adult, the bond between romantic partners. Disruptions in attachment are related to numerous correlates of family violence and IPV, such as intense emotional dependence (Dutton and Painter, 1993a; Holtzworth-Munroe and Hutchinson, 1993).

- **Religious factors**: Some current religious groups in the United States rob women of equality with men, going so far as to embed male dominance into their by-laws (Niebuhr, 1998). "The major religions legitimize the power of men over women as a God-given right, and there are strong historical traditions indicating approval of men beating their wives—within certain limits—as a way of controlling their behavior" (Archer, 2006, p. 149). Mormons, for instance, usually

> believe in rigid gender roles that give preference to men. A smattering of Mormons operating under the radar appear to cling to bygone and illegal practices, such as forced early marriage of teenage girls and polygamy (Tresniowski, Atlas, Lang, and Cardwell, 2009). Because of the dual combination of religious freedom and an emphasis on parental rights in the United States, authorities hesitate to interfere with child-rearing practices that are simply unusual. On a more positive note, several studies of female IPV victims judged spiritual beliefs to be beneficial and important to their ability to cope (Farrell, 1996; Goodman, Dutton, Weinfurt, and Cook, 2003; Humphreys, Lee, Neylan, and Marmar, 1999).

To care for service members and veterans experiencing or using intimate partner violence, it is imperative to understand the culture of that client. IPV within veteran and military populations is consistent in that all incidents share some common characteristics as it relates to basic core factors of IPV. Characteristics of service, stigma, and military lifestyle can result in unique risk factors, and transitional and combat/deployment experience may exacerbate IPV, or cause an increase in frequency of events.

Military branches, installations, and veteran service providers often operate independently, and differ in response and intervention. Community providers may often be unfamiliar with the military and veteran healthcare system. Community advocates and providers play a unique role in sharing expertise of local services, state laws, and policies with veteran healthcare providers. Community providers often are in a position to assist service members, family members, and veterans in accessing comprehensive care. Sharing training, education, and information will lay the groundwork for developing a strong community of practice.

In December 2013, the Veteran Health Administration finalized the VHA Plan for Implementation of the DV/IPV Assistance Program. This included suggestions for developing a community of practice with community service providers. In 1999, the Department of Defense created a Task Force on Domestic Violence that included both military and community experts. Recommendations from this task force have been integrated throughout military services and include an emphasis on strong civilian/military partnership to prevent and assist with IPV. Many military installations and VHA services continue to develop practice methods and policies to include collaboration with community service providers within the IPV community. Community providers can affect the services provided to our service members and veterans. The goals and objectives for the identification and treatment for IPV include:

- Review IPV services and response within the military and veteran community.
- Review barriers to accessing IPV treatment within these populations.
- Discuss service member/veteran-specific healthcare concerns that may correlate with IPV concerns.
- Identify appropriate treatment methods and intervention strategies for veterans who are using/experiencing IPV.

- Discuss basic history and key elements of IPV as they relate to the Department of Defense, VHA, and those who served.

A Complex Culture, Not Your Average Job

Each branch has its own primary mission, symbolism, and core values. Branches of service will share a focus on:

- Discipline/structure
- Pride in service
- Professional ethos of loyalty
- Self-sacrifice
- Code of honor
- Focus on hierarchy and rank structure
- Emphasis on group cohesion

Esprit de corps connects service members and veterans to each other, and the individual is secondary to the unit. These service members are tied together by a series of common threads associated with loyalty and honor, courage, physical challenges, community/peer support, recognition, college benefits, income, vocational training, and pride. Many are encouraged to pursue teachers/recruiters/family members when they seek direction or just need to do something different before stepping out into the real world.

Understanding the Language

Use of language/acronyms may indicate services your client has accessed, or could potentially access, and identify possible risk factors. Individual service members, military branches, VHA, Veterans Benefit Administration (VBA), and family or community members may inter-use terms and definitions.

Terms may have different meanings within different contexts and understanding. An important way to discern, understand, and treat IPV is learning to recognize terminology and when to ask for clarification on the following: 1) What does this term mean? 2) What service/benefit is your client correlating the term to? 3) Most importantly, what does the term mean to them?

An example of these unique concepts and terms may be the phrase "post-traumatic stress disorder." This term's context may vary according to the following recipient:

- To an active-duty, deployed service member
- To a Vietnam veteran
- To a recently returned combat veteran
- To a spouse of a service member/veteran
- To a community provider treating a service member/veteran for childhood trauma
- To the Veterans Benefits Department
- To a veteran healthcare provider
- To a community service provider

Ultimately, the primary goal and objective is to have a common understanding that the terms have the same meaning and implication when we are discussing the treatment for the individuals involved.

For the military service member, understanding his/her battle mindset involves the many strengths and skills developed during military service that will solidify a veteran's identity. Service members and veterans have been significantly trained in vigilance, resilience, and responsive behavior. Aggression and hypervigilance are useful tools within military service, but often translate into social and behavioral difficulties when returning home. Learn to assist your client in identifying behavior as a strength versus a barrier. Based upon a study presented by Shae Allen, an IPV program coordinator, the "battlemindness and "battlemind" can be defined as follows:

- A framework developed by the military to understand that the combat skills and mindset that prepared service members for deployment and combat may now negatively affect social and behavioral health at home
- The soldier's inner strength to face fear and adversity in combat with courage
- May become hazardous to social and behavioral health in the home zone

This relates to many aspects of the service member's transition, but can specifically have an impact on IPV.

This "battlemind" differs in the war zone and the home zone. The impact varies as much as the location in that in the war zone, it results in survival and longevity. In the war zone, attributes include buddies (cohesion), accountability, targeted aggression, tactical awareness, lethally armed, emotional control, mission operational security (OPSEC), individual responsibility, nondefensive (combat) driving, and discipline/order. However, change the location to the home zone and these attributes that once were assets now become liabilities in the form of withdrawals, controlling behavior, inappropriate aggression, hypervigilance, "locked and loaded" demeanor at home, anger/detachment, secretiveness, guilt, aggressive driving, and conflict.

This is particularly evident within the military subconscious when you factor in the "military norm" embodied by all military participants, to include:

- You can't quit, even when it hurts.
- You can't call in sick, you can walk it off.
- If you are sick, you have to go to "sick call."
- You will miss important family events, and your family will be proud to support you.
- You will face danger.
- You will never leave a comrade behind.
- You never quit, never show pain, never give up, and never give in.

Learn to assist clients in differentiating between military/veteran norms and common elements of IPV. Within veteran and military culture, it is common for someone to tell you what to wear, when to sleep, where to go, where to live, who you can call, what to eat, and when to eat. Each member has a mission, and that mission is the needs of the Army, Navy, and Air Force. Focus on the mission and group survival. The individual is often not considered, in addition to stigma relating to identifying "individual" concerns, such as physical pain, stress or depression, and financial problems. These often translate into transitional concerns or barriers to seeking care as a service member or veteran. To resolve these barriers or obstacles to a normal life and sense of belonging, those responsible for identifying these indicators and directing the individual to the right resource need to do the following:

- Assist in decreasing stigma relating to seeking treatment
- Increase provider knowledge of obstacles/barriers to reporting IPV within military and veteran populations
- Provide an understanding of the impact that military service and veteran benefits can indicate, as both a strength and a barrier to seeking care
- Allow the provider to develop a stronger rapport with client, and assist in comprehensive care coordination

These actions need to occur while the client is still within the military structure, but the same process or tactics, techniques, and procedures (TTP) need to continue as we transition to retirement or veteran status within the larger community. We will address the same process as we next understand our veteran community and the IPV influence.

UNITED STATES VETERANS AND INTIMATE PARTNER VIOLENCE

According to the 2010 US Census Data, there are 22,658 million veterans in the United States. More than 1.3 million of these veterans have served in multiple wars. Veterans are at risk for unique concerns, such as combat-related PTSD, TBI, military sexual trauma (MST), transitional difficulties, homelessness, and higher rates of divorce and IPV within certain populations. "For the purposes of VA health benefits and services, a person who served in the active military service and who was discharged or released under conditions other than dishonorable is a Veteran" (Giersch et al., 2013).

Many veteran services and benefits will correlate with specific factors relating to individual service. Veterans may not identify with these services based upon factors or misunderstandings such as "I did not serve in combat" or "I am not over sixty-five." Currently, there are nine recognized eras for individuals designated as veterans:

1) World War I (April 6, 1917–November 11, 1918)
2) World War II (December 7, 1941–December 31, 1946)
3) Korean conflict (June 27, 1950–January 31, 1955)
4) Vietnam era (February 28, 1961–May 7, 1975 for veterans who served in the Republic of Vietnam during that period; otherwise August 5, 1964–May 7, 1975)

5) Gulf War (August 2, 1990–August 1991)
6) Bosnia Campaign (April 6, 1992–December 14, 1995)
7) Somalia Campaign (August 1992–March 1994)
8) Operation Iraqi Freedom (OIF) (March 19, 2003–December 17, 2011)
9) Operation Enduring Freedom (OEF) (October 7, 2001–December 28, 2014, or through a future date to be set by law or presidential proclamation)

All veterans are entitled to support and resources provided by federal law and managed by the Department of Veterans Affairs. This organization is composed of the Veteran Benefits Administration (VBA), Veteran Health Administration (VHA), and National Cemetery Administration (NCA). Service members may use one benefit and not have applied or be eligible for another. Enrollment in the VHA is not a guarantee of VBA benefits (such as service-connected disability). Those with awarded service-connected disabilities or use of VBA benefits may have never utilized VHA services. VHA and VBA do not always share record and chart systems, and veterans may be required to release information for correlation. Additional data and information on the resources provided by these agencies can be acquired online at the VA website.

The VBA provides benefits and services to service members, family members, and veterans, and may include:

- Service-connected disability payments
- Education benefits
- Home loan eligibility
- Survivor benefits
- Vocational rehabilitation programs

For access to the VHA resources, minimum-duty requirements are often determined in consideration with discharge type, service-related disabilities, medical conditions, and specific war-era contextual factors. Veteran healthcare services often include in-patient services, outpatient services, specialty care, mental health treatment, and substance abuse treatment. Not every VHA will provide identical services, or have identical processes for accessing care. For veterans of the current conflicts over the past fifteen to twenty years, the federal government offers the following programs that include treatment and counseling for IPV-related issues: Operation Enduring Freedom, Operation Iraqi Freedom, and Operation New Dawn (OIF/OEF/OND). Developed to meet the needs of troop members returning from recognized Global War on Terrorism theaters of combat or countries in support of these efforts and to allow for a transition from the Department of Defense to the Veteran Health Administration, the VA provides five free years of healthcare to eligible veterans and case-management services to allow for navigation of available healthcare and benefits.

There are also special programs related to female veterans as well due to the rapid increase of females' roles in all aspect of the military, including combat. Intimate partner violence is particularly addressed as it relates to our female veterans and service members. Among women veterans, the lifetime prevalence of IPV is 33 percent. Thirty-nine percent of women veterans report having experienced IPV, a rate much higher than the national average. Those who have experienced military sexual trauma (MST) are at an even higher risk for experiencing IPV (National Center for PTSD). Other high risk factors include those females who have experienced multiple deployments, family separation, and exposure to physical and mental trauma while deployed (Giersch et al., 2013).

LGBT VETERANS AND INTIMATE PARTNER VIOLENCE

Federal and state laws recognizing same-sex partnership often preclude accurate reporting or appropriate services. The US Department of Veterans Affairs Domestic Abuse Fact Sheet states that "11% of women in homosexual relationships and 23% of men in homosexual relationships report being raped, physically assaulted, and/or stalked by an intimate partner." "Don't Ask, Don't Tell" was repealed in 2013, but the stigma of reporting IPV within LGBT populations remains a barrier. Veterans previously discharged dishonorably under "Don't Ask, Don't Tell" were not eligible for VA benefits. These veterans can now request services, but may be unaware of how to do so. Previous military and veteran service responses to LGBT populations have been limited, and are often associated with lack of privacy.

Encourage the service member or veteran to contact a VA staff to review benefits and services. One suggestion is to review advance directive planning to ensure the appropriate partner or desired partner has access to care and to ensure the completed document maintains safety. Additionally, be aware of common myths, and that veterans with previous history of MST or IPV may be uncomfortable discussing past violence. Finally, establish rapport, understand the history, and develop a cohesive, care-coordination relationship, if the veteran requests.

IPV TREATMENT FOR ACTIVE SERVICE MEMBERS AND VETERANS

Males experiencing IPV have received little attention within the healthcare field. In May 2012, VA chartered the DV/IPV Task Force to develop a national program. The VHA Plan for Implementation of the DV/IPV Assistance Program was finalized December 2013 and includes fourteen recommendations. Implementation of the plan across the VHA will expand screening, prevention, and intervention to veterans and will strengthen partnerships with community providers/resources. It focuses on developing a culture of safety and adopting a holistic, veteran-centered psychosocial rehabilitation framework to inform all facets of the national DV/IPV assistance program: "veterans who experience DV/IPV" versus "victim" or "survivor," and "veterans who use DV/IPV" versus "batterer" or "abuser."

IDENTIFYING BARRIERS TO IPV TREATMENT

Military culture contributes to forming the identity of the veteran. Veterans and service members may fear labels or stigma, and often perceive treatment as a failure of mission. Service members and veterans were proud to have served, and may alternate between periods of active-duty service. The following identified barriers may be realistic concerns:

- Position
- Promotion/career
- Loss of access to weapons
- Security clearance
- Exposure (matters are not private)
- Economic factors

Understand increased risk factors with veterans and service members, such as control of finances, isolation, lack of community or family support, sexual aggression, threat to report to command/security clearance/peers. Secondly, using shame/guilt/blame when the veteran or service member desires to seek medical or mental health treatment. Access or familiarity with weapons is also common.

INTIMATE PARTNER VIOLENCE AND COMBAT EXPERIENCE

The majority of service members returning from combat do not engage in intimate partner violence. However, many will have adjustment and stress reactions. Combat experience and military stressors can exacerbate or increase the frequency and/or intensity of intimate partner violence. The battle mindset can often turn minor incidents into overreactions. Most combat veterans will readjust successfully. However, supporters must learn to identify warning signs. Intimate partner violence can impact mental and physical health outcomes, increase of depression, suicide, and substance use and abuse. Chapter 11 will further expound on this aspect of IPV.

Treatment organizations and subject matter experts (SME) must have an understanding of the behavioral and health concerns related to military experience. Post-traumatic stress disorder, as a result of the longevity of and the exposure to the war on terrorism, is highly prevalent within military culture, as the previous data have indicated. And although it can create barriers to living a normal life, post-traumatic stress disorder is an often treatable condition that results from a traumatic event. Symptoms include:

- Intrusive bad memories or nightmares of the event
- Avoiding events and locations that may "trigger" thoughts of the event
- Hypervigilance and arousal
- Sleep problems, irritability, anger, aggression, and fear
- Aggression to multiple situations or individuals
- Traumatic brain injury

- Suicide
- Depression
- Substance abuse
- Self-medicating
- Guilt/shame

Not all veterans experiencing PTSD will become violent. Learn to identify the current pattern of behavior, along with the relationship history/behavioral pattern before military service or combat. PTSD may increase the intensity of IPV or increase physical aggression, or vice versa.

Learn to review for a comprehensive history and specific behaviors/patterns of behavior if you believe this is a concern.

SCREENING FOR PTSD/IPV

If a service member or veteran returns from combat with complex health conditions, injuries, PTSD, or mental health concerns, they are not treated by one individual person. They are treated by a team of specialized providers who are trained in military/veteran-specific concerns and utilize strong care coordination. If you believe IPV is exacerbated or caused by a transitional or combat-related concern, comprehensive screening and care coordination is recommended.

From a community standpoint, the following guidance is provided for those who are related to or involved with veterans or service members: Thank veterans and service members for their service. Be aware of services and benefits that may provide specialized treatment or unique resources. Identify the role that the family member or caregiver may play. Identify potential economic or legal concerns that may present a barrier to requesting care. Additionally, utilize office space to reflect openness. For example, exhibit military or veteran posters/flyers, VHA information, or pamphlets and identify common military observations (Veterans Day, Marine Corps Birthday, Military Spouse Appreciation Day, Military Sexual Assault Awareness Month).

Do not assume:

- That combat was difficult, or that the military was difficult (many individuals will have enjoyed aspects of deployment and military service)
- That every experience was the same
- That every veteran is "broken"
- That a veteran, service member, or family member will desire to leave the relationship
- That stigma or fears of repercussions are not real
- That all veteran IPV will be related to military or combat experience
- That the service member or veteran has the support of their peers

Do not assume the veteran has not used VA services because they are not eligible or do not desire to do so. Many veterans are unaware of how to access services, or what services they are eligible for. Identify common locations of information on veteran eligibility and education to assist the veteran in clarifying questions. Gain a release of information (ROI) if you will be assisting in care coordination. Become familiarized with the requirements of DOD and VHA ROI requirements. Integrate screening questions that will allow for specialized care coordination:

- Have you served in the military?
- Were you or your spouse/partner deployed?
- Have you accessed veteran healthcare or benefits?
- Do you have a veteran healthcare primary care provider?
- Do you have a copy of your DD 214/medical records/etc.?
- What were your dates of service, combat era, etc.?

Veterans or service members may be in relationships with other veterans or service members, who may use or access the same services. The individual perpetrating IPV may have access to higher levels of technology and security access. Be able to identify how this can increase safety concerns or stalking behaviors. The individual perpetrating IPV may carry, have access to, or use threats of a weapon. A veteran or service member experiencing IPV may have the same. Clarify all weapons in the home, regardless of whom they may belong to. And, individuals perpetrating IPV may be trained in hostage situations and restraint.

Do not fake knowledge, experience with services, or interest in military experience; be genuine. Be honest about lack of knowledge and clarify why you are asking additional questions. Focus on the strengths that service members, veterans, and family members will have developed. Work together to navigate the military system and integrate goal planning. Do not assume all combat experience will result in PTSD, or require mental health treatment. Be direct and validate their experience. Overall, be specific about your knowledge and available services. You do not have to memorize each service and benefit to assist a veteran or service member. Learn simple questions to ask, and be honest about what information you can identify together. Focus on strengths and achievements. A simple way to open the door to conversation is to thank them for their service! This includes spouses and partners. Remember and never forget that all stakeholders involved with the military services, including wives, husbands, children, and other family members, serve directly or indirectly.

Lastly, all are impacted by ignoring or failing to recognize the symptoms and red flags of intimate partner violence. The data and the research speak volumes and confirm that the same IPV concern from which this manuscript derives mirrors the military cultural experience.

Cumulatively, the Army, Navy, Air Force, and Marine Corps averaged just under eight thousand IPV complaints per year between 2009 and 2014, from families including at least one active-duty service member (*Military Times*, 2014). Repeated deployments may result in post-traumatic stress disorder (PTSD) and TBI, which manifest in IPV, leading to an uptick in domestic violence statistics. A primary focus on other issues within the military in recent years—sexual assault, combat operations, and resetting and rebuilding for warfare—has resulted in a corresponding lack of focus on IPV issues.

According to Bannerman (2014), combat veterans are responsible for almost 21 percent of intimate partner violence nationwide, linked to the development of post-traumatic stress disorder. This is comparable to the fact that veterans alone account for 20 percent of US suicides. We call the problem of veteran suicide an epidemic, funding research, convening conferences, and creating new programs, hotlines, and therapies aimed at prevention, intervention, and reducing the stigma of seeking mental healthcare. But we don't talk about veteran intimate partner violence at all, effectively ensuring the catastrophic consequences remain largely unacknowledged and unaddressed.

Even as the overall frequency of IPV in the United States declined, levels of intimate partner violence within the post-9/11 military and veterans' communities began to explode. Calls from people affiliated with the military more than tripled from 2006 to 2011. During roughly the same period at Fort Carson near Colorado Springs, the number of soldiers charged with intimate partner violence surged, domestic abuse in the Army skyrocketed as an increasing number of soldiers returned from lengthy, repeat tours in Iraq and Afghanistan, and rates of PTSD began to rise (Bannerman, 2014).

Additionally, the total number of IPV annual reports dipped in the middle years of the last decade during the height of the wars in Iraq and Afghanistan, to as low as 6,619 in 2008. But the data show that the annual total has since returned almost to the levels seen in the early years of the last decade. While the majority of cases involve female victims, the thousands of male victims face a unique challenge in the military community, some experts say. "There is not much acknowledgment that men in the military can actually be victims," says Denise Hines, a professor at Clark University who has studied domestic violence. Hines says she believes that in the general population about one quarter of IPV incidents involve men as victims, one quarter involve women as victims, and about one half involve "mutual aggression" in which both the man and the woman are to some degree guilty of abuse (*Military Times*, 2014) Despite the culture, it's a problem that can't be ignored and must be addressed accordingly.

CHAPTER 10

THE BOOMERANG EFFECT

DR. CATHERINE GAYLE

According to the Centers for Disease Control (2016), intimate partner violence (IPV) is a serious, preventable public health problem that affects millions of Americans. The term "intimate partner violence" describes physical violence, sexual violence, stalking, and psychological aggression (including coercive acts) by a current or former intimate partner. Violent crimes by intimate partners (both male and female) accounted for almost 11.9 percent of violent crimes reported to the National Crime Victimization Survey (NCVS) in 2012 (total 810,790) (Truman, Langton, and Planty, 2012). An intimate partner is a person with whom one has a close personal relationship that is characterized by the following:

- Emotional connectedness
- Regular contact
- Ongoing physical contact and sexual behavior
- Identity as a couple
- Familiarity and knowledge about each other's lives

The relationship doesn't have to involve all of these dimensions. Examples of intimate partners include current or former spouses, boyfriends or girlfriends, dating partners, or sexual partners. IPV can occur between heterosexual or same-sex couples and does not require sexual intimacy. Incidences can vary in frequency and severity. It occurs on a continuum, ranging from one episode that might or might not have lasting impact to chronic and severe episodes over a period of years.

Formerly known as domestic violence, I describe intimate partner violence as an easily treatable phenomenon. After all, you have two intelligent people in a meaningful relationship; they should know how to solve their problems without resorting to violence as a means of controlling one another. Both parties should respect the fact that they are both beautiful creatures created by God with talents and gifts, which make the natural world a better place for all. The problem in the case of intimate partner violence is that sometimes, both parties view each other as objects they must govern, or they risk losing control of the relationship. Though some might consider it stereotyping, in my experience as a therapist I have become aware that some women might find themselves as the recipient of the three "Bs": the Black Eye, the Bruised Lips, or the Broken Bones. It may be commonplace to hear through the gossip mill that "They fighting again" or "so-and-so" is going upside "so-and-so's head." From 2002 to 2011 almost 50 percent of women who reported being physically assaulted by an intimate partner reported an injury. Of those women, 45.7 percent reported bruises, cuts, or other injuries; and 13 percent reported a serious injury (sexual violence, gunshot, knife wounds, internal injuries, unconsciousness, and broken bones) (Truman, Langton, and Planty, 2012). This scenario is exacerbated with the speculation that after a fight, some men do not allow their wives to appear in the community because they regret their violent actions, while some men view abusing their wives as a badge of honor and to show that they know how to keep "their women" in line.

Another observation from my experience is that with some women, the abusers strike their victims on places normally covered with clothing or force the women to wear shades to conceal an injury. In both scenarios, the reality is that women remain in horrible conditions because they fear for their lives and the lives of other members of the family. The abusers make threats toward their children and extended families, even promising to take their own lives if the women leave the relationship. These men cannot conceptualize the physical, emotional, and spiritual trauma their exploitation has on the lives of their victims. Spiritual damage is included because many times these women begin to question their faith and wonder why their God would allow or keep them trapped in those situations. Moreover, the abuser does not consider the collateral damage that emanates from their deeds in the form of the children who become victims of that abuse as well. These are scenarios I have witnessed in my professional activities and that are also played out in movies and within the arts and theatrics; the truth is that these disturbing facts are also real to many who are subjected to IPV.

From my therapeutic experience and perspective in working with this public health issue, it appears that when the abusers are in the "rage state," they do not usually focus on a special target; in fact, anyone who lands in their peripheral view becomes the object of their intensive anger. I repeat again that children are not exempt from the negative impact of this saga. Therefore, an essential tool every parent needs to teach his or her children is to hide when violence is inevitable. Interestingly enough, though, children absorb the trajectory and develop their own safety plan. Law enforcement have found children hiding under beds, in pantries, and outside in doghouses. Children run away from home because they can no longer endure the pain of seeing their mother being abused. The impact of the abuse causes many children, especially male children, to vow that they will never treat their spouse or significant other in this manner; however, due to the extremely high statistics stemming from intimate partner violence perpetrated by male abusers, data authenticates this is not the case. Conversely, a Boomerang Effect has surfaced within this cohort.

In social psychology, the Boomerang Effect refers to the unintended consequences of an attempt to persuade, resulting instead in the adoption of an opposing position (Brehm and Brehm, 1981). For the purpose of this discussion, I relate the concept of the Boomerang Effect to illustrate how abusers declare they will treat their spouse or significant other with respect. When the realities of life start to collide with their coping skill sets, however, they realize they do not have the capacity to cope as a mature adult; subsequently, they revert to incorporating the only way they know how to muddle through a situation, which is through using force. I introduce to you one of the main agents of socialization and a critical avenue for learned behavior: family. The abusers recognize, like their parents or caretakers, that when violence is used the action does not bring about a solution, but compounds the problem, because now one has to deal with psychological and physiological fallout that comes from the abuse. In essence, the one who made the vow has now become the perpetrator of abuse.

The family of origin is the most important socialization group in our society. It transmits the culture of a group from one generation to the next. The values, norms, and beliefs concerning how one navigates through life depends on who and how that family of origin frames the instruction (E-learning Support Initiative, 2016). Trained individuals, who originated from a culture that successfully transmitted the values of that linage, impart how to live out one's role in society. For example, if a child is raised by family members who believe every day is a "Turn Up Moment," unless that child acquires the discipline not to follow that pattern, eventually, they could manifest an epicurean trait or some form of obsessive compulsive disorder. A case in point is that children of alcoholics may not abuse alcohol, but may develop an eating disorder instead. Thus, the abused becomes the perpetrator because issues stemming from their life cycle (family of origin) now influence their psyche and the sociological arrows (substance abuse, anger, etc.).

The above information provides an explicit analysis of the Boomerang Effect, as many of the perpetrators are childhood victims of physical and psychological violence in their family of origin as the statistics presented in the previous chapters have confirmed. As a therapist, I find these two types of aggression originating from both males and females; however, the reported cases of female abusers pales in comparison to male abusers because of the negative backlash against a male acknowledging his victimizations.

According to a 2010 national survey by the Centers for Disease Control and the US Department of Justice, in the last twelve months more men than women have been victims of intimate partner physical violence and over 40 percent of severe physical violence was directed at men. Men were also more often the victim of psychological aggression and control over sexual or reproductive health. Studies show that men are less likely than women to seek help, and those who do have to overcome internal and external hurdles (Galdas et al., 2005; Cook, 2009). There has been little research on responses to male victims of intimate partner violence, in part because agencies have been reluctant to fund such research, although some aspects are starting to change in this regard.

An example of the lack of support for male victims stems from the US Department of Justice solicitation of proposals for "Justice Responses to Intimate Partner Violence and Stalking" requests for funding (RFP), which states in the criteria on page 8 that "what will not be funded: Proposals for research on intimate partner violence against, or stalking of, males of any age or females under the age of 12." Additionally, George (1994) in his manuscript "Riding the Donkey Backwards" states that in the few studies completed, many men report that hotline workers say they only help women, imply or state the men must be the instigators, ridicule them, or refer them to batterers' programs. Additionally, police often fail to respond and sometimes ridicule or arrest the men when they complain of battering by their partner (Cook, 2009; Douglas and Hines, 2011). However, the gap is finally starting to be addressed, as the following statistics about women and men indicate.

According to Truman, Langton, and Planty (2012), from 2002 to 2011, 66.6 percent of female victims reported being physically attacked by an intimate partner. Of these victims, 44.6 percent were hit, slapped, or knocked down; 36.1 percent were grabbed, held, tripped, jumped, or pushed; 8.2 percent were attacked sexually; 5.4 percent were hit by an object or knocked down; and 3.8 percent were shot at, stabbed, or hit with a weapon. In that same time frame, 64.6 percent of men reported having been physically attacked by an intimate partner. Of these victims, 43.3 percent were hit, slapped, or knocked down; 19.3 percent were hit by an object held in a hand or thrown; 14.0 percent were grabbed, held, tripped, jumped, or pushed; and 8.2 percent were shot at, stabbed, or hit with a weapon.

While persons with certain risk factors are more likely to become victims or perpetrators of intimate partner violence, those risk factors contribute to IPV but might not be direct causes. Not everyone who identifies as "at risk" becomes involved in violence. Some risk factors for IPV victimization and perpetration are the same, while others are associated with one another.

Not surprising, childhood physical or sexual victimization is a risk factor for future IPV perpetration and victimization; consequently, we have the Boomerang Effect. The research presented throughout this book indicates that a combination of individual, relational, community, and societal factors contributes to the risk of becoming an IPV victim or perpetrator. Understanding these multilevel factors can help identify various opportunities for prevention.

According to Breiding et al. (2008), factors for intimate partner violence and individual risk factors are:

- Low self-esteem
- Low income
- Low academic achievement
- Young age
- Aggressive or delinquent behavior as a youth
- Heavy alcohol and drug use
- Depression
- Anger and hostility
- Antisocial personality traits
- Borderline personality traits
- Prior history of being physically abusive

- Having few friends and being isolated from other people
- Unemployment
- Emotional dependence and insecurity
- Belief in strict gender roles (e.g. male dominance and aggression in relationships)
- Desire for power and control in relationships
- Perpetrating psychological aggression
- Being a victim of physical or psychological abuse *(consistently one of the strongest predictors of perpetration)*
- History of experiencing poor parenting as a child
- History of experiencing physical discipline as a child
- Relationship instability
- Dominance and control of the relationship by one partner over the other
- Economic stress
- Unhealthy family relationships and interactions
- Marital conflict—fights, tension, and other struggles

How do we break the Boomerang Effect in our society? It is not impossible, but it will not be easy, because many societal issues begin in the womb and manifest themselves throughout the maturation process while parents and forces in the environment serve as socializing agents of that child. If parents did not have a successful childhood and endured hardships because of the lack of internal and external resources that relegated them to having deficits in their character, then the social learning theory analogy becomes evident and clear as it pertains to prior and subsequent generations. Through every conversation a therapist poses with clients, he/she is led back to that person's childhood.

Additionally, in analyzing various groups in our society, we find individuals who appear to hide behind status, while others appear to freely express their imperfections. As life would have it, the latter group gets blamed for the problems in society, when it is those individuals who hide behind their facades who create problems for the masses. Also, it is not an easy cycle to break, as one can find this phenomenon occurring in every facet of our environment among every social structure and in every corner of the globe. Therapists understand that much of the issues that arise in a person's life evolve from situations that occur in the family of origin and the family of procreation. Thus, the lack of direct and in-kind resources is a factor that influences how successful one will be in fostering positive relationships.

Best practices lead us to conduct a bio-psychosocial assessment, including the genogram, and to evaluate the rearing process and what issues surface from the family tree. It is also important to acknowledge where the deficiencies are and to develop a plan for working through those factors that are presently affecting the lives of those who exhibit tendencies of the Boomerang Effect.

From my professional experience, a couple of recommended best practices that are simple but significant entail wisdom and premarital counseling. Wisdom indicates that individuals should institute an extended "courtship." Here, they engage with the members of each other's family and discover some of the "isms" that govern that family. It is important to know if the men in your partner's family feel it is acceptable to beat their women so they can keep them "in line." Likewise, it is important for the women in your partner's family to feel it is not acceptable to manipulate or use cursing to control their mates. When persons give themselves a chance to observe their mate or attend a family reunion, they procure an opportunity to study the "issues" that are germane to their partner's family. Wisdom shows that we live what we learn, until we obtain new methods for living.

Premarital counseling with a therapist who offers intensive counseling can lead to disclosure of couples' individual coping skills and how they solve life problems. A competent therapist will address concerns that surface in that relationship. Thus, it is important to acknowledge where the deficiencies are and to develop a plan for working through those factors that are presently affecting the lives of those who exhibit tendencies of the Boomerang Effect.

Finally, as a society, we must eliminate the cover-ups and stop protecting those who are violent. Men and women who are great people but possess horrible coping skills are incarcerated. They were unable to deal with their anger or the frustration of the daily grind. They resorted to using physical and psychological aggression to affect their environment. The lifetime prevalence of physical violence by an intimate partner is 31.5 percent for women, with 22.3 percent of women experiencing at least one act of severe physical violence by an intimate partner in their lifetime (Frandsen et al., 2010). The lifetime prevalence of physical violence by an intimate partner is 27.5 percent for men, with 14 percent experiencing at least one act of severe physical violence by an intimate partner in their lifetime (Briedling et al., 2014). It is time to effect change; let us provide opportunities for others to learn how to deal with their issues without using physical and psychological aggression. It is possible if we try!

CHAPTER 11

INTIMATE PARTNER VIOLENCE: A MISCALCULATED WEAPON OF MASS DESTRUCTION (THE BEHAVIORAL HEALTH IMPLICATIONS AND CAVEATS)

DR. OLIVER JOHNSON AND DR. IRMA J. GIBSON

The past forty years have seen a substantive acceleration in research documenting the widespread prevalence of intimate partner violence (IPV) and other lifetime trauma among African American men and women accessing services through mental health settings, as well as the range of mental health conditions uniquely associated with current and past abuse. Significantly, research and practice-oriented advances in the fields of traumatic stress, child development, genetics, and neuroscience are generating new models for understanding the impact of early experience on subsequent health, mental health, and life trajectories, as well as the psychobiological impact of adult traumatic events (Warshaw, Brashler, and Gil, 2009).

Consequently, our conceptual frameworks for understanding and treating the effects of chronic interpersonal abuse across the lifespan have been expanded significantly (Felitti et al., 1998; Debellis et al., 2005; Classen et al., 2006; Lanius, Blumer, and Lanius, 2006; Lyons-Ruth et al., 2006). This growing body of knowledge, particularly when rooted unequivocally in survivor and advocacy perspectives, provides a more practical framework for understanding the range of mental health outcomes experienced by African American survivors of IPV than do earlier approaches that failed to link social context with psychiatric symptoms and disorders, particularly with reference to how these dynamics adversely impact the lives of African American men.

The focus on current research about the mental and behavioral health consequences of IPV, and the relationship between IPV, lifetime trauma, and mental health among African American males and other victims, is crucial to moving ahead with preventive efforts to combat this public health dilemma. It also provides a critical perspective on the limits of these data for understanding the African American male's experience of IPV. Frameworks can increase the understanding and responding to the traumatic effects of IPV and lifetime abuse and the comprehension for addressing mental health issues in the context of IPV among this vulnerable, though largely underappreciated, segment of persons affected by the same.

"Male victims of intimate partner violence have become a serious issue in the United States. According to Ménard, Anderson, and Godboldt (2008); approximately 3.8 women and 1.3 men per 1,000 are victims of intimate partner violence each year. The Bureau of Justice Statistics (2007) noted that each year approximately 1,181 women and 329 men are victims of intimate partner homicides. Even though the numbers are not as high for men as for women, these victims cannot be ignored" (Schuler, 2010). Although heterosexual males remain the largest segment of offenders, there is a growing recognition of the adverse impact of IPV committed by heterosexual women on their male partners as well as IPV occurrences within same-sex relationships. The stigma associated with IPV may be particularly pervasive among African American male victims, especially among people in same-sex relationships, or transgendered individuals. These victims may be especially hesitant to report IPV to law enforcement, resulting in a cycle of abuse in which violent partners avoid the criminal justice system and, consequently, become repeat offenders.

MENTAL HEALTH IN THE CONTEXT OF TRAUMA AND INTIMATE PARTNER VIOLENCE

There is a large and growing body of evidence documenting the associations between IPV and mental health conditions, including substance use, abuse, and dependence. This includes findings from population-based studies, meta-analyses, and systematic reviews, along with evidence from smaller community-based studies.

Trauma and violence are widespread, harmful, and costly public health concerns. They have no boundaries with regard to age, gender, socioeconomic status, race, ethnicity, or sexual orientation. Trauma is a common experience for adults and children in American communities, and it is especially common in the lives of people with mental and substance use disorders. Direct and indirect exposure to intimate partner violence is a type of trauma that includes extreme violence by or between individuals including exposure to homicide, suicide, and other extreme events. For this reason, the need to address trauma is increasingly seen as an important part of effective behavioral healthcare and an integral part of the healing and recovery process (SAMHSA, 2018).

The Substance Abuse and Mental Health Services Administration (SAMHSA, 2018) describes individual trauma as resulting from "an event, series of events, or set of circumstances that is experienced by an individual as physically or emotionally harmful or life threatening and that has lasting adverse effects on the individual's functioning and mental, physical, social, emotional, or spiritual well-being." The effects of traumatic events place a heavy burden on individuals, families, and communities. Although many people who experience a traumatic event will go on with their lives without lasting negative effects, others will have difficulties and experience traumatic stress reactions. How someone responds to a traumatic experience is personal. If there is a strong support system in place, little or no prior traumatic experiences, and if the individual has many resilient qualities, it may not affect his or her mental health.

Research has shown that traumatic experiences are associated with both behavioral health and chronic physical health conditions, especially those traumatic events that occur during childhood. Substance use (such as smoking, excessive alcohol use, and taking drugs), mental health conditions (such as depression, anxiety, or PTSD), and other risky behaviors (such as self-injury and risky sexual encounters) have been linked with traumatic experiences. Because these behavioral health concerns can present challenges in relationships, careers, and other aspects of life, it is important to understand the nature and impact of trauma, and to explore healing. Ferrari et al. (2016) found severe IPV abuse usually results in poor social coping, increased levels of anxiety, as well as post-traumatic stress symptoms. The cost of intimate partner violence, which disproportionately affects women and girls, was estimated to be $8.3 billion in 2003. This total includes the costs of medical care, mental health services, and lost productivity (SAMHSA, 2018).

Intimate partner violence is present in every state and every community and it impacts people of all ages, socioeconomic statuses, sexual orientation, gender, race, religion, and nationality (NCADV, 2015). IPV is linked to an increase in mental illness for victims and survivors. It can be associated with depression, anxiety, post-traumatic stress disorder, and substance abuse. In cases where the female survivors of intimate partner violence seek advocacy and mental health supports, they reported high levels of depression as well as loneliness. Yet, many professionals in the social work, psychology, and helping professions believe that employment, higher education, socioeconomic status, and the duration of the abuse can all be protective factors against IPV (Ferrari et al., 2016).

Post-Traumatic Stress Disorder (PTSD) and Depression

Studies have consistently found higher rates of PTSD and depression among survivors of IPV, as compared to those who have not experienced IPV, and rates are higher among survivors who experience other types of trauma in addition to IPV.

In the context of IPV, PTSD is associated with an increased risk of experiencing other mental health conditions, in particular depression (Classen, 2006; Fedoski, 2008; Cerilli et al., 2011). It is important to stress again that survivors' experiences of mental health symptoms will vary based on a number of factors, including their own personal strengths and resources, the duration and severity of abuse, their experience of other lifetime trauma, and their access to services and social support. Furthermore, PTSD symptoms may affect the relationship between IPV and depression, in part due to the ways that PTSD symptoms can disrupt survivors' use of important personal and social resources (Classen, 2006; Houry, 2006). To reiterate, depression and PTSD may be influenced by other factors, including the type, duration, severity, and chronicity of the abuse.

Research has shown that experiencing multiple types of abuse (e.g. physical, sexual, psychological) may significantly magnify the risk of developing mental health symptoms; one study suggests that experiencing multiple forms of abuse can increase the odds for depression, PTSD, and suicidality by six to seventeen times (Lanius, 2006). Increased risk of depression has been found among men who have experienced any recent IPV (physical, sexual, or nonphysical) and among men who have experienced any lifetime IPV (DeJonghe et al., 2008; Mitchell et al.,

2006; Bundock et al., Afifi et al., 2012). However, the development of depression and PTSD may be influenced by the type of abuse experienced; a community-based study suggests that experiencing psychological abuse is a more significant predictor of both PTSD and depression than experiencing physical aggression (Cerulli, 2011).

IPV and Other Emotional and Mental Health Conditions

The following data is tantamount to the development of similar symptoms found among African American male victims. In addition to depression and PTSD, evidence strongly suggests that experiencing IPV increases the risk of other mental health conditions.

Deliberate Self-Harm. Women exposed to IPV are up to three times more likely to engage in deliberate self-harm than nonabused women (Lyons-Ruth et al., 2006), with factors such as PTSD numbing symptoms or more severe sexual violence associated with current, deliberate self-harm (Warsaw et al., 2014).

Suicidality. IPV is also associated with increased suicidal ideation (Lanius, 2006) and suicide attempts (Mitchell et al., 2006). A large study conducted by the World Health Organization found that women who report partner violence at least once in their lifetime are nearly three times as likely to have suicidal thoughts and nearly four times as likely to attempt suicide, compared to women who have not been abused by a partner (Woods, Kozachik, and Hall, 2010). Seventy-two percent of all murder-suicides involve an intimate partner, and 94 percent of the victims of these murder-suicides are female (Violence Policy Center, 2012).

Additionally, one in six women (16.2 percent) and one in nineteen men (5.2 percent) in the United States have experienced stalking victimization at some point during their lifetime in which they felt fearful or believed they or someone close to them would be harmed or killed (by any perpetrator) (CDCP, 2010). In 2010, 241 males and 1,095 females were murdered by an intimate partner (Leserman and Drossman, 2007).

Eating Disorders. The results of a systematic review suggest a relationship between experiencing IPV and being diagnosed with an eating disorder. As compared to those without such a diagnosis, women and men with an eating disorder are significantly more likely to have experienced any lifetime IPV (Maman et al., 2013).

Other Anxiety and Mood Disorders. Both community-based studies and systematic reviews have found evidence for increased risk of other anxiety and mood disorders among survivors (Johnson, Zlotnick, and Perez, 2008; Devries et al., 2013; Dillon et al., 2013; Bundock et al., 2013). Compared to those who have not experienced IPV, survivors are nearly three times more likely to be diagnosed with an anxiety disorder (Bundock et al., 2013).

Substance Use and Abuse. Exposure to IPV is associated with increased odds of substance abuse, binge drinking, and tobacco use for both female and male survivors (Jacquier, Hellmuth, and Sullivan, 2013; Bundock et al., 2013; Afifi et al., 2012; Trevillion et al., 2012). One study suggests that survivors are nearly six times as likely to have a substance use disorder as compared to those who have never been abused (Bundock et al., 2013).

Poor Sleep. Experiencing IPV is associated with poor overall sleep quality, frequent disruptive nighttime behaviors (e.g. memories or nightmares of a traumatic experience; anxiety or panic), and sleep disorders (Debellis et al., 2005; Devries et al., 2013; Duran, Oetzel, Parker et al., 2009; Bonomi et al., 2009). The impact of IPV on the overall health and well-being of individuals, families, and communities is far reaching and extends beyond mental and emotional hurts, habits, and hang-ups.

THE PHYSICAL AND MEDICAL CONSEQUENCES OF INTIMATE PARTNER VIOLENCE

Nearly one in four women (23 percent) and one in seven men (14 percent) aged eighteen and older in the United States have been the victim of severe physical violence by an intimate partner in their lifetime. Nearly 14 percent of women and 4 percent of men have been injured as a result of IPV that included contact sexual violence, physical violence, or stalking by an intimate partner in their lifetime (Breiding, Black, Ryan, 2004).

Apart from death and injuries, physical violence by an intimate partner is associated with a number of adverse health outcomes (Appel and Holden, 1998; Tjaden and Thoennes, 2000). Several health conditions associated with intimate partner violence may be a direct result of the physical violence (for example, bruises, knife wounds, broken bones, traumatic brain injury, back or pelvic pain, headaches). Other conditions are the result of the impact of intimate partner violence on the cardiovascular, gastrointestinal, endocrine, and immune systems through chronic stress or other mechanisms (Appel and Holden, 1998).

According to the CDCa, examples of health conditions associated with IPV include:

- Asthma
- Bladder and kidney infections
- Circulatory conditions
- Cardiovascular disease
- Fibromyalgia
- Irritable bowel syndrome
- Chronic pain syndromes
- Central nervous system disorders
- Gastrointestinal disorders
- Joint disease
- Migraines and headaches

Reproductive issues:

- Gynecological disorders
- Pelvic inflammatory disease
- Sexual dysfunction
- Sexually transmitted infections, including HIV/AIDS
- Delayed prenatal care
- Preterm delivery

- Pregnancy difficulties like low-birth-weight babies and perinatal deaths
- Unintended pregnancy

Health Behaviors

Women with a history of IPV are more likely to display behaviors that present further health risks (e.g. substance abuse, alcoholism, suicide attempts) than women without a history of IPV.

IPV is associated with a variety of negative health behaviors. Studies show that the more severe the violence, the stronger its relationship to negative health behaviors by victims (CDCa).

- Engaging in high-risk sexual behavior
  - Unprotected sex
  - Decreased condom use
  - Early sexual initiation
  - Choosing unhealthy sexual partners
  - Multiple sex partners
  - Trading sex for food, money, or other items
- Using harmful substances
  - Smoking cigarettes
  - Drinking alcohol
  - Drinking alcohol and driving
  - Illicit drug use
- Unhealthy diet-related behaviors
  - Fasting
  - Vomiting
  - Abusing diet pills
  - Overeating
- Overuse of health services

Both physical and psychological IPV are associated with significant physical and mental health consequences for both male and female victims (Coker et al., 2002). And to reiterate a third time, survivors' experiences of mental health symptoms will vary based on a number of factors, including their own personal strengths and resources, the duration and severity of abuse, their experience of other lifetime trauma, and their access to services and social support (Warsharp, Brashler, and Gil, 2009). Unfortunately, effective interventions to combat this nightmare are also thwarted by the inability to effectively access services and social support by some victims.

ADDITIONAL CAVEATS

As the behavioral health aspect of intimate partner violence is addressed, it is critical to note that IPV advocates and African American male survivors have voiced concerns about the ways that survivors' mental health– and substance use–related needs are used against them, not only by abusers but also by the systems in which they seek help (e.g. batterers using mental health–related needs to control their partners; undermine them in custody battles; discredit them with friends, family, child protective services, and the courts) (Boyle, Jones, and Lloyd, 2006). In turn, considerable evidence suggests that individuals who experience mental health–related needs or have a psychiatric disability are at increased risk for being victimized by an abusive partner (Buller et al., 2014; Beydoun et al., 2012). These significant findings are mirrored and also discussed in chapter 12.

As the data indicate, the societal and economic effects of IPV are profound. The cost exceeds $8.3 billion per year (Hathaway et al., 2007). Approximately one quarter of a million hospital visits occur as a result of IPV annually (NCIPC, 2003). The cost of intimate partner rape, physical assault, and stalking totals more than $8.3 billion each year for direct medical and mental healthcare services and lost productivity from paid work and household chores (NCIPC, 2003; FVPE, 2010). Additional medical costs are associated with ongoing treatment of alcoholism, attempted suicide, mental health symptoms, pregnancy, and pediatric-related problems associated with concomitant child abuse and witnessing abuse. Intangible costs include women's decreased quality of life, undiagnosed depression, and lowered self-esteem. Destruction of the family unit often results in loss of financial stability or lack of economic resources for independent living, leading to increased populations of homeless women and children (OG, 2010). Efforts to control healthcare costs should focus on early detection and prevention of IPV (FVPE, 2010).

A substantial proportion of survivors also report other negative impacts as a result of IPV, and there is wide variation in the proportions of female and male survivors reporting these impacts. Population-based surveys indicate that among women and men in the US who have experienced contact sexual violence, physical violence, or stalking by an intimate partner during their lifetimes, 73 percent of the women and 36 percent of the men report at least one measured negative impact related to these victimization experiences (e.g. fear, concern for safety, missing school or work, needing services) (NCADV, 2015). Among the female IPV survivors, 62 percent reported feeling fearful, 57 percent reported being concerned for their safety, 25 percent missed at least one day of school or work from the IPV, 19 percent reported needing medical care, and 8 percent needed housing services. Among the male survivors, 18 percent reported feeling fearful, 17 percent reported being concerned for their safety, 14 percent missed at least one day of school or work from the IPV, 5 percent reported needing medical care, and 2 percent needed housing services (NCIVP, 2003).

Increasingly, we are becoming aware of the scope of the intimate partner violence problem and the extent to which it can and does impact an individual's mental and physical health, and the overall mental health and well-being of a family. Everyone who is a part of society must come to terms with the prevalence of intimate partner violence and better understand the overwhelming impact on families, society, and even our economy. We must also step up to support those who have experienced it and, as importantly, find ways to prevent it (Nealon-Woods, 2016). Given that IPV survivors have a wide variety of life experiences with a range of mental health effects, there is no single treatment model that will fit the needs of all survivors (Warshaw, Brashler, and Gil, 2009). However, based upon the research presented in this chapter as well as others, these are implications that impact us all; therefore, being of the mindset that it doesn't impact you is a false persona. It is your business, and it does impact "my world" and yours in one way or another.

CHAPTER 12

INTIMATE PARTNER VIOLENCE, SOCIAL WORK, AND THE LAW: THE DILEMMA OF VICTIMHOOD

ROWENA DANIELS AND DR. JERRY DANIEL

This chapter provides an analysis of social work and legal issues as related to intimate partner violence (IPV). It will address the concept of victimhood and its effect on men as they attempt to engage and navigate the criminal justice system. We use a bifurcated approach to highlight the legal significance of IPV to social work practice. The legal ramifications of IPV are understood from a micro-level perspective. Specifically, we examine how legal issues impact social work practice with IPV victims. Additionally, we elucidate legal issues related to IPV at the macro level. Historical and contemporaneous data are used to highlight the magnitude of IPV on various population groups, with a particular emphasis being placed on male victims. In doing so, incidence and trends related to the types of IPV are examined to show how the face of IPV has evolved. Finally, the legal landscape—including statutes and case law—is examined as a potential means to address IPV. Implications for social work education, research, and practice are provided.

CASE EXAMPLE

James, a thirty-seven-year-old African American male, is in the employee break area with his friend. Since there are no other employees around at the time, James takes the opportunity to respond to his friend's questions about why he has been so down lately. James shares the following about his home life:

"The nagging is constant. I am belittled daily and told constantly how inadequate I am as a father and as a husband. Sarah tells me all the time that we are barely making ends meet and that I need to take on a second job because 'real men' take care of their family. She says she does not enjoy having sex with me anymore and questions whether I am having an affair. And she says if I am not having an affair, I need to deal with my issue because I am no longer able to meet her needs. In the evenings when I go home, it is my responsibility to help the children with their homework while Sarah prepares dinner.

"Several months ago, Alex, our youngest son, brought home a bad grade on an assignment. Since then, Sarah has taken over helping the children with their homework because she says I am stupid and blamed

me for the score Alex received. She said I am worthless and not contributing anything of value to the family. I cannot believe she said all of this in front of the children. I was so angry, but I did not say anything to Sarah.

"The morning after her tirade, I got up early hoping to avoid any further discussion about the issue. However, she was up already and waiting for me in the kitchen. She was sitting at the table, and as soon as I walked in she stood with a knife and backed me into the corner. I could have overtaken her, but I did not want to hurt her and I certainly did not want to alarm the children. She told me I was worthless and that I deserved to die. She told me the children deserved a better father and she deserved a better husband.

"On the way to work, I called to make a report to the police. Because the children were home when the incident occurred, the police agreed to come to the house and talk to us that evening. Because there were no physical injuries, no witnesses, and Sarah denied the incident, the officer did not even make a written report. However, the officer did make two observations. He noted I was a rather large man and that he thought it was odd that I would be filing a complaint against my wife, especially since she did not look like she could cause me any harm. Also, he told me Sarah informed him about my past legal issues. This was the beginning of my hell with Sarah. I never called the police again."

CASE SYNOPSIS

Generally, men have difficulty contextualizing their experiences of victimization. Oftentimes, the difficulty is attributed to the angst they experience when attempting to disclose their feelings about situations that are distressing to them. In this case example, James' account is intended to illuminate a few of the many challenges faced by males who experience intimate partner violence.

Although the challenges come to the forefront when the act of violence transpires, they are often exacerbated when the male contemplates asserting a claim of victimization. As evidenced in the case example, men often grapple with factors related to gender roles and how they influence perceptions of what behaviors are expected of them; emotional and psychological abuse, which are thought to be prevalent forms of abuse experienced by men; the routine absence of physical injuries, which complicate reporting to and responsiveness of officers; stereotypes about men; men and their increased likelihood of having a criminal record and how this might impact their attempt to seek help through the criminal justice system; fear that the man will be identified as the perpetrator instead of the victim; disbelief by the officer; and the degree to which men endorse hegemonic masculine ideals. When all of these factors converge, they provide insight about how a male might contextualize his experience as a victim. It is this contextualization of victimhood that will likely have significant implications for whether a man is willing to engage the criminal justice system to seek solace from intimate partner violence.

INTIMATE PARTNER VIOLENCE: A SERIOUS PUBLIC HEALTH PROBLEM

Intimate partner violence is a serious, preventable public health issue that negatively impacts millions of Americans annually. Breiding et al. (2015) defines IPV as incidents of physical violence, sexual violence, stalking, and psychological aggression (including coercive acts) by a current or former intimate partner. An intimate partner is someone who has a close relationship with another person and is usually characterized by emotional connectedness, regular contact, ongoing physical contact and/or sexual behavior, identity as a couple, and familiarity and knowledge about each other's lives (Centers for Disease Control, 2017).

Given the prevalence of intimate partner violence, social workers and other mental health providers will likely encounter a victim while engaged in practice. An estimated ten million cases of intimate partner violence are reported each year (CDC, 2017). These incidents underlie numerous emergency room visits and therapy sessions each year.

Homicide

CASE EXAMPLE

July 4, 2018—Albany, Georgia. Police arrested a woman they said killed two people at an Albany apartment complex on Wednesday night. Officers said forty-year-old Janice Truelove shot her estranged husband and his new girlfriend. Truelove was arrested in the complex's parking lot. Investigators said they found an assault weapon inside the apartment. Two other people, including Truelove's ten-year-old son, were in the apartment. The others were not physically injured. Investigators said the wife and husband had not lived together in more than three months.

Intimate partner homicide is characterized by death against a current or former cohabitant, romantic partner, or spouse by his or her intimate partner (Catalano et al., 2009). A history of intimate partner violence is a significant risk factor for intimate partner homicide (Campbell et al., 2000). The literature is mixed on whether victims can accurately assess their own risk of IPV; however, victims and healthcare professionals together can provide a more accurate picture. Notwithstanding differences in the literature, it is imperative that individuals and professionals become educated regarding risk factors among potential perpetrators of IPV.

Nonfatal Injuries

While the magnitude of intimate partner homicide provides a dramatic picture, in terms of actual numbers, the number of males and females who suffer nonfatal injuries is significantly higher (Catalano et al., 2009). In a study conducted by Truman and Morgan (2014), approximately 45 percent of IPV resulted in some form of injury. Close intimate partners accounted for 48 percent of injuries sustained by victims. The study also revealed that the majority of nonfatal injuries are bruises and cuts.

From 2003 to 2012, IPV accounted for 21 percent of all violent crime. The majority of IPV incidents were committed by a current mate at the time of the incident. Overall, violence perpetrated by close partners (48 percent) resulted in injuries more often than violence perpetrated by immediate family members (37 percent) and extended family members (36 percent). Also, in 2003–12, the majority of IPV was simple assault (64 percent), compared to serious violence (36 percent). This pattern held for all victim-offender relationship categories (Truman and Morgan, 2014).

The majority of violence toward victims of IPV was classified as simple assault. Nonetheless, approximately 184,800 separate incidents of IPV occurred by the use of a weapon. Consistent with having a large number of incidents classified as simple assault, Truman and Morgan (2014) noted that when IPV incidents involved weapons, firearms constituted a smaller percentage than knives and other weapons.

Historical Backdrop

Although this chapter highlights the legal aspects of IPV, it is useful to examine historical aspects of IPV and its connection to the mental health and criminal justice system. IPV has a long history in the United States, but has a much shorter history of being seen as a criminal offense (Fegan, 1996; Snyder and Morgan, 2005). Hence, the criminal aspect of IPV is a fairly new phenomenon when compared to other aspects.

It was not until the 1970s that policy makers began to address the legal dimensions of IPV, particularly as related to female victims. Early policies addressing the criminalization of IPV focused on improving legal responses to protect women and punish offenders (Fagan, 1996). States developed legislation with a goal to reduce IPV, focusing specifically on the effects of punishment costs against perpetrators. The overall goal of early legislation was to create a deterrent effect and suppress violence between individuals who had an "intimate" relationship, a similar goal for other types of violence (e.g. stranger violence) (Sherman, 1992).

Legal and Ethical Aspects of IPV

Similar to other acts of violence, IPV is now codified as a criminal offense. According to Dressler (1987), criminal law "represents the community's voice regarding which behaviors are right and wrong, acceptable and unacceptable, legitimate and illegitimate" (Nolan Jr. and Westervelt, 2000, p. 624). However, laws and court processes are both susceptible to social norms (Basile, 2005). According to Nolan Jr. and Westervelt (2000), there is a direct relationship between law and culture, as one influences the other. "As culture impacts and gives meaning to the law, so the law directs, informs, and instructs culture" (2000).

In understanding IPV and the law, it is imperative to understand the legal context of IPV. The Centers for Disease Control (CDC) defines IPV as violence or aggression that occurs in a close relationship. Intimate partners include current and former spouses and dating partners. IPV can vary in frequency and severity and occurs on a continuum, ranging from one episode that might or might not have lasting impact, to chronic and severe episodes over a period of years (CDC, 2017).

Beginning in the 1970s, a number of states implemented policies that focused on "warrantless arrests," with the goal of deterring IPV. These early laws were primarily targeted toward male perpetrators, but now are gender neutral and target female perpetrators as well. The reviews of the effectiveness of these policies have been mixed. While some commentators believe these laws have been effective in increasing rates of arrest, prosecution, and conviction of IPV perpetrators (National Research Council, 2004), others believe the laws actually may have been more harmful to IPV victims (Crime and Justice News, 2014). Despite these mixed reviews, state laws vary regarding circumstances related to the warrantless arrest. A summary of each state is listed in Table 3, Appendix 14.

Pursuant to *mandatory arrest policies*, police officers are required by statute to make arrests based on probable cause that a crime (IPV) was committed. Jurisdictions that have some form of mandatory arrest provisions include Alaska, Arizona, California, Colorado, Connecticut, DC, Iowa, Kansas, Louisiana, Maine, Massachusetts, Mississippi, Missouri, Nevada, New Hampshire, New York, Ohio, Oregon, Rhode Island, South Dakota, Utah, and Washington. Unlike mandatory arrest policies, *preferred arrest statutes* are less strict; these policies encourage officers to make arrests as the favored action when there is probable cause IPV has occurred. Jurisdictions with preferred arrest policies include Arkansas, California, Massachusetts, Montana, North Dakota, and Tennessee. The policies that allow for the greatest leniency when faced with IPV are *discretionary arrest policies*. These statutes fully allow officers to use their discretion under certain circumstances where probable cause is evident. Jurisdictions with discretionary arrest provisions include Alabama, Arizona, Delaware, Florida, Georgia, Hawaii, Idaho, Illinois, Indiana, Iowa, Kentucky, *Louisiana, Maryland, Michigan, Minnesota, Missouri, *Montana, Minnesota, Missouri, Montana, Nebraska, *Nevada, New Hampshire, New Mexico, New York, North Carolina, Oklahoma, *Tennessee, Texas, *Utah, Vermont, Virginia, *Washington, and West Virginia.

It should be noted that a number of states (identified via asterisks) employ more than one policy, creating a blend of policies for its jurisdiction. Blended policies may cause the responding officers to sort out varying facts of the reported incident, hence creating a lack of clarity on how to handle the situation. Such an approach could possibly result in fewer arrests when needed, yet it could also place individuals at more risk, even when it appears that these individuals are not at risk.

Specifically at issue in this review is the fact that cultural ideals shape what it means to be a man and to be a victim (Burcar, 2013; Mejia, 2013), thereby shaping the legal response to a man's claim of victimization. Understanding how discourses related to manhood and ideals of hegemonic masculinity interface with victimhood is integral to making meaningful and sustainable changes to the way victimization of males is viewed by society and treated within the criminal justice system. These discourses are likely to direct a man's decision of whether to assert a claim of victimization. Further, the narratives surrounding the concept of victimhood are likely to shape the response he might receive from actors within the criminal justice system.

The criminal justice system is likely to be the first formal source of support accessed by a person seeking to ameliorate abuse in a relationship. However, intimate partner violence has not always been a criminal offense, and legal intervention has not always been a priority of the state. Historically, visibility and accountability were lacking and intimate partner violence was considered private and a matter between a husband and a wife. As a private, family matter, intimate partner violence was protected from legal intrusion because typically it occurred within the confines of the home. The notion of the sanctity of the home is best illustrated in early case law, such as in *Bradley v. State* (1824), where the court affirmatively stated that family arguments were best left inside the walls of the home and were not proper matters in which the court should intervene, and in *State v. Black* (1864), where the courts stated matters of a husband and a wife are best left for them to resolve and the court should not encroach upon the domestic sphere unless the violence is excessive or results in permanent injury.

In response to major shifts in the sociopolitical landscape, discourse about the criminalization of intimate partner violence emerged from the efforts of robust advocacy and activism (Lucal, 1992). For example, the anti-violence and feminist movements called upon advocates to take a stand for issues that would transform the nation. The "anti-violence movement used litigation, research and the political process" to engage state actors in efforts to address intimate partner violence (Goodmark, 2017). And the feminist movement, supported by activists, social scientists, and social service professionals, launched a public campaign to proclaim intimate partner violence, as it is referred to in this review, as a social problem. Lucal (1992, Social Problems) noted that Spector and Kitsuse (1977) defined social problems as the "activities of groups or individuals making assertions of grievances and claims with respect to some putative conditions." These movements contextually changed the nation's response to intimate partner violence and effectively moved the issue from a private, family matter (Goodmark, 2017) to a public concern that many believed could best be mitigated by engaging the criminal justice system (2017).

In the 1980s, movement toward using existing laws that addressed assault and the passage of laws specifically targeting intimate partner violence made way for police officers and the courts to begin to leverage existing authority and resources to address violence between intimates (Erez, 2002). Specifically, claims of intimate partner violence, primarily considered a male-perpetrated offense, now warranted a response from agents of the criminal justice system. Initially, the response was sluggish.

The cause was further championed by lawmakers and politicians through the enactment of the Violence Against Women Act (VAWA) in 1994 (Cho and Wilke, 2005). VAWA and the subsequent reauthorizations is public policy that has primarily focused on shaping the criminal justice system's response to intimate partner violence perpetrated by males against females. The implementation of this policy brought sweeping changes to the criminal justice system's response to intimate partner violence. The most notable changes included an increase in the number and types of victim services offered for women, accountability for perpetrators, and trainings for agents of the criminal justice system (2005).

Through these efforts to address violence perpetrated against women, significant accomplishments were achieved in law and policy. However, until recently, the plight of male victims of intimate partner violence was less visible and garnered no more than a modicum of attention. Most likely, the lack of visibility has in the past and continues to forestall efforts to effect changes in policy and law that directly impact how men experience the criminal justice system (Artime, McCallum, and Peterson, 2014). To overcome the issue of visibility, the question of where are the men who have experienced intimate partner violence must be asked and answered. It is likely the answer will be found behind the veil of victimhood.

It is necessary to pierce the veil currently obscuring a major element that reinforces men's right and desire to remain silent about intimate partner violence. This very salient element, victimhood, is likely to influence the potentiality of a man seeking intervention through the criminal justice system. Specifically, the idea of victimhood is believed to shape how or whether a man will access the criminal justice system as well as establish a framework for how he will conceptualize his own experience of intimate partner violence.

VICTIMHOOD: A GENDERED PERSPECTIVE

Claiming the status of victimhood is required for the assertion of a claim through the criminal justice system. Gendered perspectives and constructions are integral to the process of determining who is perceived as a perpetrator or a victim (Hester, 2012). Further, these constructions dictate how victimhood is defined (Durfee, 2011). Identifying a male as a victim forces a paradigm shift that challenges two notions that are deeply engrained within society's infrastructure, the idea of who can be a victim and hegemonic masculinity (Mejia, 2005). Men must juxtapose victimhood and masculine ideals in an effort to secure a balance between the two. If balance is successfully achieved, there is a greater likelihood that men will conceptualize their experience with intimate partner violence in a way that will enhance their ability to effectively assert a claim of victimization.

A victim is conceptualized as one who is passive, helpless (Durfee, 2011, p. 320, citing Holstein and Miller, 1990, p. 119), dependent, and weak (Burcar and Akerstrom, 2009). The conceptualization of victimhood also includes vulnerability, as it is key to understanding victimization (Gilson, 2016). Vulnerability is often associated with femininity, "weakness, dependency, passivity, incapacitation, incapability and powerlessness" (2016, p. 74). Literature suggests that men do not conform to this traditional definition of a victim (Tsui, Cheung, and Leung, 2010; Cheung, Leung, and Tsui, 2009). Even though current views have evolved to some degree, how a victim is conceptualized is still reflective of attributes that are more commonly associated with femininity than masculinity. The focus on feminine notions is evidenced in the long-held belief that intimate partner violence is male-perpetrated abuse against a female victim.

The characterization of a victim usually runs afoul to gender role expectations of men, as these roles are cloaked in hegemonic masculine ideals. Samulowitz, Gremyr, Eriksson, and Hensing (2018, Theoretical Framework, citing Connell and Messerschmidt, 2005) state that "hegemonic masculinity describes a pattern of masculine attributes, behaviors and practices which are constructed as the prevailing and idealized norm and against which both men and women are evaluated." Traditionally, boys and men have been socialized to conform to masculine gender roles. Gender roles are embedded in cultural values, norms, and ideologies and reflect society's expectation of what it means to be a man (Addis and Mahalik, 2003). These male gender roles which are encapsulated by hegemonic masculine ideals are cultural constructions of masculinity. Through these constructions, masculinity is conceptualized as having power, strength, control (Burcar, 2013; Burcar and Akerstrom, 2009), domination (Schuler, 2010), and is not associated with emotionality, independence, vulnerability, or weakness (Burcar and Akerstrom, 2009; Pederson and Vogel, 2007). The hegemonic masculine ideals are central to establishing the framework of how men are expected to behave (cited in Samulowitz et al., 2017, Connell and Messerschmidt, 2005). However, the framework may be expanded by individual and situational characteristics such as race, ethnicity, and cultural factors (Griffith and Cornish, 2018), as well as sexual orientation and social class (Smith, 2008).

With hegemonic masculine ideals as a backdrop, current thoughts about victimhood might lead a man to conclude that if he claims victim status as a result of intimate partner violence then he is not a "real man" (Migliaccio, 2001). According to Morgan and Wells (2016, p. 405–406, citing Eckstein, 2009), men dislike claiming victimization and have difficulty conceptualizing themselves as a victim (Cheung et al., 2009; Tsui et al., 2010). For many men, claiming victimization leads to shame, embarrassment, and threats to masculinity (Tsui et al., 2010; Cheung et al., 2009). Therefore, men are often reluctant to characterize their experience with intimate partner violence as victimization. DePuy, Abt, and Romain-Glassey (2017) note that men are more reluctant than women to disclose that they are a victim of intimate partner violence. According to Christie (1986), men resist being portrayed as a "needy victim" because when cast in this light, the dominant norms of masculinity are diminished (cited in De Puy et al., 2017, p. 437). In a study conducted by De Puy et al. (2017), "Men who reported a physical assault from a partner identified more with the notion of victims as being entitled to protections of their rights rather than as victims in need of help" (p. 437).

There is a clear line of demarcation between the social conception of what it means to be a man and what it means to be a victim. The distinction between a man and a victim remains clear, even though more men are publicly declaring they have been victimized, thus creating a paradox where men are seen as perpetrators while at the same time increasingly claiming victimization (Durfee, 2011). Men can find themselves in a precarious set of circumstances when trying to conform to gender constructions, namely hegemonic masculine ideals, while also asserting victimization. This is a crucial point, because the framework of hegemonic masculinity does not support the notion that men can be victimized. Further, the framework ignores the fact that men can experience vulnerability, distress, and suffering.

It is important to note that the constructions of masculinity are not static and can vary among groups and individuals and can change over time (Addis and Mahalik, 2003). It is also important to note that men may vary in the degree to which they adopt and internalize these constructions. However, these hegemonic ideals provide a lens through which reporting tendencies can be analyzed and understood. This is critical because the initiation of a formal report is the mechanism by which the criminal justice system is activated.

ASSERTING A CLAIM

Today, the criminal justice system is fundamental to addressing intimate partner violence in the United States (Goodmark, 2017). However, the success of the criminal justice system's response to intimate partner violence has been challenged by many scholars and some have even questioned the "continued utility of criminal justice intervention"(Goodmark, 2017). The challenge with the criminal justice system's responsiveness does not hinge solely on the system itself, but is reinforced by the man's decision of whether to accept the status of victimhood as required for the initiation of a claim in the criminal justice system.

The criminal justice system is firmly established in a victim and offender (perpetrator) dichotomy (Shuler, 2010, p. 165, citing Miller, 2005). In order to effectively file a complaint about intimate partner violence, a claim of victimhood must be asserted and established. As previously mentioned, men are often reluctant to file a claim. Therefore, it is necessary to consider the dynamics involved in a man's decision to seek help. According to Addis and Mahalik (2003), "the study of men's help seeking has direct implications for developing effective interventions informed by a psychology of gender." It is well documented that men are reluctant to seek help and sometimes this reluctance is inextricably tied to masculinity norms, stereotypes and ideologies (2003). More specifically, hegemonic masculine ideals influence whether a man reports his experience of intimate partner violence as well as whether he assigns meaning to his experience by drawing upon the notions traditionally associated with victimhood.

When a man experiences intimate partner violence, he may feel constrained by the aforementioned hegemonic masculine ideals because victimization challenges these traditional notions of what is expected of him as a man (Artime et al., 2014). For example, relying on others, admitting a need for help, and recognizing and labeling an emotional problem are typically associated with help seeking (Addis & Mahalik, 2003). However, these behaviors do not align with messages communicated to men about how they should behave when they are faced with a distressing situation such as intimate partner violence (2003). "The experience of victimization produces intense biological states of fear, grief and distress, the very states that masculine ideology was designed to expunge" (Mejia, 2005, p. 34). For this reason, in order to avoid gender role conflict, men may choose not to report their abuse to authorities (Cheung et al., 2009).

As the man attempts to weigh ideals of hegemonic masculinity against his own experiences, an internal conflict is likely to materialize leaving the man at odds with gendered ideology and compelling him to contemplate whether his claim will be taken seriously or believed (Allen-Collinson, 2009); how to manage feelings of shame (Erez, 2002); fear of being laughed at, scorned, or ridiculed (Schuler, 2010, p.165); whether he will be labeled the aggressor and incarcerated as a result of this wrongful identification (Shuler, 2010, p.165); as well as whether he will be viewed as less masculine (Durfee, 2011 p. 319 citing Eckstein, 2009). It is likely that some, if not all, of these conflicts will have to be resolved before a man can move forward with reporting abuse.

Addis and Mahalik (2003) provided additional insights related to the discourse of hegemonic masculinity and its effect on reporting by outlining a social psychological process that is reportedly triggered in response to a man's contemplation of seeking help. Central to this process is the determination of whether the problem is normal, whether the problem is a central part of the man, how others will act if he seeks help, and what may be lost if he asks for help (2003). The conclusion drawn from this perspective suggests that "a man is least likely to seek help for problems that he sees as unusual, especially when he also sees them as central to his identity. He is also unlikely to seek help if groups of men who are important to him endorse norms of self-reliance or other norms that suggest his problem is non-normative (2003)."

According to Burcar (2013), "a general victim discourse underlines the importance of notifying the police while hegemonic masculinity discourse emphasizes being strong, not backing down, and being able to sort things out by oneself." Balancing the two discourses may lead to psychological distress until the abuse is either resolved or accepted. In lieu of reporting, the literature indicates that men may tend to normalize the abuse (Migliaccio, 2002), minimize the severity of the abuse (Kury, OberfellFuchs and Wurger, 2000, cited in Allen-Collinson, 2009, p. 29), experience guilt about contribution to the conflict (Erez, 2002), and avoid talking about the abuse (Vogel and Wester, 2003, cited in Lindinger-Sternart, 2014) in order to avoid experiencing painful emotions associated with the violence (Komiya et.al, 2000, cited in Lindinger-Sternart, 2014). Javaid (2016) referencing his prior research noted that "men may conceal their emotions, fragility or psychological pain so as to maintain their hegemonic masculinity." When a man's response to intimate partner violence converges with society's notion of who can legitimately claim a status of victimization, then he must be prepared to navigate the criminal justice system, an institution that is constructed to reflect the values and beliefs of the dominant society.

NAVIGATING THE SYSTEM

"Understanding how gender and victimization operate at the institutional level is critical in understanding how men talk about their victimization" (Durfee, 2011). Continued consideration of intimate partner violence as male-perpetrated abuse against a female victim leads to further victimization of males through societal institutions, such as the criminal justice system (Hogan, Hegarty, Ward, and Dodd, 2012). Within these systems set up to support female victims of intimate partner violence, bias is institutionalized in the infrastructure (Basile, 2005). Stigmatization and discrimination against male victims may come from external sources by way of individual beliefs or social paradigms which manifest in institutional infrastructure as well as from the men themselves as they construct a definition which characterizes their own experience of victimization (Tsui, Cheung, and Leung, 2010, p. 777).

The criminal justice community did not in the past and in many cases does not embrace the notion of the victimization of males through intimate partner violence. As a result of the community's hesitance to accept that men can be victimized, criminal law has been less than effective in legitimizing claims from males. Further, "Men are not likely to seek help for problems that their larger community deems non-normative or determines that they should have been able to solve or control themselves" (Addis and Mahalik, 2003).

How men present at the time they make contact with a member of law enforcement or an officer of the court can be a determining factor in how they are received when asserting a claim of victimization. If men do not present in a manner that reflects hegemonic ideals, their claim of victimization may be invalidated (Durfee, 2011) or received with disbelief, insensitivity, or even hostility (Allen-Collinson, 2009, p. 35, citing Macchietto, J., 1992). A man must be able to clearly and concisely articulate that he has been victimized. Articulating the victimization may be a major challenge for men because they may see complaining about being abused as a major personal weakness (Tsui, Cheung, and Leung, 2010, p. 777) and believe labeling their experience as abuse evidences a failure of their masculinity (Artime, 2014).

In framing their conceptualization of victimhood, men often encounter problems because what they are attempting to make meaning of is not codified in state and federal law. Goodmark (2011) notes that the criminal statutes are consistent in that intimate partner violence is usually inclusive of physical violence and threats of physical violence. Although men experience physical violence as well as other forms of abuse, the most prevalent type of abuse experienced by men is psychological followed by physical and economic abuse (Tsui, 2014). Typically, forms of violence such as psychological and emotional abuse in isolation are not considered criminal and, therefore, are not actionable under the law.

Psychological abuse includes mental, verbal, and emotional violence, the effects of which are less visible and may not be readily identifiable. This is significant for males because these forms of abuse may be as or more debilitating than physical violence (Goodmark, 2011). And, the effects may manifest in other ways, such as alcoholism and suicidality (Kumar, 2012). Additionally, a claim of intimate partner violence may be further complicated because social perceptions about the severity of intimate partner violence are affected by gender stereotypes and gender norms (Dutton and White, 2013, cited in Machado, Santos, Graham-Kevan, and Matos, 2017, p. 514). When a claim of victimization is made, whether consciously or unconsciously, agents of the criminal justice system weigh the type as well as the severity of the abuse experienced.

INTERSECTION OF MASCULINITY, RACE, VICTIMHOOD, AND LAW

Abuse and violence against a male by his intimate partner must be contemplated as an event or pattern of events influenced by the intersectionality of masculinity, race, victimhood, and the law. When a man asserts a claim that he has been victimized, the efficacy of the legal process hinges upon the agents' as well as the victim's understanding of this intersectionality. Each of the aforementioned factors on its own has significant implications for a male who has experienced intimate partner violence. However, when the factors coalesce, further harm and possible revictimization are nearly inevitable.

Rentoul and Appleboom (1997, cited in Cheung, Leung, and Tsui, 2009, p. 448) state that men experience dissonance as they attempt to reconcile their masculine identity with the experience of being victimized. This dissonance is pervasive among male victims who seek help. Most likely, men wrestle with masculinity and victimhood because their endorsement of masculine norms increases their reluctance to see themselves as victims (Cheung et al., 2009; Tsui et al., 2010). "The traditional male gender role schema has no place for the experience of being a male abuse victim" (Gold and Pitariu, 2004, p. 184). In fact, Burcar (2013) notes that "being a victim is the antithesis of masculinity" (p. 172, citing Sundaram et al., 2004). Likewise, Burcar and Akerstrom (2009) note that men and victims are two culturally conflicting categories. Javaid (2016, p. 734, citing Connell, 2005) further addresses the issue by stating that a man cannot be both powerful and helpless at the same time because he would not be able to achieve the ideal of hegemonic masculinity. Hegemonic masculinity is believed to be counterintuitive to victimhood, and when taken together, the two are considered an unacceptable combination (George, 1994).

The criminal justice system is not exempt from the influence of masculinity, victimhood, and race. Muller, Desmarais, and Hamel (2009, p. 626, citing Dutton and Nicholls, 2005) state that a gender paradigm has shaped policy on arrest as well as treatment and victim services for several decades. How the gender paradigm shapes policy on arrest is evidenced in the victim's initial contact with the criminal justice system. For example, a police officer is often the first point of contact for individuals seeking to file a report or claim of victimization. Hester (2012, p. 1068, citing Hester, 2010) notes that an officer's response may be guided by meanings attributed to and expectations associated with gender. Further, the officer's behavior may be associated with stereotypes about perpetrators of crime.

The interfacing of masculinity, victimhood, and the law is further complicated when the male victim is a person of color. Stereotypes about men of color increase the likelihood of them being perceived as perpetrators of intimate partner violence (Lacy, 2008, cited in MacDowell, 2013, p. 548) rather than as victims. Specifically, African American males are often stereotyped as violent, aggressive, and angry (Powell, 2008), traits which are more often assigned to a perpetrator rather than a victim.

Additionally, African American men are more often regarded as perpetrators of criminal offenses because a significant number of them have a criminal history, or are under the supervision of the criminal justice system. According to Goodmark (2017, p. 68, citing Clear and Frost, 2014), one in eleven African American men are being monitored in some form through the criminal justice system, either through imprisonment, probation, parole, or other correctional supervision. Since perceptions of criminality are often associated with race, men of color frequently encounter barriers that are not a part of a Caucasian male's victimization experience. Racism, whether actual or perceived, is a reality most men of color must confront when they engage with the criminal justice system, regardless of their status as a victim or a perpetrator. In addition to the perceptions of criminality, African American men who experience intimate partner violence may encounter challenges because they are expected to conform with the hegemonic ideals which are typically associated with Caucasian males while also adhering to culturally specific ideals of what it means to be a man. The cultural realities of African American men augment traditional hegemonic notions and offer a broader scope of how masculinity can be understood (Hammond and Mattis, 2005).

Griffith and Cornish (2018, p. 79, citing Hunter and Davis, 1992) note that an important factor in defining manhood for African American men is their relationship with others. In a subsequent study, Hammond and Mattis (2005) note similar findings. Later, Hunter and Davis (1994) provide additional context to the understanding of how African American men define masculinity by relating that central to the construction of manhood are issues of identity and self-development. Since relationships, identity, and self-development are thought to define the essence of an African American male, if he experiences intimate partner violence, his decision of whether to assert a claim may be more burdensome than that of other males because of the conflict that exists between balancing his thoughts about masculinity and his connectedness to significant others against his contemplation of filing a claim.

A constructive response of the criminal justice system as well as society at large is imperative for the overall well-being of a man who is affected by intimate partner violence. The quality of a man's experience when seeking help is thought to have lasting effects on his mental health, and may be instrumental in staving off such issues as post-traumatic stress disorder, alcohol abuse (Douglas and Hines, 2011), depression, suicidal ideation, and psychosomatic symptoms (Machado et al., 2016). Acknowledgment of the potential lasting effects is crucial because it is well documented that society scripts traditional gender role messages which may lead men to disown their own emotions in order to appear tough and competent (Gold and Pitariu, 2004). Ignoring or minimizing feelings and emotions can lead to additional negative experiences for the African American male victim. A study conducted by Rose et al. 2000 (cited in Cheatham et al., 2008, p. 557) revealed that African American male participants reported feeling like they should be able to handle anything and worried about feeling weak or less of a man when they encountered a problem they perceived was beyond their ability to resolve. The participants' belief that they could handle anything likely resulted in restricted emotionality and self-reliance, both of which are associated with an increased rate of suicide among African American males (Lindinger-Sternart, 2014).

Men are revictimized when their experiences are not validated (Morgan and Wells, 2016). In order to validate the victimization experiences of men, actors within the criminal justice system need a keen understanding of hegemonic masculine ideals and victimhood. If men who experience intimate partner violence are not viewed by society as victims, this denial of status is likely to influence the type of service they receive (Javaid, 2016), as well as reinforce the invisibility that currently exists (Artime, 2014). Men must acknowledge victimization, or the pervasiveness of the issue among males will remain hidden (Artime, 2014).

CONCLUSIONS AND IMPLICATIONS FOR SOCIAL WORK AND LEGAL PRACTICE

Attorneys, judges, social workers, policy makers, and others who interact with the courts on a routine basis are able to directly influence the experiences of males affected by intimate partner violence. A primary mechanism for effecting change is through advocacy and activism. The law has long been responsive to activism and advocacy, and these efforts have been fundamental to the criminal justice system's response to women affected by intimate partner violence. Raising awareness about how men are affected by intimate partner violence will increase information about the prevalence of this issue and quash any myths about who is or can be victimized. Increased visibility of the issue can be achieved through a social movement evidenced through targeted mass media campaigns, professional research, and education (Lucal and Betsy, 1992). Lastly, change can be instituted by reframing and redefining masculinity and victimhood, or at least conceptualizing the discourses of masculinity and victimhood in a way that is more fluid, and also by implementing more intentional strategies which will resort in a meaningful departure from gender norms. These efforts are likely to garner the attention of policy makers and directly impact the current criminal justice system's response to intimate partner violence.

CHAPTER 13

A COMPREHENSIVE, PSYCHOEDUCATIONAL, THERAPEUTIC SOCIAL WORK RESPONSE

DR. IRMA J. GIBSON

Intimate partner violence (IPV) is a serious, preventable public health problem that affects millions of Americans. The term "intimate partner violence" describes physical, sexual, or psychological harm by a current or former partner or spouse. This type of violence can occur among heterosexual or same-sex couples and does not require sexual intimacy (Frieden, 2014). Data in the prior chapters has consistently confirmed that the signs and the symptoms can be recognized early. In fact, the Centers for Disease Control data indicates IPV starts early in the lifespan. And data from the National Intimate Partner and Sexual Violence Survey (NISVS) demonstrate that IPV often begins in adolescence. An estimated 8.5 million women in the US (7 percent) and over 4 million men (4 percent) reported experiencing physical violence, rape (or being made to penetrate someone else), or stalking from an intimate partner in their lifetime and indicated they first experienced these or other forms of violence by that partner before the age of eighteen (Smith et al., 2017). Furthermore, research indicates IPV is most prevalent in adolescence and young adulthood and then begins to decline at age twenty-three, demonstrating the critical importance of early prevention efforts. This data, as well as the research data presented in previous chapters, consistently point to the individual subjects and their environment in determining cause and effect. As I proceed to address these critical factors and the best practices that have demonstrated evidence-based progress of mitigating this public health issue, I want to educate the reader about the uniqueness of the social work response and why it is a crucial component to positively change these dismal statistics.

THE SOCIAL WORK RESPONSE: A PROMISING AVENUE FOR CHANGE

The primary mission of the social work profession is to enhance human well-being and help meet basic and complex needs of all people, with a particular focus on those who are vulnerable, oppressed, or living in poverty. Social work is different from other professions, because we focus both on the persons and their environment. Social workers deal with the external factors that impact a person's situation and outlook, and we create opportunities for assessment and intervention to help clients and communities cope effectively with their reality, and change of that reality when necessary. Social workers help clients deal not only with how they feel about a situation, but also with what they can do about it (NASW, n.d.).

Additionally, the social work generalist program curriculum is designed to equip students with the skill set to be practitioners who view problems holistically and are prepared to plan interventions aimed at multiple levels of systems related to client concerns. A holistic approach considers multiple dimensions of human functioning, such as biological, social, and psychological factors, among others. Client goals and needs specifically suggest appropriate interventions, rather than letting interventions inspire the selection of compatible client goals. In other words, social workers base their interventions on findings from the assessment rather than fitting clients into intervention models regardless of identified problems and goals (Kirst-Ashman et al., 2015). In short, we avoid the cookie-cutter approach and treat each case uniquely.

We strategically remain cognizant of the fact that the client problems are also influenced by factors that exist in the micro, mezzo, and macro systems, including individual relationships, relationships with organizations and groups, and social norms or larger policies that affect clients' everyday lives. More recently, the strengths perspective and social justice have become enduring elements in social work practice (Gasker and Fischer, 2014; Saleebey, 2013).

In the classroom, the focus is on foundational knowledge, which includes understanding the interaction between the biological, psychological, social, cultural, and spiritual aspects of human development and the impact on human functioning to include an understanding of the helping process. Foundational social work skills include interviewing, assessing, and intervening in problematic interactions involving individuals, couples, families, and groups.

Our professional comprehension and strategic interventions are also strongly aligned with theories. Theories are generalized sets of ideas that describe and explain our knowledge of the world in an organized way. They help us understand and contest ideas and the world around us, offer a framework for practice, and help us to be accountable, self-disciplined, and professional (Payne, 2014, p. 3). Theories are overall explanations of the person-in-environment, as we are all products of our environment, from birth to present. The growing use and support of these evidence-based best practices suggest that social work practices must be informed by results derived from the scientific method, including both quantitative and qualitative designs. Findings from social work practice are used to inform research through organizational or government reports and publications of scholarly work, such as this book. Chapter 10 introduced you to the Boomerang Effect, which is one theoretical explanation about the dynamics of IPV. Within the following content, I introduce you to additional research/evidence-based frameworks that provide additional clarity about the risk factors that contribute to the IPV epidemic. The nature versus nurture theoretical framework is the first. It raises another crucial perspective about IPV, the perpetrators, and the victims, and supports the suggested prevention strategies proposed by the CDC.

THE NATURE VERSUS NURTURE THEORETICAL FRAMEWORK

The nature versus nurture theoretical debate is about the relative influence of an individual's innate attributes as opposed to the experiences from the environment one is brought up in, in determining individual differences in physical and behavioral traits. In layman's terms, it states we are all born with certain genetic traits that shape who we are from birth to the present, including but not limited to our personality, our mannerisms, our drive, and our physical appearance. Sir Francis Galton argued that intelligence and character traits come from hereditary factors and was in clear opposition to earlier scholars such as philosopher John Locke, who is well known for the theory that children are born a "blank slate," with their traits developing completely from experience and learning. Both gentlemen shared the view that the environment and a person's unique experiences, i.e. nurture, were the prevailing forces in development (Rettew, 2017). Thus, the environment to which we are exposed and projected as we progress throughout our lifespan provides opportunities to learn, grow, mature, and change accordingly. Through these experiences and via this exposure to a plethora of negative and positive encounters, risk and protective factors emerge and saturate the environment daily beginning from birth.

ENVIRONMENTAL (NURTURE) RISK AND PROTECTIVE FACTORS THAT IMPACT INTIMATE PARTNER VIOLENCE

Intimate partner violence is associated with several risk and protective factors. In fact, research indicates a number of factors increase risk for perpetration and victimization of IPV. The risk and protective factors discussed thus far focus on the risks for IPV perpetration, although many of the same risk factors are also relevant for victimization (Capaldi et al., 2012; Stith et al., 2004). Factors that put individuals at risk for perpetrating IPV include but are not limited to demographic factors such as age (adolescence and young adulthood), low income, low educational attainment, and unemployment; childhood history factors such as exposure to violence between parents, experiencing poor parenting, and experiencing child abuse and neglect, including sexual violence, are also significant.

Other individual factors that put people at risk for perpetrating IPV include factors such as stress, anxiety, and antisocial personality traits; attitudinal risk factors, such as attitudes condoning violence in relationships and belief in strict gender roles; and other behavioral risk factors, such as prior perpetration and victimization of IPV or other forms of aggression, such as peer violence, a history of substance abuse, a history of delinquency, and hostile communication styles (Capaldi et al., 2012; Stith et al., 2004; Vagi et al., 2013; CDCPa, 2016). Relationship-level factors include hostility or conflict in the relationship, separation/ending of the relationship (e.g. break-ups, divorce/separation), aversive family communication and relationships, and having friends who perpetrate/experience IPV (Vagi et al., 2013; CDCPa, 2016).

Although less studied than factors at other levels of the social ecology, community or societal level, other factors include poverty, low social capital, low collective efficacy in neighborhoods (e.g. low willingness of neighbors to intervene when they see violence) (Smith, 2008), and harmful gender norms in societies (i.e. beliefs and expectations about the roles and behavior of men and women) (Reyes et al., 2016; CDCPa, 2016). Additionally, a few protective factors have been identified that are associated with lower chances of perpetrating or experiencing teen dating violence (TDV), which is a precursor to IPV. These include high empathy, good grades, high verbal IQ, *a positive relationship with one's mother*, and attachment to school (Vagi et al., 2013). Less is known about protective factors at the community and societal level, but research is emerging indicating environmental factors such as lower alcohol outlet density (Kearns et al., 2015) and community norms that are intolerant of IPV (Browning, 2002) may be protective against IPV. Although more research is needed, there is some evidence suggesting increased economic opportunity and housing security may also be protective against IPV (Pronyk et al., 2006; Matjasko, 2013; Baker et al., 2010).

OTHER FORMS OF VIOLENCE WITHIN THE ENVIRONMENT AND THEIR CONNECTION TO INTIMATE PARTNER VIOLENCE

Intimate partner violence is connected to many other forms of violence as well, and experience with these other forms of violence puts people at risk for perpetrating and experiencing IPV. Children who are exposed to IPV between their parents or caregivers are more likely to perpetrate or experience IPV, as are individuals who experience abuse and neglect as children (Capaldi et al., 2012; Vagi et al., 2013; Temple et al., 2013). Additionally, adolescents who engage in bullying or peer violence are more likely to perpetrate IPV (Vagi et al., 2013; Niolon et al., 2015). Empirical studies about IPV have shown how complex and impactful this public health nuisance is in an environment plagued by violence, which is a risk factor that targets not only perpetrators but also victims. In fact, those who experience sexual violence and emotional abuse are more likely to be victims of physical IPV (Stith et al., 2004). Research also suggests IPV may increase risk for suicide in victims. Both boys and girls who experience TDV are also at greater risk for suicidal ideation (Exner-Cortens et al., 2013; Silverman, 2001). Women exposed to partner violence are nearly five times more likely to attempt suicide as women not exposed to partner violence (WHO, 2013). Intimate partner problems, which include IPV, were also found to be a precipitating factor for suicide among men in a review of violent death records from seven US states (Schiff et al., 2015). Research also shows that experience with IPV (either perpetration or victimization) puts people at higher risk for experiencing IPV in the future (Exner-Cortens et al., 2017; Capaldi et al., 2012; Vagi et al., 2013).

What is noteworthy is the different forms of violence often share the same individual, relationship, community, and societal risk factors (Wilkins et al., 2014). *The interconnections between the different forms of violence suggest multiple opportunities for prevention* (CDCPb, 2016). Many of the strategies addressed include example programs and policies that have demonstrated impacts on other forms of violence, as reflected in the CDC's other data for prevention of child abuse and neglect, sexual violence, youth violence, and suicide (Fortsen, et al., 2016; Basile et al., 2016; David-Ferdon et al., 2016; Cooper and Smith, 2011). Recognizing and addressing these interconnections will help us better prevent all forms of violence. However, prevention has to focus on interventions during the early phase of the lifespan. "Children are like wet cement. Whatever falls on them makes an impression" (Haim Ginott, as cited in NYARCP, 2011). Additional theories of importance that align with the CDC's prevention strategies are presented in the next section.

CRUCIAL THEORETICAL FRAMEWORKS: THE ECOLOGICAL SYSTEM'S THEORY AND ERICK ERIKSON'S STAGES OF PSYCHOSOCIAL DEVELOPMENT

Bronfenbrenner's ecological systems theory views an individual's development within the context of the system of relationships that form his/her environment. Bronfenbrenner's theory has been historically applied to child development. By defining complex layers of environment, each having an effect on children's development, this theory emphasizes that children's interaction between factors in their maturing biology, their immediate family/community environment, and the societal landscape fuels and steers their development. Furthermore, changes or conflict in any one layer will ripple throughout other layers. To study a child's development, then, we must look not only at the child and his/her immediate environment, but also at the interaction of the larger environment (Kuna, 2014).

These system transactions consist of lifestyle and philosophy of life factors such as heredity, life experiences, and environmental influences (nature vs. nurture). "All behavior has heritable components and all behavior is the joint product of heredity and environment, but differences in behavior can be apportioned between differences in hereditary and environment" (Wine, 2000, para. 4). Understanding the above dynamics and how these factors affect day-to day functioning, including how one survives and gets along with others as well as contemplation of feelings of self-worth and inadequacy, are critical to these systematic transactions.

Erikson's psychosocial theory of development offers another model for understanding socialization and learned behaviors. In each stage, there are influences or agents of socialization that have an impact on the child and the messages of socialization they receive. These factors were alluded to in prior chapters. This theory considers the impact of external factors, parents, and society on personality development from childhood to adulthood. According to Erikson's theory, every person must pass through a series of eight interrelated stages over the entire life cycle. Up until the fifth stage (12–18 years, identity vs. role confusion), development depends on what is done to a person. At this point, development now depends primarily upon what a person does. An adolescent must struggle to discover and find his or her own identity, while negotiating and struggling with social interactions and "fitting in," as well as developing a sense of morality. Erikson believed much of life is preparing for the middle adulthood stage (seventh), and the last (eighth) stage involves much reflection. As older adults, some can look back with a feeling of integrity (contentment and fulfillment), having led a meaningful life and provided a valuable contribution to society. Others may have a sense of despair during this stage, reflecting upon their experiences and failures (Learning Theories, 2016).

From a theoretical stance, critical thinking emerges and raises some valid points about the origins of this extremely serious public health issue identified as intimate partner violence and the significance of the environmental and social learning context as an influential factor among the perpetrators and even the victims. How important are the factors pertaining to early-childhood development in determining why some perpetrate and why others become victims? Although there are always exceptions to the rule, Maslow's hierarchy of needs is another major piece of the puzzle in providing additional clarity about the environment in which we are born and exposed to throughout our human development. It is a crucial theoretical framework for supporting the hypothesis that the environment is a powerful factor in either deterring or promoting many of the ills of society, including IPV. However, the most significant connection/relationship is with the basic family (Learning Theories, 2016).

MASLOW'S HIERARCHY OF NEEDS

"Maslow's hierarchy of needs is a theory of motivation and personality developed by the psychologist Abraham H. Maslow (1908–1970). Maslow's hierarchy explains human behavior in terms of basic requirements for survival and growth. These requirements or needs are arranged according to their importance for survival and their power to motivate the individual. The most basic physical requirements, such as food, water, or oxygen, constitute the lowest level of the need hierarchy. Needs at the higher levels of the hierarchy are less oriented towards physical survival and more toward psychological well-being and growth. These needs have less power to motivate persons, and they are more influenced by formal education and life experiences. The resulting hierarchy of needs is often depicted as a pyramid, with physical survival needs located at the base of the pyramid and needs for self-actualization located at the top"(Krapp, 2010). Every person is capable and has the desire to move up the hierarchy toward a level of self-actualization. Unfortunately, progress is often disrupted by failure to meet lower-level needs (McLeod, 2016). The following chart (Krapp, 2010) exhibits what is needed according to Maslow to eventually and developmentally reach self-actualization throughout the lifespan: physiological needs to include food, water, shelter, and clothing; security and safety needs provided by family and society; love and belonging to give and receive love, appreciation, and friendship; self-esteem needs, i.e. self-respect and individuality; and self-actualization, to include experiencing purpose, meaning, and realizing all inner potential.

Figure 6. Maslow's Hierarchy of Needs

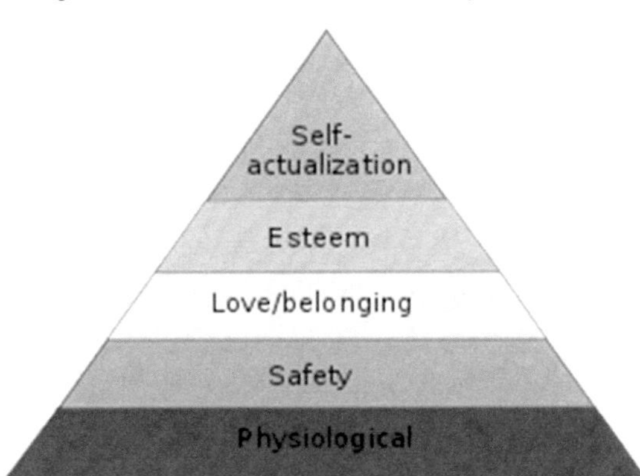

As the importance of a stable family foundation is addressed, a crucial point is studies have shown that "children who do not get the early intervention, permanence and stability they need are more likely to act out and fail in school because they lack the skills necessary to succeed. Researchers of early childhood emphasize the importance of early childhood nurturing and stimulation to help the brain grow, *especially between birth and age seven*, and even beyond and thus help children to thrive and to be on a positive path toward successful adulthood. The importance of stimulation in the first years of life is dramatically underlined in the U.S. Department of Education's study of 22,000 kindergartners in the kindergarten class of 1998–99, which found that Black and Hispanic children were substantially behind when they entered kindergarten" (Children's Defense Fund, 2008). Theoretically speaking, this is a crucial factor in regard to IPV and the family connection.

In layman's terms, thousands of children in the child welfare system are already considered at risk of failing to reach self-actualization and become productive citizens of society as early as zero to seven years of age. Thousands more are not in the child welfare system, but nevertheless join the ranks and fail to have their basic human needs met as a result of the impact of poverty on their lives. Particularly with young children, their needs cannot be satisfied without a relationship with another person. The cradle-to-prison pipeline quotes Chief Judge Patricia Clark of the Juvenile Division of King County Superior Court, Seattle, Washington, as saying: "The United States of America does not value and protect all of its children equally or ensure them the basic hope, health care, safety, education and family supports all children need to envisage and achieve a productive future." The statistics paint a disturbing but accurate picture about the state of child and family welfare and its prognosis. It is no secret that the basic needs of many of our children and youth are not met. Primary and secondary intervention methods are desperately needed for effective change. Until these ideas are embraced, the state of child and family welfare will remain in crisis, and the ripple effect includes the impact of and the connection to IPV.

SOCIALIZATION, THE SOCIAL LEARNING THEORY, AND INTIMATE PARTNER VIOLENCE

One of a society's most important functions is the socialization of children. From birth, individuals are socialized via the main agents of socialization: family, school, peers, media, social media, religion, and employers. While school, peers, and the media belong under the primary socialization category, the workplace and the government are secondary means of socialization that are also considered specialized statutes as we move through our life course. "Socialization is the process of learning over time how to function in a group or society. It is a set of paradigms, rules, procedures and principles that govern perception, attention, choices, learning and development" (Doff, 1982, as cited in AECT, 2001). This socialization is based upon race, ethnicity, class, religious preference, and region.

According to Macionis (2009), socialization is a process by which the cultural heritage of a society is transmitted to the next generation. Crucial to the socialization of children are family, school, peers, and the media. For young children in most societies, the family is the primary world for the first few years of life. From infancy, families transmit cultural social values and are the primary source of emotional support and social position. Unfortunately and to the detriment of many innocent children, the wobbly foundation (socialization) established during those crucial first seven years of life serves as a precursor to what could be a tumultuous future that impacts every facet of the lifespan, including adolescence and young adulthood. Although family has been slated as the most influential among these socialization agents, twenty-first-century technology appears to be changing the dynamics of the equation via increased exposure to the media. Gone are the days when wandering eyes and inquiring minds were met with a rendition of the Star-Spangled Banner, the flying of Old Glory, and the static from the television network's end-of-the-day broadcasting signal. It's definitely a new day. Reality television, as discussed in chapter 6, is listed under this category and is a case in point. Many social critics claim today's youth face more serious and critical risks than any previous generation, and parents are convinced their children face a major crisis. In recent years, attention has increasingly focused on issues such as youth crime and violence, substance abuse, gangs, school dropouts, academic performance, and other issues associated with "at-risk youth." In fact, most experts will agree that violence in schools, deteriorating family structure, substance abuse, alarming media images, and gang activity put teens at risk. This analysis is consistent with research regarding the main agents of socialization and the significance of each in all of our lives from birth to present.

The social learning theory and social-cognitive models address how individuals come to imitate behavior observed in the media and develop mental "primes" and "scripts" from material viewed on television, which can then guide their later behavior. These theoretical models also address the ways in which exposure to violent material (acts and behaviors) can lead to people becoming desensitized to violence and disinhibited from behaving aggressively (Bastian et al., 2013). Regardless of the settings, not only is imitation the highest form of flattery, but it appears that the lack of self-examination and fragile emotions may play a crucial part in the overall decision to do so.

This specific study about the social learning theoretical framework formally introduces the essence of and the main theoretical component of this policy/practice analysis. Perhaps the most widely accepted account of the way in which family and televised content affect the attitudes and behaviors of the developing child is Bandura's social learning theory (Bandura, 1971, 1986, as cited in Bastian et al., 2013). According to Albert Bandura (1976), the originator of what has become perhaps the most prominent theory of learning and human development, "Most human behavior is learned observationally through modeling: from observing others one forms an idea of how new behaviors are performed, and on later occasions this coded information serves as a guide for action. He indicated that learning can occur simply by observing the actions of others."

Bandura also argued that people learn behavioral responses such as aggression either by direct experience, in which their own aggressive behavior is reinforced, or by observing that such behavior brings rewards to others (that is, through vicarious reinforcement). Further, media characters along with parents, peers, and others are the sources that provide the text for modelling specific attitudes and behaviors, and attitudes and behaviors learned at a young age through habitual exposure to such models are argued to be relatively resistant to change (Bastian et al., 2013).

The point is that family is a crucial aspect of socialization, and family socialization begins a process through which humans learn to be the adult persons they become. For some, the effects of family socialization are evident and long lasting; for others, there is not much obvious effect; and for still others, it looks like there's no relationship at all. With scrutiny, one can observe that some adults choose to adopt behaviors and values that are completely opposite from those of their families. The socialization is just as strong, but it has a different effect. For some adults, their interactions with family continue in such a close relationship that the family maintains a dominant role in their ongoing socialization (Driscoll and Nagel, 2008).

IMPLICATIONS FOR SOCIAL WORK

The years between six and fourteen—middle childhood and early adolescence—are a time of important developmental advances that establish children's sense of identity. During these years, children make strides toward adulthood by becoming competent, independent, self-aware, and involved in the world beyond their families. Biological and cognitive changes transform children's bodies and minds. Social relationships and roles change dramatically as children enter school, join programs, and become involved with peers and adults outside their families. During middle childhood, children develop a sense of self-esteem and individuality, comparing themselves with their peers. They come to expect they will succeed or fail at different tasks. They may develop an orientation toward achievement that will color their response to school and other challenges for many years. *In early adolescence, the tumultuous physical and social changes that accompany puberty, the desire for autonomy and distance from the family, and the transition from elementary school to middle school or junior high can all cause problems for young people* (Eccles, 1999). Please keep in mind the facts that were introduced in chapter 7, when the authors presented the research indicating the age when problems with bullying are identified, as early as elementary school. Bullying is a precursor to teen dating violence and intimate partner violence. What is occurring emotionally, socially, and mentally as early as primary and elementary school is crucial, as the following factors indicate. The emotional-social learning component is significant and will be critical in developing interventions that effectively address the prevention of IPV.

Three key forces combine to influence children's self-confidence and engagement in tasks and activities during the middle childhood years: (1) cognitive changes that heighten children's ability to reflect on their own successes and failures; (2) a broadening of children's worlds to encompass peers, adults, and activities outside the family; and (3) exposure to social comparison and competition in school classrooms and peer groups. Middle childhood gives children the opportunity to develop competencies and interests in a wide array of domains. For most children this is a positive period of growth: with the right kinds of experiences, they develop a healthy sense of industry and a confidence that they can master and control their worlds (Eccles, 1999). The Children's Defense Fund (2008) reports that seven million youngsters—one in four adolescents—have only limited potential for becoming productive adults because they are at high risk for encountering serious problems at home, in school, or in their communities. This is one of the disturbing findings in what is known about young people aged ten to seventeen growing up in the United States today.

And research has consistently shown that teenagers who have trouble coping with the stresses of life are more likely to abuse drugs and alcohol, engage in criminal activity and haphazard sexual behaviors, and experience emotional instability. Many of these at-risk teens become runaways and eventually find themselves locked up in detention centers or homeless (Gottesman and Schwarz, 2011). Considering the world as it exists today, all youth are at risk. These challenges are experienced by young people globally. They are exposed to ever-increasing violence, sex, drugs, and alcohol to a much larger degree than in the past through peer experiences, communities, and the media, as well as their families. What today's youth have to cope with on a daily basis is mind boggling. This is why it is crucial their human growth and development essentials are addressed specifically utilizing Maslow's theory of hierarchical needs relative to their age and life situation to motivate them toward social goals.

Life experiences including neglect, abuse, trauma, divorce, losses, and other significant issues can cause an individual to fluctuate between levels of the hierarchy. Reflect on the bearing of these and other factors to children and youth in their most impressionable years, zero to eight, and beyond. An unstable and unhealthy foundation can result in adjustment problems and issues across the lifespan if sufficient mental and emotional support mechanisms are not implemented. Perpetrators and victims of intimate partner violence and social aggression are products of their environments and deserve to be assessed and evaluated uniquely and as individuals. Thus, it is necessary to eliminate the "cookie-cutter" approach to assisting this population and utilize psychological evaluations to pinpoint the origin of the problem. "Many psychologists agree that to design effective bullying-prevention and intervention programs, they need to understand that a child's tendency toward bullying is influenced by individual, familial and environmental factors" (Crawford, 2002). "Our children are our only hope for the future, but we are their only hope for their present" (Zig Ziglar, as cited in NYARCP, 2011).

PREVENTION STRATEGIES

Collective collaborations with families (traditional and nontraditional), guardians, teachers, social workers, counselors, and administrators, and partnerships with community agencies including child welfare agencies, law enforcement, and programs that address the root of the problems associated with IPV, beginning with our youth, are crucial to assisting this population from a primary prevention stance.

Numerous theories exist in the quest to explain human behavior; however, the theories that are addressed in this discussion add credence to the fact that the scope of the origin of bullying and aggression in children and youth that eventually lead and progress to other antisocial behaviors, such as TDV and IPV, must focus on the ecological influences in the perpetrator's environment, more specifically the influences with which they are impacted, whether directly or indirectly. "Efforts to both reduce violence and the effects of exposure to violence need to include individuals, families, school systems, communities, and public policy and legislation" (Thomas et al., 2012, p. 64). Ideally, primary prevention is preferable at the early phase of the lifespan; however, statistics and the evidence discussed in this book confirm that adult perpetrators are still in serious need of attention. Therefore, tertiary prevention is also and continues to be a necessity. The intervention model for adult perpetrators, which has been widely used and with mixed reactions, is the Duluth Model.

THE DULUTH MODEL OF INTERVENTION

Domestic Abuse Intervention Programs (DAIP) began in 1980 as an initiative to reform the criminal justice system in Duluth, Minnesota. At that time, victims of intimate partner violence had little recourse when being assaulted. Perpetrators were rarely arrested unless the assault happened in front of an officer or the injuries sustained by the victim were serious. Choices for victims were limited: initiate criminal justice charges, endure the abuse, or flee the relationship.

DAIP organizers—activists in the battered women's movement—set out to understand the laws, policies, and procedures of the criminal justice system, as well as understand the cultures of each of the involved agencies. In doing so, they built relationships that allowed new interventions to be proposed and tested. The results were strikingly effective in keeping batterers from continuing their abuse. Eventually, eleven community agencies agreed to continue to formally work together to continue to make positive change in the criminal justice system around battering. This effort became known as the Duluth Model. (Chapter 12 provides a more detailed analysis of the legal history of IPV and the response from the law and criminal justice aspect.)

According to Miller et al., 2013, the Duluth Model curriculum is one of a number of interventions that are common in the treatment of IPV offenders. This prominent clinical intervention employs a feminist psychoeducational approach and proposes that the principal cause of intimate partner violence is a social and cultural patriarchal ideology that historically has allowed men to control women through power and violence. Violence perpetrated on women and children originates from their relative positions of weakness and vulnerability socially, politically, economically, and culturally. As such, the curriculum acknowledges that there are often co-occurring issues like substance abuse and mental health concerns, but for cases that come to the attention of law enforcement, most involve men who are battering women. Issues such as anger, stress, or dysfunctional relationships don't tend to cause an ongoing pattern of coercion and violence with the intent to dominate an intimate partner. The Duluth Model curriculum is considered less of a therapy and more of a psychoeducational program for IPV perpetrators. This educational process focuses on providing a process where men gain a critical understanding of how they are socially constructed to believe they have a right to dominate their female intimate partner and punish her for not submitting to their demands. Despite this factor, Babcock and colleagues (2004) found that the Duluth intervention demonstrates a significant positive effect on recidivism.

The Domestic Abuse Intervention Program's Men's Nonviolence Program uses the "Power and Control Wheel" as the framework to understand patterns of abusive behavior, including acts and threats of physical and sexual violence. These behaviors are used by the abuser to control IPV victims. The wheels include the following eight items that are significant to the cognitive-behavioral psychoeducation interventions (PIE).

Figure 7. Violence versus Nonviolence

(1) intimidation	(1) negotiation and fairness
(2) emotional abuse	(2) economic partnership
(3) isolation	(3) shared responsibility
(4) economic abuse	(4) responsible parenting
(5) male privilege	(5) honesty and accountability
(6) coercion and threats	(6) trust and support
(7) using children	(7) respect
(8) minimizing, denying, and blaming	(8) nonthreatening behavior
The wheel was designed by advocates and women who were battered, so they could show the system of tactics and violence that gives the perpetrator power and control over the victim.	**These are seen as the foundations for a strong and egalitarian relationship. The aim of the intervention is to expose men to using nonviolent actions, intents, beliefs, and effects that support the "Equality Wheel."**

"It is important to note that despite some clear differences in underlying treatment targets and methods, both Duluth Model interventions and more traditional Cognitive-Behavioral Therapy (CBT) programs for IPV are often labeled as 'cognitive behavioral,' and some scholars suggest that they both pursue the ultimate goal of violence reduction via modification of cognitive processes" (Gardner et al., 2016; Smedslund et al., 2007).

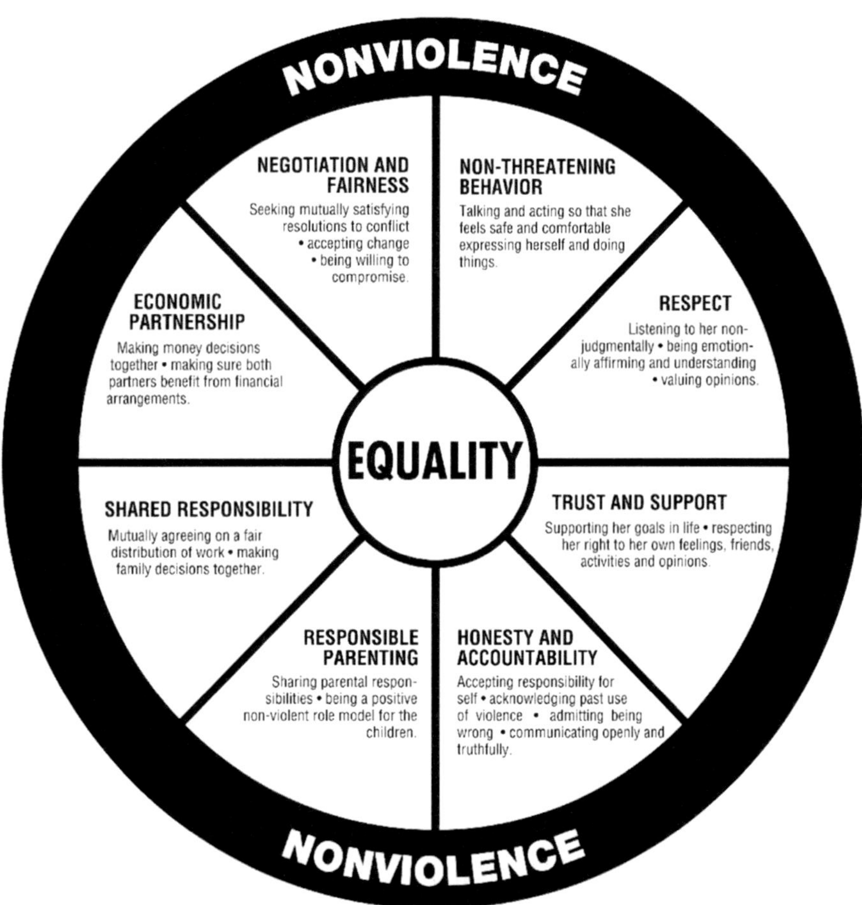

DOMESTIC ABUSE INTERVENTION PROGRAMS
202 East Superior Street
Duluth, Minnesota 55802
218-722-2781
www.theduluthmodel.org

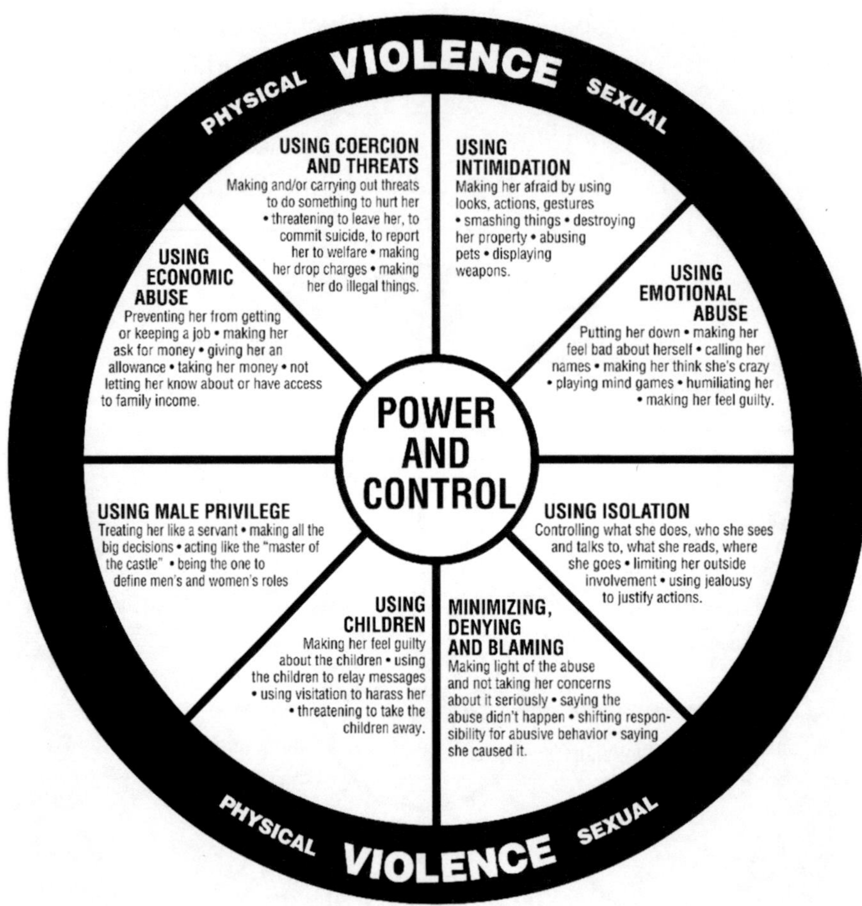

DOMESTIC ABUSE INTERVENTION PROGRAMS
202 East Superior Street
Duluth, Minnesota 55802
218-722-2781
www.theduluthmodel.org

Furthermore, investigators have long argued that the foundational Duluth Model constructs do not sufficiently attend to female-to-male IPV (Dutton and Corvo, 2006; Dutton and Nicholls, 2005; Felson, 2002; Straus, 2009). Additionally, it has been (wrongly) suggested that the Duluth Model's exclusive focus on patriarchal beliefs (a) continues despite limited empirical support (Dixon and Graham-Kevan, 2011; Dutton and Nicholls; Sugarman and Frankel, 1996), (b) fails to adequately consider and address a range of psychological issues and risk factors (e.g. exposure to abuse, problematic anger, emotional control, and other related variables) found in perpetrators of IPV, and (c) is a major obstacle to the development of more effective batterers' interventions (Dutton and Corvo, 2007). Thus, alternative IPV treatments to the Duluth Model have been introduced.

While the above model of intervention focuses on changing the mindset of batterers (specifically male perpetrators) with an eventual change in behavior, the overall answers are found in the ecological theoretical framework the CDC has strategically adopted. Its application transcends gender, age, and other cultural specifics and includes addressing the specific needs of all persons in the environment in response to IPV. Because the social work mission, philosophy, principles, and values are directly aligned with the CDC's evidence-based response to prevention and treatment of this public health nuisance, it places our response in a crucial position.

The Duluth Model has evolved and changed over the last thirty years and has spread across the globe. Although DAIP continues to work toward ending violence against women through its programs in Duluth and in partnership with IPV practitioners around the world, what is extremely noteworthy is the fact that empirical research suggests intimate partner violence has been falsely framed as exclusively male-initiated violence. The literature of one particular article concludes with a discussion of the similarities and differences between male and female IPV offenders and identifies areas where treatment for female offenders might be improved also. Additionally, as the literature on women as perpetrators of violence in their intimate relationships (i.e. domestically violent women) is becoming more common, the literature on intervention programs for these women is scant, although particular attention is paid to the cultural influences that shape our conceptualization of "intimate partner violence" (Carney, Butrell, and Dutton, 2007). The essence of this book is to bring attention to this issue and is on point in the effort to begin the quest to effectively address this problem on behalf of all victims, regardless of their gender, sexual preference, or sexual orientation.

THE CDC'S CONTEXTUAL AND CROSS-CUTTING THEMES

Just as the declaration of the social work ideology of addressing social and public health issues, the CDC's strategies and approaches for preventing IPV represent different levels of the social ecology, with efforts intended to impact individual behaviors and also the relationships, families, schools, and communities that influence risk and protective factors for IPV. These strategies and approaches are intended to work in combination and reinforce one another to prevent IPV. While individual skills are important and research has demonstrated preventive effects in reducing IPV, approaches addressing peer, family, school, and other environments as well as societal factors are equally important for a comprehensive approach that can have the greatest public health impact. The following is a list of the strategies and the approaches that have proven to be effective.

STRATEGY	APPROACH
Teach safe and healthy relationship skills	• Social-emotional learning programs for youth • Healthy relationship programs for couples
Engage influential adults and peers	• Men and boys as allies in prevention

	• Bystander empowerment and education • Family-based programs
Disrupt the developmental pathways toward partner violence	• Early-childhood home visitation • Preschool enrichment with family engagement • Parenting skill and family relationship programs • Treatment for at-risk children, youth, and families
Create protective environments	• Improve school climate and safety • Improve organizational policies and workplace climate • Modify the physical and social environments of neighborhoods
Strengthen economic supports for families	• Strengthen household financial security • Strengthen work-family supports
Support survivors to increase safety and lessen harms	• Victim-centered services • Housing programs • First responder and civil legal protections • Patient-centered approaches • Treatment and support for survivors of IPV, TDV

Intimate partner violence represents a significant public health issue that has considerable societal costs. Supporting the development of healthy, respectful, and nonviolent relationships has the potential to reduce the occurrence of IPV and prevent its harmful and long-lasting effects on individuals, families, and their communities. A variety of strategies and approaches can ideally be used in combination with a multilevel, multisector approach to preventing IPV. Consistent with the CDC's emphasis on the primary prevention of IPV, there are multiple strategies to stop perpetration of partner violence before it starts, in addition to approaches designed to support survivors and diminish the short- and long-term harms of IPV. The hope is that multiple sectors, such as public health, healthcare, education, business, justice, social services, IPV coalitions, and the many other organizations that comprise the civil society sector, will use the recommended model proposed by the CDC to prevent IPV and its consequences.

The strategies and approaches identified by the CDC represent the best available evidence to address the problem of IPV. It is based on research which suggests that the strategies and approaches described have a demonstrated impact on rates of IPV or on risk and protective factors for IPV. Although the evidence on what works to stop IPV is not as expansive as it is for other areas (e.g. youth violence), ongoing monitoring and evaluation of existing or newly developed strategies and approaches will create opportunities for building upon the current evidence. As new evidence emerges, it will be incorporated, disclosed, and used to inform and guide communities seeking to address the problem of IPV. Violence between intimate partners is a costly public health issue, but it is also preventable. Through continued research and evaluation of promising approaches for preventing IPV, we can strengthen our understanding of how to support healthy relationships between intimate partners and alleviate the burden of IPV to society as a whole (McCullom et al., 2008).

And while the ultimate goal is to model ideal behaviors in an effort to address violence and bullying before it begins, prevention requires an understanding of the factors that influence this public health annoyance. The intervention and strategies proposed by the CDC can be implemented in the early stages of child development and the lifespan. It uses a four-level social-ecological model to better understand violence and the effect of potential prevention strategies (CDC, n.d.). This model considers the complex interplay between individual, relationship, community, and societal factors (micro, mezzo, and macro factors). It allows for the risk factors that impact people who are experiencing or perpetrating violence to be addressed. Please note that children in the United States are more likely to be exposed to violence and crime than are adults (Finklehor, 2008). Additionally, the majority of US nonfatal intimate partner victimizations of women (two-thirds) occur at home, and children are residents of the households experiencing intimate partner violence in 43 percent of incidents involving female victims (USDJ, 2006). The statistics speak volumes about the effects on the youth, and the proof is in the pudding.

The individual level (micro) identifies biological and personal history factors that may perpetuate violence, including age, education, income, substance use, or history of abuse. The relationship level (mezzo) examines the influence of close peers, partners, and family members that might increase aggressive and violent behaviors. "The third level (macro), community, explores the settings, such as schools, workplaces, and neighborhoods, in which social relationships occur and seeks to identify the characteristics of these settings that are associated with becoming victims or perpetrators of violence" (CDC, n.d.). The final component focuses on societal factors (macro) that exacerbate and create a culture that is conducive to violence and includes social and cultural norms. Just as prevention strategies should include a continuum of activities that address multiple levels of the social-ecological model that are developmentally appropriate and conducted across the lifespan, pinpointing and focusing on the origin of the problem of bullying and aggression should also be a top priority—spoken in true social work language.

CHAPTER 14

CLOSING REFLECTIONS: A CALL TO ACTION

DR. IRMA J. GIBSON

And the truth shall make you free . . .

—John 8:32, KJV

Many children living in America in a time of "peace" are exposed to community conditions characteristic of a war zone, with commensurate psychological impacts. The spread of gun culture is a part of the children's "war zone" experience, and the experience of community violence occurs within a larger context of risk for most children. They often are poor, live in father-absent families, contend with parental incapacity due to depression or substance abuse, are raised by caretakers with little education or employment prospects, and as the literature has indicated, are exposed to intimate partner violence. In coping with the traumatic events of a "war zone," the child is forced into patterns of behavior, thought, and feelings that are themselves "abnormal" when contrasted with that of the untraumatized, healthy child. Children are particularly vulnerable to the trauma caused by threat and fear. Steps must be taken to intervene and change such exposure to violence and its devastating consequences (Garbarino, J. G., and Kostenly, K., 1997). And so as we strategize solutions to combat the crisis of intimate partner violence via the mass destruction of our violent culture, I challenge you with the following charge.

The plethora of information that has been presented in this book confirms that this public health epidemic is systemic, starts early within the lifespan, and is indeed a complicated travesty that warrants a different kind of attention. Although it is a common topic in the forefront of the media and the public, it usually generates attention only after the damage has been done. Yet some of us have become numb to the disturbing statistics broadcasted daily via the mass media. However, the goal is to stop IPV before it begins. And this can only be initiated with primary prevention measures instead of the secondary and tertiary approaches that are now prevalent. Perhaps avenues such as this book and other opportunities and forums to educate, teach, and impact change are a necessity. While there is a lot to learn about how to prevent IPV, we do know that strategies that promote the importance of healthy behaviors in relationships as well as programs that teach young people skills for dating can also prevent violence. These programs can stop violence in dating relationships before it occurs (Brieding et al., 2014). But how can we move forward with a realistic and promising strategy without an accurate and truthful working knowledge of the origins of the problem?

As a practitioner and an educator who has conducted numerous assessments that pertain to a diverse number of public health issues, the common theme that leads to a resolution and some type of relief is always an accurate diagnosis of the historical facts of the subjects in their environment across the lifespan. As the prior chapter specifically asserts via theoretical explanations, the environmental exposure on so many levels is crucial. And after being exposed to the many facets of child and family welfare, the saga and the shroud of confusion in regard to IPV and its devastating effects upon society, it starts to make more sense. First of all, social policy doesn't always match or support simple resolutions or early-stage interventions. Simply stated, policy doesn't match practice. Secondly, because of this misguided approach, the problems presented are misdiagnosed and inappropriately assessed, and the symptoms of these problems continue to be ineffectively addressed, thus resulting in a continuous failure to analyze the "roots." This is also where a part of the problem lies.

Ineffectively assessing the problem (not addressing the root) can result in ineffective treatment interventions. A simple analogy is this: Whenever gardeners (social workers, counselors, and other advocates) want to rid the harvest ("dysfunctional" family foundations and social relationships across the lifespan) of unwanted and problematic weeds (perpetrators, violence, symptoms of the problems, and other precursors), they treat the weeds from the visible tip to the root (the problems and the true barriers). If only the top and the surface of the weeds are treated, and the roots are left in place and unaddressed, chances are the weeds will return. So, instead of effectively treating the true problem in its entirety, only the top of the weeds (the symptoms associated with the problem) receive attention. So the cycle continues, until the root receives sufficient attention. Until the stakeholders (and that is every capable human being) in the fight against this ugly and relentless social ill begin the process of truly addressing the true origin of IPV, the services and programs provided will continue to remain insufficient and ineffective. Again, "Youth don't usually change because of programs, they change because of people" (Allen Mendler and Moe Bickweat, as cited in NYARCP, 2011).

The prior chapters are strategically saturated with the definitions of the various forms of IPV. As a result, each reader may be more prone to recognize it even in its most subtle form, including the mass media, which sometimes has a tendency to misguide and stereotype. According to the findings of Bastian et al. (2013), the role of media in modern life is indispensable, providing information, education, and entertainment. Due to the critical nature of this epidemic and the unfortunate alarming statistics that are evident of its wrath, factual information must be disseminated to avoid minimizing the seriousness of this problem. It can no longer be undermined or mistaken for entertainment in some forms of reality television. Society can no longer be misinformed and remain uneducated and dumbfounded to the plethora of disturbing yet factual information being disseminated on the world stage.

Thus, the debate continues about the nature and the extent of the negative impact of some aspects of the media on individuals' values, beliefs, attitudes, and behaviors, and on society in general. Starting with "the man in the mirror" is a crucial solution piece that can no longer be ignored. The purpose is twofold: not only should the IPV solution pertain to and focus solely upon the youth who are at risk, but the adults who are instrumental in their environment should embrace and apply the same measures to their own self-examination. Adults are crucial resources for children who are attempting to cope with chronic danger and stress. When adults begin to deteriorate, decompensate, and panic, children suffer. Efforts to help children exposed to a "war zone" should include programmatic efforts to alter the "legitimization of aggression" among children and youth, responses to trauma in early childhood, and the mobilization of prosocial adult and youth members of the community to become involved in changing community and family conditions (Garbarino, J. G., and Kostenly, K., 1997). Youth seek our attention in negative ways when we provide them too few positive ways to communicate and to get the attention and love they need. And we choose to punish and lock them up rather than take the necessary, more cost-effective steps to prevent and intervene early to ensure them the healthy, safe, fair, and moral start in life they need to reach successful adulthood (Edelman, 2007).

THE VILLAGE IS IN DISARRAY—YOU ARE YOUR BROTHER'S KEEPER!

In the US, it is estimated that more than fifteen million children are exposed to intimate partner violence each year, and researchers believe witnessing IPV may be just as harmful to children as being victims of abuse themselves. Studies consistently show that kids exposed to IPV are more likely to be in abusive relationships, even as early as adolescence. Likewise, their own children end up in the same setting of abuse and violence (Callahan, 2014).

In a national online survey, one in five tweens—ages eleven to fourteen—said their friends are victims of dating violence and nearly half who are in relationships know friends who are verbally abused. Two in five of the youngest tweens, ages eleven and twelve, reported that their friends are victims of verbal abuse in relationships (Teenage Research Unlimited, 2006). One in three adolescent girls in the United States is a victim of physical, emotional, or verbal abuse from a dating partner—a figure that far exceeds victimization rates for other types of violence affecting youth. Though more than four in five parents (82 percent) feel confident they could recognize the signs if their child was experiencing dating abuse, a majority of parents (58 percent) could not correctly identify all the warning signs of abuse (Teenage Research Unlimited, 2009).

The old African proverb "It takes a village to raise a child" rings as true today as it did many years ago. However, as a result of technology (which is a blessing and a curse), a change in family values, family dynamics, community demographics, and other factors, the village as we know it today has changed dramatically from what it used to be. The "village" from which this philosophical phrase originated was a close-knit, intertwined community whose members demonstrated personal responsibility for the basic needs of every child, regardless of the biological parents. Today, some of the members who make up the village structure have failed miserably and continue to traumatize our youth on a daily basis with their idiosyncratic ways of thinking and operating. Today, the village is indeed in disarray!

The task of dealing with the aforementioned factors and the effects of community violence falls to the people who teach the children of that society—their parents and other relatives, teachers, counselors, authority figures, and role models. When children grow up witnessing intimate partner violence, they carry a lifelong burden. This early trauma may impact their development, emotional regulation, and mental health. But one of the saddest outcomes is that children who witness IPV grow up to have a greater risk of living in violent relationships themselves, whether as victims or as perpetrators. Without more awareness of this problem and help for these families, the burden of IPV will continue to be passed from one generation to the next (Callahan, 2014).

As the research has consistently demonstrated, IPV is a problem that starts early despite the fact much of the focus has been geared toward adults. Moving forward with effective interventions must include every facet of society. And while the ideal world would be problem free, let's face the ugly truth. As long as children are born into families who are not able to provide the basic intrinsic needs that ensure stability, self-actualization, and a sound and solid foundation, there will be a need for a "village"-focused intervention. As long as the risk factors of children who are born into these unfortunate and adverse circumstances are not sufficiently addressed across their lifespan as they become adults, there will be a need to intervene, collaborate, promote, and create innovative preventive measures. "It is easier to build strong children than to fix broken [adults]" (Frederick Douglass).

The CDC calls for a collaborative approach that includes the community and the organizations within. Over the years, I have witnessed numerous failures to cut through the red tape, to go that extra mile, and even the inability to let go of egos and the status quo by those who choose to work on behalf of our children but do so haphazardly. And so I set out on a mission to address the issues in the best way I know how: exposing the issue, promoting research, and challenging policies in an effort to decrease the gap between policy and practice. Interventions to which our youth will respond are desperately needed, and it has to happen collaboratively. It is about recognizing that the traditional way of addressing child and family welfare issues has not been fully effective.

We have to take the much-needed approach to unselfishly work together and dare to think outside the box, utilizing a variety of forums and measures if we are serious about reaching and saving our youth from the pains of poverty, violence, and failure. It requires twenty-first-century approaches and interventions to address twenty-first-century problems. According to social work values, we have to meet our youth where they are, and it starts with addressing our own prejudices as advocates and providers of our most precious resources: our children, our youth, our future. "Children are great imitators. So give them something great to imitate" (NYAR, Anonymous, 2011).

This is truly a wake-up call! As the various authors of this book have established via a plethora of crucial information to raise our level of consciousness and critical thinking, it is no doubt that the twenty-first century presents with a unique set of problems and concerns. A lot has changed over the years, and the "village" is in disarray. But I can assure you, as I "preach to the choir" and to you, the elders of the village, our children and families are in crisis. And if we, who are a part of the village, are really serious about the future of our youth, business as usual must change. If we want to equip them with the tools to effectively maneuver throughout their lifespan, become productive citizens of society, and achieve excellence, we all have to change the culture within the village. Failing to do so has catastrophic consequences in addition to IPV, and it's called the *cradle-to-prison pipeline*. This serious saga is initially and briefly introduced in Chapter 1: Torn AND Driven. I would be remiss if I didn't conclude with a more detailed view of the serious implications associated with it.

THE CRADLE-TO-PRISON PIPELINE CONNECTION: THE STRUGGLE IS REAL

The Children's Defense Fund's Cradle to Prison Pipeline Campaign, which is a national and community crusade to engage families, youth, communities, and policy makers in the development of healthy, safe, and educated children, indicates that poverty, racial disparities, and a culture of punishment rather than prevention and early intervention are key forces driving the pipeline. The pipeline is directly related to the IPV crisis. Pervasive poverty, inadequate access to health coverage, gaps in early childhood development, disparate educational opportunities, intolerable abuse and neglect, unmet mental and emotional problems, rampant substance abuse, and an overburdened, ineffective juvenile justice system are the main factors that define the problems we have to address with our children and families. These are the problems that help define our roles as human service providers in the twenty-first century. "The most dangerous place for a child to try to grow up in America is at the intersection of race and poverty" (CDF, 2008).

The cradle-to-prison pipeline statistics continue to mirror and represent what became a constant theme in the numerous comprehensive child and family assessments and home evaluations I conducted during my tenure as a family consultant. Since that time, I have discovered that many of the youth who are failing in school and experiencing problems are coping with issues that have not been accurately introduced to and effectively addressed by the child welfare system. Much of what is being addressed is done during the tertiary stages of prevention, as opposed to the primary and/or secondary stages of prevention. This is due, in part, because we, as policy makers, administrators, and service providers, are not all on the same sheet of music. We as advocates are not all communicating with each other. This has to change! The point is this: our society is going to either have to pay for the disarray in the village now or we will pay for it later, and I promise you, later is more costly. We are witnessing it in the IPV crisis wherein research has shown that the issues and the problems begin as early as elementary school. "Alone we can do so little, together we can do so much" (NYAR, 2011).

To witness repeated generational afflictions of poverty, neglect, helplessness, illiteracy, and vocational deficits, along with the inability to dream, sparked a passion in me several years ago to explore innovative avenues by which to address the problems being faced by the child welfare system as well as the consumers it serves. Research has shown that in addition to a collaborative effort among child and family advocates, twenty-first-century interventions to which our youth will respond are desperately needed. It is time to dismiss our individual agendas and work collaboratively, regardless of whether you are on the private, local, state or federal level. "Our children are our only hope for the future, but we are their only hope for their present" (NYAR, Zig Ziglar, 2011).

One-size-fits-all zero-tolerance school discipline policies are transforming schools into a major point of entry into the juvenile justice system as children are increasingly arrested on school grounds for subjectively and loosely defined behaviors. Most juvenile correctional facility programs focus on punishment rather than treatment and rehabilitation, often creating environments that further harden youth. This makes it more difficult for them to productively reintegrate into their families and communities. "The effects of abuse, poverty and neglect that some kids carry with them to school can be like an extra backpack weighing heavily on weak shoulders. Educators say that explains why some fail, fight or simply shut down" (Dodd, 2010).

We must speak out against policies that contribute to criminalizing children at younger and younger ages, and fight for policies that help children thrive and put them on track to a productive adulthood. If you are experiencing behavioral problems with a child, check out the total environment, particularly outside of the school setting. I guarantee you will find the barriers that, in part, are hindering the socialization, educational, and learning processes. I'm stressing and focusing on education because research has shown that lack of a stable foundation during those most impressionable years will produce an environment that is not conducive to thriving and succeeding, leading to poverty and the trajectory to prison. Without a quality education, our youth are being set up for failure. The village is in crisis and our future (the voices) is at stake! As we look ahead, let's reassess ourselves, our agenda, and what role we play in restoring the village.

Again, we have to WAKE UP! We have to meet our youth where they are, and it starts with a collaborative effort from each entity of advocates and providers who are concerned about the welfare of our most precious resources: our children, our youth, our future. It is time for the social institutions, human service agencies, and communities to connect, and it is time for the elders in the broken village to effectively address the crisis and make reparations to restore it one voice, one child, one hope, and one dream at a time. This is a wake-up call unlike any other; it is time for a change, and that change begins with me and you. An essential element in adult learning is to challenge our own ingrained perceptions and examine our insights critically.

Edelman (2007) challenges us as parents, adults, citizens, and leaders to examine ourselves regularly to determine whether we are contributing to the crisis our children face or to the solutions they urgently need. And if we are not a part of the solution, we are a part of the problem and need to do better. Our children don't need or expect us to be perfect. They do need and expect us to be honest, to admit and correct our mistakes, and to share our struggles about the meanings and responsibilities of faith, parenthood, citizenship, and life. Before we can pull up the moral weeds of violence, materialism, and greed in our world that are strangling so many of our children, we must pull up the moral weeds in our own homes, backyards, neighborhoods, institutions, and public policies. So many children are confused about what is right and wrong because so many adults talk right and do wrong in our personal, professional, and public lives.

The saying "Children do as we do and not as we say" is real and factual, as the main agents of socialization shape and mold us from birth to present. None of the aforementioned agents of socialization are exempt from the infamous acts of shame that appear in multimedia. This is evident by a variety of recent media sources that describe the appalling demeanor of "professionals" as well as ordinary people. The following are recent headlines that were broadcasted via the MSN website: "Three Teachers Resign Over Insulting Disparaging and Profanity-laden Chat Messages About Students"; "Professor among 4 fired in UNC academic fraud"; "U.S. senators call for federal judge to resign over wife beating"; "'Tennis Greats were fined $10,000 apiece on Saturday at Wimbledon for Unsportsmanlike Conduct"; "School Cafeteria Lady Charged With Stealing 'Large Sum of Money' From Student Accounts"; "Daycare Worker Pleads Guilty to Raping 4 Children"; "Judge Reprimanded for Jailing Domestic Violence Victim" (MSN website, n.d.). Headlines are saturated with internet news stories such as these, and adults are the casting players in the theater of life for society's youth, the viewing audience for these "productions."

I again repeat the following quote: "America's future will be determined by the home and the school. The child becomes largely what he is taught; hence we must watch what we teach and how we live" (NYAR, Jane Addams, 2011).

We, along with families, educators, human service providers, law enforcement, and the other elders in the village, no doubt have an extremely difficult and challenging role to play as providers in these changing times. And budget cuts and political constraints and expectations don't help. But the fact remains, we are all responsible, and some of us chose careers and titles that place us in powerful and influential positions where lives are being impacted every day. The human services field embodies professions that impact human lives, and it has to be entered into with the whole heart. This means regardless of the paycheck, you should be willing to give your 110 percent each and every day. "We are what we repeatedly do. Excellence, then, is not an act, but a habit" (NYAR, Aristotle, 2011).

As we critically examine the IPV crisis and its connection to the present state of the village, please don't forget to know thyself, then commit, strategize, and do your part in repairing the voices in the village: our children and our youth. I believe that every child, every voice in the village has potential and deserves to be given a chance to experience a level playing field in reaching it. "There is a brilliant child locked inside every student" (NYAR, Marva Collins, 2011). Thus, as I reflect on the rationale for this book and what the literature has expectantly revealed, it is no doubt that the timing is perfect, as research lends credence to this call for a new pathway and a twenty-first-century perspective for effectively evaluating and responding to IPV, one that has not received much attention in the past. While primary prevention of IPV would ideally be effective at the origin of the beginning symptoms and before children become perpetrating adults, the disturbing statistics indicate prior interventions have not been effective in yielding these promising results. And so I have to once again divert my attention to the adult perpetrators as well as the victims, the research-focused literature, and the rationale for raising awareness of this public health saga.

Ideally, we should work to prevent intimate partner violence before it starts to breed, which benefits both parents and their children. This can be done in various settings where social and emotional learning can be modeled. According to Callahan (2014), effective prevention programs can start in schools, providing education to kids about healthy relationships and conflict resolution. However, programs can also target at-risk couples and parents, giving them training in conflict management and connecting them with services to alleviate other sources of family stress, which can increase risk for IPV. Remember, the literature reflects the fact that IPV is an intricate problem that will require a multidimensional solution and additional research to validate and assess evidence-based responses.

NEW DIRECTIONS FOR IPV RESEARCH: WHERE DO WE GO FROM HERE?

The impact of intimate partner violence is multifaceted and varied. It can impact individual victims, their children, third parties, and society as a whole (Hart and Klein, 2013). Research suggests the level of IPV, including frequency and severity, influences the impact on the victim, with more severe, more frequent incidences increasing the impact (Campbell, 2002). The National Intimate Partner and Sexual Violence Survey (NISVS) reports that lifetime IPV caused 18.8 percent of women to report at least one IPV-related impact (the survey measured), while the highest percent, 25.7 percent, reported being fearful and 10 percent reported missing at least one day of work or school as a result. For women specifically, 1.5 percent reported contracting a sexually transmitted disease and 1.7 percent reported becoming pregnant after being raped by an intimate partner. For men, the largest percent, 9.9 percent, reported at least one IPV-related impact, and the highest, 5.2 percent, reported being fearful, with 3.9 percent missing at least a day of work or school (Black et al., 2011).

In my conviction to expose the prevalence of male victims of IPV, I would be negligent to ignore in my closing remarks the vast amount of literature that has been presented throughout this book. Although a gap still exists, this population is slowly gaining the attention that is long overdue among the research agenda protocol. According to Schuler (2010), taking into account the large amount of empirical investigations conducted in the area of intimate partner violence, very few studies have examined male victims. Unfortunately, scholars in the field of criminal justice have been relatively silent on this subject, with most empirical research published from non-criminal justice scholarly journals about the criminal justice system. Graham-Kevan (2007, as cited in Schuler, 2010) argues, "The scholarly neglect of this topic has limited our overall understanding of violence in intimate relationships" (p. 3). It is very difficult to get male victims of intimate partner violence to come forward due to the societal stigma that might be placed on them (Graham-Kevan, 2007, as cited in Schuler, 2010). Male victims fear this stigma. No man wants to be considered weak. As a result, like many crimes of intimate partner violence that have women victims, men are equally or even more silent about this crime.

In a review of various studies about perpetrators, multiple forms of intimate partner violence were examined, including women's use of violence. It argues for development of more complex conceptualizations of intimate partner violence. As new victims are identified, partner violence has been reconceptualized. Research findings indicate women are both victims and perpetrators in intimate partner violence, challenging previous conceptualizations and explanations. The authors argue that how researchers conceptualize intimate partner violence influences how they study and measure it. The authors also call for researchers to develop more complex constructions of gender, and to distinguish between distinct forms of intimate partner violence (McHugh and Frieze, 2006).

Female-to-male IPV recently has become a recognized healthcare issue. In one study, a heterosexual male Emergency Department population was screened for IPV using the Hurt/Insult/Threaten/Scream (HITS) scale, a four-question survey. This study enrolled 282 men. Basic demographics, along with the answers to the HITS scale, were analyzed. Of the men screened, 29.3 percent had a positive history of IPV. Men who were positive for IPV were more likely to score higher on questions regarding the frequency of verbal aggression than actual or threatened physical violence. This study reinforces the need to screen both genders for IPV in the Emergency Department (Mills et al., 2003).

> Another study in which the objective was to determine the accuracy of two brief surveys for detection of male victims of intimate partner violence (IPV) in the Emergency Department (ED), was conducted prospectively in an urban, teaching hospital over 6 weeks; all men triaged to the acute care portion of the ED were eligible for enrollment. Exclusion criteria included age less than 18 years, refusal, altered mental status, or condition requiring lifesaving intervention. Data included demographics, The Revised Conflict Tactics Scale (CTS2) score, and scores on two brief surveys of IPV: the HITS ("Hurt/Insult/Threaten/Scream") scale and the Partner Violence Screen (PVS). The CTS2 uses previously validated population scores for female to male psychological aggression and physical assault. Neither the HITS nor the PVS has been validated for use in the ED for detecting male victims of IPV. There were 116 men approached for enrollment; nearly half completed all surveys. Mean age was 41.8 years, and the sample was 73% African-American and 20% white. Thirty-nine percent had positive scores on the psychological aggression portion of the CTS2, whereas 20% had positive scores on the physical assault subscale. While neither the HITS nor the PVS accurately screens male victims of IPV in the ED, [it is a start] and further research is needed to develop a valid, brief screening test to identify male victims of IPV in an acute setting. (Mills et al., 2006)

What you the reader needs to know is IPV can be prevented. I can't stress this point enough. Primary prevention of IPV, including TDV, means preventing IPV before it begins. Primary prevention strategies are key to ending partner violence in adolescence and adulthood and protecting people from its effects. And partner violence in adolescence can be a precursor or risk factor for partner violence in adulthood. Many strategies to prevent IPV therefore see adolescence as a critical developmental period for the prevention of partner violence in adulthood. It is also important to assist survivors and their children and protect them from future harm. Although there is less evidence of what works to prevent IPV compared to other areas of violence, such as youth violence or child maltreatment, a growing research base demonstrates there are multiple strategies to prevent IPV from occurring in the first place and to lessen the harms for survivors (Jennings, 2017). Strategies are available that can benefit adolescents and adults regardless of their level of risk, as well as individuals and environments at greatest risk. A comprehensive approach that simultaneously targets multiple risk and protective factors is critical to having a broad and sustained impact on IPV. Even though more research is needed (e.g. to strengthen the evidence addressing community and societal level factors), we cannot let the need for further research impede efforts to effectively prevent IPV within our communities (Niolon et al., 2017).

LASTING IMPRESSIONS

Last but certainly not least, I would like to discuss an issue that was not thoroughly addressed in the contents of this book. This was done so intentionally, because I wanted to leave the readers with the answers to one of the most judgmental and infamous questions victims have to face: *Why does she/he stay?* The answers are just as complex as the problem and the solutions. Socialization, which is addressed extensively in chapter 13 and referenced in other chapters, creates a powerful unwillingness in relationships. People feel they must stay in a relationship and are highly resistant to change as a means of problem solving. Socialization and/or religious or cultural beliefs demand the victim maintain the facade of a good marriage or a good relationship.

You will discover that there are many reasons why someone stays, and commitment, finances, and religion are just a few. However, some victims have frequently reported an answer that is both simple and powerful: victims stay for love and the hope that the abuser will change. They also stay because of fear, and for good reason—the most dangerous time in a violent relationship is when a victim is leaving. Sometimes, there just doesn't seem to be a way out. It is important to remember that any relationship is difficult to leave, but a violent one has many extra layers of complexity and fear. Thus, leaving is a process, and not a one-time event. So, as a society, we must support and empower victims in this process and hold the abuser accountable for the violence he/she chooses to inflict (BPA, 2014).

According to Whiting (2016), based upon the analysis of real-world, true-to-heart feedback from survivors, the following reasons were entailed as the top responses from victims:

1. **Distorted Thoughts.** Being controlled and hurt is traumatizing, and this leads to confusion, doubt, and even self-blame. Perpetrators harass and accuse victims, which wears them down and causes despair and guilt. For example, women shared: "I believed I deserved it," and "I was ashamed, embarrassed, and blamed myself because I thought I triggered him." Others minimized the abuse as a way to cope with it, saying: "[I stayed] because I didn't think that emotional and financial abuse was really abuse. Because words don't leave bruises," and "Because I didn't know what my boyfriend did to me was rape."
2. **Damaged Self-Worth.** Related was the damage to the self that is the result of degrading treatment. Many women felt beaten down and of no value, saying: "He made me believe I was worthless and alone," and "I felt I had done something wrong and I deserved it."
3. **Fear.** The threat of bodily and emotional harm is powerful, and abusers use this to control and keep women trapped. Female victims of violence are much more likely than male victims to be terrorized and traumatized. One said: "I was afraid of him . . . I knew he'd make leaving an ugly, drawn-out nightmare." Attempting to leave an abuser is dangerous. One woman felt trapped because of her husband's "threats of hunting me down and harming all my loved ones including our kids while I watched and then killing me."
4. **Wanting to Be a Savior.** Many described a desire to help or love their partners with the hopes they could change them: "I believed I could love the abuse out of him." Others described internal values or commitments to the marriage or partner, with tweets like: "I thought I would be the strong one who would never leave him and show him loyalty. I would fix him and teach him love." Others had pity and put their partner's needs above their own: "His father died, he became an alcoholic and said that God wouldn't want me to leave him because he needed me to make him better."
5. **Children.** These women also put their children first, sacrificing their own safety: "I was afraid if he wasn't beating me he would beat his kids. And I valued their lives more than my own." And, "I stayed for twenty years while I protected our children, all while I was being abused." Others mentioned staying to benefit the children: "I wanted my son to have a father."
6. **Family Expectations and Experiences.** Many posted descriptions of how past experiences with violence distorted their sense of self or of healthy relationships: "I watched [my dad] beat my mom. Then I found someone just like dad," and "[When you are] raised by animals, you partner with wolves." Some mentioned family and religious pressures: "My mother told me God would disown me if I broke my marriage."
7. **Financial Constraints.** Many referred to financial limitations, and these were often connected to caring for children: "I had no family, two young children, no money, and guilt because he had brain damage from a car accident." Others were unable to keep jobs

because of the abuser's control or their injuries, and others were used financially by their abuser: "[My] ex racked up thousands of debt in my name."

8. **Isolation.** A common tactic of manipulative partners is to separate their victim from family and friends. Sometimes this is physical, as one woman experienced: "I was literally trapped in the backwoods of WV, and he would use my little boy to keep me close." Other times isolation is emotional, as one woman was told: "You can either have friends and family or you can have me."

Although these eight reasons for staying are common, they do not describe every victim and situation. Women can also be perpetrators, and there are many patterns of violence (Johnson, 2008). Yet, these posts provide compelling insider's views of the difficulties of making decisions in a violent relationship, and this is helpful for outsiders to understand. One reason many victims hesitate to speak up is because they are afraid of being judged and pressured by friends and professionals (Merchant and Whiting, n.d.) If more people responded to victims' stories of abuse with concern and compassion, instead of with criticism, more victims might speak up and find the support they need to live a life free of abuse (Whiting, 2016). Whatever the reason they decide to stay, which appears to be either strong emotional, psychological, and situational factors that keep the victim tied to the abuser, please remember leaving and staying aren't the factors that cause abusive behavior.

WAKE UP AND STAY WOKE!

In the book review of Dr. Don Dutton's *Rethinking Domestic Violence*, a striking revelation indicates that "after twenty years of viewing intimate partner violence as generated by gender and focusing on a punitive 'law and order' approach, Dutton now argues that this approach must be more varied and flexible. Treatment providers, criminal justice system personnel, lawyers, and researchers have indicated the need for a new view of the problem—one less invested in gender politics and more open to collaborative views and interdisciplinary insights" (Matthews, 2018). It is my prayer and my hope that the contents of this book have set the stage for that sensitive but much-needed conversation and that it has served its purpose: to educate, edify, encourage, and inspire you to another level of empowerment in regard to exposing and thwarting this public health crisis. Let this be the unique call to action needed to create a phenomenal response to impacting a major change in arresting the senseless violence that has consumed past and present generations, our families, our communities, our society, and our world. It is a complex problem; however, I have attempted to keep the content and the language as simple as possible. Therefore in layman's terms, it's apparent that the eight listed reasons why victims stay resonate with the statistics the various chapters have disclosed about the implications of ineffectively addressing and ignoring the root cause of IPV: it's learned behavior that impacts all genders; the state of the environment is critical; the impact on children starts early; and the overall behavioral, mental, and emotional health of those involved are complicated and costly. Thus, as the literature has confirmed, it will require a collaborative and unique effort on every level of intervention: micro, mezzo, and macro.

Every chapter depicts real-world scenarios and/or life stories. These true life events and experiences heavily mirror the evidence-based research and findings presented, which speaks volumes. The purpose is not to minimize the seriousness of IPV and the conditions to which the female victim continues to be subjected and whose statistics remain at alarming and disturbing numbers; it is to raise awareness about the male victims who are also impacted. The statistical numbers are lower but inaccurate, also due to the stigma attached. Please take heed to the content, whether as a practitioner or future practitioner with a desire to improve your knowledge, values, and skill set to bring about change for all who are impacted. The trajectory of a life can be changed and saved even if you are an individual whose sole purpose is to sponge up the opportunity to gain a new perspective on this public health nuisance via increased self-awareness, self-assessment, and self-regulation. Therefore, I challenge you to "put down the finger puppets, turn off the television and visit that destination called 'reality'"(Onusic, 2013)!

In closing, I want to direct your attention to the appendices, where you will be provided with a glance of additional demographic statistics about IPV, the warning signs and symptoms, and authentic documents that chronicle the actions taken to arrest this debilitating issue. I also placed in the lineup some fond family memories of Terrell and some of my most teachable and inspirational quotes and readings, which I often share with my students as I attempt to equip them with not only academic content, but life lessons geared toward enhancing their overall well-being and their practical knowledge. A strong and supportive family foundation is one of the protective factors that is consistently identified in statistical data about IPV. To reiterate my final point, the essence of this manuscript "is not meant to downplay in any way domestic violence among women. Unfortunately, it continues to be a horrible disparity! It is, however, intended to add to the growing conversation that anyone can be the victim of domestic abuse and everyone who needs protection deserves access to it" (Weinberger, 2015). Always know that real love isn't violent, words do hurt, and no one deserves to be abused.

Your character is what you do when you think no one is looking,
so be the change you want to see.

APPENDICES

APPENDIX 1: DEMOGRAPHICS OF IPV VICTIMS BY SEXUAL ORIENTATION

Intimate partner violence

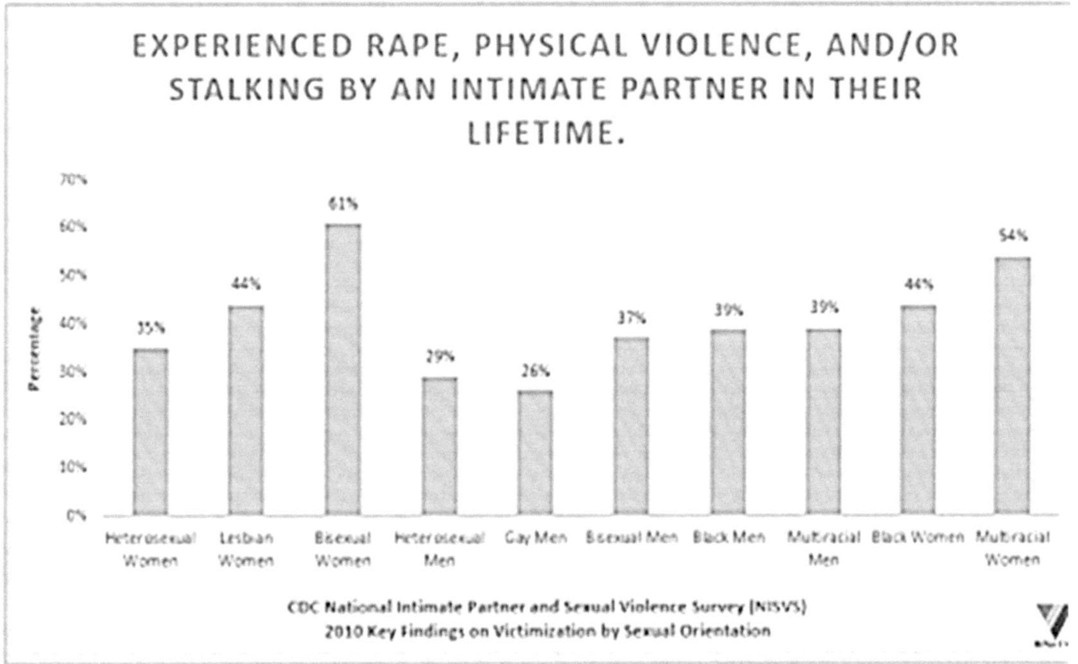

APPENDIX 2: THE WARNING SIGNS OF INTIMATE PARTNER VIOLENCE

The Warning Signs of Intimate Partner Violence

- △ Extreme jealousy
- △ Controlling behavior
- △ Quick involvement
- △ Alcohol and drug use
- △ Explosive temper
- △ Isolates you from friends and family
- △ Uses force during argument
- △ Blames others for his/her problems
- △ Extreme jealousy
- △ Cruelty to animals
- △ Uses force during argument
- △ Abused former partners

APPENDIX 3: ANTI-BULLYING SUPPORT RESPONSE

November 2, 2001

To The Staff of Cedar Grove Middle:

I am writing this letter as a concerned parent on behalf of my son, Terrell J. Gibson, who was involved in a physical altercation on 10-31-01 in his math class. I am also requesting that a copy be placed in his file with the discipline form that was sent to me on 11-1-01. The teacher for the class, in which the initial altercation took place, is Ms. R[illegible], who I have been corresponding with since the beginning of the school year. In fact, I initiated the phone call on the day that Terrell informed me of the incident as well as the subsequent meeting that following morning.

Our initial conversation was at the beginning of the school year and was regarding concern that Terrell was laughing in class and following the crowd who appeared to be disruptive and unruly. Upon meeting with Terrell and Ms R[illegible], we were able to resolve the issue and my son issued an apology to Ms. R[illegible] for being disruptive. I even offered advice as a parent and as a social worker for improving conditions in the classroom. Ms. R[illegible] appeared very receptive to and appreciative of the feedback. I asked her to contact me if Terrell presented any more problems and extended my 100% support for her.

Although reports from school indicated that Terrell had improved his behavior, he continued to express concern for how some of the other children in the classroom disrespected Ms. R[illegible] and her class. He also spoke about how this made it difficult for the learning process to take place and how Ms. R[illegible] would teach to the good side of the classroom while the unruly side was left to itself. He reportedly even asked to move to the "good side" on one occasion so that he could keep up. His request was granted, but I still had concern about why these kids who were allegedly acting out were not sent to the office to have the issues addressed. I assumed that if they were, they would not continue the behavior that I was hearing about each week. My mistake as a parent is that I did not pursue the concerns further, at least, not until my son was involved in the altercation that turned physical.

Everyday, I discuss school with my son and a week doesn't go by when he doesn't report that someone cursed him, called him names, threatened to beat him up, called him a tattle tale, talked about his clothes and shoes, invaded his personal space, and taunted him for one reason or another. Yes, bullying is alive and well in Cedar Grove Middle, regardless of the recent happenings that have occurred at Columbine High and other schools. And it was allegedly occurring in Ms. R[illegible]'s room as well as the bus stop and on the bus. In the midst of all of these concerns, I encouraged Terrell to tell the teacher, tell an adult, tell it, tell it, tell it!!! So did his grandmother, who he often talks to and who asked how long I was going to allow this to happen. I would get responses such as "Moma, they don't listen or they'll say I'm tired of you telling, I don't like tattle tells, sit down, go back to your seat" or just totally ignore what is going on. In a time such as this, I don't think that any of us need to close our ears to what our children are trying to tell us, whether we be parents, educators, mentors or other types of child advocates. By doing so, we may be contributing to a bigger problem.

This is why I spend time with my son daily discussing school and how his day is going. No matter how many times he tells me that some of his classmates were saying mean and insensitive comments to him, I continue to listen and discuss what is going on. You see, words do hurt, in spite of what some may think. I know, because I've been there and I hear it from the personal experiences of my clients daily. Even though there is not much that we can do about adults who say things to hurt other people, I'm of the belief that with children, it is a different story. We can stop turning our heads and address it, find out where the insensitive and cold-hearted behavior is coming from. Perhaps the person is miserable and misery loves company, or possibly and most often home and or the community are failing the child miserably. I can only speculate, but do know that allowing children to continue to taunt and threaten other kids who appear vulnerable and easy-going can result in one of two scenarios. The perpetrator gets worse and is eventually lost in the system and/or the victim becomes frustrated because no one appears to care and gives up on being positive, resulting in two young lives giving up on hope. I consider my son to be a victim in all of this and I want all of you to know that I feel that we have failed him miserably. He has been punished with two days of in school suspension because he finally got tired of being bullied and fought back. This isn't the first time that this has happened, but I plan to make it the last.

I am raising Terrell to be non-violent and I have always taught him that he should never start fights or make fun of anyone who is different and I have also taught him to fear God and I am not ashamed to tell you this. However, for the past two years, middle school is making me rethink my philosophy. This period in his life is the first time that he has had to endure treatment of this sort and certainly the first time that he has had to serve detention!! This concerns me very much and just as I am sold out for Jesus, I am also sold out to being the best parent to my son and giving him the attention, nurture and support that he needs to make it through this challenging and trying time of his adolescence years. You see, our black boys and men are at a disadvantage and they face an uncertain future. I refuse to allow the system and society to make my son a statistic of the penal system or an early grave. This is why I expend so much energy trying to raise him properly and engaging myself in his school life. This is why I work so hard to give him what he needs at home, because I don't expect for you to have to be his parent at school. However, I do expect for you to carry out your duties as if your heart is in your profession and I do expect for you to protect my son when he is in your care.

I realize that teaching is a very difficult profession, so is mine. They both are professions that reward very little and expect much. This is why our hearts have to be in what we do, because it is not just a job. We have other people's lives in our hands. Saying the wrong thing, making the wrong decision can sometimes damage a person for life. I trust that in the future, you will respect my wishes to look after my son while he is in your care just as I have taught him to respect your authority and what you do for a living. No, he's not perfect and he makes mistakes sometimes, even follows the crowd every now and then, but he is a good boy and I know my child. And I believe that you would agree with me if you were asked to give an honest opinion. No, I'm not saying that he is not different when he is not around me, and that he never does any wrong, but I do strongly believe that because of his timidness, he probably won't start a fight, but he will defend himself. I've asked him to do so lately because I felt as though he needed to. Turning the other cheek for the school year 2001-2002 has only caused him humility, more threats and certainly more teasing by his classmates. In fact the threats usually start when he responds verbally to their taunts or he ignores them, which usually makes them angry.

I'm writing this letter because I love my son and I want him to be treated fairly. Last year, he was written up because he defended himself. During this altercation, he was accused of hitting first and admitted to defending himself from a young man who not only had been taunting him, but felt bold enough to knock his books from his desk. He also left a scratch on Terrell's face. How much is he supposed to take? He's only human!! Ask yourself if you have ever been in a situation where you were so frustrated that you made an irrational decision. You see I am talking about an age group that needs assistance in making decisions, structure, mediation, proper guidance and positive role modeling. I can only hope and pray that this young man as well as his cousin who made threats against Terrell were disciplined in the same manner as my son. Because the message that Terrell has been receiving is one of non-support and unconcern and that he was absolutely out of line for defending himself in a classroom where the teacher is present but failed to observe the commotion that was occurring in that small classroom. Ask yourself if this is fair to label him with "simple battery" because he felt the need to take a stand against bullying and harassment. Something has to change and soon.

In the future, if he is allowed to be taunted, physically attacked and punished because no one would address his concerns, I have no other choice but to seek legal advice. I consider this to be a serious matter and I consider my son's future to be at stake. I can't imagine what this is doing to him emotionally. It has to be draining to have to go to school, study, concentrate and be on guard for the bullies and other disruptive groups, who have nothing better to do but make threats and degrade someone's appearance because they appear different or don't want to be a part of the "click". By the way, these bullies are slick, cunning and innovative in doing their actions behind the teacher's back. This is why it is good to get both sides of the story and to listen. I plan to continue to stay very vocal and involved for my son's sake, and I wanted you to know what I'm feeling right now as well as my frustration as a parent. I respect educators and I have taught Terrell to do the same and we thank you for all that you do. But again, I feel as though the system punished him unfairly and I just wanted you to know that I want the best for him as any caring parent would for his or her child. Thanks for taking the time out to read my concerns and I look forward to assisting you in any way possible to make education a success for my son and others who aspire to beat the odds.

Sincerely,

Irma J. Gibson

cc: Mr. A[illegible]
cc: counselor
cc: Ms. R[illegible]
cc: Mr. L[illegible]
cc: Ms. B[illegible]
cc: Mr. D[illegible]
cc: Terrell Gibson's disciplinary file

APPENDIX 4: SAVANNAH DA VICTIM ADVOCACY LETTERS

Office of District Attorney Larry Chisolm
Victim-Witness Assistance Program
Chatham County Courthouse 6th Floor
133 Montgomery Street, Room 625
Savannah, Georgia 31401

Phone (912) 652 - 7329
1 (800) 477 5959
Fax 912 652-7321
Date: 9/20/2012

TERRELL GIBSON
4111 ALTA TOWNE CIRCLE
UNIVERSITY COMMONS
#1104A
POOLER, GA 31322

State of Georgia
vs.

Case No: R12040380 *Case Type:* CRIMINAL - STATE COURT
DIN: P1110164 *Judge:* HONORABLE HERMANN W. COOLIDGE
ADA: GRACE HA

Dear TERRELL GIBSON :
This letter is to inform you the above case is tentatively scheduled for Arraignment in State Court 10/5/2012at 9:00 am. At this time the defendant and/or his attorney and the Assistant District Attorney for State Court appear before a Judge. You will not receive a subpoena for this Arraignment date, and you are not required to be present; however, you are welcome to attend. The defendant is formally told the charges pending and given a list of witnesses for the State. The defendant will either plead guilty or ask for a trial.

Additional important information and forms concerning our program can be found online at **districtattorney.chathamcounty.org**. Please download and fill out the appropriate forms and return to our office; or, if you do not have computer access, please call Victim-Witness, and we will send you the necessary information. Also call me if you have additional information or opinions to add to the case before the arraignment.

Arraignments are held on the fourth floor of the Chatham County Courthouse in either courtroom G or H. If you decide to come to the courthouse or visit our office, you may park for free at the Chatham County garage on the 4th, 5th, or 6th floors if space is available. The Chatham County garage is located next door to the courthouse.

Please contact our Victim-Witness Assistance Program at (912) 652-7329 if you have any questions or if we can be of assistance. Our hours are 8:00 am to 5:00 pm Monday through Friday and our services are free of charge.
Para informacion en Español, por favor llame al 912-652-8059
VWAP does not discriminate on the basis of race, color, national origin, religion, sex, disability, or age for any of our program participants.

Sincerely,

JJ Haire

JJHaire@chathamcounty.org
912-652-8066

Office of District Attorney Larry Chisolm
Victim-Witness Assistance Program
Chatham County Courthouse 6th Floor
133 Montgomery Street, Room 625
Savannah, Georgia 31401

Phone (912) 652 - 7329
1 (800) 477 5959
Fax 912 652-7321
Date: 7/19/2012

TERRELL GIBSON
4111 ALTA TOWNE CIRCLE
UNIVERSITY COMMONS
#1104A
POOLER, GA 31322

State of Georgia
vs.

Case No: R12040380 Case Type: CRIMINAL - STATE COURT
DIN: P1110164 Judge: HONORABLE HERMANN W. COOLIDGE
ADA: MARK J BOYD

Dear TERRELL GIBSON :
This letter is to inform you the above case is tentatively scheduled for Arraignment in State Court 8/2/2012at 9:00 am. At this time the defendant and/or his attorney and the Assistant District Attorney for State Court appear before a Judge. You will not receive a subpoena for this Arraignment date, and you are not required to be present; however, you are welcome to attend. The defendant is formally told the charges pending and given a list of witnesses for the State. The defendant will either plead guilty or ask for a trial.

Additional important information and forms concerning our program can be found online at **districtattorney.chathamcounty.org**. Please download and fill out the appropriate forms and return to our office; or, if you do not have computer access, please call Victim-Witness, and we will send you the necessary information. Also call me if you have additional information or opinions to add to the case before the arraignment.

Arraignments are held on the fourth floor of the Chatham County Courthouse in either courtroom G or H. If you decide to come to the courthouse or visit our office, you may park for free at the Chatham County garage on the 4th, 5th, or 6th floors if space is available. The Chatham County garage is located next door to the courthouse.

Please contact our Victim-Witness Assistance Program at (912) 652-7329 if you have any questions or if we can be of assistance. Our hours are 8:00 am to 5:00 pm Monday through Friday and our services are free of charge.
Para informacion en Español, por favor llame al 912-652-8059
VWAP does not discriminate on the basis of race, color, national origin, religion, sex, disability, or age for any of our program participants.

Sincerely,

JJ Haire

JJHaire@chathamcounty.org
912-652-8066

APPENDIX 5: SSU STUDENT AFFAIRS ADVERSE ACTION

OFFICE OF THE STUDENT ETHICS

Box 20521
3219 College Street
Savannah, GA 31404
P: (912) 358-3122
F: (912) 356-2464

October 13, 2011

Mr. Terrell Gibson -
University Commons 1104-A
Savannah State University
(Hand Delivered & Emailed

Dear Mr. Gibson:

The Office of Student Ethics is in receipt of a report from the Savannah State University DPS CRN (111012001) that outlines violations of the Savannah State University Code of Student Ethics; specifically indicating your arrest for **Level I.1 'Zero Tolerance' Misconduct (Assault)** on 13 October 2011. Therefore, it is my determination that your continual presence on campus constitutes a serious threat of harm to the campus community. In accordance with the Code of Student Rights, Responsibilities and Ethics, I am issuing a Summary Suspension from the University. You are to vacate all University premises IMMEDIATELY.

> **Note the following statement regarding Disciplinary Suspension:**
> "A student who has been summarily suspended after mid-term of the semester pursuant to the *Savannah State University Student Conduct Code* pending the outcome of a disciplinary hearing **will not** be eligible for withdrawal from the University until the final disposition of the case. Should the student be found guilty of violating the Student Conduct Code or plead "no contest," the student will receive failing grades from the date of the summary suspension and forfeit the semester. Should the student be found not guilty, the Vice President for Student Affairs will provide written notification to the Vice President for Academic Affairs of the disposition. Should the student desire to withdraw, the Vice President for Academic Affairs will accept a petition from the student and grant an automatic withdrawal without penalty and forward the withdrawal approval to the appropriate offices."(***Savannah State University On-Line Catalog, 2011-2012, page 35***).

Should you wish to appeal these sanctions, you may do so by submitting a written appeal to the Special Assistant to the Vice President for Student Affairs within five business days of the original decision on the grounds for appeal as stated on pages 75 of the *2011-2012 Savannah State University Student Handbook.*

Sincerely,

, Interim Coordinator

APPENDIX 6: SSU STUDENT AFFAIRS APPEAL LETTER (TERRELL)

October 14, 2011

I Terrell Gibson am appealing the charges of Affray on the grounds of: The findings are not supported by substantial evidence or the sanctions are not supported by the findings and whether the sanction imposed by the adjudicating body was excessive, in light of the nature of the offense and the students disciplinary record. I reported an incident just about a year ago to date where the same exact thing happened but she was in my apartment in the commons uninvited. During the incident on October 13th she had been harassing me as she knocked on my door all night long. My roommate will verify this information. I also gave a note that she had left on my door to the officer who escorted me on campus (please see police report). She constantly follows me on campus and lately [redacted] has been harassing and making threats to numerous of people on campus including me, from social networks to text messages and voicemails and I have evidence to prove this.

Even after the altercation today she continued to make threats while sitting in the processing area of the jail. Of course they removed me and placed me in the cell but it was she who was verbally making threats. This is the same behavior that she has shown in the past and has gotten away with it. The police even got to see her temper when she found out that we were both being charged. (She thought I was the only one that was going to be charged) She had to be restrained because she believes that she is above the law.

After being released from jail I got 4 calls from a private number and it was her uncle leaving a message telling me that I was going to go back to jail and to get used to it. Her entire family has always made threats to me and has not tried to discourage her from attacking me in and out of the relationship. They have convinced her that no matter what, males don't have a right to defend themselves in any circumstances against females. I have been taught not to hit females but my parents have told me that if I felt like I was in danger to try to get away from the person and if I can't then try to keep him or her away from me or from hurting me and this is what I was doing. I have reached out to campus police on some occasions and on other occasions I have managed to talk her down. This time that did not work. I ran until I couldn't but I had a witness who realized that I was in danger and she assisted me. That did not stop her from attacking me or from destroying a laptop computer, ipod touch (which she replaced), and other items. The relationship with her has put me through a lot and I have been the victim of intimate partner violence. A lot of people can't understand that but it happens more often than you think or know. That is why I got out of the relationship over a year ago.

I have worked hard to get back on track from the distractions of an abusive relationship and I am a senior expected to graduate in May 2012. Until I missed class today I was doing very well academically and other wise. I am not guilty of the charges and know this will be a set back and a miscarriage of justice if [redacted] is allowed to get away with her plots and this charge is upheld. So my future is at your mercy and I hope and pray that you make the right decision. I appreciate if you can make a fast decision. Thank You.

Terrell Gibson

APPENDIX 7: SSU STUDENT AFFAIRS APPEAL SUPPORT LETTER (IRMA)

October 14, 2011

To All Concerned Parties:
I am writing this letter to provide additional feedback regarding the incidents that occurred prior to the altercation on today that involved my son, Terrell Gibson and G[redacted] G[redacted]. In addition to campus police reports of various incidents in which this young lady was the aggressor, I, my colleagues in the Social Work Department and even students who are matriculating in the program can verify that Miss G[redacted] has reeked havoc in Terrell's life, not only during their relationship as girlfriend and boyfriend, but also after he mustered up the courage to dissolve the relationship. They witnessed incidents on campus. Although his father and I and others believed that his life was in danger due to the nature of her behavior whenever she would lose her temper and attack him, his decision was a difficult one because she had become an important part of our family. She often was included in family trips, outings and vacations. Upon discovering that Terrell was being emotionally and physically abused, his father and I intervened and discouraged the continuation of the relationship. Although we loved G[redacted] and had become very fond of her, we feared that Terrell would either be physically hurt and/or his future destroyed because of her mental instability. (She will stop at nothing to get her way). And she was very insecure, possessive, controlling and quick tempered. I recognized the warning signs and talked her into seeking help from the counseling center on campus. She even listed me as next of kin during an incident in the Spring semester when she had to be hospitalized. The stronger Terrell became in avoiding contact with her, the more unstable she became.

I spoke with her father on yesterday (he called me twice), who constantly insists that Terrell should just take G[redacted]'s blows and attacks and call it a day. I became even more concerned because he is oblivious to the fact that she needs psychiatric help as is the entire family. In their minds, Terrell abandoned her and is a coward for putting his own safety first. As parents, Terrell's father and I beg to differ. We are seriously concerned about this family's mental state. Although we changed Terrell's cell number a few months ago, G[redacted] managed to acquire it recently and the threatening phone calls have once again started as they did when the two of them were a couple. Terrell has endured a lot and is on track to graduate in May 2012. This incident is her "sick" plan to "get him back" for refusing to acknowledge her, particularly since the trip to Florida did not include her; (she celebrated with my family in Florida last year, a decision that haunts me to this day) and her recent birthday was not celebrated by Terrell. She assured him that she was going to destroy him and that he was going to "go to jail". She prevailed!! It is not unusual for her to stress the point that her father is a former policeman and can find out anything that he desires about anyone on campus. So, "don't mess with her or her family".

I believe that she will continue with this attitude that clearly sends the message that she can do anything that she desires and suffer no consequences. Case and point. As I was waiting for Terrell to be discharged from the detention center earlier, G[redacted]'s friend was involved in a conversation with another SSU student who announced that he had been suspended from campus. She was not aware that I was Terrell's mother and stated to the

young man: ""Oh my friend was too but she is going to appeal to Dr. G[redacted]. He'll let you back on." She was referring to G[redacted] G[redacted]. Needless to say, it has impacted Terrell and my entire family and I hope that this letter provides you with some additional information that will help to clarify the true nature of the incident. Please don't allow this sick game that this young lady and her family are playing to disrupt Terrell's life any further. There is an enormous amount of evidence that supports everything that has been reported. If it is needed, please feel free to solicit it. Thanks.

Irma J. Gibson

APPENDIX 8: SSU STUDENT AFFAIRS APPEAL DECISION

OFFICE OF THE VICE PRESIDENT FOR STUDENT AFFAIRS

Box 20521
3219 College Street
Savannah, GA 31404
P: (912) 356-2194
F: (912) 356-2464

October 17, 2011

Mr. Terrell Gibson - [redacted] **Hand delivered**
University Commons, Apt. 1104A
Savannah State University
Savannah, Georgia 31404
(E-mailed to: tgibson7@student.savannahstate.edu)

Dear Mr. Gibson,

I have reviewed your appeal request, and the supporting information related to the incident alleging a Student Code of Ethics **Level 1.1 'Zero Tolerance' Misconduct (Assault)** violation per the Appeal Procedures noted in the *Student Code of Ethics.* In reviewing this matter, I considered whether or not the decision to suspend you was reached in a fair and impartial manner; whether or not the action taken was too severe for the nature of the infraction; whether or not you were denied due process; and whether or not the evidence presented was insufficient to support the findings.

After a thorough review of the written documents from the SSUPD Incident Report(s) and your written statements, subsequent correspondences, discussions and consideration of the issues discussed with you on Friday, October 14, 2011 at Hill Hall with your parents in attendance, I **did** find cause to **modify** the sanctions issued by Mr. [redacted], Interim Coordinator of Student Ethics as noted below.

SANCTIONS:

1. **Summary Suspended from Savannah State University lifted immediately!**
2. To avoid future conflict, you are **MANDATED** to refrain from having any written, oral, telephonic, pictorial, electronic and/or physical contact with **Ms.** [redacted]. You are to immediately contact the Office of Student Ethics and Public Safety should Ms. [redacted] makes any contact with you in the manner as noted above.
3. **Mandated to attend Healthy Choices Session(s) with Ms.** [redacted], **Director of Counseling Services no later than October 21, 2011.** Contact Ms. [redacted], Secretary at 912.358.3129 to schedule appointment. The Office of Counseling will notify the Office of Student Ethics of your attendance
4. **WARNED.** You will face possible suspension and/or expulsion for violations of the Student Code of Ethics or the 2011-2012 Residence Handbook for incidents of the same nature.

Please understand that failure to satisfy any of the above required sanctions will be interpreted as violation of the terms of set forth and will be grounds for further sanctions up to suspension and/or permanent expulsion.

Should you wish to appeal these sanctions, you may do so by submitting a written appeal to the Vice President for Student Affairs within five business days of the original decision on the grounds for appeal as stated on page 75 of the 2011-2012 Savannah State University Handbook, otherwise these sanctions are effective immediately.

Sincerely,

[redacted]
Special Assistant to the Vice President

cc: Dr. [redacted], Vice President for Student Affairs
Mr. [redacted], Interim Coordinator of Student Ethics
Mr. [redacted], Chief, SSUPD
Ms. [redacted], Director for Residential Services & Programs
Ms. [redacted] Director, Office of Counseling Services
Mr. [redacted], Resident Director, University Commons
Student Ethics File

APPENDIX 9: FAMILY PICTURES

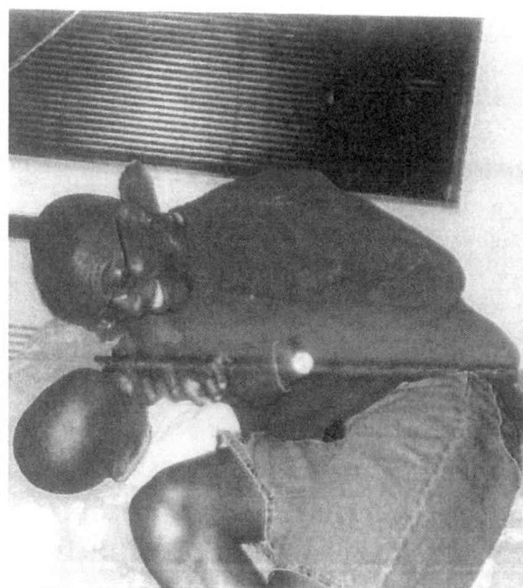

FAMILY

APPENDIX 10: NEGOTIATION LETTER FROM FIVE-YEAR-OLD TERRELL

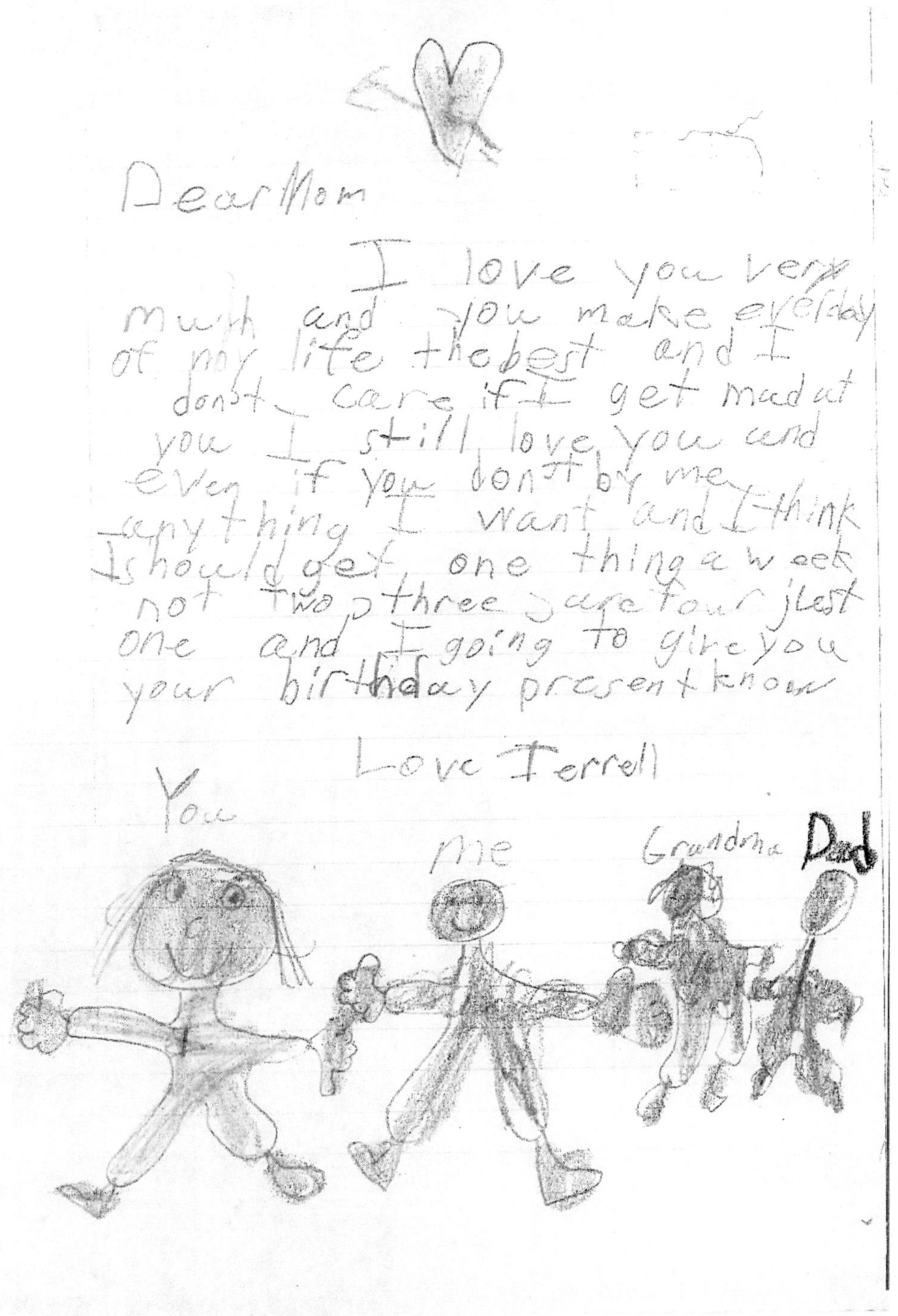

Dear Mom

I love you very
mush and you make everday
of my life the best and I
don't care if I get mad at
you I still love you and
even if you don't by me
anything I want and I think
I should get one thing a week
not two, three, are four, just
one and I going to give you
your birthday present know

Love Terrell

Terrell's first attempt to use his "Let's make a deal" skills.
Out of the mouth of babes . . .

APPENDIX 11: GREETING CARDS FROM TERRELL TO MOM

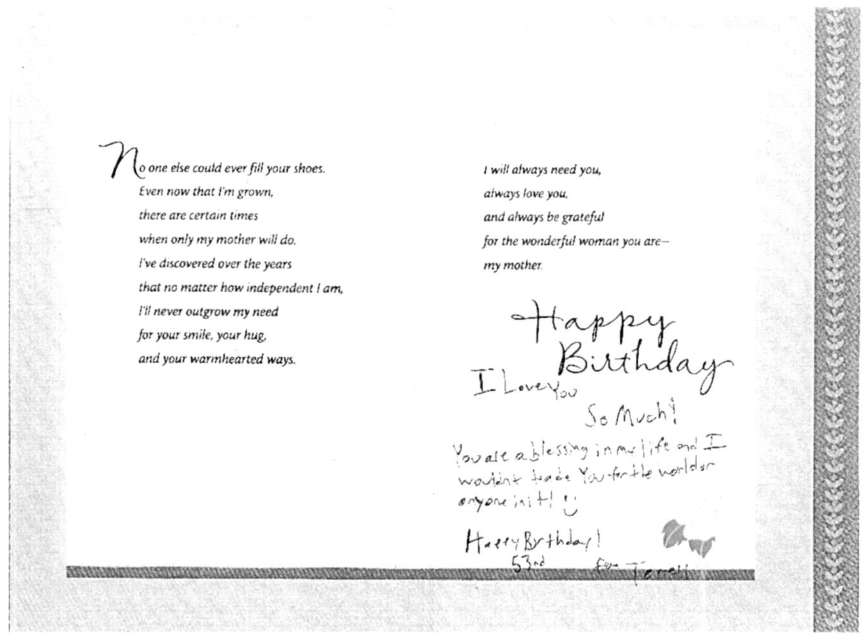

"There's only one you, Mom."

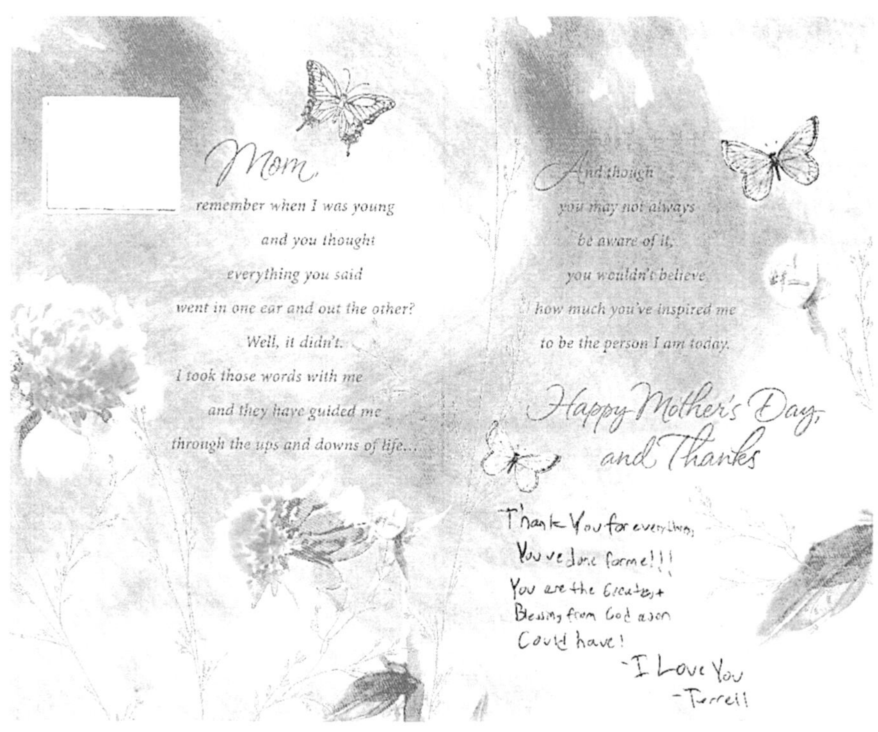

"It's great to be your son."

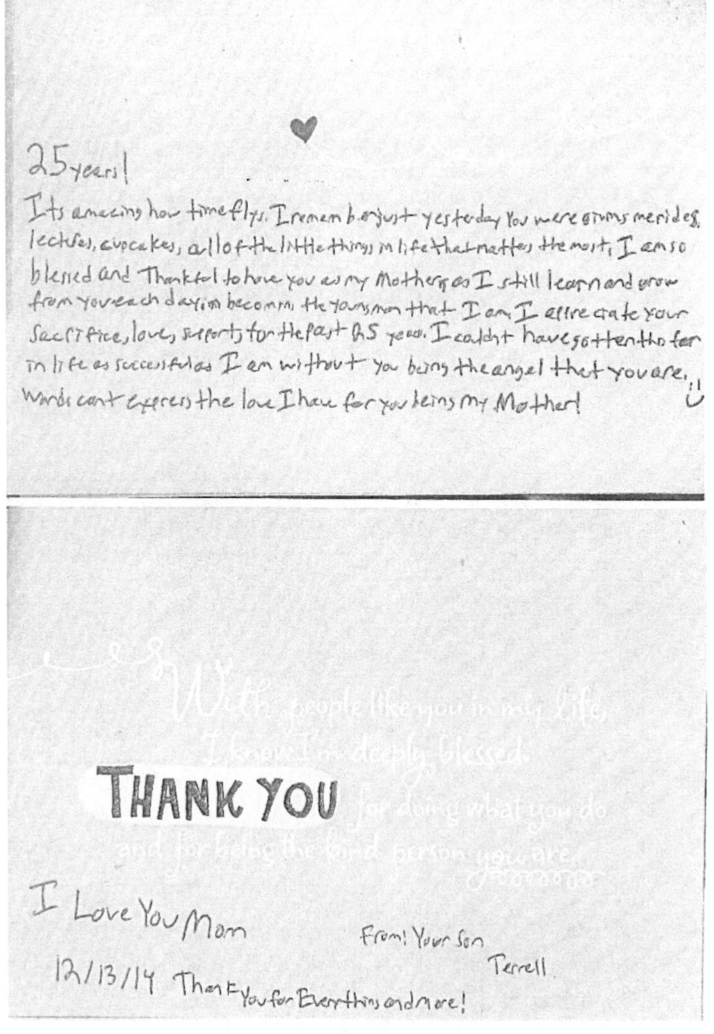

25 years!
Its amazing how time flys. I remember just yesterday you were giving me rides, lectures, cupcakes, all of the little things in life that matters the most. I am so blessed and Thankful to have you as my Mother as I still learn and grow from you each day in becoming the young man that I am. I appreciate your sacrifice, love, support for the past 25 years. I couldn't have gotten this far in life as successful as I am without you being the angel that you are.
Words can't express the love I have for you being my Mother! :)
With people like you in my life, I know I'm deeply blessed.
THANK YOU for doing what you do and for being the kind person you are.
I Love You Mom
From! Your Son Terrell
12/13/14 Thank You for Everything and more!

A card from Terrell to his mom on his *twenty-fifth birthday. Who does that?*

APPENDIX 12: "THE GOOD IN YOU"

THE GOOD IN YOU

"Character Strengths are the positive parts of your personality that impact how you think, feel and behave and are the keys to you being your best self. When applied effectively, they are beneficial both to you and society as a whole. They are different than your other strengths, such as your unique skills, talents, interests and resources, because character strengths reflect the 'real' you—who you are at your core" (The VIA Institute on Character, 2019).

Courtesy, practicing good manners; Civic responsibility and social consciousness

Honesty and integrity; Humility

Attitude (your attitude determines your Altitude)

Responsibility (taking ownership of your actions); Restraint/temperance

Accountability and Appreciation for differences and diversity

Compassion, Caring, and Choosing love and peace over hate

Treating others the way you want to be treated; Taking the high road

Excellence in your mindset and all that you establish and attempt as a goal

Respect for self and others; Release of grudges

YOUR CHARACTER IS WHAT YOU DO WHEN NO ONE IS LOOKING
(THE INWARD VALUES THAT DETERMINE OUTWARD ACTIONS)

Weigh Your Moral Compass

VIA Institute on Character. (N.d.). "Character Strengths Fact Sheets." Retrieved from http://www.viacharacter.org/www/Character-Strengths.

APPENDIX 13: "LIFE IS A THEATER"

Life Is a Theater

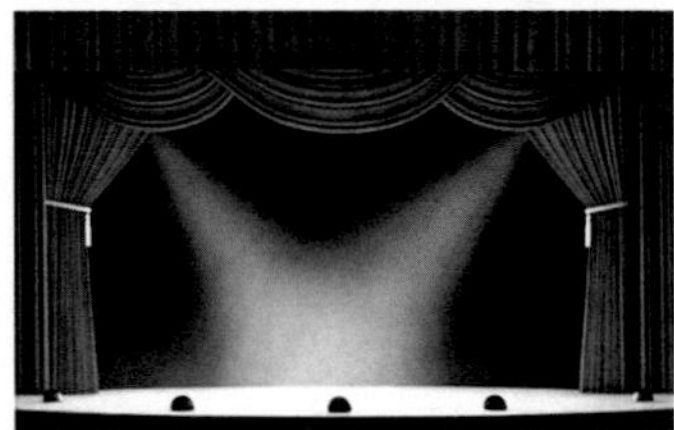

Life is a theater, so invite your audience carefully.
Not everyone can or should have a front row seat.
And *you* get to decide who will sit there.
Observe the relationships around you.
Which ones lift, which ones lean, and which ones limit?
Which ones encourage and which ones dishearten?
When you leave certain people, do you feel better or worse?
Are they leading you up a path of growth, going nowhere . . . or worse, taking you downhill?
Are there people who don't really know or understand you, and never take the time to try?
What about critics, those who judge you and all that you do?
And are there those near you who only want to upstage you?
Know this: some people in your life are best loved from a distance.
It's amazing what you can accomplish when you let go of, or at least minimize, your time spent with draining, negative, incompatible, not-going-anywhere friendships.
Observe the relationships around you. Pay attention!
Who are the directors, working to bring out the best in you?
Is there a supporting cast, helping you in your role?
Which ones make up your loyal fan club, applauding your efforts, and even giving an occasional standing ovation? Who affirms and appreciates all your hard work?
These are the people worthy of your attention, your time and your energy.
The more you seek respect, growth, peace of mind, love and truth, the easier it will become for you to decide who sits in the front row and who should be moved to the balcony. In the finale, you cannot "change" most of the people around you, so you have to change the people you are around the most! Life is a theater, and **YOU** are the star.

APPENDIX 14: IPV ARREST POLICIES BY STATE

State	IPV Arrest Policy	Relevant Statute	Circumstances
Alabama	Officer's Discretion	Ala. Code 1975 § 15-10-3 (8)	An officer may arrest a person when an offense involves domestic violence, and the arrest is based on probable cause, regardless of whether the offense is a felony or misdemeanor.
Alaska	Mandatory Arrest; Mutual is discretionary	Alaska Stat. § 18.65.530 (A)and (B)	An officer shall arrest a person when there is probable cause to believe that a crime of domestic violence has been committed in past 12 hours. When there are mutual accusations, policy of determination based upon the primary aggressor.
Arizona	Discretionary Arrest/ Mandatory Arrest	Ariz. Legis. Serv. Ch. 90 §13–3601(B)	An officer shall arrest where infliction of physical injury or involving the discharge, use, or threatening exhibition of a deadly weapon or dangerous instrument. Otherwise, discretionary.
Arkansas	Pro-Arrest; Mutual is discretionary	Ark. Code Ann. § 16-81-113 (a)(1)(A) and (a)(2)(A)	Where probable cause exists, arrest is the preferred action. Mutual accusations to be evaluated separately, policy of determination based upon primary aggressor.
California	Pro-Arrest/ Mandatory Arrest; Mutual is discouraged	Cal. Penal Code § 13701(B)	Arrest encouraged where probable cause. Mandatory arrest when claiming violation of domestic violence protective or restraining order. Dual arrests are discouraged, but not prohibited. Reasonable efforts shall be made to identify primary aggressor.

Colorado	Mandatory Arrest; Mutual is discretionary	Colo. Rev. Stat. § 18-6-803.6	An officer shall arrest where probable cause to believe that a crime involving domestic violence was committed. Mutual accusations to be evaluated separately.
Connecticut	Mandatory Arrest; Mutual is discretionary	Conn. Gen. Stat.§ 46b-38b (a)	An officer shall arrest whenever the officer determines upon speedy information that an act of domestic violence has occurred.
Delaware	Officer's Discretion	Del. Code Ann. Tit 11 § 1904 (A)(4)	An officer may arrest whenever there are reasonable grounds to believe that any misdemeanor involving physical injury or the threat thereof or any misdemeanor involving illegal sexual contact or attempted sexual contact has taken place.
DC	Mandatory Arrest	D.C. Code Ann. § 16-1031 (a)	An officer shall arrest where probable cause to believe physical injury or the threat thereof has occurred.
Florida	Officer's Discretion; Mutual is discouraged	Fla. Stat. Ann. § 741.29 (3) and 4(a) and 4(b)	An officer may arrest whenever the officer determines upon probable cause that an act of domestic violence has been committed. Mutual accusations to be evaluated separately; mutual arrests strongly discouraged, policy of determination based upon primary aggressor.
Georgia	Officer's Discretion	Ga. Code Ann., § 17-4-20 (A) and Ga. Code Ann., § 17-4-20.1 (A) and (B)	An officer may arrest where probable cause to believe an act of family violence occurred, without the consent of the victim and without consideration of the relationship between the parties. Where mutual accusations,

			policy of determination based upon primary aggressor.
Hawaii	Officer's Discretion	Haw. Rev. Stat § 709-906 (2)	An officer may arrest a person if the officer has reasonable grounds to believe that the person is physically abusing, or has physically abused, a family or household member.
Idaho	Officer's Discretion	I.C. § 19-603 (6)	An officer may arrest when upon immediate response to a report of a commission of a crime there is probable cause to believe that the person arrested has committed a violation of 18-918 (domestic assault or battery).
Illinois	Officer's Discretion	725 Ill. Comp. Stat. 5/112A-30	Whenever a law enforcement officer has reason to believe that a person has been abused by a family or household member, the officer shall immediately use all reasonable means to prevent further abuse, including arresting the abusing party, where appropriate.
Indiana	Officer's Discretion	IC 35-33-1-1 (A)(5)(B)	An officer may arrest when there is probable cause to believe a domestic battery has been committed.
Iowa	Discretionary Arrest/Mandatory Arrest	Iowa Code Ann. §§ 236.12 (2)(a) and (2)(b)	Arrest is discretionary where probable cause to believe domestic abuse assault has been committed, not resulting in physical injury. Arrest is mandatory where probable cause to believe domestic abuse assault has been committed that resulted in physical injury, or was committed with intent to inflict serious injury; or with display of a dangerous weapon.

Kansas	Mandatory Arrest	Kan. Stat. Ann. § 22-2307 (b)(1)	Officers shall make an arrest when they have probable cause to believe that a crime is being committed or has been committed.
Kentucky	Officer's Discretion	Ky. Rev. Stat. § 431.005 (2)(a)	Any peace officer may arrest a person without warrant when the peace officer has probable cause to believe that the person has intentionally or wantonly caused physical injury to a family member or member of an unmarried couple.
Louisiana	Mandatory Arrest; Mutual is discretionary	La. Rev. Stat. Ann. § 46-2140 A(1), A(2), and B(1)	An officer shall arrest where reason to believe family/household member has been abused and (1) probable cause to believe that there has been aggravated or second-degree battery or (2) reasonable belief that impending danger to victim exists where aggravated or simple battery/assault has occurred. Mutual accusations to be evaluated separately, policy of determination based upon primary aggressor.
Maine	Mandatory Arrest	Me. Rev. Stat. Ann. Tit 19-A § 4012 (5)	An officer shall arrest where probable cause to believe there has been a violation of Title 17-A § 208 (aggravated assault) between members of the same family/ household.
Maryland	Officer's Discretion; Mutual is discretionary	Md. Crim. Proc. § 2-204 (A)(1), (A)(2), and (B)	(A) A police officer may arrest a person if: (1) the police officer has probable cause to believe that: (i) the person battered the person's spouse or household member; (ii) there is evidence of physical injury; and (iii) unless arrested

			immediately, the person: 1. may not be apprehended; 2. may cause physical injury or property damage to another; or 3. may tamper with, dispose of, or destroy evidence; and (2) A report to police was made within 48 hours of the alleged incident. (B) Policy of determination based upon primary aggressor.
Massachusetts	Pro-Arrest/ Mandatory Arrest	Mass. Gen. Laws Ann. Ch. 209a § 6 (7)	Arrest shall be the preferred response whenever an officer witnesses or has probable cause to believe that a person has committed a felony, a misdemeanor involving abuse, or an assault and battery. Mandatory arrest when a law officer has probable cause to believe person has violated a temporary or permanent vacate, restraining, or no-contact order or judgment.
Michigan	Officer's Discretion	Mich. Comp. Laws § 764.15a	An officer may arrest if the officer has reasonable cause to believe both of the following: (a) The violation ("domestic assault") has occurred or is occurring and (b) the individual has had a child in common with the victim, resides or has resided in the same household as the victim, has or has had a dating relationship with the victim, or is a spouse or former spouse.
Minnesota	Officer's Discretion	Minn. Stat. Ann. § 629.341 Subd.1	A peace officer may arrest a person anywhere without a warrant, including at the person's residence, if the peace officer has probable cause to

			believe that within the preceding 24 hours the person has committed domestic abuse.
Mississippi	Mandatory Arrest	Miss. Code Ann. § 99-3-7 (3)	Any law enforcement officer shall arrest a person when he has probable cause to believe that the person has, within 24 hrs, knowingly committed a misdemeanor act of domestic violence or knowingly violated provisions of an ex parte protective order, protective order after hearing or court-approved consent.
Missouri	Officer's Discretion/ Mandatory Arrest; Mutual is discretionary	Mo. Rev. Stat. §455.085.1, 455.085.3	Officer may arrest when probable cause to believe there has been abuse or assault against a family or household member has been committed. Mandatory arrest when a law enforcement officer has probable cause to believe that a party, against whom a protective order has been entered and who has notice of such order entered, has committed an act of abuse in violation of such order. Policy of determination based upon primary aggressor.
Montana	Pro-Arrest; Mutual is discretionary	Mont. Code Ann. § 46-6-311 (2)(A) and (2)(B)	Arrest is the preferred response in partner or family member assault cases involving injury to the victim, use or threatened use of a weapon, violation of a restraining order or other imminent danger to the victim. Policy of determination based upon primary aggressor.
Nebraska	Officer's Discretion	Neb. Rev. Stat. § 29-404.02 (1)(C)	A peace officer may arrest a person without a warrant if (s)he has reasonable cause to believe

			that such person has committed one or more of the following acts to one or more household members: (a) Attempting to cause or intentionally, knowingly, or recklessly causing bodily injury with or without a deadly weapon; or (b) Threatening another in a menacing manner.
Nevada	Mandatory Arrest; Mutual is discretionary	Nev. Rev. Stat. § 171.137	A peace officer shall arrest when the peace officer has probable cause to believe that the person has committed a battery in the last 24 hours.
New Hampshire	Officer's Discretion/ Mandatory Arrest	N.H. Rev. Stat. Ann. § 594:10 (I)(B); N.H. Rev. Stat. Ann. § 173-B:9	An officer may arrest if there is probable cause to believe that in the last 12 hours a person has committed an abuse, including domestic violence. An officer shall arrest if person violates a temporary or permanent restraining order.
New Jersey	Mandatory Arrest (under certain circumstances)	N.J. Stat. Ann. § 2c: 25-21	An officer shall arrest if there is probable cause to believe domestic violence has occurred and either victim shows signs of injury, there is probable cause to believe that a weapon was involved, or there is probable cause to believe the person has violated a judicial or protective order.
New Mexico	Officer's Discretion	N.M.S.A. 1978, § 31-1-7 (A)	A peace officer may arrest a person and take that person into custody without a warrant when the officer is at the scene of a domestic disturbance and has probable cause to believe that the person has committed an assault

			or a battery upon a household member.
New York	Discretionary Arrest/ Mandatory Arrest	N.Y. Crim. Proc. Law § 140.10 (1) and (4)(a) and (b)	An officer may arrest a person when there is probable cause to believe the person has committed an offense. An officer shall arrest when there is probable cause to believe the person has committed a felony against a member of the same household or when there is probable cause to believe a protective order has been violated.
North Carolina	Officer's Discretion	N.C.G.S.A. § 15a-401 (b) (1) (2)	An officer may arrest a person when there is probable cause to believe the person has committed 1. A felony, 2. A misdemeanor and will not be apprehended unless immediately arrested or may cause physical injury to himself or others, or damage to property unless immediately arrested, or 3. Has committed one of the listed misdemeanors.
North Dakota	Pro-Arrest	N.D. Cent. Code § 14-07.1-10	If probable cause to believe that a person has committed a crime involving domestic violence, whether the offense is a felony or misdemeanor, and whether or not the crime was committed in the presence of the officer, then the law enforcement officer shall presume that arresting.
Ohio	Mandatory Arrest; Mutual is discretionary	Ohio Rev. Code Ann. § 2935.032 (A)(1)(a); Ohio Rev. Code Ann. § 2935.03 (A)(1)(a)(ii)	An officer shall arrest if there are reasonable grounds to believe that a person knowingly caused physical harm to another or another's unborn or knowingly caused or attempted to cause physical harm with a deadly

			weapon unless there are mutual accusations, in which case there is a policy of determination based upon primary aggressor.
Oklahoma	Officer's Discretion	Okl. Stat. §22-196 (6), (7), and (8)	A police officer may arrest a person if the officer has probable cause to believe that the person has committed and act of domestic violence in the last 72 hours and there are physical signs of injury, impairment of physical condition, a threat made to the victim, or a violation of a protective order.
Oregon	Mandatory Arrest	Or. Rev. Stat. § 133.055 (2)(a),(b),(c)	A police officer shall arrest a person if the officer has probable cause to believe that a felonious assault or an assault resulting in physical injury occurred or action has placed another to reasonably fear imminent serious bodily injury or death.
Pennsylvania	Officer's Discretion	18 Pa. Cons. Stat. Ann. § 2711(a)	A police officer may arrest a person where there is probable cause to believe the person has committed simple assault, aggravated assault, reckless endangerment of another person, or harassment or stalking against a family or household member.
Rhode Island	Mandatory Arrest; Mutual is discretionary	R.I. Gen. Laws § 12-29-3 (b), (c)	A police officer shall arrest whenever there is probable cause to believe any of the following has occurred: felonious assault, assault resulting in injury (physical pain, illness, or an impairment of physical condition), action intending to cause fear of imminent serious bodily injury or death, or

			violation of a protective order or no-contact order. There is a policy of determination of primary aggressor in cases of mutual accusations.
South Carolina	Mandatory Arrest (with physical injury; discretionary without)	S.C. Code Ann. § 16-25-70	A police officer must arrest if physical injury is present and there is probable cause to believe a person is committing or has freshly committed a misdemeanor/felony assault or battery. A police officer may arrest when there is probable cause but no physical injury. There is a policy of determination of primary aggressor in cases of mutual accusations.
South Dakota	Mandatory Arrest	S.D. Codified Laws Ann. §§ 23a3-2.1	A police officer shall arrest a person if officer has probable cause to believe a protective order has been violated. An officer shall arrest when officer has probable cause to believe that a person 18+ yrs and within last 48 hrs has assaulted a spouse, former spouse, the parent of that person's child, or any person with whom the offender resides or has formerly resided and that an aggravated assault or assault resulting in bodily injury has occurred, or an attempt has been made to put another in fear of imminent serious bodily harm.
Tennessee	Pro-Arrest; Mutual is discretionary	Tenn. Code Ann. § 36-3-619 (a) and (b)	Arrest is the preferred response when a law enforcement officer has probable cause to believe that a person has committed a crime involving domestic abuse,

			whether a misdemeanor or felony. If an officer has probable cause to believe that 2+ persons committed a crime, or 2+ persons make complaints to the officer, the officer shall try to determine the primary aggressor. Arrest is the preferred response only with respect to the primary aggressor.
Texas	Officer's Discretion	Tex. C.C.P. Art. 14.03 (A)(4)	A peace officer may arrest a person whom the officer has probable cause to believe has committed an offense involving family violence.
Utah	Mandatory Arrest; Mutual is discretionary	Utah Code Ann. § 77-36-2.2 (2)and (3)	If the peace officer has probable cause to believe that there will be continued violence against the alleged victim, or if there is evidence that the perpetrator has either recently caused serious bodily injury or used a dangerous weapon in the domestic violence offense, the officer shall arrest the alleged perpetrator into custody. Policy of determination based upon primary aggressor.
Vermont	Officer's Discretion	Vt. R.Cr.P. Rule 3	An officer may arrest for a misdemeanor where the officer has probable cause to believe that the person to be arrested has committed an assault against a family or household member, or a child of a family or household member.
Virginia	Discretionary Arrest	Va. Code Ann. § 19.2-81.3	Any officer may arrest without a warrant for an alleged violation (assault, battery, violation of protective order) regardless of whether such violation was

			committed in his presence, if based on probable cause or upon personal observations or the reasonable complaint of a person who observed the alleged offense or upon personal investigation. An officer having probable cause to believe that a violation occurred shall arrest and take into custody the person he has probable cause to believe, based on the totality of the circumstances, was the predominant physical aggressor unless there are special circumstances which would dictate a course of action other than an arrest.
Washington	Mandatory Arrest; Mutual is discretionary	Wash. Rev. Code Ann. §10.31.100 (1), (2)(a),(b),(c)	A police officer shall arrest a person if 16+ and within the preceding four hours has assaulted a family or household member and the officer believes: (i) A felonious assault has occurred; (ii) an assault has occurred which has resulted in bodily injury to the victim observable or not; or (iii) that any physical action has occurred which was intended to cause another person reasonably to fear imminent serious bodily injury or death. An officer shall arrest for violation of protection order. Policy of determination based upon primary aggressor.

West Virginia	Officer's Discretion	W. Va. Code, § 48-27-1002 (a) and (b)	A law-enforcement officer may arrest a person if the officer has observed credible corroborative evidence that an offense has occurred and either the law-enforcement officer has received, from the victim or a witness, an oral or written allegation of facts constituting a violation of section twenty-eight, article two, chapter sixty-one of this code (domestic violence offense) or the law-enforcement officer has observed credible evidence that the accused committed the offense.

BIBLIOGRAPHY

PREFACE AND INTRODUCTION

Brehm, S., and Brehm, J. W. (1981). *Psychological Reactance: A Theory of Freedom and Control.* New York: Academic Press.

Centers for Disease Control and Prevention. (N.d.). "Intimate Partner Violence: Definitions." Retrieved from http://www.cdc.gov/violenceprevention/intimatepartnerviolence/definitions.html.

Centers for Disease Control and Prevention. (N.d.). "Intimate Partner Violence: Consequences." Retrieved from: https://www.cdc.gov/violenceprevention/intimatepartnerviolence/consequences.html.

Weinberger, B. Z. Esq. (2015). "It's Time to Acknowledge Male Victims of Domestic Violence." Retrieved from https://www.huffingtonpost.com/bari-zell-weinberger-esq/its-time-to-acknowledge-m_b_8292976.html.

CHAPTER 1

Aratani, Y. (2009). "Homeless Children and Youth: Causes and Consequences." New York: National Center for Children in Poverty.

Breiding, M. J., Basile, K. C., Smith, S. G., Black, M. C., and Mahendra, R. R. (2015). "Intimate Partner Violence Surveillance: Uniform Definitions and Recommended Data Elements, Version 2.0." Atlanta, GA: National Center for Injury Prevention and Control, Centers for Disease Control and Prevention. https://www.cdc.gov/violenceprevention/pdf/ipv/intimatepartnerviolence.

Breiding, M. J., Chen J., and Black, M. C. (2014). "Intimate Partner Violence in the United States 2010." Atlanta, GA: National Center for Injury Prevention and Control, Centers for Disease Control and Prevention.

Christle, C., Jolivette, K., Nelson, C. M., and Scott, T. M. (2007). "Moving beyond What We Know: Risk and Resilience Factors and the Development of EBD: The National Center on Education, Disability and Juvenile Justice."

Enander, V., and Holmberg, C. (2008). "Why Does She Leave? The Leaving Process(es) of Battered Women." *Health Care for Women International* 29, no. 3: 200–226.

Facts for Life. (2010). (4th ed.). Retrieved from http://www.factsforlifeglobal.org/03/.

Giedd, J. N. (2004). "Structural Magnetic Resonance Imaging of the Adolescent Brain." Adolescent Brain Development: Vulnerabilities and Opportunities: 77–85.

Gitterman, A. (2014). *Handbook of Social Work Practice with Vulnerable and Resilient Populations* (3rd ed.). New York: Columbia University Press. Retrieved from https://inpublicsafety.com/2015/10/domestic-violence-and-intimate-partner-violence-whats-the-difference/.

Hutchison, E. D. (2015). *Dimensions of Human Behavior: The Changing Life Course* (5th ed.). Thousand Oaks, CA: Sage Publication, Sage, Inc.

James, S. D. (2012). "'Mama's Boy Myth': Sons Who Are Close to Mom Are Stronger (ABC News)." *Good Morning America*. Retrieved from https://www.yahoo.com/gma/mamas-boy-myth-sons-close-mom-stronger-201451350--abc-news.html.

Johnson, S. B., Blum, R., and Giedd, J. N. (2009). "Adolescent Maturity and the Brain: The Promise and Pitfalls of Neuroscience Research in Adolescent Health Policy." *Journal of Adolescent Health* 45, no. 3 (September 2009): 216–221. doi: 10.1016/j.jadohealth.2009.05.016.

Lahey, J. (2014). "Raising Teenagers: Protect When You Must, Permit When You Can." *NY Times*. Motherlode. Adventures in Parenting. https://parenting.blogs.nytimes.com/2014/09/18/raising-teenagers-protect-when-you-must-permit-when-you-can/.

Little, W. (2016). *Introduction to Sociology: 2nd Canadian Edition*. Retrieved from https://opentextbc.ca/introductiontosociology2ndedition/.

Nealon-Woods, M. (2016). "The Realities of Domestic Violence and Its Impact on Our Society." The Chicago School of Professional Psychology.

Physicians for Human Rights. "Adolescent Brain Development: A Critical Factor in Juvenile Justice Reform." Retrieved from physiciansforhumanrights.org/juvenilejustice/factsheets/braindev.pdf.

Smith, S. G., Chen, J., Basile, K. C., Gilbert, L. K., Merrick, M. T., Patel, N., Walling, M., and Jain, A. (2017). *The National Intimate Partner and Sexual Violence Survey (NISVS): 2010–2012 State Report.* Atlanta, GA: National Center for Injury Prevention and Control, Center for Disease Control and Prevention.

Tjaden, P., and Thoennes, N. (2000). "Full Report of the Prevalence, Incidence, and Consequences of Violence against Women: Findings from the National Violence against Women Survey." Research report.

Wallace, R. (2015). "Domestic Violence and Intimate Partner Violence: What's The Difference?" Public Safety. National Center for PTSD. Intimate Partner Violence. United States Department of Veteran Affairs. Retrieved from Washington, DC, and Atlanta, GA: US Department of Justice, National Institute of Justice, and US Department of Health and Human Services, Centers for Disease Control and Prevention.

Zastrow, C., and Kirst-Ashman, K. (2015). *Empowerment Series: Understanding Human Behavior and the Social Environment* (10th ed.). Belmont, CA: Thomson.

CHAPTER 3

Black Demographics. (N.d.). "The African American Population Report: Black Male Statistics." Retrieved from http://blackdemographics.com/population/black-male-statistics/.

Children's Defense Fund. (2008). "Child Research Data." Retrieved from http://cdf.childrensdefense.org/site/DocServer/state-of-americas-children-2008-report.pdf?docID=9061.

Cook, C. (2005). "Going Home: Formerly Incarcerated African American Men Return to Families and Communities." *Journal of Family Nursing* 11, no. 4: 388–404.

Dublin, H. (2018). "Endangered Species." *Encyclopedia Britannica*. Retrieved from https://www.britannica.com/science/endangered-species.

Federal Bureau of Investigation. (2011). "Crime in the United States, 2010." Uniform Crime Reports, US Department of Justice. Retrieved from https://ucr.fbi.gov/crime-in-the-u.s/2010/crime-in-the-u.s.-2010.

Gitterman, A. (2014). *Handbook of Social Work Practice with Vulnerable and Resilient Populations* (3rd ed.). New York: Columbia University Press.

National Center for Injury Prevention and Control, Division of Violence Prevention (NCIPCDVP). (2017). "Intimate Partner Violence: Risk and Protective Factors." Retrieved from https://www.cdc.gov/violenceprevention/intimatepartnerviolence/riskprotectivefactors.html.

National Center for Injury Prevention and Control, Division of Violence Prevention (NCIPCDVP). (2017). "Preventing Intimate Partner Violence." Retrieved from https://www.cdc.gov/violenceprevention/pdf/ipv-factsheet.pdf.

The Annie E. Casey Foundation. (2010). "Early Warning! Why Reading by the End of Third Grade Matters." Baltimore, MD: A Kids Count Special Report from the Annie E. Casey Foundation. Retrieved from http://www.aecf.org/resources/early-warning-why-reading-by-the-end-of-third-grade-matters/.

CHAPTER 4

Wallace, R. (2015). "Identifying Signs of Intimate Partner Violence." Public Safety. Retrieved from https://inpublicsafety.com/2015/01/identifying-signs-of-intimate-partner-violence/.

CHAPTER 5

Archer, J. (1999). "Assessment of the Reliability of the Conflict Tactics Scales: A Meta-Analytic Review." *Journal of Interpersonal Violence* 14, no. 12: 1263–1289.

Archer, J. (2000). "Sex Differences in Aggression between Heterosexual Partners: A Meta-Analytic Review." *Psychological Bulletin* 126: 651–680.

Arnocky, S., and Vaillancourt, T. (2014). "Sex Differences in Response to Victimization by an Intimate Partner: More Stigmatization and Less Help-Seeking among Males." *Journal of Aggression, Maltreatment & Trauma* 23: 705–724. doi: 10.1080/10926771.2014.933465.

Basile, S. (2005). "A Measure of Court Response to Requests for Protection." *Journal of Family Violence* 20: 171–179. doi: 10.1007/s10896-005-3653-x.

Brown, G. A. (2004). "Gender as a Factor in the Response of the Law Enforcement System to Violence against Partners." *Sexuality and Culture* 8, no. 3–4: 3–139. doi:10.1007/s12119-004-1000-7.

Carlyle, K. E., Scarduzio, J. A., and Slater, M. D. (2014). "Media Portrayals of Female Perpetrators of Intimate Partner Violence." *Journal of Interpersonal Violence* 29, no. 13: 2394–2417. doi:10.1177 /0886260513520231.

Cook, P. W. (2009). *Abused Men: The Hidden Side of Domestic Violence* (2nd ed.). Westport, CT: Praeger.

Coney, N. S., and Mackey, W. C. (1999). "The Feminization of Domestic Violence in America: The Woozle Effect Goes beyond Rhetoric." *Journal of Men's Studies* 8: 45–58.

Copp, J., Giordano, P., Longmore, M., and Manning, W. (2016). "The Development of Attitudes toward Intimate Partner Violence: An Examination of Key Correlates among a Sample of Young Adults." *Journal of Interpersonal Violence* 30, no. 17: 3112–3132. doi: 10.1177/0886260516651311.

Eckstein, J. (2016). "IPV Stigma and Its Social Management: The Roles of Relationship-Type, Abuse-Type, and Victims' Sex." *Journal of Family Violence* 31: 215–225. doi: 10.1007/s10896-015-9752-4.

Glaser, B. G., and Strauss, A. L. (1967). *The Discovery of Grounded Theory: Strategies for Qualitative Research*. Chicago: Aldine Publishing Company.

Grant, J. (2004). "A 'REAL BOY' and Not a Sissy: Gender, Childhood and Masculinity, 1890–1940." *Journal of Social History*: 830–851.

Henning, K., Jones, A., and Holdford, R. (2005). "'I Didn't Do It, but If I Did I Had a Good Reason': Minimization, Denial, and Attributions of Blame among Male and Female Domestic Violence Offenders." *Journal of Family Violence* 20, no. 3: 131–139.

Hertzog, J., and Rowley, R. (2014). "My Beliefs of My Peers' Beliefs: Exploring the Gendered Nature of Social Norms in Adolescent Romantic Relationships." *Journal of Interpersonal Violence* 29, no. 2: 348–368. doi:10.1177/0886260513505145.

Hines, D. A., and Douglas, E. M. (2010). "A Closer Look at Men Who Sustain Intimate Terrorism by Women." *Partner Abuse* 1: 286–313. doi: 10.1891/1946-6560.1.3.286.

Hines, D. A., and Douglas, E. M. (2009). "Women's Use of Intimate Partner Violence against Men: Prevalence, Implications, and Consequences." *Journal of Aggression, Maltreatment & Trauma* 18: 572–586. doi: 10.1080/10926770903103099.

Hines, D. A., Douglas, E. M., and Berger, J. L. (2015). "A Self-Report Measure of Legal and Administrative Aggression within Intimate Relationships." *Aggressive Behavior* 41: 295–309. doi:10.1002/ab.21540.

Hines, D. A., Douglas, E. M., and Berger, J. L. (2014). "The Measurement of Legal/Administrative Aggression with Intimate Relationships." *Aggressive Behavior* 41, no. 4: 295–309. doi: 10.1002/ab.21540.

Kernsmith, P. (2005). "Exerting Power or Striking Back: A Gendered Comparison of Motivations for Domestic Violence Perpetration." *Victims and Violence* 20, no. 2: 173–185. doi:10.1891/088667005780905605.

Kim, J., and Kim, J. (2017). "Fathers' Indirect Contribution to Children's Social-Emotional Development via Mothers' Psychological Parenting Environment." *Social Behavior & Personality* 45, no. 5: 833–844. Retrieved from https://doi.org/10.2224/sbp.6187.

Kimmel, M. S. (2006). *Manhood in America: A Cultural History* (2nd ed.). New York: Oxford University Press.

Leonard, J. (2003). "The Hidden Victims of Domestic Violence." *Victimology* 7: 1–22.

Muftic, L., and Bouffard, J. (2007). "An Evaluation of Gender Differences in the Implementation and Impact of a Comprehensive Approach to Domestic Violence." *Violence Against Women* 13, no. 1: 46–69. doi:10.1177/1077801206295131.

Muller, H. J., Desmarais, S. L., and Hamel, J. M. (2009). "Do Judicial Responses to Restraining Order Requests Discriminate against Male Victims of Domestic Violence?" *Journal of Family Violence* 24, no. 8: 625–637. doi:10.1007/s10896-009-9261-4.

Murray, C. E., Crowe, A., and Brinkley, J. (2015). "The Stigma Surrounding Intimate Partner Violence: A Cluster Analysis Study." *Partner Abuse* 6, no. 3: 320–336. doi:10.1891/1946-6560.6.3.320.

Murray, C. E., Crowe, A., and Overstreet, N. M. (2015). "Sources and Components of Stigma Experienced by Survivors of Intimate Partner Violence." *Journal of Interpersonal Violence*. doi:10.1177/0886260515609565.

Nybergh, L., Enander, V., and Krantz, G. (2016). "Theoretical Considerations on Men's Experiences of Intimate Partner Violence: An Interview-Based Study." *Journal of Family Violence* 31:191–202. doi: 10.1007/s10896-015-9785-8.

Overstreet, N. M., Earnshaw, V. A., Kalichman, S. C., and Quinn, D. M. (2013). "Internalized Stigma and HIV Status Disclosure among HIV-Positive Black Men Who Have Sex with Men." *AIDS Care* 25, no. 4: 466–471. doi:10.1080/09540121.2012.720362.

Rhatigan, D. L., Stewart, C., and Moore, T. M. (2011). "Effects of Gender and Confrontation on Attributions of Female-Perpetrated Intimate Partner Violence." *Sex Roles* 64, no. 11: 875–887. doi:10.1007/s11199- 011-9951-2.

Robertson, K., and Murachver, T. (2009). "Attitudes and Attributions Associated with Female and Male Partner Violence." *Journal of Applied Sociology* 39, no. 7: 1481–1512. doi: 10.1111/j.1559- 1816.2009.00492.x.

Scarduzio, J. A., Carlyle, K. E., Harris, K. L., and Savage, M. W. (2016). "Maybe She Was Provoked: Exploring Gender Stereotypes about Male and Female Perpetrators of Intimate Partner Violence." *Violence Against Women*. doi:10.1177/1077801216636240. Advance online publication.

Shernock, S., and Russel, B. (2012). "Gender and Racial/Ethnic Differences in Criminal Justice Decision Making in Intimate Partner Violence Cases." *Partner Abuse* 3, no. 4: 501–530. doi:10.1891/1946-6560.3.4.501.

Smith, S., Chen, J., Basile, K., Gilbert, L., Merrick, M., Patal, N., Walling, M., and Jain, A. (2017). "The National Intimate Partner and Sexual Violence Survey (NISVS): 2010–2012 State Report." Atlanta, GA: National Center for Injury Prevention and Control, Centers for Disease Control and Prevention.

Sorenson, S. B., and Taylor, C. A. (2005). "Female Aggression toward Male Intimate Partners: An Examination of Social Norms in a Community-Based Sample." *Psychology of Women Quarterly* 29, no. 1: 78–96. doi:10.1111/j.1471-6402.2005.00170.x.

Squires, J., Bricker, D., and Twombly, E. (2001). *The ASQ:SE User's Guide for the Ages & Stages Questionnaire: Social Emotional (ASQ:SE): A Parent-Completed, Child-Monitoring System for Social-Emotional Behaviors*. Baltimore, MD: Brookes.

Straus, M. A. (2006). "Future Research on Gender Symmetry in Physical Assaults on Partners." *Violence Against Women* 12, no. 11: 1086–1097.

Straus, M. A., and Gelles, R. J. (1990). *Physical Violence in American Families: Risk Factors and Adaptations to Violence in 8,145 Families*. New Brunswick, NJ: Transaction Publishers.

Sylaska, K. M., and Edwards, K. M. (2014). "Disclosure of Intimate Partner Violence to Informal Social Support Network Members: A Review of the Literature." *Trauma, Violence, & Abuse* 15, no. 1: 3–21. doi: 10.1177/1524838013496335.

Sylaska, K. M., and Walters, A. S. (2014). "Testing the Extent of the Gender Trap: College Students' Perceptions of and Reactions to Intimate Partner Violence." *Sex Roles* 70, no. 3: 134–145. doi:10.1007/s11199-0140344-1.

Tilbrook, E., Allan, A., and Dear, G. (2010). *Intimate Partner Abuse of Men*. Perth, Western Australia: Men's Advisory Network.

Tjaden, P., and Thoennes, N. (2000). "Prevalence and Consequences of Male-to-Female and Female-to-Male Intimate Partner Violence as Measured by the National Violence against Women Survey." *Violence Against Women* 6: 142.

Trotter, J. L., and Allen, N. E. (2009). "The Good, the Bad, and the Ugly: Domestic Violence Survivors' Experiences with Their Informal Social Networks." *American Journal of Community Psychology* 43, no. 3-4: 221–231.

Tsiko, R. (2016). "A Spatial Latent Gaussian Model for Intimate Partner Violence against Men in Africa." *Journal of Family Violence*, 31:443–459. doi: 10.1007/s10896-015-9784-9.

Tsui, V., Cheung, M., and Leung, P. (2010). "Help-Seeking among Male Victims of Partner Abuse: Men's Hard Times." *Journal of Community Psychology* 38, no. 6: 769–780. doi: 10.1002/jcop.20394.

Tsui, V., Cheung, M., and Leung, P. (2012a). "Help-Seeking among Male Victims of Partner Abuse: Men's Hard Times." *Journal of Community Psychology* 38, no. 6: 769–780. doi:10.1002/jcop.20394.

Tsui, V., Cheung, M., and Leung, P. (2012b). "Male Victims in Heterosexual Intimate Partner Violence: A Framework Explaining Help-Seeking Reluctance." *International Journal of Psychology Research* 7, no. 1: 1–21.

White, A. (2009). "Big Boys Really Don't Cry: Considering Men's Reluctance to Engage in Counseling." *Psychology Review* 24, no. 3–4; 11, no. 1: 16–22. doi: 10.1111/cdep.12218.

CHAPTER 6

Bradshaw, C. (2013). "Domestic Violence and Self-Esteem." Retrieved from https://silencingsociety.blogspot.com/2015/04/.

Bradshaw, C. P., and Hazan, C. (2006). "Examining Views of Self in Relation to Views of Others: Implications for Research on Aggression and Self-Esteem." *Journal of Research in Personality* 40, no. 6: 1209–1218. https://doi.org/10.1016/j.jrp.2005.11.004.

Chandra, A., Martino, S. C., and Collins, R. (2012). "The 'Reality' of Health: Reality Television and the Public Health." *Pediatrics* 122, no. 5 (2008): 1047–1054.

Edelman, M. W. (2007). "A Call to End Adult Hypocrisy, Neglect and Abandonment of Children and America's Cradle to Prison Pipeline." Children's Defense Fund. Retrieved from https://www.childrensdefense.org/wp-content/uploads/2018/08/cradle-prison-pipeline-report-2007-full-lowres.pdf.

Fahner, M. (2012). "The Real Effects of Reality TV." *USA College Today*. Retrieved from http://college.usatoday.com/2012/04/18/the-real-effects-of-reality-tv/.

Garbarino, J. (2006). *See Jane Hit: Why Girls Are Growing More Violent and What Can Be Done about It*. New York: The Penguin Press.

Hall, T. L. (2012). "How Would You Feel? Stigma and Self-Esteem in Student Responses to Intimate Partner Violence Vignettes." Graduate Masters Theses 97. Retrieved from https://scholarworks.umb.edu/masters_theses/97.

Harris, S., Petrie, G., and Willoughby, W. (2002). "Bullying among 9th Graders: An Exploratory Study." *NASSP Bulletin*: 86, 1630.

Hodges, E. V. E., and Perry, D. G. (1996). "Victims of Peer Abuse: An Overview." *Journal of Emotional and Behavioral Problems* 5: 23–28.

Hutchison, E. D. (2015). *Dimensions of Human Behavior: The Changing Life Course* (5th ed.). Thousand Oaks, CA: Sage Publication, Sage, Inc.

Lehmann, C. (2012). "Reality TV: A Blessing or a Curse? An Analysis of the Influence of Reality TV on U.S. Society." Rhetoric and Composition IILAX017B1010.

Library.thinkquest.org and thedailymail.net. (N.d). "Female Bullies." Bullying Statistics: Anti-Bullying Help, Facts, and More. Retrieved from http://www.bullyingstatistics.org/content/female-bullying.html.

Limber, S. P. (2002). "Addressing Youth Bullying Behaviors." Published in the Proceedings of the Educational Forum on Adolescent Health on Youth Bullying. Chicago: American Medical Association.

Melton, G. B., Limber, S. P., Cunningham, P., Osgood, D. W., Chambers, J., Flerx, V., Henggeler, S., and Nation, M. (1998). "Violence among Rural Youth." Final report to the Office of Juvenile Justice and Delinquency Prevention.

Nansel, T. R., Overpeck, M., Pilla, R. S., Ruan, W. J., Simons-Morton, B., and Scheidt, P. (2001). "Bullying Behavior among U.S. Youth: Prevalence and Association with Psychosocial Adjustment." *Journal of the American Medical Association* 285: 2094–2100.

National Institute of Justice. (2015). "Risk and Protective Factors, Psychosocial Health Behaviors and Teen Dating Violence." Retrieved from https://www.nij.gov/topics/crime/intimate-partner-violence/teen-dating-violence/Pages/risk-factors.aspx.

National Institute of Justice. (2017). "Understanding Risks in Adolescence and Partner Influences That Lead to Intimate Partner Violence in Young Adulthood." Retrieved from https://nij.gov/topics/crime/intimate-partner-violence/Pages/risks-in-adolescence-that-lead-to-intimate-partner-violence-in-young-adulthood.aspx.

National Youth-At-Risk Conference Program (NYARCP). (2011). "Successful Programs for Empowering Youth: Overcoming Poverty, Violence and Failure." National Youth-At-Risk Conference.

NPR Staff. (2014). "Viewer Beware: Watching Reality TV Can Impact Real-Life Behavior." National Public Radio US. Retrieved from https://www.npr.org/2014/08/24/342429563/viewer-beware-watching-reality-tv-can-impact-real-life-behavior.

Rankin, A. (N.d). "Realty TV: A Race to the Bottom: A Content Analysis of Prime Time Broadcast Reality Series." Retrieved from http://www.parentstv.org/PTC/publications/reports/realitytv2/main.asp.

Rigby, K. (1996). *Bullying in Schools and What to Do about It.* Bristol, PA: Jessica Kingsley Publishers.

Seabrook, L. A., and Walcott, Q. (2017). "Let's Stop Referring to Domestic Violence and Sexual Assault as 'Women's Issues.'" The Blog. *Huffington Post*. Retrieved from https://www.huffingtonpost.com/linda-a-seabrook/lets-stop-referring-to-do_b_9800250.html.

Shuler Ivey, Caroletta. (2010). "Male Victims of Intimate Partner Violence in the United States: An Examination of the Review of Literature through the Critical Theoretical Perspective." *Journal of Criminal Justice Sciences* 5: 973–5089.

Reiss, S., and Wiltz, J. (2001). "Why America Loves Reality TV." *Psychology Today*. Retrieved from https://www.psychologytoday.com/us/articles/200109/why-america-loves-reality-tv.

Yeo, S. (2017). "Teen Boys Discuss the Pressures of Becoming a Man: 'Confusing' and 'Frustrating.'" *Good Morning America*. Retrieved from https://www.yahoo.com/gma/teen-boys-discuss-pressures-becoming-man-confusing-frustrating-123304563--abc-news-parenting.html.

Zastrow, C., and Kirst-Ashman, K. (2015). *Empowerment Series: Understanding Human Behavior and the Social Environment* (10th ed.). Belmont, CA: Thomson.

CHAPTER 7

Angold, A., Copeland, W., Costello, E., and Wolfe, D. (2013). "Impact of Bullying in Childhood on Adult Health." *Psychological Science* (August 2013). doi: 10.1177/09567976108.

APA Council of Representatives. (2004). "APA Resolution on Bullying among Children and Youth." Retrieved from http://www.apa.org/topics/bullying/.

Bosworth, K., Espelage, D. L., and Simon, T. (1999). "Factors Associated with Bullying Behavior in Middle School Students." *Journal of Early Adolescence* 19: 341–362.

Centers for Disease Control and Prevention (2017). "Teen Dating Violence." Retrieved from https://www.cdc.gov/violenceprevention/intimatepartnerviolence/teendating.html.

Centers for Disease Control and Prevention. "Youth Risk Behavior Surveillance—United States, 2011." MMWR, Surveillance Summaries 2012: 61, no. SS-4. Retrieved from www.cdc.gov/mmwr/pdf/ss/ss6104.pdf.

Centers for Disease Control and Prevention. "Youth Risk Behavior Surveillance—United States, 2015." MMWR, Surveillance Summaries 2016: 65, no. SS-9. Retrieved from http://www.cdc.gov/mmwr/volumes/65/ss/ss6506a1.htm.

Diliberti, M., Jackson, M., and Kemp, J. (2017). "Crime, Violence, Discipline, and Safety in U.S. Public Schools: Findings From the School Survey on Crime and Safety: 2015–16 (NCES 2017122)." US Department of Education, National Center for Education Statistics. Washington, DC. Retrieved August 7, 2017, from http://nces.ed.gov/pubsearch.

Edelman, M. W. (2007). "A Call to End Adult Hypocrisy, Neglect and Abandonment of Children and America's Cradle to Prison Pipeline." Children's Defense Fund. Retrieved from https://www.childrensdefense.org/wp-content/uploads/2018/08/cradle-prison-pipeline-report-2007-full-lowres.pdf.

Espelage, D. L., Holt, M. K., and Henkel, R. R. (2003a). "Examination of Peer Group Contextual Effects on Aggressive Behavior during Early Adolescence." *Child Development* 74: 205–220.

Espelage, D., and Swearer, S. M. (2003b). "Research on School Bullying and Victimization: What Have We Learned and Where Do We Go from Here?" *School Psychology Review* 32: 365–383.

Florida Laws. (N.d.). Florida statutes.

Fredland, N. (2008). "Sexual Bullying Addressing the Gap between Bullying and Dating Violence." *Advances in Nursing Science* 31, no. 2: 95–105.

Gastic, B. (2008). "School Truancy and the Disciplinary Problems of Bullying Victims." *Educational Review* 60: 391–404. doi: 10.1080/00131910802393423.

Georgia Laws. (N.d.). O.C.G.A.-Official code of Georgia, annotated.

Haynie, D. L., Nansel T., Eitel P., et al. "Bullies, Victims, and Bully/Victims: Distinct Groups of At-Risk Youth." *Journal of Early Adolescence* 21, no. 1 (2011): 29-49.

Kalish, R., and Kimmel, M. (2010). "Suicide by Mass Murder: Masculinity, Aggrieved Entitlement, and Rampage School Shootings." *Health Sociology Review* 19, no. 4: 451–464.

Klein, J. (2012). *The Bully Society: School Shootings and the Crisis of Bullying in America's Schools.* New York: New York University Press.

L. L., Marshall, K. J., Rainford, N., and Hall, J. E. (2016). "A Comprehensive Technical Package for the Prevention of Youth Violence and Associated Risk Behaviors." Atlanta, GA: National Center for Injury Prevention and Control, Centers for Disease Control and Prevention. Retrieved from https://www.cdc.gov/violenceprevention/pdf/yv-technicalpackage.pdf.

Massat, C. R., Kelley, M. S., and Constable, R. (2016). *School Social Work: Practice, Policy, and Research* (8th ed.). Chicago: Lyceum Books.

Munsey, C. (2011). "APA Is Front and Center at White House Bullying Conference." *Monitor on Psychology* 42, no. 5 (May 2011): 18.

National Center for Injury Prevention and Control, Division of Violence Prevention. (2017). "Preventing Bullying." Retrieved from https://www.cdc.gov/violenceprevention/pdf/bullying-factsheet508.pdf.

National Center for Injury Prevention and Control, Division of Violence Prevention. (2018). "Preventing Intimate Partner Violence." Retrieved from https://www.cdc.gov/violenceprevention/pdf/ipv-factsheet.pdf.

National Youth-At-Risk Conference Program (NYARCP). (2011). "Successful Programs for Empowering Youth: Overcoming Poverty, Violence and Failure." National Youth-At-Risk Conference.

Olweus, D. (1993). *Bullying at School: What We Know and What We Can Do.* New York: Blackwell.

Olweus, D. (2001). *Olweus' Core Program against Bullying and Antisocial Behavior: A Teacher Handbook.* Bergen, Norway: Author.

Olweus, D., Limber, S., and Mihalic, S. (1999). The Bullying Prevention Program. "Blueprints for Violence Prevention." Boulder, CO: Center for the Study and Prevention of Violence.

O'Malley Olsen, E., Kann, L., Vivolo-Kantor, A., Kinchen, S., and McManus, T. (2014). "School Violence and Bullying among Sexual Minority High School Students, 2009–2011." *Journal of Adolescent Health* 1–7.

Reid, K. (2008). "The Causes of Non-Attendance: An Empirical Study." *Educational Review* 60, no. 4: 345–357. Retrieved from https://www.researchgate.net/publication/240525780_The_causes_of_nonattendance_An_empirical_study.

Rigby, K. (2002). *New Perspectives on Bullying.* London: Jessica Kingsley.

Robers, S., Kemp, J., and Truman, J. "Indicators of School Crime and Safety: 2012" (NCES 2013-036/NCJ 241446). Washington, DC: National Center for Education Statistics, US Department of Education, and Bureau of Justice Statistics, Office of Justice Programs, US Department of Justice; 2013. Retrieved from http://nces.ed.gov/pubs2013/2013036.pdf.

Temkin, D. (2015). "All 50 States Now Have a Bullying Law. Now What?" Education Research, Child Trends. Retrieved from https://www.huffingtonpost.com/deborah-temkin/all-50-states-now-have-a_b_7153114.html.

Upton Patton, D., Sung Hong, J., Ranney, M., Patel, S., Kelley, C., Eschmann, R., and Washington, T. (2014). "Social Media as a Vector for Youth Violence: A Review of the Literature." *Computers in Human Behavior* 35: 548–553.

Woods, R. (2015). "Policy for Prohibiting Bullying, Cyberbullying, Harassment and Intimidation." Georgia Department of Education.

Woods, S., and Wolke, D. (2003). "Does the Content of Anti-Bullying Policies Inform Us about the Prevalence of Direct and Relational Bullying Behaviour in Primary Schools?" *Educational Psychology* 23: 381–401.

CHAPTER 8

AP-NORC Center. (2017). "Phasing into Retirement Survey." Retrieved from http://www.apnorc.org/projects/Pages/Phasing-into-Retirement.aspx.

Archer, J. (2000). "Sex Differences in Aggression between Heterosexual Partners: A Meta-Analytic Review." *Psychological Bulletin* 126: 651–680.

Bruel, N., and Smith, M. (2015). "Deadly Calls and Fatal Encounters." Office of Community Oriented Policing Services. National Law Enforcement Officers Memorial Fund. US Department of Justice.

Brush, L. D. (1990). "Violent Acts and Injurious Outcomes in Married Couples: Methodological Issues in the National Survey of Families and Households." *Gender Society* 4: 56–67.

Centers for Disease Control and Prevention. (2012). "Behavioral Risk Factors Surveillance System (BRFSS)." Retrieved from https://www.cdc.gov/brfss/annual_data/annual_data.htm.

Centers for Disease Control and Prevention. (2000). "Extent, Nature and Consequences of Intimate Partner Violence: Findings from the National Violence against Women Survey." National Institute of Justice.

Davis, Baron. (2011). "Breaking the Cycle of Inner-City Gang Violence." Retrieved from https://www.huffingtonpost.com/baron-davis/breaking-the-cycle-of-inn_b_196785.html.

Davis, R. L. (2009). "Exploring Law Enforcement's Response to 'Intimate Partner Violence.'" Law Enforcement and Intimate Partner Violence. Retrieved from https://www.policeone.com/patrol-issues/articles/1788033-Exploring-law-enforcements-response-to-intimate-partner-violence/.

DeJong, C., Burgess-Proctor, A., and Elis, L. (2008). "Police Officer Perceptions of Intimate Partner Violence: An Analysis of Observational Data." Violence and Victims. Springer Publishing Company. Department of Justice. (N.d.). "Identifying and Preventing Gender Bias in Enforcement Response to Sexual Assault and Domestic Violence." Retrieved from http://www.justice.gov/ovw/identifying-and-preventing-gender-bias.

Dobash, R. E., and Dobash, R. P. (1979). *Violence against Wives*. New York: Free Press.

Feder, L. "Police Handling of Domestic Violence Calls: An Overview and Further Investigation." *Women and Criminal Justice* 10, no. 2 (1999): 49–68, NCJ 177884. Retrieved from http://www.ncjrs.gov/App/Publications/abstract.aspx?ID=177884.

Finn, M., Blackwell, B., Stalans, L., Studdard, S., and Dugan, L. "Dual Arrest Decisions in Domestic Violence Cases: The Influence of Departmental Policies." *Crime and Delinquency* 50, no. 4 (October 2004): 565–589, NCJ 207463. Retrieved from http://www.ncjrs.gov/App/Publications/abstract.aspx?ID=207463.

Friday, P., Lord, V., Exum, M., and Hartman, J. (2006). "Evaluating the Impact of a Specialized Domestic Violence Police Unit." National Institute of Justice, Washington, DC: US Department of Justice.

Hirschel, D., Buzawa, E., Pattavina, A., Faggiani, D., and Reuland, M. "Explaining the Prevalence, Context, and Consequences of Dual Arrest in Intimate Partner Cases." Final report for National Institute of Justice, grant number 2001-WT-BX-0501. Washington, DC: US Department of Justice, National Institute of Justice, April 2007, NCJ 218355. Retrieved from http://www.ncjrs.gov/App/Publications/abstract.aspx?ID=240055.

Kaeble, D., and Cowhig, M. (2018). "Correctional Populations in the United States, 2016." Washington: US Bureau of Justice Statistics. Retrieved from https://www.bjs.gov/content/pub/pdf/cpus16.pdf.

Klein, A. (2009). "Practical Implications of Current Domestic Violence Research: For Law Enforcement, Prosecutors and Judges." Special report for National Institute of Justice. Washington, DC: US Department of Justice, National Institute of Justice. Retrieved from https://www.ncjrs.gov/pdffiles1/nij/225722.pdf.

Law Enforcement, Justice System, and Domestic Violence. (2015). "Leading Facts and Statistics on Law Enforcement, the Justice System and Domestic Violence." Retrieved from https://www.domesticshelters.org/domestic-violence-statistics/law-enforcement-and-domestic-violence.

Ménard, K. S., Anderson, A. L., and Godboldt, S. M. (2009). "Gender Differences in Intimate Partner Recidivism." *Criminal Justice and Behavior* 36, no. 1: 61–76. Retrieved from https://ifls.osgoode.yorku.ca/wp-content/uploads/2015/02/DeJong-et-al-2008-Police-Officer-perceptions-of-IPV-An-analysis-of-observational-data.pdf.

Rigakos, G. "Situational Determinants of Police Responses to Civil and Criminal Injunctions for Battered Women." *Violence Against Women* 3, no. 2 (April 1997): 204–216. Available online at http://vaw.sagepub.com/cgi/content/abstract/3/2/204.

Shuler Ivey, Caroletta. (2010). "Male Victims of Intimate Partner Violence in the United States: An Examination of the Review of Literature through the Critical Theoretical Perspective." *Journal of Criminal Justice Sciences* 5: 973–5089.

Smith, S., Fowler, K., and Niolon, P. (2014). "Intimate Partner Homicide and Corollary Victims in 16 States: National Violent Death Reporting System, 2003–2009."

Smithey, M., Green, S., and Giacomazzi, A. "Collaborative Effort and the Effectiveness of Law Enforcement Training toward Resolving Domestic Violence." Final report for National Institute of Justice, grant number 97-WE-VX-0131. Washington, DC: US Department of Justice, National Institute of Justice, November 2000, NCJ 191840. Retrieved from http://www.ncjrs.gov/App/Publications/abstract.aspx?ID=191840.

Straus, M. A. (2004). "Women's Violence toward Men Is a Serious Social Problem." In Gelles, R. J., and Loseke, D. R., eds. *Current Controversies on Family Violence* (2nd ed.). Newbury Park, CA: Sage, 55–77.

Straus, M. A, and Gelles, R. J. (1995). "How Violent Are American Families? Estimates from the National Family Violence Resurvey and Other Studies." In Straus, M. A., and Gelles, R. J., eds. *Physical Violence in American Families: Risk Factors and Adaptations to Violence in 8,145 Families*. New Brunswick, NJ: Transaction Publishers, 95–112.

Sumner, A. (2014). "A Different Response to Intimate Partner Violence." The e-newsletter of the COPS Office 7, no. 9. Retrieved from http://www.nij.gov/topics/crime/intimate-partner-violence/pages/extent.aspx.

Teicher, R. (2017). "A Better Way to Deal with Intimate-Partner Violence." Director of the Intimate Partner Violence Intervention Program. National Network for Safe Communities. Retrieved from http://www.governing.com/gov-institute/voices/col-intimate-partner-violence-procedural-justice.html.

The Sentencing Project. (2015). "Trends in U.S. Corrections." Retrieved from https://sentencingproject.org/wp-content/uploads/2016/01/Trends-in-US-Corrections.pdf.

Tjaden, P., and Thoennes, N. (1998). "Prevalence, Incidence, and Consequences of Violence against Women: Findings from the National Violence against Women Survey." Washington, DC: US Department of Justice.

US Department of Justice. (2003). "Criminal Victimization." Bureau of Justice Statistics.

US Department of Justice. (2017). "Federal Domestic Violence Laws." Office of the US Attorneys. Retrieved from https://www.justice.gov/usao-wdtn/victim-witness-program/federal-domestic-violence-laws.

US Department of Justice, Office of Justice Programs, Bureau of Justice Statistics, Truman, J., and Morgan, R. "Nonfatal Domestic Violence, 2003–2012." (2014).

Wakefield, S., and Wildeman, C. (2011). "Mass Imprisonment and Racial Disparities in Childhood Behavioral Problems." *Criminology and Public Policy* 10, no. 3: 793–817. Retrieved from https://doi.org/10.1111/j.1745-9133.2011.00740.x.

Whitaker, D. J., Haileyesus, T., Swahn, M., and Saltzman, L. S. (2007). "Differences in Frequency of Violence and Reported Injury between Relationships with Reciprocal and Nonreciprocal Intimate Partner Violence." *American Journal of Public Health* 97, no. 5: 941–947. doi: 10.2105/AJPH.2005.079020.

CHAPTER 9

Archer, J. (2006). "Cross-Cultural Differences in Physical Aggression Between Partners: A Social-Role Analysis." *Personality and Social Psychology Review* 10, no. 133. doi: 10.1207/s15327957pspr1002_3. Retrieved from http://psr.sagepub.com/cgi/content/abstract/10/2/133.

Avon Foundation for Women. (2015). "Victim Advocate Guide: Intimate Partner Violence (IPV) and Combat Experience." Battered Women's Justice Project.

Bannerman, S. (2014). "When the War Came Home: High Risk of Military Domestic Violence on the Home Front." Continuum Publishing. Retrieved from https://www.sfgate.com/opinion/article/High-risk-of-military-domestic-violence-on-the-5377562.php.

Barnett, O., Miller-Perrin, C., and Perrin, R. (2010). "History and Definitions of Family Violence." *Family Violence across the Lifespan: An Introduction*. 3rd ed. California: Sage Publications, Inc. Retrieved from https://www.sagepub.com/sites/default/files/upm-binaries/38654_Chapter1.pdf.

Bradford, J., ed. (2003). *Atlas of American Military History*. New York: Oxford University Press.

Breiding, M. J., Basile, K. C., Smith, S.G., Black, M. C., and Mahendra, R. R. (2015). "Intimate Partner Violence Surveillance: Uniform Definitions and Recommended Data Elements, Version 2.0." Atlanta, GA: National Center for Injury Prevention and Control, Centers for Disease Control and Prevention. Retrieved from http://www.cdc.gov/violenceprevention/pdf/ipv/intimatepartnerviolence.pdf.

Brinkerhoff, M. B., and Lupri, E. (1988). "Interspousal Violence." *Canadian Journal of Sociology* 13: 407–431.

Bushman, B. J., and Anderson, C. A. (2001) "Effects of Violent Video Games on Aggressive Behavior, Aggressive Cognition, Aggressive Affect, Physiological Arousal, and Prosocial Behavior: A Meta-Analytic Review of the Scientific Literature." Retrieved from https://doi.org/10.1111/1467-9280.00366.

Caliber Associates. (1996). "The Final Report on the Study of Spousal Abuse in the Armed Forces." The Department of Defense: Washington, DC.

Campbell, J. C., and Wolf, A. D. (2002). "Intimate Partner Violence and Physical and Mental Health Consequences among Active Duty Military Women."

Centers for Disease Control and Prevention. (March 11, 2016). "Intimate Partner Violence: Definitions." Retrieved from http://www.cdc.gov/violenceprevention/intimatepartnerviolence/definitions.html.

Centers for Disease Control and Prevention. (2001). "Updated Guidelines for Evaluating Public Health Surveillance Systems: Recommendations from the Guidelines Working Group." *MMWR* 50, no. RR-13 (2001): 1–51. Retrieved from http://www.cdc.gov/violenceprevention/intimatepartnerviolence/index.html.

Department of Defense Task Force Against Domestic Violence. (2001). "Domestic Violence." Retrieved from https://apps.dtic.mil/dtic/tr/fulltext/u2/a389984.pdf.

Department of Veteran Affairs. (n.d.). "Veterans with Lesbian, Gay, Bisexual and Transgender (LGBT) and Related Identities." Patient Care Services. Retrieved from https://www.patientcare.va.gov/LGBT/index.asp. doi: 10.1146/annurev.soc.25.1.395.

Dutton, D., and Painter, S. (1993). "Emotional Attachments in Abusive Relationships: A Test of Traumatic Bonding Theory." *Violence and Victims* 8, no. 2: 105–120. doi: 10.1891/0886-6708.8.2.105.

Ferrell, J. (1996). "Cultural Criminology." *Annual Review of Sociology* 20, no. 3. Futures without Violence. (N.d.). Retrieved from http://www.futureswithoutviolence.org/.

Gierisch, J. M., Shapiro, A., Grant, N. N., King, H. A., McDuffie, J. R., and Williams, J. W. (2013). "Intimate Partner Violence: Prevalence among U.S. Military Veterans and Active Duty Service Members and a Review of Intervention Approaches." Washington, DC, Department of Veterans Affairs. Retrieved from https://www.ncbi.nlm.nih.gov/pubmed/25232637

Goodman, L., Dutton, M. A., Weinfurt, K., and Cook, S. (2003). "The Intimate Partner Violence Strategies Index: Development and Application." *Violence Against Women*, 9: 163–186.

Hansen, C. (2001). "A Considerable Service: An Advocates Introduction to Domestic Violence and the Military." Domestic Violence Report.

Hart, B. J., and Klein, A. R. (2013). "Practical Implications of Current Intimate Partner Violence Research for Victim Advocates and Service Providers." Retrieved from https://www.ncjrs.gov/pdffiles1/nij/grants/244348.pdf.

Johnson, M. (2008). *A Typology of Domestic Violence: Intimate Terrorism, Violent Resistance, and Situational Couple Violence*. Lebanon, NH: Northeastern University Press.

Kauth, M. (2017). "An Overview of LGBT Veteran Health." US Department of Veteran Affairs. Retrieved from http://vapaa.org/resources/Documents/LGBT%20Veteran%20Health%20-%20VAPAA%202017v2.pdf.

Luby, C. (2010). "Promoting Military Cultural Awareness in an Off-post Community of Behavioral Health and Social Support Service Providers."

Marshall, A., et al. (2005). "Intimate Partner Violence among Military Veterans and Active Duty Servicemen." *Clinical Psychology Review* 25, 862–876.

Military One Source. (2012). "2011 Demographics: Profile of the Military Community." Retrieved from http://download.militaryonesource.mil/12038/MOS/Reports/2011-Demographics-Report.pdf.

Military Times. (2014). "Domestic Violence in the Military." Retrieved from http://www.militarytimes.com/story/military/2014/08/27/one-third-of-domestic-violence-victims-in-active-duty-military-families-are-men/14682985/.

Millett, A., and Maslowski, P. (1984). *For the Common Defense: A Military History of the United States of America*. New York: The Free Press.

National Center on Domestic and Sexual Violence (NCDSV). (2015). "Uniform Code of Military Justice Articles Relating to Domestic Violence." Retrieved from www.ncdsv.org/images/Attachment8--UCMJArticles.pdf.

National Domestic Violence Hotline. (N.d.). "Motivational Interviewing with Individuals Experiencing IPV." Retrieved from http://www.thehotline.org/.

Service Women's Action Network. (2012). "Rape, Sexual Assault and Sexual Harassment in the Military." New York: Service Women's Action Network. Retrieved from The Invisible War Discussion and Resource Guide. (2012). "*The Invisible War* Movie." Retrieved February 11, 2013, from https://www.nrcdv.org/wp-content/uploads/2013/06/MST-Handout-The_Invisible_War_Screenings.pdf.

United States Census Bureau. (2011). "Statistical Abstract of the United States: 2012." Retrieved from https://www2.census.gov/library/publications/2011/compendia/statab/131ed/2012-statab.pdf. US Department of Veterans Affairs. (n.d.) "Intimate Partner Violence: Let VA Help."

Veterans Affairs. "Women Veterans Health Care." Retrieved from http://www.womenshealth.va.gov/WOMENSHEALTH/outreachmaterials/abuseandviolence/intimatepartnerviolence.asp.

Victim Advocate Guide. Retrieved from https://www.bwjp.org/assets/documents/pdfs/victim-advocate-guide-2015.pdf.

Wallace, H. (2004). *Family Violence: Legal, Medical, and Social Perspectives*. Allyn & Bacon.

Weigley, R., ed. (1975). *New Dimensions in Military History: An Anthology*. Presidio Press: San Rafael, CA.

Wenger-Trayner. (March 11, 2016). Retrieved from http://wengertrayner.com/resources/what-is-a-community-of-practice.

CHAPTER 10

Brehm, S., and Brehm, J. W. (1981). *Psychological Reactance: A Theory of Freedom and Control*. New York: Academic Press.

Breiding, M. J., Black, M. C., and Ryan, G. W. (2008). "Chronic Disease and Health Risk Behaviors Associated with Intimate Partner Violence—18 U.S. States/Territories, 2005." *Annals of Epidemiology* 18, no. 7: 538–544.

Breiding, M. J., et al. (2014). "Prevalence and Characteristics of Sexual Violence, Stalking, and Intimate Partner Violence Victimization—National Intimate Partner and Sexual Violence Survey, United States, 2011." Atlanta, GA: Centers for Disease Control and Prevention, 2014. Retrieved from http://www.cdc.gov/mmwr/pdf/ss/ss6308.pdf.

Centers for Disease Control and Prevention (2016). "Intimate Partner Violence: Definitions." Retrieved from http://www.cdc.gov/violenceprevention/intimatepartnerviolence/definitions.html.

Cook, P. W. (2009). *Abused Men: The Hidden Side of Domestic Violence* (2nd ed.). Westport: Praeger.

Douglas, E. M., and Hines, D. (2011) "The Help-Seeking Experiences of Men Who Sustain Intimate Partner Violence: An Overlooked Population and Implications for Practice." *Journal of Family Violence*, no. 6 (August 26, 2011):473-485. Published online June 4, 2011. National Institute of Mental Health, grant number 5R21MH074590.

E-learning Support Initiative. (2016). *Sociology: Understanding and Changing the Social World.* University of Minnesota Libraries Publishing. Retrieved from http://open.lib.umn.edu/sociology/.

Frandsen, R., et al. (2010). "Background Checks for Firearm Transfers, 2010—Statistical Tables." Washington, DC: Bureau of Justice Statistics, US Department of Justice, 2010. Retrieved from http://bjs.gov/content/pub/pdf/bcft10st.pdf.

George, M. J. (1994). "Riding the Donkey Backwards: Men as the Unacceptable Victims of Marital Violence." *Journal of Men's Studies* 3: 137–159.

Truman, J., Langton, L., and Planty, M. (2012). "Criminal Victimization." Washington, DC: Bureau of Justice Statistics, US Department of Justice, 2013. Retrieved from http://www.bjs.gov/content/pub/pdf/cv12.pdf.

CHAPTER 11

Afifi, T. O., Henriksen, C. A., Asmundson, G. J., and Sareen, J. (2012). "Victimization and Perpetration of Intimate Partner Violence and Substance Use Disorders in a Nationally Representative Sample." *Journal of Nervous and Mental Disorders* 200, no. 8, 684–691.

Appel, A. E., and Holden, G. W. "The Co-Occurrence of Spouse and Physical Child Abuse: A Review and Appraisal." *Journal of Family Psychology* 12 (1998): 578–599.

Beydoun, H. A., Beydoun, M. A., Kaufman, J. S., Lo, B., and Zonderman, A. B. (2012). "Intimate Partner Violence against Adult Women and Its Association with Major Depressive Disorder, Depressive Symptoms and Postpartum Depression: A Systematic Review and Meta-Analysis." *Social Science & Medicine* 75, no. 6: 959–975.

Bonomi, A. E., Anderson, M. L., Reid, R. J., Rivara, F. P., Carrell, D., and Thompson, R. S. (2009). "Medical and Psychosocial Diagnoses in Women with a History of Intimate Partner Violence." *Archives of Internal Medicine* 169, no. 18: 1692–1697.

Boyle, A., Jones, P., and Lloyd, S. (2006). "The Association between Domestic Violence and Self-Harm in Emergency Medicine Patients." *Emergency Medicine Journal* 23, 604–607.

Buller, A. M., Devries, K. M., Howard, L. M., and Bacchus, L. J. (2014). "Associations between Intimate Partner Violence and Health among Men Who Have Sex with Men: A Systematic Review and Meta-Analysis." *PLoS Medicine* 11, no. 3, e1001609.

Bundock, L., Howard, L. M., Trevillion, K., Malcolm, E., Feder, G., and Oram, S. (2013). "Prevalence & Risk of Experiences of Intimate Partner Violence among People with Eating Disorders: A Systematic Review." *Journal of Psychiatric Research* 47, no. 9: 1134–1142.

Centers for Disease Control and Prevention. (2010). Interpersonal Personal Violence, National Intimate Partner and Sexual Violence Survey.

Centers for Disease Control and Prevention. (N.d.). "Intimate Partner Violence: Consequences." Retrieved from https://www.cdc.gov/violenceprevention/intimatepartnerviolence/consequences.html.

Cerulli, C., Talbot, N. L., Tang, W., and Chaudron, L. H. (2011). "Co-Occurring Intimate Partner Violence and Mental Health Diagnoses in Perinatal Women." *Journal of Women's Health* 20, no. 12: 1797–1803.

Classen, C. C., Pain, C., Field, N. P., and Woods, P. "Post-Traumatic Personality Disorder: A Reformulation of Complex Post-Traumatic Stress Disorder and Borderline Personality Disorder." *Psychiatry Clinic North America* 29, no. 1 (2006): 87–112, viii–ix.

Coker, A. L., Davis, K. E., Arias, I. L., Desai, S., Sanderson, M., Brand, H. M., and Smith, P. H. (2002). "Physical and Mental Health Effects of Intimate Partner Violence for Men and Women." *American Journal of Preventive Medicine* 23, no. 4: 260–268. Retrieved from https://doi.org/10.1016/S0749-3797(02)00514-7.

Coker, A. L., Smith, P., Fadden, M. (2005). "Intimate Partner Violence and Disabilities among Women Attending Family Practice Clinics." *Journal of Women's Health* 14, no. 9: 829–838.

De Bellis, M. D., and Van Dillen, T. "Childhood Post-Traumatic Stress Disorder: An Overview." *Child Adolescent Psychiatry Clinic North America* 14, no. 4 (2005): 745–772, ix.

DeJonghe, E. S., Bogat, G. A., Levendosky, A. A., and von Eye, A. (2008). "Women Survivors of Intimate Partner Violence and Post-Traumatic Stress Disorder: Prediction and Prevention." *Journal of Postgraduate Medicine* 54, no. 4: 294–300.

Devries, K. M., Mak, J. Y., Bacchus, L. J., Child, J. C., Falder, G., et al. (2013). "Intimate Partner Violence and Incident Depressive Symptoms and Suicide Attempts: A Systematic Review of Longitudinal Studies." *PLoS Medicine* 10, no. 5, e1001439.

Dillon, G., Hussain, R., Loxton, D., and Rahman, S. (2013). "Mental and Physical Health and Intimate Partner Violence against Women: A Review of the Literature." *International Journal of Family Medicine* (2013), 313909.

Duran, B., Oetzel, J., Parker, T., et al. (2009). "Intimate Partner Violence and Alcohol, Drug, and Mental Disorders among American Indian Women in Primary Care." *American Indian and Alaska Native Mental Health Research* 16, no. 2: 11–27.

Family Violence Prevention Fund. (2010). "The Health Care Costs of Domestic and Sexual Violence." San Francisco (CA): FVPF; Retrieved from http://www.futureswithoutviolence.org/userfiles/file/HealthCare/Health_Care_Costs_of_Domestic_and_Sexual_Violence.pdf.

Fedovskiy, K., Higgins, S., and Paranjape, A. (2008). "Intimate Partner Violence: How Does It Impact Major Depressive Disorder and Post Traumatic Stress Disorder among Immigrant Latinas?" *Journal of Immigrant and Minority Health* 10, no. 1: 45–51.

Felitti, V. J., Anda, R. F., Nordenberg, D., et al. "Relationship of Childhood Abuse and Household Dysfunction to Many of the Leading Causes of Death in Adults." The Adverse Childhood Experiences (ACE) Study. *American Journal of Preventative Medicine* 14, no. 4 (1998): 245–258.

Ferrari, G., Agnew-Davies, R., Bailey, J., Howard, L., Howarth, E., Peters, T. J., and Feder, G. S. (2016). "Domestic Violence and Mental Health: A Cross-Sectional Survey of Women Seeking Help from Domestic Violence Support Services." Global Health Action, 91–10. doi:10.3402/gha.v9.29890

Houry, D., Kemball, R., Rhodes, K. V., and Kaslow, N. J. (2006). "Intimate Partner Violence and Mental Health Symptoms in African American Female ED Patients." *American Journal of Emergency Medicine* 24, no. 4: 444–450.

Jaquier, V., Hellmuth, J. C., and Sullivan, T. P. (2013). "Post-Traumatic Stress and Depression Symptoms as Correlates of Deliberate Self-Harm among Community Women Experiencing Intimate Partner Violence." *Psychiatry Research* 206, no. 1: 37–42.

Johnson, D. M., Zlotnick, C., and Perez, S. (2008). "The Relative Contribution of Abuse Severity and PTSD Severity on the Psychiatric and Social Morbidity of Battered Women in Shelters." *Behavior Therapy* 39, no. 3: 232–241.

Lanius, R. A., Bluhm, R., Lanius, U., and Pain, C. "A Review of Neuroimaging Studies in PTSD: Heterogeneity of Response to Symptom Provocation." *Journal of Psychiatry Research* 40, no. 8 (2006): 709–729.

Leserman, J., and Drossman, D. A. "Relationship of Abuse History to Functional Gastrointestinal Disorders and Symptoms." *Trauma, Violence, and Abuse* 8 (2007): 331–343.

Lyons-Ruth, K., Dutra, L., Schuder, M. R., and Bianchi, I. "From Infant Attachment Disorganization to Adult Dissociation: Relational Adaptations or Traumatic Experiences?" *Psychiatry Clinic North America* 29, no. 1 (2006): 63–86, viii.

Maman, S., Campbell, J., Sweat, M. D., and Gielen, A. C. (2000). "The Intersections of HIV and Violence: Directions for Future Research and Interventions." *Social Science & Medicine* 50, no. 4: 459–478.

Mitchell, M. D., Hargrove, G. L., Collins, M. H., Thompson, M. P., Reddick, T. L., and Kaslow, N. J. (2006). "Coping Variables That Mediate the Relation between Intimate Partner Violence and Mental Health Outcomes among Low-Income, African American Women." *Journal of Clinical Psychology* 62, no. 12: 1503–1520.

National Center for Injury Prevention and Control (NCIPC). (2003). "Costs of Intimate Partner Violence against Women in the United States." Atlanta, GA: Centers for Disease Control and Prevention. Retrieved from http://www.cdc.gov/violenceprevention/pdf/IPVBook-a.pdf.

NCADV. (2015). "Domestic Violence National Statistics." Retrieved from www.ncadv.org.

Nealon-Woods, M. (2016). "The Realities of Domestic Violence and Its Impact on Our Society." The Chicago School of Professional Psychology.

Obstetrics and Gynecology. (2012). "Health Care for Homeless Women. Committee Opinion No. 454." *American College of Obstetricians and Gynecologists* 115: 396–399.

Obstetrics and Gynecology (OG). (2012). "Intimate Partner Violence (2012). Committee Opinion No. 518." *American College of Obstetricians and Gynecologists* 119: 412–417.

Rothman, E., Hathaway, J., Stidsen, A., and de Vries, H. (2007). "How Employment Helps Female Victims of Intimate Partner Abuse: A Qualitative Study." *Journal of Occupational Health Psychology*.

Shuler Ivey, Caroletta. (2010). "Male Victims of Intimate Partner Violence in the United States: An Examination of the Review of Literature through the Critical Theoretical Perspective." *Journal of Criminal Justice Sciences* 5: 973–5089.

Smith, S., Fowler, K., and Niolon, P. (2014). "Intimate Partner Homicide and Corollary Victims in 16 States: National Violent Death Reporting System, 2003–2009."

Substance Abuse and Mental Health Services Administration (SAMHSA). (2018). "Trauma and Violence." Retrieved from https://www.samhsa.gov/trauma-violence.

Tjaden, P., and Thoennes, N. (2000). "Extent, Nature, and Consequences of Intimate Partner Violence: Findings from the National Violence Against Women Survey." Washington, DC: US Department of Justice. Publication No. NCJ 181867. Retrieved from https://www.ncjrs.gov/pdffiles1/nij/181867.pdf.

Trevillion, K., Oram, S., Feder, G., and Howard, L. M. (2012). "Experiences of Domestic Violence and Mental Disorders: A Systematic Review and Meta-Analysis." *PLoS ONE* 7, no. 12: e51740.

Violence Policy Center. (2012). "American Roulette: Murder-Suicide in the United States." Retrieved from www.vpc.org/studies/amroul2012.pdf.

Warshaw, C., Brashler, P., and Gil, J. (2009). "Mental Health Consequences of Intimate Partner Violence." In Mitchell, C., and Anglin, D., eds. *Intimate Partner Violence: A Health Based Perspective*, chapter 12. New York: Oxford University Press. Retrieved from http://www.nationalcenterdvtraumamh.org/wp-content/uploads/2015/10/Mitchell-Chapter-12.pdf.

Warshaw, C., Lyon, E., Bland, P., Phillips, H., and Hooper, M. "Mental Health and Substance Use Coercion Survey: Report on Findings from the National Center on Domestic Violence, Trauma & Mental Health and the National Domestic Violence Hotline, 2014."

Woods, S. J., Kozachik, S. L., and Hall, R. J. (2010). "Subjective Sleep Quality in Women Experiencing Intimate Partner Violence: Contributions of Situational, Psychological, and Physiological Factors." *Journal of Traumatic Stress* 23, no. 1: 141–150.

CHAPTER 12

Addis, M. E., and Mahalik, J. R. (2003). "Men, Masculinity, and the Contexts of Help Seeking." *American Psychologist* 58, no. 1: 5–14.

Allen-Collinson, J. (2009). "A Marked Man: Female Perpetrated Intimate Partner Abuse." *International Journal of Men's Health* 8, no. 1: 22–40.

Artime, T. M., McCallum, E. B., and Peterson, Z. D. (2014). "Men's Acknowledgement of Their Sexual Victimization Experiences." *Psychology of Men and Masculinity* 15, no. 3: 313–323.

Basile, S. (2005). "A Measure of Court Response to Requests for Protection." *Journal of Family Violence* 20, no. 3: 171–179. doi: 10.1007/s10896-005-3653-x.

Breiding, M. J., Basile, K. C., Smith, S. G., Black, M. C., Mahendra, R. R. *Intimate Partner Violence Surveillance: Uniform Definitions and Recommended Data Elements, Version 2.0.* Atlanta, GA: National Center for Injury Prevention and Control, Centers for Disease Control and Prevention. 2015.

Burcar, V. (2013). "Doing Masculinity in Narratives about Reporting Violent Crime: Young Male Victims Talk about Contacting and Encountering the Police." *Journal of Youth Studies* 16, no. 2: 172–190. Retrieved from http://dx.doi.org/10.1080/13676261.2012.704992.

Burcar, V., and Akerstrom, M. (2009). "Negotiating a Victim Identity: Young Men as Victims of Violence." *Journal of Scandinavian Studies in Criminology and Crime Prevention* 10: 37–54. doi: 10.1080/14043850902815073.

Campbell, J. C., Sharps, P. W., and Nancy Glass. "Risk Assessment for Intimate Partner Violence," in Pinard, G. F., and Pagani, L., eds. *Clinical Assessment of Dangerousness: Empirical Contributions*. New York: Cambridge University Press, 2000, 136–157.

Catalano, S., Smith, E., Snyder, H., and Rand, M. (2009). *Female Victims of Violence*. Bureau of Justice Statistics Selected Findings. Retrieved August 5, 2018, from https://www.bjs.gov/content/pub/pdf/fvv.pdf.

Centers for Disease Control (2017). "Preventing Intimate Partner Violence." Retrieved September 16, 2018, from https://www.cdc.gov/violenceprevention/pdf/ipv-factsheet.pdf.

Cheatham, C. T., Barksdale, D. J., and Rodgers, S. G. (2008). "Barriers to Health Care and Health-seeking Behaviors Faced by Black Men." *Journal of American Academy of Nurse Practitioners* 20: 555–562.

Cheung, M., Leung, P., and Tsui, V. (2009). "Asian Male Domestic Violence Victims: Services Exclusive for Men." *Journal of Family Violence* 24, no. 7: 447–462. Retrieved from https://doi.org/10.1007/s10896-009-9240-9.

Cho, H., and Wilke, D. (2005). "How Has the Violence Against Women Act Affected the Response of the Criminal Justice System to Domestic Violence?" *Journal of Sociology & Social Welfare* 32, no. 4): 125–139.

Crime and Justice News. (May 21, 2014). "Do Mandatory Domestic Violence Arrests Hurt Victims?" Retrieved September 16, 2018, from https://thecrimereport.org/2014/05/21/2014-05-domestic-violence-policing-for-wed-icj/.

De Puy, J., Romain-Glassey, N., and Abt, M. (2017). "Coping with Multiple Adversities: Men Who Sought Medico-Legal Care Because of Physical Violence from a Partner or Ex-Partner." *Psychology of Violence* 7, no. 3: 428–439.

Douglas, E. M., and Hines, D. A. (2011). "The Help-Seeking Experiences of Men Who Sustain Intimate Partner Violence: An Overlooked Population and Implications for Practice." *Journal of Family Violence* 26: 473–485. doi: 10.1007/s10896-011-9382-4.

Durfee, A. (2011). "I'm Not a Victim. She's an Abuser: Masculinity, Victimization, and Protection Orders." *Gender and Society* 25, no. 3: 316–334.

Epstein, D. (1999). "Redefining the State's Response to Domestic Violence: Past Victories and Future Challenges." Case Law: State v. Black 60 N.C. 266 (1864). Georgetown Law Library. Georgetown Journal of Gender and Law. 127–143. Retrieved from https://scholarship.law.georgetown.edu/facpub.

Erez, E. (2002). "Domestic Violence and the Criminal Justice System: An Overview." *Online Journal of Issues in Nursing* 7, no. 1, manuscript 3. Retrieved from https://www.ncbi.nlm.nih.gov/pubmed/12044215.

Fagan, J. (1996). *The Criminalization of Domestic Violence: Promises and Limits*. Washington, DC: US Department of Justice.

George, J. (1994). "Riding a Donkey Backwards: Men as the Unacceptable Victims of Marital Violence." *Journal of Men's Studies* 3, no. 2: 137–159.

Gilson, E. C. (2016). "Vulnerability and Victimization: Rethinking Key Concepts in Feminist Discourses on Sexual Violence." *Journal of Women in Culture and Society* 42, no. 1: 71–98.

Gold, J. M., and Pitariu, G. V. (2004). "Opening the Eyes of Counselors to the Emotional Abuse of Men: An Overlooked Dynamic in Dysfunctional Families." *Journal of Humanistic Counseling, Education and Development* 43: 178–187.

Goodmark, L. (2017). "Should Domestic Violence Be Decriminalized?" *Harvard Journal of Law and Gender* 40: 53–113. Retrieved from https://ssrn.com/abstract=2985139.

Griffith, D. M., and Cornish, E. K. (2018). "What Defines a Man?: Perspectives of African American Men on the Components and Consequences of Manhood." *Psychology of Men & Masculinity* 19, no. 1: 78–88.

Hammond, W. P., and Mattis, J. S. (2005). "Being a Man About It: Manhood Meaning Among African American Men." *Psychology of Men & Masculinity* 6, no. 2: 114–126.

Hester, M. (2012). "Portrayal of Women as Intimate Partner Domestic Violence Perpetrators." *Violence Against Women* 18, no. 9: 1067–1082.

Hogan, K. F., Hegarty, J. R., Ward, T., and Dodd, L. J. (2012). "Counsellors' Experiences of Working with Male Victims of Female-Perpetrated Domestic Abuse." *Counselling and Psychotherapy Research* 12, no. 1: 44–52.

Hunter, A. G., and Davis, J. E. (1994). "Hidden Voices of Black Men: The Meaning, Structure, and Complexity of Manhood." *Journal of Black Studies* 25, no. 1: 20–40.

Javaid, A. (2016). "Voluntary Agencies' Responses to, and Attitudes toward Male Rape: Issues and Concerns." *Sexuality and Culture* 20: 731–748. doi: 10.1007/s12119-016-9348-2.

JustiaUS Law. (1968). Case Law: Bradley v. State, 1 Miss (1 Walker) 156 (1824). Retrieved from https://law.justia.com/cases/mississippi/supreme-court/1968/44949-0.html.

Kumar, A. (2012). "Domestic Violence against Men in India: A Perspective." *Journal of Human Behavior in the Social Environment* 22: 290–296. doi: 10.1080/10911359.2012.655988.

Lindinger-Sternart, S. (2015). "Help-Seeking Behaviors of Men for Mental Health and the Impact of Diverse Cultural Backgrounds." *International Journal of Social Science Studies* 3, no. 1. Retrieved from http://ijsss.redfame.com.

Lucal, Betsy (1992). "Battered Husbands and Battered Wives: Why One Is a Social Problem and the Other Is Not." Abstract of a paper presented at the Annual Meeting of the Society for the Study of Social Problems (42nd, Pittsburgh, PA).

MacDowell, E. L. (2013). "Theorizing from Particularity: Perpetrators and Intersectional Theory on Domestic Violence." *The Journal of Gender, Race & Justice* 16: 531–576.

Machado, A., Matos, M., and Hines, D. (2016). "Help-Seeking and Needs of Male Victims of Intimate Partner Violence in Portugal." *Psychology of Men & Masculinities* 17, no. 3: 255–264. doi: 10:1037/men0000013.

Machado, A., Santos, A., Graham-Kevan, N., and Matos, M. (2017). "Exploring Help Seeking Experiences of Male Victims of Female Perpetrators of IPV." *Journal of Family Violence* 32: 513–523.

Mejia, X. E. (2005). "Gender Matters: Working with Adult Male Survivors of Trauma." *Journal of Counseling and Development* 83: 29–40.

Migliaccio, T. A. (2001). "Marginalizing the Battered Male." *Journal of Men's Studies* 9: 205–206.

Morgan, W., and Wells, M. (2016). "It's Deemed Unmanly: Men's Experiences of Intimate Partner Violence (IPV)." *Journal of Forensic Psychiatry & Psychology* 27, no. 3: 404–418. Retrieved from http://dx.doi.org/10.1080/14789949.2015.1127986.

Muller, H. J., Desmarais, S. L., and Hamel, J. M. (2009). "Do Judicial Responses to Restraining Order Requests Discriminate against Male Victims of Domestic Violence?" *Journal of Family Violence* 24: 625–637. doi: 10.1007/s10896-009-9261-4.

Nolan, J. L., Jr., and Westervelt, S. D. (2000). "Justifying Justice: Therapeutic Law and the Victimization Defense Strategy." *Sociological Forum* 15, no. 4: 617–646.

Samulowitz, A., Gremyr, I., Eriksson, E., and Hensing, G. (2018). "'Brave Men' and 'Emotional Women': A Theory Guided Literature Review on Gender Bias in Health Care and Gendered Norms towards Patients with Chronic Pain." *Pain Research and Management* (2018). Retrieved from https://doi.org/10.1155/2018/6358624.

Shuler, C. A. (2010). "Male Victims of Intimate Partner Violence in the United States: An Examination of the Review of Literature through the Critical Theoretical Perspective." *International Journal of Criminal Justice Sciences* 5, no. 1: 163–173.

Smith, E. (2008). "African American Men and Intimate Partner Violence." *Journal of African American Studies* 12: 156–179. doi: 10.1007/s12111-008-9039-4.

Snyder, E. S., and Morgan, L. W. (2005). "Domestic Violence Ten Years Later." *Family Law*, no. 1: 4.

Truman, J. L., and Morgan, R. E. (2014). "Nonfatal Domestic Violence, 2003–2012." Retrieved September 15, 2018, from https://www.bjs.gov/content/pub/pdf/ndv0312.pdf.

Tsui, V. (2014). "Male Victims of Intimate Partner Abuse: Use and Helpfulness of Services." *Social Work* 59, no. 2: 121–130. Retrieved from http://dx.doi.org/10.1093/sw/swu007.

Tsui, V., Cheung, M., and Leung, P. (2010). "Help-Seeking among Male Victims of Partner Abuse: Men's Hard Times." *Journal of Community Psychology* 38: 769–780. Retrieved from http://dx.doi.org/10.1037/a0023688.

Vogel, D. L., Wester, S. R., and Larson, L. M. (2007). "Avoidance of Counseling: Psychological Factors That Inhibit Seeking Help." *Journal of Counseling and Development* 85: 410–422.

CHAPTER 13

Association for Educational Communications and Technologies (AECT). (2001). "Research on Learning from Television." *The Handbook of Research for Educational Communications and Technology*. Retrieved from http://members.aect.org/edtech/ed1/firstedition.asp.

Babcock, Julia C., Green, Charles E., and Robie, Chet. (2004) "Does Batterers' Treatment Work? A Meta-Analytic Review of Domestic Violence Treatment." *Clinical Psychology Review* 23: 1023–1053.

Baker, C. K., Billhardt, K. A., Warren, J., Rollins, C., and Glass, N. E. (2010). "Domestic Violence, Housing Instability, and Homelessness: A Review of Housing Policies and Program Practices for Meeting the Needs of Survivors." *Aggression and Violent Behavior* 15 (2010): 430–439.

Bandura, A. (1976). *The Social Learning Theory* (1st ed.). Prentice-Hall Publishers.

Basile, K. C., DeGue, S., Jones, K., Freire, K., Dills, J., Smith, S. G., and Raiford, J. L. (2016). "STOP SV: A Technical Package to Prevent Sexual Violence." Atlanta, GA: National

Center for Injury Prevention and Control, Centers for Disease Control and Prevention. "Preventing Intimate Partner Violence across the Lifespan: A Technical Package of Programs, Policies, and Practices," 49.

Bastian, B., Nielsen, M., Riggs, D., Due, C., Louis, W., Burke, S., Pham, H., and Gridley, H. (2013). "Media Representations and Responsibilities: Psychological Perspectives." The Australian Psychological Society Unlimited.

Browning, C. R. (2002). "The Span of Collective Efficacy: Extending Social Disorganization Theory to Partner Violence." *Journal of Marriage and Family* 64, no. 4: 833–850.

Capaldi, D. M., Knoble, N. B., Shortt, J. W., and Kim, H. K. (2012). "A Systematic Review of Risk Factors for Intimate Partner Violence." *Partner Abuse* 3, no. 2: 231–280.

Carney, M., Buttell, F., and Dutton, D. (2007). "Women Who Perpetrate Intimate Partner Violence: A Review of the Literature with Recommendations for Treatment." *Aggression and Violent Behavior* 12, no. 1: 108–115. Retrieved from https://doi.org/10.1016/j.avb.2006.05.002.

Centers for Disease Control. (N.d.). "The Social-Ecological Model: A Framework for Prevention." Retrieved from https://www.cdc.gov/violenceprevention/publichealthissue/social-ecologicalmodel.html?CDC_AA_refVal=https%3A%2F%2Fwww.cdc.gov%2Fviolenceprevention%2Foverview%2Fsocial-ecologicalmodel.html.

Centers for Disease Control. (2018). "Understanding Bullying." Injury Prevention and Control: Division of Violence Prevention. Retrieved from https://www.cdc.gov/violenceprevention/pdf/bullying-factsheet508.pdf.

Centers for Disease Control. (N.d.). "Youth Bullying: What Does the Research Say?" Injury Prevention and Control: Division of Violence Prevention. Retrieved from http://www.cdc.gov/violenceprevention/youthviolence/bullyingresearch/index.html.

Centers for Disease Control and Prevention. (2016). "Intimate Partner Violence: Risk and Protective Factors." Retrieved July 2016 from http://www.cdc.gov/violenceprevention/intimatepartnerviolence/riskprotectivefactors.html.

Centers for Disease Control and Prevention (2016). "Preventing Multiple Forms of Violence: A Strategic Vision for Connecting the Dots." Atlanta, GA: National Center for Injury Prevention and Control, Centers for Disease Control and Prevention.

Cooper, A., and Smith, E. L. (2011). "Homicide Trends in the United States, 1980–2008." Washington, DC: Bureau of Justice Statistics. NCJ 236018.

Crawford, N. (2002). "New Ways to Stop Bullying." *Monitor on Psychology* 33, no. 9: 64.

David-Ferdon, C., Vivolo-Kantor, A. M., Dahlberg, L. L., Marshall, K. J., Rainford, N., and Hall, J. E. (2016). "A Comprehensive Technical Package for the Prevention of Youth Violence and Associated Risk Behaviors." Atlanta, GA: National Center for Injury Prevention and Control, Centers for Disease Control and Prevention.

Domestic Abuse Intervention Programs. (2017). "The Duluth Model." Retrieved from https://www.theduluthmodel.org/.

Driscoll, A., and Nagel, N. G. (2008). *Early Childhood Education: Birth–8: The World of Children, Families, and Educators*. New York: Pearson Education Inc., 175–176.

Dutton, D. (2007). "Female Intimate Partner Violence and Developmental Trajectories of Abusive Females." *International Journal of Men's Health* 6, no. 1. Retrieved from https://www.questia.com/library/p535/international-journal-of-men-s-health.

Eccles, J. S. (1999). "The Development of Children Ages 6–14." *The Future of Children: When School Is Out* 9, no. 2.

Exner-Cortens, D., Eckenrode, J., Bunge, J., and Rothman, E. (2017). "Revictimization after Adolescent Dating Violence in a Matched, National Sample of Youth." *Journal of Adolescent Health* 60, no. 2: 176–183.

Exner-Cortens, D., Eckenrode, J., and Rothman, E. (2013). "Longitudinal Associations between Teen Dating Violence Victimization and Adverse Health Outcomes." *Pediatrics* 131, no. 1: 71–78.

Finklehor, D. (2008). *Childhood Victimization: Violence, Crime and Abuse in the Lives of Young People.* The Oxford Press.

Fortson, B. L., Klevens, J., Merrick, M. T., Gilbert, L. K., and Alexander, S. P. (2016). "Preventing Child Abuse and Neglect: A Technical Package for Policy, Norm, and Programmatic Activities." Atlanta, GA: National Center for Injury Prevention and Control, Centers for Disease Control and Prevention.

Frieden, T. R. (2014). "Six Components Necessary for Effective Public Health Program Implementation." *American Journal of Public Health* 104, no. 1: 17–22.

Gardner, F. L., Birkley, E., Moore, Z., and Eckhardt, C. (2016). "History, Comparative Outcomes, and Future Directions for Intimate Partner Violence Intervention Programs." *Behavior Therapist* 39: 168–174.

Gottesman, D., and Schwarz, S. W. (2011). "Juvenile Justice in the U.S.: Facts for Policymakers." National Center for Children in Poverty.

Kearns, M. C., Reidy, D. E., and Valle, L. A. (2015). "The Role of Alcohol Policies in Preventing Intimate Partner Violence: A Review of the Literature." *Journal of Studies on Alcohol and Drugs* 76, no. 1: 21–30.

Krapp, E. K. (2010). *Gale Encyclopedia of Nursing and Allied Health* 3: 1500–1503. From Gale Virtual Reference Library.

Kuna, J. (2014). "An Overview of Bronfenbrenner's Ecological Systems Theory, with Practical Applications." *Self-Improvement*. Retrieved from http://www.slideshare.net/John_Kuna_PsyD/bronfenbrenner-34175734.

Learning Theories. (2016). "Erickson's Stages of Psychosocial Development." Retrieved from http://www.learning-theories.com/eriksons-stages-of-development.html.

Macionis, J. J. (2009). *Society: The Basics* (10th ed.). Upper Saddle River, NJ: Pearson Education.

Matjasko, J. L., Niolon, P. H., and Valle, L. A. (2013). "The Role of Economic Factors and Economic Support in Preventing and Escaping from Intimate Partner Violence." *Journal of Policy Analysis and Management* 32, no. 1, 122128.

McLeod, S. A. (2016). "Maslow's Hierarchy of Needs." Retrieved from www.simplypsychology.org/maslow.html.

Miller, M., Drake, E., and Nafziger, M. (2013). "What Works to Reduce Recidivism by Domestic Violence Offenders? (Document No. 13-01-1201)." Olympia, WA: Washington State Institute for Public Policy. Interventions for Domestic Violence Offenders: Duluth Model. Retrieved from https://www.crimesolutions.gov/PracticeDetails.aspx?ID=17.

National Association of Social Work (NASW). (N.d.). "Why Choose the Social Work Profession?" Retrieved from https://www.socialworkers.org/Careers/Career-Center/Explore-Social-Work/Choose-the-Social-Work-Profession.

National Youth-At-Risk Conference Program (NYARCP). (2011). "Successful Programs for Empowering Youth: Overcoming Poverty, Violence and Failure." National Youth-At-Risk Conference.

Niolon, P. H., Kearns, M., Dills, J., Rambo, K., Irving, S., Armstead, T., and Gilbert, L. (2017). "Preventing Intimate Partner Violence across the Lifespan: A Technical Package of Programs, Policies, and Practices." Atlanta, GA: National Center for Injury Prevention and Control, Centers for Disease Control and Prevention.

Niolon, P. H., Vivolo-Kantor, A. M., Latzman, N. E., Valle, L. A., Kuoh, H., Burton, T., Taylor, B. G., and Tharp, A. T. (2015). "Prevalence of Teen Dating Violence and Co-Occurring Risk Factors among Middle School Youth in High-Risk Urban Communities." *Journal of Adolescent Health* 56, no. 2: S5–S13.

Payne, M. (2014). *Modern Social Work Theory* (4th ed.). New York: Palgrave Macmillan.

Pronyk, P. M., Hargreaves, J. R., Kim, J. C., Morison, L. A., Phetla, G., Watts, C., Busza, J., and Porter, J. D. (2006). "Effect of a Structural Intervention for the Prevention of Intimate-Partner Violence and HIV in Rural South Africa: A Cluster Randomized Trial." *The Lancet* 368, no. 9551: 1973–1983.

Rettew, D. (2017). "Nature versus Nurture: Where We Are in 2017." *Psychology Today*. Retrieved from https://www.psychologytoday.com/us/blog/abcs-child-psychiatry/201710/nature-versus-nurture-where-we-are-in-2017.

Reyes, H. L. M., Foshee, V. A., Niolon, P. H., Reidy, D. E., and Hall, J. E. (2016). "Gender Role Attitudes and Male Adolescent Dating Violence Perpetration: Normative Beliefs as Moderators." *Journal of Youth and Adolescence* 45, no. 2: 350–360.

Silverman, J. G., Raj, A., Mucci, L. A., and Hathaway, J. E. (2001). "Dating Violence against Adolescent Girls and Associated Substance Use, Unhealthy Weight Control, Sexual Risk Behavior, Pregnancy, and Suicidality." *Journal of the American Medical Association* 286, no. 5: 572–579.

Smith, D. L. (2008). "Disability, Gender and Intimate Partner Violence: Relationships from the Behavioral Risk Factor Surveillance System." *Sexuality and Disability* 26, no. 1: 15–28.

Smith, S. G., Chen, J., Basile, K. C., Gilbert, L. K., Merrick, M. T., Patel, N., Walling, M., and Jain, A. (2017). "The National Intimate Partner and Sexual Violence Survey (NISVS): 2010–2012 State Report." Atlanta, GA: National Center for Injury Prevention and Control, Centers for Disease Control and Prevention.

Stith, S. M., Smith, D. B., Penn, C. E., Ward, D. B., and Tritt, D. (2004). "Intimate Partner Physical Abuse Perpetration and Victimization Risk Factors: A Meta-Analytic Review." *Aggression and Violent Behavior* 10, no. 1: 65–98.

Temple, J. R., Shorey, R. C., Tortolero, S. R., Wolfe, D. A., and Stuart, G. L. (2013). "Importance of Gender and Attitudes about Violence in the Relationship between Exposure to Interparental Violence and the Perpetration of Teen Dating Violence." *Child Abuse & Neglect* 37, no. 5: 343–352.

Thomas, A. J., Carey, D., Prewitt, K. R., Romero, E., Richards, M., and Velsor-Friedrich, B. (2012). "African-American Youth and Exposure to Community Violence: Supporting Change from the Inside." *Journal for Social Action in Counseling and Psychology* 4, no. 1: 54–68.

"Trajectories of Abusive Females." *International Journal of Men's Health* 6, no. 1: 54–70.

US Department of Justice, Bureau of Justice Statistics. (2006). "Intimate Partner Violence in the United States."

Vagi, K. J., Olsen, E. O., Basile, K. C., and Vivolo-Kantor, A. M. (2015). "Teen Dating Violence (Physical and Sexual) among U.S. High School Students: Findings from the 2013 National Youth Risk Behavior Survey." *JAMA Pediatrics* 169, no. 5: 474–482.

Vagi, K. J., Rothman, E. F., Latzman, N. E., Tharp, A. T., Hall, D. M., and Breiding, M. J. (2013). "Beyond Correlates: A Review of Risk and Protective Factors for Adolescent Dating Violence Perpetration." *Journal of Youth and Adolescence* 42, no. 4: 633–649.

Wine, J. J. (2000). "All Behavior Has Heritable Components." Notes for Wine Lecture. Cognitive Neuroscience: Genes and Behavior. Retrieved from https://web.stanford.edu/~wine/202/g-and-b.html.

World Health Organization. (2013). *Global and Regional Estimates of Violence against Women: Prevalence and Health Effects of Intimate Partner Violence and Non-Partner Sexual Violence.* Geneva: World Health Organization.

Zastrow, C., and Kirst-Ashman, K. (2015). *Empowerment Series: Understanding Human Behavior & the Social Environment* (10th ed.). Belmont, CA: Thomson.

CHAPTER 14

Bastian, B., Nielsen, M., Riggs, D., Due, C., Louis, W., Burke, S., Pham, H., and Gridley, H. (2013). "Media Representations and Responsibilities: Psychological Perspectives." The Australian Psychological Society Unlimited.

Battered Persons' Advocacy (BPA). (2014). "Why Does a Victim Stay?" Retrieved from http://peaceathome.com/learn-more/why-does-she-stay/.

Black, M., Basile, K., Breiding, M., Smith, S., Walters, M., Merrick, M., Chen, J., and Stevens M. "National Intimate Partner and Sexual Violence Survey, 2010 Summary Report." Atlanta, GA: National Center for Injury Prevention and Control, Centers for Disease Control and Prevention, 2011.

Breiding, M. J., Chen J., and Black, M. C. (2014). "Intimate Partner Violence in the United States—2010." Atlanta, GA: National Center for Injury Prevention and Control, Centers for Disease Control and Prevention.

Callahan, A. (2014). "Domestic Violence: An Unwanted Family Legacy." The Urban Child Institute. Retrieved from http://www.urbanchildinstitute.org/articles/features/domestic-violence-an-unwanted-family-legacy.

Campbell, J. (2002). "Health Consequences of Intimate Partner Violence." *The Lancet* 413: 1331–1336.

Children's Defense Fund. (2008). Retrieved from: http://cdf.childrensdefense.org/site/DocServer/state-of-americas-children-2008-report.pdf?docID=9061.

Davis, A. (2008). "Interpersonal and Physical Dating Violence among Teens." The National Council on Crime and Delinquency Focus.

Dodd, D. A. (April 2010). "Troubled Students Learn to Cope with Hurt at Home While at School." *The Atlanta Journal-Constitution.* Retrieved from https://www.ajc.com/lifestyles/troubled-students-learn-cope-with-hurt-home-while-school/E0zCQjiUMIQeyWxydmKfol/.

Edelman, M. W. (2007). "A Call to End Adult Hypocrisy, Neglect and Abandonment of Children and America's Cradle to Prison Pipeline." Children's Defense Fund. Retrieved from https://www.childrensdefense.org/wp-content/uploads/2018/08/cradle-prison-pipeline-report-2007-full-lowres.pdf.

Garbarino, J. G., and Kostenly, K. (1998). "What Children Can Tell Us about Living in a War Zone." In Osofsky, J., ed. *Children in a Violent Society*. New York: Guilford.

Hart, B. J., and Klein, A. R. (2013). "Practical Implications of Current Intimate Partner Violence Research for Victim Advocates and Service Providers." US Department of Justice.

Jennings, W. G., Okeem, C., Piquero, A. R., Sellers, C. S., Theobald, D., and Farrington, D. P. (2017). "Dating and Intimate Partner Violence among Young Persons Ages 15–30: Evidence from a Systematic Review." *Aggression and Violent Behavior* (e-publication ahead of print). doi: 10.1016/j.avb.2017.01.007.

Johnson, M. (2008). *A Typology of Domestic Violence: Intimate Terrorism, Violent Resistance, and Situational Couple Violence*. Boston: Northeastern University Press.

Mahatma, Gandhi. (N.d.). Good Reads. Retrieved from https://www.goodreads.com/author/quotes/5810891.

Mathew, D. A. (2018). Book review of *Rethinking Domestic Violence*. Retrieved from https://drdondutton.com/portfolio/rethinking-domestic-violence/.

McHugh, M. C., Frieze, I. H., and Ann, N. Y. (2006). "Intimate Partner Violence: New Directions." *Academy Science* 87: 121–141. doi: 10.1196/annals.1385.011.

Merchant, L. V., and Whiting, J. B. (In submission). "Factors in Couples' Desistance from Domestic Violence." Retrieved from https://www.researchgate.net/publication/321442468_A_Grounded_Theory_Study_of_How_Couples_Desist_from_Intimate_Partner_Violence.

Microsoft Network (MSN) Website. (N.d). Retrieved from http://www.msn.com/?ocid=iehp.

Mills, L. D., Mills, T. J., Taliaferro, E., Zimbler, A., and Smith, D. (2003). "The Prevalence of Female-to-Male Intimate Partner Violence in an Urban Emergency Department." *Journal of Emergency Medicine*, no. 2: 215–218.

Mills, T. J., Avegno, J. L., and Haydel, M. J. (2006). "Male Victims of Partner Violence: Prevalence and Accuracy of Screening Tools." *Journal of Emergency Medicine* 1, no. 4: 447–452.

Niolon, P. H., Kearns, M., Dills, J., Rambo, K., Irving, S., Armstead, T., and Gilbert, L. (2017). "Preventing Intimate Partner Violence across the Lifespan: A Technical Package of Programs, Policies, and Practices." Atlanta, GA: National Center for Injury Prevention and Control, Centers for Disease Control and Prevention.

Onusic, S. (2013). "Violent Behavior: A Solution in Plain Sight." *Journal of Wise Traditions in Food, Farming, and the Healing Arts*. Retrieved from http://www.westonaprice.org/uncategorized/violent-behavior-a-solution-in-plain-sight/.

Shuler, I. C. (2010). "Male Victims of Intimate Partner Violence in the United States: An Examination of the Review of Literature through the Critical Theoretical Perspective." *Journal of Criminal Justice Sciences* 5: 973–5089.

Weinberger, B. Z., Esq. (2015). "It's Time to Acknowledge Male Victims of Domestic Violence." Retrieved from https://www.huffingtonpost.com/bari-zell-weinberger-esq/its-time-to-acknowledge-m_b_8292976.html.

Whiting, J. (2016). "Eight Reasons Women Stay in Abusive Relationships." Family Studies. Retrieved from http://family-studies.org/eight-reasons-women-stay-in-abusive-relationships.

Teenage Research Unlimited. (2009). "Impact of the Economy and Parent/Teen Dialogue on Dating Relationships and Abuse." Family Violence Prevention Fund and Liz Claiborne.

Teenage Research Unlimited. (2008). "Tween and Teen Dating Violence and Abuse Study." Teenage Research Unlimited for Liz Claiborne Inc. and the National Teen Dating Abuse Helpline.

ABOUT THE AUTHOR

IRMA J. GIBSON, PHD, MSW

Dr. Irma J. Gibson is a visiting associate professor of social work at the Florida A&M University and an international professor teaching study-abroad students at the University of the West Indies in Trinidad and Tobago. She is a speaker, a writer, and an advocate in the area of child and family welfare. Thirteen years ago, she entered into academia full time at Savannah State University, after twenty-two years of clinical and administrative practice with the federal government, nationally and internationally. She made history in 1992 as the first and youngest African American female to serve as team leader of the Readjustment Counseling Northeast Region's Hartford Veterans Outreach Center. Throughout her career, she has served and continues to pursue research interests with various populations, including children and families impacted by poverty and other public health problems, the homeless, those suffering from addiction and mental health challenges including post-traumatic stress disorder, active-duty military, veterans of the armed services and their families, and international social work. She teaches across the social work curriculum and has been blessed with opportunities to present regionally and nationally on the topics of service learning, child and family welfare, and a variety of other social work topics and themes.

She received a bachelor's in sociology from Paine College (magna cum laude), a master's in social work from the University of Georgia, and a PhD in social work with a concentration in public health from Clark Atlanta University.

BIOS OF CONTRIBUTORS

JERRY B. DANIEL, JD, PHD, MPH, MSW, MS, LCS

Dr. Jerry B. Daniel joined Albany State University in January 2014 as an associate professor and teaches in the Bachelor and Master of Social Work Programs. He holds an AS (Criminal Justice) from Middle Georgia College, a BS (Criminal Justice) from Mercer University, an MS (Counseling Psychology/School Counseling) from Fort Valley State University, an MSW (Health/Mental Health) from Clark Atlanta University, an MPH (Health Services Administration) and a PhD (Social Work: Research, Policy Analysis, and Administration) from the University of Pittsburgh, and a JD (Law) from the University of Georgia.

Prior academic experience includes Mercer University School of Medicine, where he held joint appointments as an assistant professor of community medicine and assistant professor of psychiatry. He was the founding director of the Center for Rural Health and Health Disparities and assistant director of the Community Medicine Program. He also served in adjunct positions with the University of Georgia and Fort Valley State University. Dr. Daniel has also taught and conducted research at Volga Region State University of Service (Togliatti, Russia) as a Fulbright Scholar. He is a licensed clinical social worker, licensed attorney, certified school social worker, and certified school counselor (all in Georgia). He has published in the areas of criminal justice, social work, law, and public health.

ROWENA DANIELS, LCSW, MBA, ESQ.

Ms. Rowena Daniels is licensed to practice law in Georgia and Florida. She holds four academic degrees: the juris doctorate from Florida A&M University College of Law; a master's degree in business administration and a bachelor's degree in arts sociology, both from Albany State; and a master's degree in social work from Florida State University. Additionally, she is a licensed clinical social worker and has been licensed as such in Georgia since 1998. Ms. Daniels has worked as an administrator and a clinician, and has extensive experience working with individuals, families, and groups.

SAMMIE L. DAVIS JR. (LTC RETIRED), DOCTORAL CANDIDATE AT CAPELLA UNIVERSITY

Sammie L. Davis Jr. is a thirty-seven-year military veteran of the US Army. His military background and experiences include logistics, acquisition and procurement, contracting, and training and development. Sammie is an ROTC scholarship recipient and recently retired from active federal service as of December 31, 2017. In addition to his nine deployments (six combat tours of Desert Storm, Iraq, and Afghanistan), he has been stationed at eighteen duty locations here in the US and abroad. He has a strong and exceptional gift for training and personal development and enjoys working with people, especially youth. He is an ordained minister who holds degrees in physics and mathematics (Dillard University) as well as a master's in education (Central Michigan University; Curriculum Development and Adult Learning). He is currently working on his PhD (ABD) (Capella University) in education, with a focus on performance improvement and training. He continues to lecture and train as a consultant on Continuous Process Improvement (CPI) with the Army Contracting Command and teaches physics and mathematics at the College of Southern Maryland.

He is married (thirty-four years) to Zelda R. Gaylord-Davis, another retired veteran, and is the father of two daughters, Jessica and Joslynn. He is also the "Big Poppa" of one infant granddaughter. His training philosophy is simple: each one teaches one, and allow the chain of success to develop through the process of mentoring and coaching, coupled with effective feedback and guidance.

ROENIA DELOACH, PHD, MSW, BSW

Dr. Roenia DeLoach received her BSW degree from Jackson State University (Jackson, Mississippi) and completed a practicum in a community mental health center. She received her MSW degree with a concentration in mental health from Ohio State University (Columbus, Ohio). She also received her PhD in social work and a graduate interdisciplinary specialization in aging from Ohio State University. Dr. Roenia Deloach has been a faculty member in the Department of Social Work at Savannah State University since 2002. She has held several administrative roles at Savannah State University: chair of the Department of Social Work, coordinator of Bachelor of Social Work Program, and coordinator of the Master of Social Work Program. She has over fifteen years of clinical experience, to include work in community mental health and medical (hospital, dialysis center, and hospice).

CATHERINE GAYLE, PHD, MSW, LCSW, CCFC

Dr. Catherine Gayle is a native of Savannah, Georgia. As an academician, she is a maven for change and has used her professional acumen to catapult others toward excellence, obtaining a bachelor's, a master's, and a PhD from Tuskegee University, Florida University, and Clark Atlanta University, respectively, in the area of social work. Dr. Gayle has used her skills to empower various social groups throughout the world. She has a passion for serving victims of sexual assault and provides workshops on a number of topics. She has also authored a book entitled *I Did Not Ask for This: A Candid Discussion on Sexual Assault*, and is completing her second book, *When Men Piss on the Cloth*.

She is an ordained minister and the former chair of the Department of Social Work at Tuskegee University. Presently Dr. Gayle is a tenured associate professor and serves as chair of the Department of Social Work at Savannah State University. A former board member of the Baccalaureate Program Directors (BPD) and recently reappointed as a commissioner on the Accreditation Board for the Council on Social Work Education (CSWE), Dr. Gayle is also a licensed clinical social worker, a certified masters level addiction counselor, and a Fulbright-Hays scholar who has traveled to Ghana, where she is conducting a comparative analysis on domestic violence in Ghana and the United States of America. Dr. Gayle is a sought-after speaker, has ministered in Nairobi, Kenya, and spearheads a weekly radio broadcast on 94.9 FM in Hinesville, Georgia, entitled, *Stepping Out on Faith Ministries*.

TERRELL JAMAR GIBSON, BA

Terrell JaMar Gibson was born on December 13, 1989, in Bamberg, Germany, and moved to Wethersfield, Connecticut, at the age of two and a half. He then moved to Atlanta, Georgia, in 1994. His educational foundation is rooted in the Christian curriculum provided by Faith Academy, where he matriculated until the second grade. He then attended various public and charter schools within the Dekalb County vicinity, including Cedar Grove High School, until his senior year. He then moved to Hinesville, Georgia, and graduated from Liberty County High School in May 2007. To further his education, he attended Savannah State University and graduated May 2012 with a bachelor's in mass communications, with a concentration in radio and television and a minor in political science. He received his first position in the mass communications profession at WFXL Fox 31 in 2013 and has worked in various positions, TV markets, and news stations in the states of Georgia and Iowa, including WMGT in Macon as a production assistant and photojournalist. His current position is as a remote event crew member/director for a major news channel in Florida. Some of his personal hobbies include listening to music, playing and watching sports, traveling, and spending time with his family.

MRS. TONICA GLEATON

Mrs. Tonica Gleaton is a devoted wife of thirty years and the proud mother of two well-loved, smart, and handsome sons: Bobby Jr. (age twenty-five at death in 2015) and Brandon (age twenty-six). She is a federal employee working at the Centers for Disease Control and Prevention. She and her family currently reside in Decatur, Georgia, where she and her husband raised their sons. Both sons are high school graduates and attended college at Albany State University. They are also US Army Reservists.

In her spare time, she enjoys planning events, which she decided to pursue as a business venture that keeps her as busy as she chooses. One of her dreams is to retire from the federal government so she can indulge in event-planning full time. Coordinating events is therapeutic and a welcome distraction since the loss of Bobby Jr.

OLIVER J. JOHNSON, PHD, LCSW, LCAS, CCS

Dr. Oliver J. Johnson holds a PhD in social work from Clark Atlanta University and has lectured widely in a variety of forums on issues pivotal to the promotion of health and wellness among African American families. His workshops include Psychotherapy with Black Men, Healing the Inner Child of the African American Male, Achievement Conflicts in Hospitalized Black Adolescent Males, The Invisibility Syndrome and The African American Male, Depression as a Risk Factor for HIV Disease among African American Men and Women, Effective Clinical Practice with Dually Diagnosed African American Men, Reducing Cardiovascular Disease among African American Men, and Substance Abuse Treatment and Black Men. Dr. Johnson has served as an adjunct lecturer at the University of Michigan School of Social Work, Ashland Theological Seminary/Pastoral Counseling Program, Lewis College of Business, Marygrove College, Spring Arbor College, University of Phoenix, and Wayne State University's College for Lifelong Learning, where he has designed courses that include Cultural Competency in Social Work Practice. In August 2018, Dr. Johnson was promoted to full professor in the School of Social Work at Fayetteville State University. Dr. Johnson is also the author of a bestseller entitled *Breaking the Chains of Cocaine: Black Male Addiction and Recovery*. He holds memberships with the National Association of Social Workers and the National Association of Black Social Workers.

MR. LEON JONES

Mr. Leon Jones is a Macon, Georgia, coroner who believes, "It's my responsibility to do more for my community." I also have a passion for our youth."

Mr. Jones is a Macon native, was one of the first fifty black students to integrate Willingham High School, and is a graduate of Southwest High School. He received his EMT (Emergency Medical Technician) certification from Macon Vocational Technical Institute and his Cardiac Technician Certifications from the Medical Center of Central Georgia (Basic Cardiac Life Support Provider and Advanced Cardiac Life Support Provider). He is also certified in homicide investigations by the University of St. Louis School of Medicine and holds certification in death investigations from the Cobb County Police Department in Marietta, Georgia.

Jones retired after thirty-two years of service as an EMT with the Medical Center of Central Georgia and has also worked in emergency medical services throughout the region. He has served as deputy coroner for Bibb County since 1990 and as Bibb County's elected coroner since 2004. He is a member of Beulahland Bible Church and is married to the lovely Sheila Bryant Jones.

Despite his busy schedule, Jones finds time to serve his community, speaking at Bibb County schools on a regular basis.
"My faith in Christ is what brings me through, and it's what keeps me going."

Jones' personal philosophy is: "If you want it, work for it; never forget who you are and where you came from."

TREVIS KILLEN, EDD, EDS, MSW

Dr. Trevis Killen is executive director of student services for Jones County Schools. Prior to that role, he served as the school social work consultant for the Student Support Services Project collaboration between the University of South Florida and Florida Department of Education. Before that appointment, he was a school social worker for the Houston County School District. Dr. Killen is the former state president and vice president for the School Social Workers Association of Georgia. Dr. Killen has been an adjunct instructor for Lanier Technical College, where he taught GED classes to detained youth and adults. When requested, Dr. Killen teaches social work course for Southern Regional Technical College, and human services courses for Mercer University.

MS. SABRINA MANNING-PRINCE

Sabrina Manning-Prince is the founder of the Georgia-based firm YourSPACE (Special Projects Administrative Consulting Executives). She is a published author, freelance writer/reporter, motivational speaker, small business consultant, and youth development specialist. In 2015, she published her first book, which details her personal experience with domestic violence, and uses the book as a platform to address healthy relationships and safe dating for teens. She has spent over thirty years advocating for children, youth, and women. As a youth development specialist, she has managed and monitored student services grants in several rural Georgia counties. She serves/has served on a local Head Start Policy Council, a Steering Committee of a future Boys and Girls Club unit, and the Advisory Board of the Albany State University Social Work Department.

JEROME H. SCHIELE, PHD

Dr. Jerome H. Schiele is a professor and chair of the PhD department in the School of Social Work at Morgan State University. A native of Hampton, Virginia, Dr. Schiele received his bachelor's degree in sociology from Hampton University in 1983, and attained both his master's and doctoral degrees in social work from Howard University. Dr. Schiele has almost thirty years of higher-education experience and has served in both faculty and administrative positions. Before arriving at Morgan State University, he was professor and dean of the College of Professional Studies at Bowie State University and a professor and associate dean in the School of Social Work at the University of Georgia. He also has taught and served in administrative roles at Norfolk State University, Clark Atlanta University, and the State University of New York at Stony Brook. He also previously served as professor and inaugural director of the PhD program at Morgan State University. Dr. Schiele's research focuses on social policy analysis, racial oppression, and cultural diversity/competence. He has published numerous scholarly articles, essays, and book chapters, which appear in major academic periodicals and publications. Dr. Schiele also is the author of *Human Services and the Afrocentric Paradigm*, editor of *Social Welfare Policy: Regulation and Resistance among People of Color*, and coauthor with Phyllis Day of *A New History of Social Welfare, 7th edition*. Dr. Schiele's primary teaching areas are social policy analysis, cultural diversity/competence, and social work practice theory. He is a member of several professional organizations.

MAJOR TONNIE ALFONZO WILLIAMS SR.

Major Tonnie Williams Sr. presents with thirty-one years of law enforcement service, starting with the Macon Police Department in July 24, 1984. Since that time, he has served in a number of ranks and positions, including patrol officer, sergeant, bureau detective, property detective, pawn detail supervisor, drug unit supervisor, lieutenant/assistant commander of Precincts 1 and 2, Area 2 assistant commander of Property and Drug Unit Investigations, captain/commander of Precinct 4, and major/commander of youth and intervention services.

After consolidation of the Macon Police Department and the Bibb County Sheriff's Office, Major Williams served in the Sheriff's Outreach Section, Patrol Administration/Patrol Districts and Traffic Division, Corrections Administration for all jail/detention operations, and currently in Court Services responsible for Security of the Courthouse, Juvenile Justice Center, and State Court Probation Office.

He graduated from the FBI Academy on March 14, 2008, and has proudly served as commander of the Special Weapons Assault Team (SWAT), including the opportunity to carry out SWAT details via security detail at the forty-fifth presidential inauguration ceremonies and the president's visit to Macon, Georgia, as commander and honor guard.

He is the first person to be honored as Officer of the Year for the Macon Police Department. Additional awards include Peace Officer Association of Georgia Peace Officer of the Year and the Medal of Valor. He has received accolades and honors from the Exchange Club, Optimist Club, Shield Club, the United States Marine Corps, and local businesses and churches in the community.

MR. RICARLO D. WILLIAMS, MPA, MSW

Ricarlo D. Williams is a school social worker for Decatur County Schools. In addition to this role, he serves as a city councilmember in Colquitt, Georgia, and is an active member of Alpha Phi Alpha Fraternity, INC, Sons of Colquitt Masonic Lodge #580, the Southwest Georgia Regional Commission, the School Social Workers Association of Georgia Executive Board, and the Colquitt/Miller County Volunteer Fire Department. Prior to the role of school social worker, he served as an independent living specialist for the Georgia Department of Human Services. Mr. Williams has received the Georgia 40 under 40 Achievement Award and Leadership Colquitt. Mr. Williams is also the cofounder of Men Leaning Forward, Inc.